A WRITER'S READER

A WRITER'S READER

SECOND EDITION

Donald Hall

D. L. Emblen
Santa Rosa Junior College

LITTLE, BROWN AND COMPANY
Boston   Toronto

For William R. Booth

Library of Congress Catalog Card No. 78–73831

FOURTH PRINTING

*Published simultaneously in Canada
by Little, Brown & Company (Canada) Limited*

Printed in the United States of America

Preface

Reading well precedes writing well. Of all the ancestors claimed by a fine piece of prose, the most important is the prose from which the writer learned his craft. Writers learn craft, not by memorizing rules about restrictive clauses, but by striving to equal a standard formed from reading.

A composition course, then, must be two courses: one in reading, another in writing. If students lack practice in writing, they are usually unpracticed readers as well. Most students lack quality of reading as well as quantity; and if we assert that good models help us, we admit that bad models hurt us. People who read bad prose twelve hours a week — newspapers, popular fiction, textbooks — are as ill-served as people who read nothing at all. Surely most textbooks, from freshman handbooks through the text for Psych 101, encourage the illusion that words merely stand in for ideas, or carry information on their backs — that words exist for the convenience of thinking much as turnpikes exist for the sake of automobiles.

This barbarism underlies the vogue of speed reading, which urges us to scan lines for comprehension, ignoring syntax and metaphor, ignoring image and feeling and sound. If we are to grow and to learn — and surely if we are to write well — we must learn to read slowly and intimately, and to read good writing. We must learn to read actively, even aggressively, without the passivity derived from watching television. The active reader questions as he reads, subjects each author's ideas to skeptical scrutiny, and engages the writer in dialogue as part of the reading process.

For language embodies the human psyche. Learning to read — that privilege so recently extended to the ancestors of most of us — allows us to enter human history. In books we perceive the gesture, the pulse, the heartbeat, the pallor, the eye-movement, the pitch, and the tone of people who lived before us, or who live now in other places, in other skins, in other habits, customs, beliefs, and ideas.

Language *embodies* the human psyche, which includes ideas and the feelings that properly accompany ideas. There is no sleight-of-mind by which the idea may be separated from its body and remain alive. The body of good writing is rhythm and image, metaphor and syntax, order of phrase and order of paragraph.

A NOTE TO THE SECOND EDITION

Many teachers have helped us prepare this second edition of *A Writer's Reader* — in letters, in conversations at colleges all over the country, in responses to a Little, Brown survey of users. We thank more people than we can list.

We have added considerable material, far more than we have cut, and we are pleased with what we have come up with. We believe that we have made a representative sampling of good prose. We like some pieces more than others, heaven knows, but we believe that all of them provide something to learn from. We have included a wide variety of American prose, not only contemporary but historical, with high points of our history represented in their own style and syntax. We hope that young Americans will attach themselves to the body of their history by immersion in its significant utterances.

We have numbered paragraphs for ease of reference, except in short stories, where lines of numbers down the page seemed obtrusive. Although *A Writer's Reader* is a collection of essays, we have again violated coherence by including fiction, feeling that the contrast afforded by a few short stories among the essays was useful and refreshing. For this edition, we have gone further afield and included several poems, for the same reason. Perhaps we should make an argument for including poems — but let us just say that we enjoy them, and we hope you do too. To satisfy students' curiosity, we have included headnotes to the poems; but we have stopped short of suggesting questions after them, lest we seem to surround a landscape garden with a hundred-foot-high cement wall.

We have chosen to arrange our essays, stories, and poems alphabetically by author. This arrangement makes for random juxtaposition, irrational sequence, and no sense at all — which is why we chose it. We expect no one to teach these pieces in alphabetical order. (We expect teachers to find their own order — which they would do whatever order we attempted to impose.) In our first edition we struggled to make a stylistic organization, listing some essays as examples of "Sentences," others as examples of "Paragraphs." For the editors themselves, a year after deciding on our organization, it was no longer clear why essay X was to be studied for its sentences, essay Y for its paragraphs. With a rhetorical organization, one runs into another sort of problem. Although an essay may contain Division, or Process Analysis, or an example of Example, the same essay is likely to use three or four other patterns as well. No piece of real prose is ever so pure as our systems of classification. Thematic organizations, which have their attractions, have similar flaws; is E. B. White's theme, in "Once More to the Lake," Mortality? Aging? Youth and Age? or, How I Spent My Summer Vacation?

Our arrangement is more arbitrary than an arrangement by style or rhetoric or theme, and presents itself only to be ignored. At the same time, there are dozens of ways in which these essays (and poems and stories) can be used together. Our Instructor's Manual suggests several combinations. Our Rhetorical Index, printed as an appendix to the text itself, lists single-paragraph examples of rhetorical patterns as well as longer units. We hope that students will find the Rhetorical Index useful. Freshmen who return to their rooms from class, set to write a paper using Comparison and Contrast, sometimes find themselves in need of a concrete example of the assigned pattern to imitate.

Thus, we have tried to supply some useful maps to go with our arbitrary arrangement.

We must admit that we take pleasure in the strange juxtapositions the alphabet imposes. We enjoy beginning our book with Henry Adams, James Agee, Woody Allen, Maya Angelou. . . .

Acknowledgments

We thank the following users of the first edition for their helpful comments: Maureen Andrews, Meredith Berman, Ed Buckley, Sandra Burns, Jon Burton, Steven Connelly, Randy Conine, Roger Conner, Garber Davidson, Virginia de Araujo, Barbara Hamilton, John Huntington, Donald Kansch, Gregory Keeler, Jeff Kluewer, Thomas Kmetzo, Deanne Milan, Stephen O'Neill, Ray Peterson, Martha Rainbolt, Terry Shelton, Arnold Solkov, Andrew Solomon, Kathleen Sullivan, and Craig Watson. We thank Dale Anderson, Charles Christensen, Elizabeth Philipps, and Jan Welch, at Little, Brown, for their efforts on the book's behalf.

Finally, special thanks are due Clayton Hudnall for his important contributions to the book and its manual.

Contents

A WRITER'S READER

Henry Adams (1838–1918) entertained notions of a political career, in keeping with family traditions, but withdrew from Washington in distaste over the corruption of the Grant adminis-tration. For a time, he taught history at Harvard and edited the North American Review. *After publishing two anonymous novels without great success, he undertook and completed the massive* History of the United States During the Administrations of Jeffer-son and Madison. *His best works are* Mont St. Michel and Chartres *(1904) and his autobiography — written in the third person and called* The Education of Henry Adams *(1907) — from which we take this fragment of reminiscence.*

Hundreds of American writers have recollected visits to grand-father's house; few were grandson to one president and great-grandson to another. Adams's contrasts of style — eighteenth cen-tury with ninteenth, Boston with the small town of Quincy, the Brooks grandfather with the Adams grandfather — culminate in an anecdote which illuminates the fundamental contrast of pri-vate and public.

1

HENRY ADAMS
Winter and Summer

Boys are wild animals, rich in the treasures of sense, but the New England boy had a wider range of emotions than boys of more equable climates. He felt his nature crudely, as it was meant. To the boy Henry Adams, summer was drunken. Among senses, smell was the strongest — smell of hot pine-woods and sweet-fern in the scorching summer noon; of new-mown hay; of ploughed earth; of box hedges; of peaches, lilacs, syringas; of stables, barns, cow-yards; of salt water and low tide on the marshes; nothing came amiss. Next to smell came taste, and the children knew the taste of everything they saw or touched, from pennyroyal and flagroot to the shell of a pignut and the letters of a spelling book — the taste of A-B, AB, suddenly revived on the boy's tongue sixty years afterwards. Light, line, and color as sensual pleasures, came later and were as crude as the rest. The New England light is glare, and the atmosphere harshens color. The boy was a full man before he ever knew what was meant by atmosphere; his idea of pleasure in light was the blaze of a New England sun. His idea of color was a peony, with the dew of early morning on its petals. The intense blue of the sea, as he saw it a mile or two away, from the Quincy hills; the cumuli in a June afternoon sky; the strong reds and greens and purples of colored prints and children's picture-books, as the American colors then ran; these were ideals. The opposites or antipathies, were the cold grays of November evenings, and the thick, muddy thaws of Boston winter. With such standards, the Bostonian could not but develop a double nature. Life was a double thing. After a January blizzard, the boy who could look with pleasure into the violent snow-glare of the cold white sunshine, with its intense light and shade, scarcely knew what was meant by tone. He could reach it only by education.

2   Winter and summer, then, were two hostile lives, and bred two separate natures. Winter was always the effort to live; summer was tropical license. Whether the children rolled in the grass, or waded in the brook, or swam in the salt ocean, or sailed in the bay, or fished for smelts in the creeks, or netted minnows in the salt-marshes, or took to the pine-woods and the granite quarries, or chased muskrats and hunted snapping-turtles in the swamps, or mushrooms or nuts on the autumn hills, summer and country were always sensual living, while winter was always compulsory learning. Summer was the multiplicity of nature; winter was school.

3   The bearing of the two seasons on the education of Henry Adams was no fancy; it was the most decisive force he ever knew; it ran through life, and made the division between its perplexing, warring, irreconcilable problems, irreducible opposites, with growing emphasis to the last year of study. From earliest childhood the boy was accustomed to feel that, for him, life was double. Winter and summer, town and country, law and liberty, were hostile, and the man who pretended they were not, was in his eyes a schoolmaster — that is, a man employed to tell lies to little boys. Though Quincy was but two hours' walk from Beacon Hill, it belonged in a different world. For two hundred years, every Adams, from father to son, had lived within sight of State Street, and sometimes had lived in it, yet none had ever taken kindly to the town, or been taken kindly by it. The boy inherited his double nature. He knew as yet nothing about his great-grandfather,

who had died a dozen years before his own birth: he took for granted that any great-grandfather of his must have always been good, and his enemies wicked; but he divined his great-grandfather's character from his own. Never for a moment did he connect the two ideas of Boston and John Adams; they were separate and antagonistic; the idea of John Adams went with Quincy. He knew his grandfather John Quincy Adams only as an old man of seventy-five or eighty who was friendly and gentle with him, but except that he heard his grandfather always called "the President," and his grandmother "the Madam," he had no reason to suppose that his Adams grandfather differed in character from his Brooks grandfather who was equally kind and benevolent. He liked the Adams side best, but for no other reason than that it reminded him of the country, the summer, and the absence of restraint. Yet he felt also that Quincy was in a way inferior to Boston, and that socially Boston looked down on Quincy. The reason was clear enough even to a five-year-old child. Quincy had no Boston style. Little enough style had either; a simpler manner of life and thought could hardly exist, short of cave-dwelling. The flint-and-steel with which his grandfather Adams used to light his own fires in the early morning was still on the mantelpiece of his study. The idea of a livery or even a dress for servants, or of an evening toilette, was next to blasphemy. Bathrooms, water-supplies, lighting, heating, and the whole array of domestic comforts, were unknown at Quincy. Boston had already a bathroom, a water-supply, a furnace, and gas. The superiority of Boston was evident, but a child liked it no better for that.

The magnificence of his grandfather Brooks's house in Pearl Street or South Street has long ago disappeared, but perhaps his country house at Medford may still remain to show what impressed the mind of a boy in 1845 with the idea of city splendor. The President's place at Quincy was the larger and older and far the more interesting of the two; but a boy felt at once its inferiority in fashion. It showed plainly enough its want of wealth. It smacked of colonial age, but not of Boston style or plush curtains. To the end of his life he never quite overcame the prejudice thus drawn in with his childish breath. He never could compel himself to care for nineteenth-century style. He was never able to adopt it, any more than his father or grandfather or great-grandfather had done. Not that he felt it as particularly hostile, for he reconciled himself to much that was worse; but because, for some remote reason, he was born an eighteenth-century child. The old house at Quincy was eighteenth century. What style it had was in its Queen Anne mahogany panels and its Louis Seize chairs and sofas.

The panels belonged to an old colonial Vassall who built the house; the furniture had been brought back from Paris in 1789 or 1801 or 1817, along with porcelain and books and much else of old diplomatic remnants; and neither of the two eighteenth-century styles — neither English Queen Anne nor French Louis Seize — was comfortable for a boy, or for any one else. The dark mahogany had been painted white to suit daily life in winter gloom. Nothing seemed to favor, for a child's objects, the older forms. On the contrary, most boys, as well as grown-up people, preferred the new, with good reason, and the child felt himself distinctly at a disadvantage for the taste.

5   Nor had personal preference any share in his bias. The Brooks grandfather was as amiable and as sympathetic as the Adams grandfather. Both were born in 1767, and both died in 1848. Both were kind to children, and both belonged rather to the eighteenth than to the nineteenth centuries. The child knew no difference between them except that one was associated with winter and the other with summer; one with Boston, the other with Quincy. Even with Medford, the association was hardly easier. Once as a very young boy he was taken to pass a few days with his grandfather Brooks under charge of his aunt, but became so violently homesick that within twenty-four hours he was brought back in disgrace. Yet he could not remember ever being seriously homesick again.

6   The attachment to Quincy was not altogether sentimental or wholly sympathetic. Quincy was not a bed of thornless roses. Even there the curse of Cain set its mark. There as elsewhere a cruel universe combined to crush a child. As though three or four vigorous brothers and sisters, with the best will, were not enough to crush any child, every one else conspired towards an education which he hated. From cradle to grave this problem of running order through chaos, direction through space, discipline through freedom, unity through multiplicity, has always been, and must always be, the task of education, as it is the moral of religion, philosophy, science, art, politics, and economy; but a boy's will is his life, and he dies when it is broken, as the colt dies in harness, taking a new nature in becoming tame. Rarely has the boy felt kindly towards his tamers. Between him and his master has always been war. Henry Adams never knew a boy of his generation to like a master, and the task of remaining on friendly terms with one's own family, in such a relation, was never easy.

7   All the more singular it seemed afterwards to him that his first serious contact with the President should have been a struggle of will, in which the old man almost necessarily defeated the boy, but instead

of leaving, as usual in such defeats, a lifelong sting, left rather an impression of as fair treatment as could be expected from a natural enemy. The boy met seldom with such restraint. He could not have been much more than six years old at the time — seven at the utmost — and his mother had taken him to Quincy for a long stay with the President during the summer. What became of the rest of the family he quite forgot; but he distinctly remembered standing at the house door one summer morning in a passionate outburst of rebellion against going to school. Naturally his mother was the immediate victim of his rage; that is what mothers are for, and boys also; but in this case the boy had his mother at unfair disadvantage, for she was a guest, and had no means of enforcing obedience. Henry showed a certain tactical ability by refusing to start, and he met all efforts at compulsion by successful, though too vehement protest. He was in fair way to win, and was holding his own, with sufficient energy, at the bottom of the long staircase which led up to the door of the President's library, when the door opened, and the old man slowly came down. Putting on his hat, he took the boy's hand without a word, and walked with him, paralyzed by awe, up the road to the town. After the first moments of consternation at this interference in a domestic dispute, the boy reflected that an old gentleman close on eighty would never trouble himself to walk near a mile on a hot summer morning over a shadeless road to take a boy to school, and that it would be strange if a lad imbued with the passion of freedom could not find a corner to dodge around, somewhere before reaching the school door. Then and always, the boy insisted that this reasoning justified his apparent submission; but the old man did not stop, and the boy saw all his strategical points turned, one after another, until he found himself seated inside the school, and obviously the centre of curious if not malevolent criticism. Not till then did the President release his hand and depart.

The point was that this act, contrary to the inalienable rights of boys, and nullifying the social compact, ought to have made him dislike his grandfather for life. He could not recall that it had this effect even for a moment. With a certain maturity of mind, the child must have recognized that the President, though a tool of tyranny, had done his disreputable work with a certain intelligence. He had shown no temper, no irritation, no personal feeling, and had made no display of force. Above all, he had held his tongue. During their long walk he had said nothing; he had uttered no syllable of revolting cant about the duty of obedience and the wickedness of resistance to law; he had shown no concern in the matter; hardly even a consciousness of the

8

boy's existence. Probably his mind at that moment was actually troubling itself little about his grandson's iniquities, and much about the iniquities of President Polk, but the boy could scarcely at that age feel the whole satisfaction of thinking that President Polk was to be the vicarious victim of his own sins, and he gave his grandfather credit for intelligent silence. For this forbearance he felt instinctive respect. He admitted force as a form of right; he admitted even temper, under protest; but the seeds of moral education would at that moment have fallen on the stoniest soil in Quincy, which is, as every one knows, the stoniest glacial and tidal drift known in any Puritan land.

____ CONSIDERATIONS ____

1. Earlier in his autobiography, Adams gives the reader some idea of how the young Henry, because of the peculiar nature of his family and its position, was burdened with expectations growing out of the family's deep involvement in American history and politics. In this excerpt, study his vocabulary and look for words that express his constant awareness of that involvement.

2. Adams chose an unusual point-of-view for an autobiography — the third person. Change a given paragraph to the first person point-of-view to see what difference the author's decision on that technical matter can make.

3. What illustrations does Adams use to help the reader understand what is meant by "He felt his nature crudely. . . ."?

4. Adams's essay might fairly be said to be built upon a system of opposites. List several of these opposites to help you understand how a series of contrasts can serve as an organizing principle of an essay.

5. In Paragraph 6, Adams sets forth clearly and firmly his conviction about what education must be. Judging from your educational experience, to what extent can you agree with him?

6. What allowed the boy to respect his grandfather, even as the old man was disciplining him?

James Agee (1909–1955) was a journalist, critic, poet, and novelist. He was an early critic of film as art, and wrote the script for The African Queen *among other movies. A heart attack killed him at forty-five, before he had finished his novel* A Death in the Family. *Editors assembled the final manuscript, and included as a prologue the essay reprinted here. The novel was awarded the Pulitzer Prize in 1958. His prose evokes lost time; detail is described with intimate precision, landscape rendered exactly with a wash of nostalgia.*

2

JAMES AGEE
Knoxville: Summer 1915

We are talking now of summer evenings in Knoxville, Tennessee 1 in the time that I lived there so successfully disguised to myself as a child. It was a little bit mixed sort of block, fairly solidly lower middle class, with one or two juts apiece on either side of that. The houses corresponded: middle-sized gracefully fretted wood houses built in the late nineties and early nineteen hundreds, with small front and side and more spacious back yards, and trees in the yards, and porches. These were softwooded trees, poplars, tulip trees, cottonwoods. There were fences around one or two of the houses, but mainly the yards ran into each other with only now and then a low hedge that wasn't doing very well. There were few good friends among the grown people, and they were not poor enough for the other sort of intimate acquaintance, but everyone nodded and spoke, and even might talk short times, trivially, and at the two extremes of the general or the particular, and ordinarily nextdoor neighbors talked quite a bit when they happened to run into each other, and never paid calls. The men were mostly small businessmen, one or two very modestly executives, one or two worked with their hands, most of them clerical, and most of them between thirty and forty-five.

2   But it is of these evenings, I speak.

3   Supper was at six and was over by half past. There was still daylight, shining softly and with a tarnish, like the lining of a shell; and the carbon lamps lifted at the corners were on in the light, and the locusts were started, and the fire flies were out, and a few frogs were flopping in the dewy grass, by the time the fathers and the children came out. The children ran out first hell bent and yelling those names by which they were known; then the fathers sank out leisurely in crossed suspenders, their collars removed and their necks looking tall and shy. The mothers stayed back in the kitchen washing and drying, putting things away, recrossing their traceless footsteps like the lifetime journeys of bees, measuring out the dry cocoa for breakfast. When they came out they had taken off their aprons and their skirts were dampened and they sat in rockers on their porches quietly.

4   It is not of the games children played in the evening that I want to speak now, it is of a contemporaneous atmosphere that has little to do with them: that of the fathers of families, each in his space of lawn, his shirt fishlike pale in the unnatural light and his face nearly anonymous, hosing their lawns. The hoses were attached at spigots that stood out of the brick foundations of the houses. The nozzles were variously set but usually so there was a long sweet stream of spray, the nozzle wet in the hand, the water trickling the right forearm and the peeled-back cuff, and the water whishing out a long loose and low-curved cone, and so gentle a sound. First an insane noise of violence in the nozzle, then the still irregular sound of adjustment, then the smoothing into steadiness and a pitch as accurately tuned to the size and style of stream as any violin. So many qualities of sound out of one hose: so many choral differences out of those several hoses that were in earshot. Out of any one hose, the almost dead silence of the release, and the short still arch of the separate big drops, silent as a held breath, and the only noise the flattering noise on leaves and the slapped grass at the fall of each big drop. That, and the intense hiss with the intense stream; that, and that same intensity not growing less but growing more quiet and delicate with the turn of the nozzle, up to that extreme tender whisper when the water was just a wide bell of film. Chiefly, though, the hoses were set much alike, in a compro-

mise between distance and tenderness of spray (and quite surely a sense of art behind this compromise, and a quiet deep joy, too real to recognize itself), and the sounds therefore were pitched much alike; pointed by the snorting start of a new hose; decorated by some man playful with the nozzle; left empty, like God by the sparrow's fall, when any single one of them desists: and all, though near alike, of various pitch; and in this unison. These sweet pale streamings in the light lift out their pallors and their voices all together, mothers hushing their children, the hushing unnaturally prolonged, the men gentle and silent and each snail-like withdrawn into the quietude of what he singly is doing, the urination of huge children stood loosely military against an invisible wall, and gentle happy and peaceful, tasting the mean goodness of their living like the last of their suppers in their mouths; while the locusts carry on this noise of hoses on their much higher and sharper key. The noise of the locust is dry, and it seems not to be rasped or vibrated but urged from him as if through a small orifice by breath that can never give out. Also there is never one locust but an illusion of at least a thousand. The noise of each locust is pitched in some classic locust range out of which none of them varies more than two full tones: and yet you seem to hear each locust discrete from all the rest, and there is a long, slow pulse in their noise, like the scarcely defined arch of a long and high set bridge. They are all around in every tree, so that the noise seems to come from nowhere and everywhere at once, from the whole shell heaven, shivering in your flesh and teasing your eardrums, the boldest of all the sounds of night. And yet it is habitual to summer nights, and is of the great order of noises, like the noises of the sea and of the blood her precocious grandchild, which you realize you are hearing only when you catch yourself listening. Meantime from low in the dark, just outside the swaying horizons of the hoses, conveying always grass in the damp of dew and its strong green-black smear of smell, the regular yet spaced noises of the crickets, each a sweet cold silver noise threenoted, like the slipping each time of three matched links of a small chain.

But the men by now, one by one, have silenced their hoses and 5 drained and coiled them. Now only two, and now only one, is left, and you see only ghostlike shirt with the sleeve garters, and sober mystery of his mild face like the lifted face of large cattle enquiring of your presence in a pitchdark pool of meadow; and now he too is gone; and it has become that time of evening when people sit on their porches, rocking gently and talking gently and watching the street and the standing up into their sphere of possession of the trees, of birds hung havens, hangars. People go by; things go by. A horse, drawing a buggy, breaking his hollow iron music on the asphalt; a loud auto; a quiet auto; people in pairs, not in a hurry, scuffling, switching their weight of aestival body, talking casually, the taste hovering over them of vanilla, strawberry, pasteboard and starched milk, the image upon them of lovers and horsemen, squared with clowns in hueless amber. A street car raising its iron moan; stopping, belling and starting; stertorous; rousing and raising again its iron increasing moan and swimming its gold windows and straw seats on past and past and past, the bleak spark crackling and cursing above it like a small malignant spirit set to dog its tracks; the iron whine rises on rising speed; still risen, faints; halts; the faint stinging bell; rises again, still fainter; fainting, lifting, lifts, faints forgone: forgotten. Now is the night one blue dew.

Now is the night one blue dew, my father has drained, he has coiled the hose
Low on the length of lawns, a frailing of fire who breathes.
Content, silver, like peeps of light, each cricket makes his comment over and over in the drowned grass.
A cold toad thumpily flounders.
Within the edges of damp shadows of side yards are hovering children nearly sick with joy of fear, who watch the unguarding of a telephone pole.
Around white carbon corner lamps bugs of all sizes are lifted elliptic, solar systems. Big hardshells bruise themselves, assailant: he is fallen on his back, legs squiggling.
Parents on porches: rock and rock: From damp strings morning glories: hang their ancient faces.
The dry and exalted noise of the locusts from all the air at once enchants my eardrums.

6   On the rough wet grass of the back yard my father and mother have spread quilts. We all lie there, my mother, my father, my uncle, my aunt, and I too am lying there. First we were sitting up, then one of us lay down, and then we all lay down, on our stomachs, or on our sides, or on our backs, and they have kept on talking. They are not talking much, and the talk is quiet, of nothing in particular, of nothing at all in particular, of nothing at all. The stars are wide and alive, they seem each like a smile of great sweetness, and they seem very near. All my people are larger bodies than mine, quiet, with voices gentle and meaningless like the voices of sleeping birds. One is an artist, he is living at home. One is a musician, she is living at home. One is my mother who is good to me. One is my father who is good to me. By

some chance, here they are, all on this earth; and who shall ever tell the sorrow of being on this earth, lying, on quilts, on the grass, in a summer evening, among the sounds of the night. May God bless my people, my uncle, my aunt, my mother, my good father, oh, remember them kindly in their time of trouble; and in the hour of their taking away.

After a little I am taken in and put to bed. Sleep, soft smiling, draws me unto her: and those receive me, who quietly treat me, as one familiar and well beloved in that home: but will not, oh, will not, not now, not ever; but will not ever tell me who I am.   7

_____ CONSIDERATIONS _____

1. Agee is famous for the close attention he pays to the senses. In this piece, which one — seeing, hearing, smelling, tasting, touching — is exercised the most?

2. What do you make of Agee's paragraph sense? Compare, for example, Paragraph 2 with Paragraph 4. Would you recommend breaking the latter into smaller units? Where? Why, or why not?

3. The first sentence of Paragraph 1 offers an opportunity for experimentation. Copy it out *without* the following phrases: "so successfully," "disguised," and "to myself." Then replace the phrases, one at a time, considering how each addition changes the dimension, the direction, or the depth of the story begun. Which of the three works the greatest change? Why?

4. How does the first sentence embody a theme important to the whole story? Is that theme sounded elsewhere in the story?

5. Agee's evocation of a summer evening might seem strange to an apartment-dweller in Knoxville in 1979. Would it be possible to write so serenely about a summer evening in the Knoxville — or Detroit, or Minneapolis, or San Francisco — of today?

6. Agee's attempt to recapture and thus understand his childhood — or at least a moment of it — is similar to and different from the efforts of several other writers in this book. Compare and contrast "Knoxville: Summer 1915" with one of these: Henry Adams (pages 1–6); Frank Conroy (pages 93–100); Lillian Hellman (pages 178–184); Langston Hughes (pages 198–200); or E. B. White (pages 442–447).

Woody Allen (b. 1935) is a universal genius, best known for acting in, writing, and directing movies. His films range from What's New, Pussycat? *(1964) through* Love and Death *(1975) and* Annie Hall *(1977), to* Interiors *(1978). He has also published short fiction and nonfiction in* Playboy *and* The New Yorker, *and in 1978 won an O. Henry Award for the best American short story of the previous year. His prose is collected in two volumes,* Getting Even *(1971), and* Without Feathers *(1975), from which we take this essay. Students struggling with their own journals may take advice from Woody Allen: it is possible to write about serious subjects, and make fun of your own seriousness. "What is it about death that bothers me so much? Probably the hours."*

3

WOODY ALLEN

Selections from the Allen Notebooks

Following are excerpts from the hitherto secret private journal of Woody Allen, which will be published posthumously or after his death, which ever comes first.

1   Getting through the night is becoming harder and harder. Last evening, I had the uneasy feeling that some men were trying to break into my room to shampoo me. But why? I kept imagining I saw shadowy forms, and at 3 A.M. the underwear I had draped over a chair resembled the Kaiser on roller skates. When I finally did fall asleep, I had that same hideous nightmare in which a woodchuck is trying to claim my prize at a raffle. Despair.

I believe my consumption has grown worse. Also my asthma. 2
The wheezing comes and goes, and I get dizzy more and more frequently. I have taken to violent choking and fainting. My room is
damp and I have perpetual chills and palpitations of the heart. I
noticed, too, that I am out of napkins. Will it never stop?

Idea for a story: A man awakens to find his parrot has been made 3
Secretary of Agriculture. He is consumed with jealousy and shoots
himself, but unfortunately the gun is the type with a little flag that
pops out, with the word "Bang" on it. The flag pokes his eye out, and
he lives — a chastened human being who, for the first time, enjoys the
simple pleasures of life, like farming or sitting on an air hose.

Thought: Why does man kill? He kills for food. And not only 4
food: frequently there must be a beverage.

Should I marry W.? Not if she won't tell me the other letters in 5
her name. And what about her career? How can I ask a woman of her
beauty to give up the Roller Derby? Decisions . . .

Once again I tried committing suicide — this time by wetting my 6
nose and inserting it into the light socket. Unfortunately, there was a
short in the wiring, and I merely caromed off the icebox. Still obsessed
by thoughts of death, I brood constantly. I keep wondering if there is
an afterlife, and if there is will they be able to break a twenty?

I ran into my brother today at a funeral. We had not seen one 7
another for fifteen years, but as usual he produced a pig bladder from
his pocket and began hitting me on the head with it. Time has helped
me understand him better. I finally realized his remark that I am
"some loathsome vermin fit only for extermination" was said more
out of compassion than anger. Let's face it: he was always much
brighter than me — wittier, more cultured, better educated. Why he is
still working at McDonald's is a mystery.

Idea for story: Some beavers take over Carnegie Hall and perform 8
Wozzeck. (Strong theme. What will be the structure?)

Good Lord, why am I so guilty? Is it because I hated my father? 9
Probably it was the veal-parmigian' incident. Well, what *was* it doing
in his wallet? If I had listened to him, I would be blocking hats for a

living. I can hear him now: "To block hats — that is everything." I remember his reaction when I told him I wanted to write. "The only writing you'll do is in collaboration with an owl." I still have no idea what he meant. What a sad man! When my first play, *A Cyst for Gus,* was produced at the Lyceum, he attended opening night in tails and a gas mask.

10 Today I saw a red-and-yellow sunset and thought, How insignificant I am! Of course, I thought that yesterday, too, and it rained. I was overcome with self-loathing and contemplated suicide again — this time by inhaling next to an insurance salesman.

11 Short story: A man awakens in the morning and finds himself transformed into his own arch supports. (This idea can work on many levels. Psychologically, it is the quintessence of Kruger, Freud's disciple who discovered sexuality in bacon.)

12 How wrong Emily Dickinson was! Hope is not "the thing with feathers." The thing with feathers has turned out to be my nephew. I must take him to a specialist in Zurich.

13 I have decided to break off my engagement with W. She doesn't understand my writing, and said last night that my *Critique of Metaphysical Reality* reminded her of *Airport.* We quarreled, and she brought up the subject of children again, but I convinced her they would be too young.

14 Do I believe in God? I did until Mother's accident. She fell on some meat loaf, and it penetrated her spleen. She lay in a coma for months, unable to do anything but sing "Granada" to an imaginary herring. Why was this woman in the prime of life so afflicted — because in her youth she dared to defy convention and got married with a brown paper bag on her head? And how can I believe in God when just last week I got my tongue caught in the roller of an electric typewriter? I am plagued by doubts. What if everything is an illusion and nothing exists? In that case, I definitely overpaid for my carpet. If only God would give me some clear sign! Like making a large deposit in my name at a Swiss bank.

15 Had coffee with Melnick today. He talked to me about his idea of having all government officials dress like hens.

Play idea: A character based on my father, but without quite so   16
prominent a big toe. He is sent to the Sorbonne to study the harmon-
ica. In the end, he dies, never realizing his one dream — to sit up to his
waist in gravy. (I see a brilliant second-act curtain, where two midgets
come upon a severed head in a shipment of volleyballs.)

While taking my noon walk today, I had more morbid thoughts.   17
What *is* it about death that bothers me so much? Probably the hours.
Melnick says the soul is immortal and lives on after the body drops
away, but if my soul exists without my body I am convinced all my
clothes will be loose-fitting. Oh, well . . .

Did not have to break off with W. after all, for as luck would have   18
it, she ran off to Finland with a professional circus geek. All for the
best, I suppose, although I had another of those attacks where I start
coughing out of my ears.

Last night, I burned all my plays and poetry. Ironically, as I was   19
burning my masterpiece, *Dark Penguin,* the room caught fire, and I am
now the object of a lawsuit by some men named Pinchunk and Schlos-
ser. Kierkegaard was right.

____ CONSIDERATIONS _____

   1. How soon does the writer let you know that he is playing, rather than
showing you pages from an actual private journal?
   2. Allen's playfulness characteristically takes on the cutting edge of satire. Find a few examples and determine the target of that satire.
   3. Much of Allen's humor depends upon his expert use of *non sequitur.*
Look up the term, then find examples in the Allen notebooks. When is a non
sequitur a flaw, and when is it an asset?
   4. Woody Allen is an omnivorous reader, his biographers tell us. What
evidence of this can you find in his notebooks?
   5. "Universal and timeless!" we sometimes exclaim of a great work of
literature. What lines in the Allen notebooks suggest the author's lack of
concern for those grand attributes? Contrarily, do you regard anything in this
work as universal or timeless?

Maya Angelou (b. 1928) once told an interviewer, "One would say of my life — born loser — had to be; from a broken family, raped at eight, unwed mother at sixteen . . . it's a fact, but it's not the truth."

When she grew up, Maya Angelou became an actress, a singer, a dancer, a songwriter, a teacher, an editor, and a poet. She sang and danced professionally in Porgy and Bess *with a company that traveled through twenty-two countries of Europe and Asia. She wrote for the* Ghana Times *and she taught modern dance in Rome and in Tel Aviv. Her recent books are* Gather Together in My Name *(1974),* Oh Pray My Wings Are Gonna Fit Me Well *(1975), and* And Still I Rise *(1978).*

In 1970 she wrote her autobiography; I Know Why the Caged Bird Sings *was an immediate success. As she says, "I speak to the black experience, but I am always talking about the human condition." The book recounts her early life, with realism and with joy. This section describes a masterful black con man, skillful at turning white bigotry into black profits.*

4

MAYA ANGELOU

Mr. Red Leg

1   Our house was a fourteen-room typical San Franciscan post-Earthquake affair. We had a succession of roomers, bringing and taking their different accents, and personalities and foods. Shipyard workers clanked up the stairs (we all slept on the second floor except Mother and Daddy Clidell) in their steel-tipped boots and metal hats, and gave way to much-powdered prostitutes, who giggled through their make-

up and hung their wigs on the door-knobs. One couple (they were college graduates) held long adult conversations with me in the big kitchen downstairs, until the husband went off to war. Then the wife who had been so charming and ready to smile changed into a silent shadow that played infrequently along the walls. An older couple lived with us for a year or so. They owned a restaurant and had no personality to enchant or interest a teenager, except that the husband was called Uncle Jim, and the wife Aunt Boy. I never figured that out.

The quality of strength lined with tenderness is an unbeatable   2 combination, as are intelligence and necessity when unblunted by formal education. I was prepared to accept Daddy Clidell as one more faceless name added to Mother's roster of conquests. I had trained myself so successfully through the years to display interest, or at least attention, while my mind skipped free on other subjects that I could have lived in his house without ever seeing him and without his becoming the wiser. But his character beckoned and elicited admiration. He was a simple man who had no inferiority complex about his lack of education and, even more amazing, no superiority complex because he had succeeded despite that lack. He would say often, "I been to school three years in my life. In Slaten, Texas, times was hard, and I had to help my daddy on the farm."

No recriminations lay hidden under the plain statement, nor was   3 there boasting when he said, "If I'm living a little better now, it's because I treats everybody right."

He owned apartment buildings and, later, pool halls, and was   4 famous for being that rarity "a man of honor." He didn't suffer, as many "honest men" do, from the detestable righteousness that diminishes their virtue. He knew cards and men's hearts. So during the age when Mother was exposing us to certain facts of life, like personal hygiene, proper posture, table manners, good restaurants and tipping practices, Daddy Clidell taught me to play poker, blackjack, tonk and high, low, Jick, Jack and the Game. He wore expensively tailored suits and a large yellow diamond stickpin. Except for the jewelry, he was a conservative dresser and carried himself with the unconscious pomp of a man of secure means. Unexpectedly, I resembled him, and when he, Mother and I walked down the street his friends often said, "Clidell, that's sure your daughter. Ain't no way you can deny her."

Proud laughter followed those declarations, for he had never had   5 children. Because of his late-arriving but intense paternal sense, I was introduced to the most colorful characters in the Black underground. One afternoon, I was invited into our smoke-filled dining room to make the acquaintance of Stonewall Jimmy, Just Black, Cool Clyde, Tight Coat and Red Leg. Daddy Clidell explained to me that they were the most successful con men in the world, and they were going to tell me about some games so that I would never be "anybody's mark."

6   To begin, one man warned me, "There ain't never been a mark yet that didn't want something for nothing." Then they took turns showing me their tricks, how they chose their victims (marks) from the wealthy bigoted whites and in every case how they used the victims' prejudice against them.

7   Some of the tales were funny, a few were pathetic, but all were amusing or gratifying to me, for the Black man, the con man who could act the most stupid, won out every time over the powerful, arrogant white.

8   I remember Mr. Red Leg's story like a favorite melody.

9   "Anything that works against you can also work for you once you understand the Principle of Reverse.

10   "There was a cracker in Tulsa who bilked so many Negroes he could set up a Negro Bilking Company. Naturally he got to thinking, Black Skin means Damn Fool. Just Black and I went to Tulsa to check him out. Come to find out, he's a perfect mark. His momma must have been scared in an Indian massacre in Africa. He hated Negroes only a little more than he despised Indians. And he was greedy.

11   "Black and I studied him and decided he was worth setting up against the store. That means we were ready to put out a few thousand dollars in preparation. We pulled in a white boy from New York, a good con artist, and had him open an office in Tulsa. He was supposed to be a Northern real estate agent trying to buy up valuable land in Oklahoma. We investigated a piece of land near Tulsa that had a toll bridge crossing it. It used to be part of an Indian reservation but had been taken over by the state.

12   "Just Black was laid out as the decoy, and I was going to be the fool. After our friend from New York hired a secretary and had his cards printed, Black approached the mark with a proposition. He told him that he had heard that our mark was the only white man colored people could trust. He named some of the poor fools that had been taken by that crook. It just goes to show you how white folks can be deceived by their own deception. The mark believed Black.

13   "Black told him about his friend who was half Indian and half colored and how some Northern white estate agent had found out that he was the sole owner of a piece of valuable land and the Northerner wanted to buy it. At first the man acted like he smelled a rat, but from

the way he gobbled up the proposition, turns out what he thought he smelled was some nigger money on his top lip.

"He asked the whereabouts of the land but Black put him off. He told his cracker that he just wanted to make sure that he would be interested. The mark allowed how he was being interested, so Black said he would tell his friend and they'd get in touch with him. Black met the mark for about three weeks in cars and in alleys and kept putting him off until the white man was almost crazy with anxiety and greed and then accidentally it seemed Black let drop the name of the Northern real estate agent who wanted the property. From that moment on we knew we had the big fish on the line and all we had to do was to pull him in. 14

"We expected him to try to contact our store, which he did. That cracker went to our setup and counted on his whiteness to ally him with Spots, our white boy, but Spots refused to talk about the deal except to say the land had been thoroughly investigated by the biggest real estate concern in the South and that if our mark did not go around raising dust he would make sure that there would be a nice piece of money in it for him. Any obvious inquiries as to the rightful ownership of the land could alert the state and they would surely push through a law prohibiting the sale. Spots told the mark he would keep in touch with him. The mark went back to the store three or four times but to no avail, then just before we knew he would crack, Black brought me to see him. That fool was as happy as a sissy in a C.C.C. camp. You would have thought my neck was in a noose and he was about to light the fire under my feet. I never enjoyed taking anybody so much. 15

"Anyhow, I played scary at first but Just Black told me that this was one white man that our people could trust. I said I did not trust no white man because all they wanted was to get a chance to kill a Black man legally and get his wife in the bed. (I'm sorry, Clidell.) The mark assured me that he was the only white man who did not feel like that. Some of his best friends were colored people. In fact, if I didn't know it, the woman who raised him was a colored woman and he still sees her to this day. I let myself be convinced and then the mark began to drag the Northern whites. He told me that they made Negroes sleep in the street in the North and that they had to clean out toilets with their hands in the North and even things worse than that. I was shocked and said, "Then I don't want to sell my land to that white man who offered seventy-five thousand dollars for it.' Just Black said, 'I wouldn't know what to do with that kind of money,' and I said that all I wanted was to have enough money to buy a home for my old mom, to buy a 16 business and to make one trip to Harlem. The mark asked how much would that cost and I said I reckoned I could do it on fifty thousand dollars.

17   "The mark told me no Negro was safe with that kind of money. That white folks would take it from him. I said I knew it but I had to have at least forty thousand dollars. He agreed. We shook hands. I said it would do my heart good to see the mean Yankee go down on some of 'our land.' We met the next morning and I signed the deed in his car and he gave me the cash.

18   "Black and I had kept most of our things in a hotel over in Hot Springs, Arkansas. When the deal was closed we walked to our car, drove across the state line and on to Hot Springs.

19   "That's all there was to it."

20   When he finished, more triumphant stories rainbowed around the room riding the shoulders of laughter. By all accounts those storytellers, born Black and male before the turn of the twentieth century, should have been ground into useless dust. Instead they used their intelligence to pry open the door of rejection and not only became wealthy but got some revenge in the bargain.

21   It wasn't possible for me to regard them as criminals or be anything but proud of their achievements.

22   The needs of a society determine its ethics, and in the Black American ghettos the hero is that man who is offered only the crumbs from his country's table but by ingenuity and courage is able to take for himself a Lucullan feast. Hence the janitor who lives in one room but sports a robin's-egg-blue Cadillac is not laughed at but admired, and the domestic who buys forty-dollar shoes is not criticized but is appreciated. We know that they have put to use their full mental and physical powers. Each single gain feeds into the gains of the body collective.

23   Stories of law violations are weighed on a different set of scales in the Black mind than in the white. Petty crimes embarrass the community and many people wistfully wonder why Negroes don't rob more banks, embezzle more funds and employ graft in the unions. "We are the victims of the world's most comprehensive robbery. Life demands a balance. It's all right if we do a little robbing now." This belief appeals particularly to one who is unable to compete legally with his fellow citizens.

24   My education and that of my Black associates were quite different from the education of our white schoolmates. In the classroom we all learned past participles, but in the streets and in our homes the Blacks

learned to drop *s*'s from plurals and suffixes from past-tense verbs. We were alert to the gap separating the written word from the colloquial. We learned to slide out of one language and into another without being conscious of the effort. At school, in a given situation, we might respond with "That's not unusual." But in the street, meeting the same situation, we easily said, "It be's like that sometimes."

_____ **CONSIDERATIONS** _____

1. Most of Angelou's essay is devoted to Mr. Red Leg telling a story. Notice how close to pure narration that story is. Compare it with the selections in this book by Annie Dillard (pages 137–139), Virginia Woolf (pages 479–481), or Richard Wright (pages 483–491), and contrast the amount of description and narration in Mr. Red Leg's story to that in one of the others.

2. Compare Angelou's essay with Frank Conroy's (pages 93–100), who also emphasizes memorable characters. How do the two authors differ in their reasons for devoting so much space to Mr. Red Leg and to Ramos and Ricardo?

3. At the end of her essay, Angelou sets out an important linguistic principle. Paraphrase that idea and provide examples from your own experience or research.

4. "Stories of law violations are weighed on a different set of scales in the Black mind than in the white." Is a similar difference seen in the minds of two generations? Discuss relative justice versus absolute law.

5. Angelou demonstrates her versatility as a writer frequently in this essay by managing two voices. Find examples and discuss.

6. From what you learn of Angelou's upbringing in the essay, compile a *negative* report by a social worker on Angelou's childhood. Are there positive details in the essay that would allow you to refute a negative report?

Matthew Arnold (1822–1888) was the preeminent man of letters in Victorian England, famous for his essays on culture and literature, as well as for his poetry. "Dover Beach" laments the decline of religious faith, and attempts to transfer devotion from God to a human companion. Although the quandary and the response were products of the Victorian Age, "Dover Beach" still speaks to men and women a century after its making.

5

MATTHEW ARNOLD
Dover Beach

The sea is calm to-night.
The tide is full, the moon lies fair
Upon the straits; on the French coast the light
Gleams and is gone; the cliffs of England stand,
5   Glimmering and vast, out in the tranquil bay.
Come to the window, sweet is the night-air!
Only, from the long line of spray
Where the sea meets the moon-blanch'd land,
Listen! you hear the grating roar
10   Of pebbles which the waves draw back, and fling,
At their return, up the high strand,
Begin, and cease, and then again begin,
With tremulous cadence slow, and bring
The eternal note of sadness in.

15   Sophocles long ago
Heard it on the Ægean, and it brought
Into his mind the turbid ebb and flow
Of human misery; we

Find also in the sound a thought,
Hearing it by this distant northern sea.   20

The Sea of Faith
Was once, too, at the full, and round earth's shore
Lay like the folds of a bright girdle furl'd.
But now I only hear
Its melancholy, long, withdrawing roar,   25
Retreating, to the breath
Of the night-wind, down the vast edges drear
And naked shingles° of the world.   pebbled beaches

Ah, love, let us be true
To one another! for the world, which seems   30
To lie before us like a land of dreams,
So various, so beautiful, so new,
Hath really neither joy, nor love, nor light,
Nor certitude, nor peace, nor help for pain;
And we are here as on a darkling plain   35
Swept with confused alarms of struggle and flight,
Where ignorant armies clash by night.

Francis Bacon (1561–1626) was born to a famous and powerful Elizabethan family, attended Trinity College at Cambridge University, and studied the law. In his essays he is a father of our written language, often counted with Jonathan Swift among the greatest makers of English prose. In this essay, compressed and epigrammatic, Bacon sets forth enough ideas to provide most writers with half a book, and enough arguments for a dozen debates.

6

FRANCIS BACON

Of Marriage and Single Life

He that hath wife and children hath given hostages to fortune; for they are impediments to great enterprises, either of virtue or mischief. Certainly the best works, and of greatest merit for the public, have proceeded from the unmarried or childless men, which both in affection and means have married and endowed the public. Yet it were great reason that those that have children should have greatest care of future times, unto which they know they must transmit their dearest pledges. Some there are who, though they lead a single life, yet their thoughts do end with themselves, and account future times impertinences. Nay, there are some other that account wife and children but as bills of charges. Nay more, there are some foolish rich covetous men that take a pride in having no children, because they may be thought so much the richer. For perhaps they have heard some talk, "Such an one is a great rich man," and another except to it, "Yea, but he hath a great charge for children"; as if it were an abatement to his riches. But the most ordinary cause of a single life is liberty, especially in certain self-pleasing and humorous[1] minds, which are so sensible of every restraint, as they will go near to think their girdles and garters to be bonds and shackles. Unmarried men are best friends, best masters, best servants, but not always best subjects, for they are light to run away, and almost all fugitives are of that condition. A single life doth well with churchmen, for charity will hardly water the ground where it must first fill a pool. It is indifferent for judges and magistrates, for if they be facile and corrupt, you shall have a servant five times worse than a wife. For soldiers, I find the generals commonly in their hortatives put men in mind of their wives and children; and I think the despising of marriage amongst the Turks maketh the vulgar soldier more base. Certainly wife and children are a kind of discipline of humanity; and single men, though they be many times more charitable, because their means are less exhaust, yet, on the other side, they are more cruel and hard-hearted (good to make severe inquisitors), because their tenderness is not so oft called upon. Grave natures, led by custom, and therefore constant, are commonly loving husbands, as was said of Ulysses, *Vetulam suam prœtulit immortalitati.*[2] Chaste women are often proud and forward, as presuming upon the merit of their chastity. It is one of the best bonds, both of chastity and obedience, in the wife if she think her husband wise, which she will never do if she find him jealous. Wives are young men's mistresses, companions for middle age, and old men's nurses, so as a man may have a quarrel[3] to marry when he will. But yet he was reputed one of the wise men that made answer to the question when a man should marry: "A young man not yet, an elder man not at all." It is often seen that bad husbands have very good wives; whether it be that it raiseth the price of their husbands' kindness when it comes, or that the wives take a pride in their patience. But this never fails, if the bad husbands were of their own choosing, against their friends' consent; for then they will be sure to make good their own folly.

CONSIDERATIONS

1. Most modern readers find Bacon's compressed style difficult, but a little study enables them to locate and understand the sources of that diffi-

---

[1] Moody, eccentric. — ED.
[2] He preferred his aged wife to immortality. — ED.
[3] Reason, excuse. — ED.

culty. With study, the difficulties themselves become interesting. What characteristics of Bacon's style would you list as difficulties?

2. About a third of the way into the essay, Bacon uses the word "humorous" to describe the minds of those who prize above all else the liberty they enjoy as unmarried men. Something has happened to that word since Bacon used it. Consult the *Oxford English Dictionary* to find out what the word meant in Bacon's time. Do other words in the essay reflect linguistic change?

3. William Shakespeare and Bacon were contemporaries. Examine Shakespeare's famous sonnet (page 370) to see if you find any features common to both writers. Do they share anything with the King James Version of the Bible, first published a few years before Shakespeare's death? (See the excerpt from Ecclesiastes, pages 53–59.)

4. In the last third of the essay, Bacon argues that wife and children "are a kind of discipline of humanity." What kind of discipline does he have in mind? To what extent is that idea the controlling thesis of the essay?

5. According to modern standards, Bacon's essay suffers from a problem of paragraphing. If you were to edit this piece, where would you suggest breaking it into more than one paragraph? Why? Would you have similar suggestions for the first paragraph of Henry David Thoreau's essay (page 400), or Paragraph 5 in Aldous Huxley's (pages 203–205)?

James Baldwin (b. 1924) published his first novel, Go Tell It On the Mountain, *when he was still in his twenties. Son of a Harlem minister, he has written three more novels, a book of stories, one play, and several collections of essays. In these pages Baldwin summarizes his life to the age of thirty-one, then concentrates a life's ambition into one sentence.*

7

JAMES BALDWIN
Autobiographical Notes

I was born in Harlem thirty-one years ago. I began plotting novels 1 at about the time I learned to read. The story of my childhood is the usual bleak fantasy, and we can dismiss it with the restrained observation that I certainly would not consider living it again. In those days my mother was given to the exasperating and mysterious habit of having babies. As they were born, I took them over with one hand and held a book with the other. The children probably suffered, though they have since been kind enough to deny it, and in this way I read *Uncle Tom's Cabin* and *A Tale of Two Cities* over and over and over again; in this way, in fact, I read just about everything I could get my hands on — except the Bible, probably because it was the only book I was encouraged to read. I must also confess that I wrote — a great deal — and my first professional triumph, in any case, the first effort of mine to be seen in print, occurred at the age of twelve or thereabouts, when a short story I had written about the Spanish revolution won some sort of prize in an extremely short-lived church newspaper. I remember the story was censored by the lady editor, though I don't remember why, and I was outraged.

From *Notes of a Native Son* by James Baldwin. © 1955 by James Baldwin. Reprinted by permission of Beacon Press.

2   Also wrote plays, and songs, for one of which I received a letter of congratulations from Mayor La Guardia, and poetry, about which the less said, the better. My mother was delighted by all these goings-on, but my father wasn't, he wanted me to be a preacher. When I was fourteen I became a preacher, and when I was seventeen I stopped. Very shortly thereafter I left home. For God knows how long I struggled with the world of commerce and industry — I guess they would say they struggled with *me* — and when I was about twenty-one I had enough done of a novel to get a Saxton Fellowship. When I was twenty-two the fellowship was over, the novel turned out to be unsalable, and I started waiting on tables in a Village restaurant and writing book reviews — mostly, as it turned out, about the Negro problem, concerning which the color of my skin made me automatically an expert. Did another book, in company with photographer Theodore Pelatowski, about the store-front churches in Harlem. This book met exactly the same fate as my first — fellowship, but no sale. (It was a Rosenwald Fellowship.) By the time I was twenty-four I had decided to stop reviewing books about the Negro problem — which, by this time, was only slightly less horrible in print than it was in life — and I packed my bags and went to France, where I finished, God knows how, *Go Tell It on the Mountain.*

3   Any writer, I suppose, feels that the world into which he was born is nothing less than a conspiracy against the cultivation of his talent — which attitude certainly has a great deal to support it. On the other hand, it is only because the world looks on his talent with such a frightening indifference that the artist is compelled to make his talent important. So that any writer, looking back over even so short a span of time as I am here forced to assess, finds that the things which hurt him and the things which helped him cannot be divorced from each other; he could be helped in a certain way only because he was hurt in a certain way; and his help is simply to be enabled to move from one conundrum to the next — one is tempted to say that he moves from one disaster to the next. When one begins looking for influences one finds them by the score. I haven't thought much about my own, not enough anyway; I hazard that the King James Bible, the rhetoric of the store-front church, something ironic and violent and perpetually understated in Negro speech — and something of Dickens' love for bravura — have something to do with me today; but I wouldn't stake my life on it. Likewise, innumerable people have helped me in many ways; but finally, I suppose, the most difficult (and most rewarding) thing in my life has been the fact that I was born a Negro and was

forced, therefore, to effect some kind of truce with this reality. (Truce, by the way, is the best one can hope for.)

One of the difficulties about being a Negro writer (and this is not **4** special pleading, since I don't mean to suggest that he has it worse than anybody else) is that the Negro problem is written about so widely. The bookshelves groan under the weight of information, and everyone therefore considers himself informed. And this information, furthermore, operates usually (generally, popularly) to reinforce traditional attitudes. Of traditional attitudes there are only two — For or Against — and I, personally, find it difficult to say which attitude has caused me the most pain. I am speaking as a writer; from a social point of view I am perfectly aware that the change from ill-will to good-will, however motivated, however imperfect, however expressed, is better than no change at all.

But it is part of the business of the writer — as I see it — to **5** examine attitudes, to go beneath the surface, to tap the source. From this point of view the Negro problem is nearly inaccessible. It is not only written about so widely; it is written about so badly. It is quite possible to say that the price a Negro pays for becoming articulate is to find himself, at length, with nothing to be articulate about. ("You taught me language," says Caliban to Prospero, "and my profit on't is I know how to curse.") Consider: the tremendous social activity that this problem generates imposes on whites and Negroes alike the necessity of looking forward, of working to bring about a better day. This is fine, it keeps the waters troubled; it is all, indeed, that has made possible the Negro's progress. Nevertheless, social affairs are not generally speaking the writer's prime concern, whether they ought to be or not; it is absolutely necessary that he establish between himself and these affairs a distance which will allow, at least, for clarity, so that before he can look forward in any meaningful sense, he must first be allowed to take a long look back. In the context of the Negro problem neither whites nor blacks, for excellent reasons of their own, have the faintest desire to look back; but I think that the past is all that makes the present coherent, and further, that the past will remain horrible for exactly as long as we refuse to assess it honestly.

I know, in any case, that the most crucial time in my own devel- **6** opment came when I was forced to recognize that I was a kind of bastard of the West; when I followed the line of my past I did not find myself in Europe but in Africa. And this meant that in some subtle way, in a really profound way, I brought to Shakespeare, Bach, Rembrandt, to the stones of Paris, to the cathedral at Chartres and to the

Empire State Building, a special attitude. These were not really my creations, they did not contain my history; I might search in them in vain forever for any reflection of myself. I was an interloper; this was not my heritage. At the same time I had no other heritage which I could possibly hope to use — I had certainly been unfitted for the jungle or the tribe. I would have to appropriate these white centuries, I would have to make them mine — I would have to accept my special attitude, my special place in this scheme — otherwise I would have no place in *any* scheme. What was the most difficult was the fact that I was forced to admit something I had always hidden from myself, which the American Negro has had to hide from himself as the price of his public progress; that I hated and feared white people. This did not mean that I loved black people; on the contrary, I despised them, possibly because they failed to produce Rembrandt. In effect, I hated and feared the world. And this meant, not only that I thus gave the world an altogether murderous power over me, but also that in such a self-destroying limbo I could never hope to write.

7   One writes out of one thing only — one's own experience. Everything depends on how relentlessly one forces from this experience the last drop, sweet or bitter, it can possibly give. This is the only real concern of the artist, to recreate out of the disorder of life that order which is art. The difficulty then, for me, of being a Negro writer was the fact that I was, in effect, prohibited from examining my own experience too closely by the tremendous demands and the very real dangers of my social situation.

8   I don't think the dilemma outlined above is uncommon. I do think, since writers work in the disastrously explicit medium of language, that it goes a little way towards explaining why, out of the enormous resources of Negro speech and life, and despite the example of Negro music, prose written by Negroes has been generally speaking so pallid and so harsh. I have not written about being a Negro at such length because I expect that to be my only subject, but only because it was the gate I had to unlock before I could hope to write about anything else. I don't think that the Negro problem in America can be even discussed coherently without bearing in mind its context; its context being the history, traditions, customs, the moral assumptions and preoccupations of the country; in short, the general social fabric. Appearances to the contrary, no one in America escapes its effects and everyone in America bears some responsibility for it. I believe this the more firmly because it is the overwhelming tendency to speak of this problem as though it were a thing apart. But in the work of Faulkner,

in the general attitude and certain specific passages in Robert Penn Warren, and, most significantly, in the advent of Ralph Ellison, one sees the beginnings — at least — of a more genuinely penetrating search. Mr. Ellison, by the way, is the first Negro novelist I have ever read to utilize in language, and brilliantly, some of the ambiguity and irony of Negro life.

About my interests: I don't know if I have any, unless the morbid desire to own a sixteen-millimeter camera and make experimental movies can be so classified. Otherwise, I love to eat and drink — it's my melancholy conviction that I've scarcely ever had enough to eat (this is because it's *impossible* to eat enough if you're worried about the next meal) — and I love to argue with people who do not disagree with me too profoundly, and I love to laugh. I do *not* like bohemia, or bohemians, I do not like people whose principal aim is pleasure, and I do not like people who are *earnest* about anything. I don't like people who like me because I'm a Negro; neither do I like people who find in the same accident grounds for contempt. I love America more than any other country in the world, and, exactly for this reason, I insist on the right to criticize her perpetually. I think all theories are suspect, that the finest principles may have to be modified, or may even be pulverized by the demands of life, and that one must find, therefore, one's own moral center and move through the world hoping that this center will guide one aright. I consider that I have many responsibilities, but none greater than this: to last, as Hemingway says, and get my work done. 9

I want to be an honest man and a good writer. 10

____ **CONSIDERATIONS** _____

1. Why didn't the young Baldwin read the Bible? In your education, have you ever been affected by similar feelings?
2. Point out specific features of Baldwin's style that account for its slightly ironic tone. What other authors in this book make use of irony? Why?
3. Baldwin finds it difficult, he says, to distinguish the things that helped him as a writer from those that hurt him. Can you draw any parallels with your experience as a student?
4. Baldwin wrote this essay for a book that appeared in 1955, when he was thirty-one years old and had already published two successful novels. How do those facts affect your response to the last sentence in the essay?
5. Many black writers have argued that the black artist must reject all of white culture. How does Baldwin explain his acceptance of Shakespeare,

Bach, Rembrandt, the cathedral at Chartres, and the Empire State Building? With this point in mind, consider what Etheridge Knight says about *his* heritage on pages 217–218.

6. Note how many years Baldwin covers in the first half-dozen sentences of Paragraph 2. How do you explain the lack of details about those years? Is this a weakness or a strength of the essay?

Donald Barthelme (b. 1931) has published two novels, and several volumes of short pieces, like "The School," which are generally described as fiction. He grew up in Texas, lives in New York's Greenwich Village, and supports himself by writing prose which is impeccable, unpredictable, funny, absurd, and serious.

8

DONALD BARTHELME

The School

Well, we had all these children out planting trees, see, because we figured that . . . that was part of their education, to see how, you know, the root systems . . . and also the sense of responsibility, taking care of things, being individually responsible. You know what I mean. And the trees all died. They were orange trees. I don't know why they died, they just died. Something wrong with the soil possibly or maybe the stuff we got from the nursery wasn't the best. We complained about it. So we've got thirty kids there, each kid had his or her own little tree to plant, and we've got these thirty dead trees. All these kids looking at these little brown sticks, it was depressing.

It wouldn't have been so bad except that just a couple of weeks before the thing with the trees, the snakes all died. But I think that the snakes — well, the reason that the snakes kicked off was that . . . you remember, the boiler was shut off for four days because of the strike, and that was explicable. It was something you could explain to the kids because of the strike. I mean, none of their parents would let them cross the picket line and they knew there was a strike going on and what it meant. So when things got started up again and we found the snakes they weren't too disturbed.

With the herb gardens it was probably a case of overwatering, and at least now they know not to overwater. The children were very conscientious with the herb gardens and some of them probably . . . you know, slipped them a little extra water when we weren't looking. Or maybe . . . well, I don't like to think about sabotage, although it did occur to us. I mean, it was something that crossed our minds. We were thinking that way probably because before that the gerbils had died, and the white mice had died, and the salamander . . . well, now they know not to carry them around in plastic bags.

Of course we *expected* the tropical fish to die, that was no surprise. Those numbers, you look at them crooked and they're belly-up on the surface. But the lesson plan called for a tropical-fish input at that point, there was nothing we could do, it happens every year, you just have to hurry past it.

We weren't even supposed to have a puppy.

We weren't even supposed to have one, it was just a puppy the Murdoch girl found under a Gristede's truck one day and she was afraid the truck would run over it when the driver had finished making his delivery, so she stuck it in her knapsack and brought it to school with her. So we had this puppy. As soon as I saw the puppy I thought, Oh Christ, I bet it will live for about two weeks and then . . . And that's what it did. It wasn't supposed to be in the classroom at all, there's some kind of regulation about it, but you can't tell them they can't have a puppy when the puppy is already there, right in front of them, running around on the floor and yap yap yapping. They named it Edgar — that is, they named it after me. They had a lot of fun running after it and yelling, "Here, Edgar! Nice Edgar!" Then they'd laugh like hell. They enjoyed the ambiguity. I enjoyed it myself. I don't mind being kidded. They made a little house for it in the supply closet and all that. I don't know what it died of. Distemper, I guess. It probably hadn't had any shots. I got it out of there before the kids got to school. I checked the supply closet each morning, routinely, because I knew what was going to happen. I gave it to the custodian.

And then there was this Korean orphan that the class adopted through the Help the Children program, all the kids brought in a quarter a month, that was the idea. It was an unfortunate thing, the kid's name was Kim and maybe we adopted him too late or something. The cause of death was not stated in the letter we got, they suggested we adopt another child instead and sent us some interesting case histories, but we didn't have the heart. The class took it pretty hard, they began (I think; nobody ever said anything to me directly) to feel that maybe there was something wrong with the school. But I don't think there's anything wrong with the school, particularly, I've seen better and I've seen worse. It was just a run of bad luck. We had an extraordinary number of parents passing away, for instance. There were I think two heart attacks and two suicides, one drowning, and four killed together in a car accident. One stroke. And we had the usual heavy mortality rate among the grandparents, or maybe it was heavier this year, it seemed so. And finally the tragedy.

The tragedy occurred when Matthew Wein and Tony Mavrogordo were playing over where they're excavating for the new federal office building. There were all these big wooden beams stacked, you know, at the edge of the excavation. There's a court case coming out of that, the parents are claiming that the beams were poorly stacked. I don't know what's true and what's not. It's been a strange year.

I forgot to mention Billy Brandt's father, who was knifed fatally when he grappled with a masked intruder in his home.

One day, we had a discussion in class. They asked me, where did they go? The trees, the salamander, the tropical fish, Edgar, the poppas and mommas, Matthew and Tony, where did they go? And I said, I don't know, I don't know. And they said, who knows? and I said, nobody knows. And they said, is death that which gives meaning to life? and I said, no, life is that which gives meaning to life. Then they said, but isn't death, considered as a fundamental datum, the means by which the taken-for-granted mundanity of the everyday may be transcended in the direction of —

I said, yes, maybe.

They said, we don't like it.

I said, that's sound.

They said, it's a bloody shame!

I said, it is.

They said, will you make love now with Helen (our teaching assistant) so that we can see how it is done? We know you like Helen.

I do like Helen but I said that I would not.

We've heard so much about it, they said, but we've never seen it.

I said I would be fired and that it was never, or almost never, done as a demonstration. Helen looked out of the window.

They said, please, please make love with Helen, we require an assertion of value, we are frightened.

I said that they shouldn't be frightened (although I am often frightened) and that there was value everywhere. Helen came and embraced me. I kissed her a few times on the brow. We held each other. The children were excited. Then there was a knock on the door, I opened the door, and the new gerbil walked in. The children cheered wildly.

____ CONSIDERATIONS _____

1. Voice or persona is the prominent feature of Barthelme's short story. From what the voice reveals, how would you describe the narrator?

2. The story lists an apparently endless series of failures and catastrophes. Is there a significant order to those events?

3. In the last third of the story, Barthelme puts unlikely words into the mouths of the schoolchildren. Why?

4. Some readers charge that Barthelme's humor is sick. What do you understand by the term, sick humor? What might be pointed out as an example of it in this story? Is Jonathan Swift open to the same charge? (See pages 378–385.)

5. What is a gerbil (see the third paragraph), and why does Barthelme repeat the word in his concluding paragraph?

James E. Baxter (b. 1925) practices psychiatry in New York City, teaches, and works at a large medical center where he concerns himself with the psychiatric effects of surgery. He writes for medical journals, and in popular magazines sometimes interprets medical or psychiatric practice for the general public. Discussing the controversial subject of transsexual surgery, Dr. Baxter argues his case in plain language informed by technical knowledge.

9

JAMES E. BAXTER, M.D.

Why Shouldn't We Change Sex?

A lot of us have been watching — with a prurient sort of interest — the adventures of a lady who used to be a gentleman and who has made her way into the sports sections of our newspapers and magazines. There's been a big to-do about the authenticity of her new sex, fusses about chromosome tests and comments about the level of her voice, and some of her potential opponents have been willing to compete against her while others have declined.

Most of us on the sidelines have, I suspect, wished Dr. Renee Richards good luck, while uneasily realizing that she's shown more guts than we would have in his, now her, shoes.

Why shouldn't we change sex if we want to and can? We change cars, houses, jobs, spouses, hair color, and, God knows, religion. Names are changed often enough. And almost all of us have ancestors who changed nationalities.

Flux, restless rearranging, has been not only a constant in American life but essential to it. The Great Plains couldn't have become the breadbasket for much of the world unless people were willing to change their address from the East to the Middle West. And the per-acre production of wheat didn't multiply as it did without the help of scientists fully committed to the notion of hybridization.

5   Furthermore, as a people, we've long been attuned to psychological change. Trading those rags for riches required mental flexibility on the part of our beloved robber barons that would have dumfounded their peasant forebears. As succeeding generations of American parents dreamed of a different, better life for their children, succeeding generations of youth set out on a quest to "find themselves"; in other words, to modify their old identities.

6   Finding a "right identity" for ourselves is possibly what we're all ultimately after. It ought to have two major components: feeling that what we sense to be best and truest within us is pretty well expressed in our daily lives, and, second, feeling that we are involved with other people in ways that are mutually supportive and respectful and even loving.

7   What probably should move us most about Dr. Richards is the knowledge that she was terribly unhappy in her previous sexual identity. Assuming, as she undoubtedly did, that she had only one chance at life here below, she dared to do everything she could to embody the identity that she felt was truly her own. And now she's off and running, apparently in top, if modified, form.

8   Those who would cast stones at her are easily disposed of: if they cavil that sex alteration is contrary to divine edict, they're guilty of trying to read the mind of the Almighty, a theological misdemeanor. If they say that she's made a spectacle of herself by flaunting her new sexual orientation in public, ask them if she should have gone into permanent hiding. If they protest that the lady's body proportions and her muscle mass are still pretty much those of a male and that she's thus competing against females unfairly, perhaps this deserves investigation and some Solomonic resolution.

9   But I suspect that the stone throwers are mostly those whose anxieties are aroused by events that they're not prepared for. If the lady has caused awkwardness or sadness for her relatives and friends, there's nothing new about that, and surely they have their own relatives and friends who have rallied round and offered support.

10   Of what her new identity has cost her in inner struggle and physical pain, she has so far mercifully kept us ignorant. Gratuitously invading the privacy of others can be a criminal offense. Invading one's own in public can be mortally offensive and, because it's unpunishable, is less forgivable than the former.

Whatever the weight of an individual emotional burden or the 11
outcome of tennis matches, the ongoing saga of Dr. Richards will certainly have focused the attention of both the lay and the medical com-
munities on a large and provocative question: what is meant by
sexuality? It used to be so simple — female or male — just as someone
was alive or dead if his heart was beating or not. Now death is viewed
as a complex of conditions including the activity of the brain.

Endocrinologists know that a child can be born with both female 12
and male sexual tissues as well as with ambiguous external sexual
organs. And as Dr. Richards has reminded us, the standard XX and XY
chromosome differentiation is not always flawless. To compound
these uncertainties, other questions intrude. What about the psychological orientation, toward male or female longings and urges? Or the
so-called secondary sexual characteristics — beards, bosoms and muscular backhands?

Are the sex-change operations just a more sophisticated transves- 13
tism or do they actually reverse "sexuality"? But how are we using
that term? There's no consensus at this point, and chances are there
won't be for some time to come.

And this could easily lead us to convoluted speculations about 14
the nature of identity. To what extent can a person simply will himself
a new identity? How *authentic* is it? Are you who you are according to
the statistics of the Census Bureau or as your acquaintances see you?
Or should you yourself be the only judge of who you are? It would
seem that Dr. Richards's situation is making us rethink some of our
most basic suppositions about ourselves.

So perhaps we should relax and nod our tentative approval at her 15
decision and decisiveness. She will hardly have the chance to renege,
and if she behaves with the good sportsmanship that we expect of our
athletes, she might come to be a respected exemplar of the American
way: she abruptly eradicated much of her past, headed forthrightly in
a new direction and has let it be understood that she has no apologies
and no discernible misgivings.

___ **CONSIDERATIONS** _____

1. In his first sentence, Baxter uses the word "prurient," which often
figures in definitions of pornography. Carefully examine dictionary definitions
of prurient to see whether they actually clarify the word or simply send you to
other words that are also difficult, if not impossible, to define.

2. Baxter attempts, in Paragraph 8, to dispose quickly of the arguments against Dr. Richards's actions. How convincing or logical are his replies to those arguments? Are convincing arguments necessarily logical? Are logical arguments always convincing?

3. The author raises several large questions that he does not attempt to answer. He asks us to think about the nature of sexuality and the authenticity of identity, for example. How does he use those questions to further his argument?

4. To what extent are we influenced by our society in determining our notions of maleness and femaleness? Consider the examples offered by Nora Ephron (pages 150–158), Ernest Hemingway (pages 185–189), and Margaret Mead (pages 260–273).

5. Study Baxter's use of the first-person pronouns, "we" and "us" and "our." Do those words add to the persuasiveness of his plea for acceptance of Dr. Richards?

*Wendell Berry (b. 1934) was born and educated in Kentucky,
left home to teach in New York and California — and returned to
his native hill. He is a novelist —* Nathan Coulter *(1960),* A Place
on Earth *(1968), and* The Memory of Old Jack *(1974) — and a poet,
with six volumes of poetry; the most recent are* The Country of
Marriage *(1973) and* Clearing *(1977). He has also published four
collections of essays; the latest, published by the Sierra Club,
expresses in its title the range of Wendell Berry's passions:* The
Unsettling of America: Culture and Agriculture.*
"A Native Hill" appeared in* The Long-Legged House *(1969) and
uses description to make clear the emotional and intellectual center of Berry's work — the human relationship to land.*

10

WENDELL BERRY

A Native Hill

I start down from one of the heights of the upland, the town of   1
Port Royal at my back. It is a winter day, overcast and still, and the
town is closed in itself, humming and muttering a little, like a winter
beehive.

The dog runs ahead, prancing and looking back, knowing the way   2
we are about to go. This is a walk well established with us — a route
in our minds as well as on the ground. There is a sort of mystery in the
establishment of these ways. Any time one crosses a given stretch of
country with some frequency, no matter how wanderingly one begins,
the tendency is always toward habit. By the third or fourth trip, without realizing it, one is following a fixed path, going the way one went
before. After that, one may still wander, but only by deliberation, and

when there is reason to hurry, or when the mind wanders rather than the feet, one returns to the old route. Familiarity has begun. One has made a relationship with the landscape, and the form and the symbol and the enactment of the relationship is the path. These paths of mine are seldom worn on the ground. They are habits of mind, directions and turns. They are as personal as old shoes. My feet are comfortable in them.

3   From the height I can see far out over the country, the long open ridges of the farmland, the wooded notches of the streams, the valley of the river opening beyond, and then more ridges and hollows of the same kind.

4   Underlying this country, nine hundred feet below the highest ridgetops, more than four hundred feet below the surface of the river, is sea level. We seldom think of it here; we are a long way from the coast and the sea is alien to us. And yet the attraction of sea level dwells in this country as an ideal dwells in a man's mind. All our rains go in search of it and, departing, they have carved the land in a shape that is fluent and falling. The streams branch like vines, and between the branches the land rises steeply and then rounds and gentles into the long narrowing fingers of ridgeland. Near the heads of the streams even the steepest land was not too long ago farmed and kept cleared. But now it has been given up and the woods is returning. The wild is flowing back like a tide. The arable ridgetops reach out above the gathered trees like headlands into the sea, bearing their human burdens of fences and houses and barns, crops and roads.

5   Looking out over the country, one gets a sense of the whole of it: the ridges and hollows, the clustered buildings of the farms, the open fields, the woods, the stock ponds set like coins into the slopes. But this is a surface sense, an exterior sense, such as you get from looking down on the roof of a house. The height is a threshold from which to step down into the wooded folds of the land, the interior, under the trees and along the branching streams.

6   I pass through a pasture gate on a deep-worn path that grows shallow a little way beyond, and then disappears altogether into the grass. The gate has gathered thousands of passings to and fro, that have divided like the slats of a fan on either side of it. It is like a fist holding together the strands of a net.

7   Beyond the gate the land leans always more steeply toward the branch. I follow it down, and then bear left along the crease at the bottom of the slope. I have entered the downflow of the land. The way I am going is the way the water goes. There is something comfortable

and fit-feeling in this, something free in this yielding to gravity and taking the shortest way down. The mind moves through the watershed as the water moves.

As the hollow deepens into the hill, before it has yet entered the woods, the grassy crease becomes a raw gulley, and along the steepening slopes on either side I can see the old scars of erosion, places where the earth is gone clear to the rock. My people's errors have become the features of my country.

It occurs to me that it is no longer possible to imagine how this country looked in the beginning, before the white people drove their plows into it. It is not possible to know what was the shape of the land here in this hollow when it was first cleared. Too much of it is gone, loosened by the plows and washed away by the rain. I am walking the route of the departure of the virgin soil of the hill. I am not looking at the same land the first-comers saw. The original surface of the hill is as extinct as the passenger pigeon. The pristine America that the first white men saw is a lost continent, sunk like Atlantis in the sea. The thought of what was here once and is gone forever will not leave me as long as I live. It is as though I walk knee-deep in its absence.

The slopes along the hollow steepen still more and I go in under the trees. I pass beneath the surface. I am enclosed, and my sense, my interior sense, of the country becomes intricate. There is no longer the possibility of seeing very far. The distances are closed off by the trees and the steepening walls of the hollow. One cannot grow familiar here by sitting and looking as one can up in the open on the ridge. Here the eyes become dependent on the feet. To see the woods from the inside one must look and move and look again. It is inexhaustible in its standpoints. A lifetime will not be enough to experience it all.

Not far from the beginning of the woods, and set deep in the earth in the bottom of the hollow, is a rock-walled pool not a lot bigger than a bathtub. The wall is still nearly as straight and tight as when it was built. It makes a neatly turned narrow horseshoe, the open end downstream. This is a historical ruin, dug here either to catch and hold the water of the little branch, or to collect the water of a spring whose vein broke to the surface here — it is probably no longer possible to know which. The pool is filled with earth now, and grass grows in it. And the branch bends around it, cut down to the bare rock, a torrent after heavy rain, other times bone dry. All that is certain is that when the pool was dug and walled there was deep topsoil on the hill to gather and hold the water. And this high up, at least, the bottom of the hollow, instead of the present raw notch of the streambed, wore the

8

9

10

11

same mantle of soil as the slopes, and the stream was a steady seep or trickle, running most or all of the year. This tiny pool no doubt once furnished water for a considerable number of stock through the hot summers. And now it is only a lost souvenir, archaic and useless, except for the bitter intelligence there is in it. It is one of the monuments to what is lost.

12   Like the pasture gates, the streams are great collectors of comings and goings. The streams go down, and paths always go down beside the streams. For a while I walk along an old wagon road that is buried in leaves — a fragment, beginningless and endless as the middle of a sentence on some scrap of papyrus. There is a cedar whose branches reach over this road, and under the branches I find the leavings of two kills of some bird of prey. The most recent is a pile of blue jay feathers. The other has been rained on and is not identifiable. How little we know. How little of this was intended or expected by any man. The road that has become the grave of men's passages has led to the life of the woods.

> And I say to myself: Here is your road
> without beginning or end, appearing
> out of the earth and ending in it, bearing
> no load but the hawk's kill, and the leaves
> building earth on it, something more
> to be borne. Tracks fill with earth
> and return to absence. The road was worn
> by men bearing earth along it. They have come
> to endlessness. In their passing
> they could not stay in, trees have risen
> And stand still. It is leading to the dark,
> to mornings where you are not. Here
> is your road, beginningless and endless as God.

13   Now I have come down within the sound of the water. The winter has been rainy, and the hill is full of dark seeps and trickles, gathering finally, along these creases, into flowing streams. The sound of them is one of the elements, and defines a zone. When their voices return to the hill after their absence during summer and autumn, it is a better place to be. A thirst in the mind is quenched.

14   I have already passed the place where water began to flow in the little stream bed I am following. It broke into the light from beneath a rock ledge, a thin glittering stream. It lies beside me as I walk, overtaking me and going by, yet not moving, a thread of light and sound. And now from below comes the steady tumble and rush of the water of

Camp Branch — whose nameless camp was it named for? — and gradually as I descend the sound of the smaller stream is lost in the sound
of the larger.

The two hollows join, the line of the meeting of the two spaces   15
obscured even in winter by the trees. But the two streams meet precisely as two roads. That is, the stream *beds* do; the one ends in the
other. As for the meeting of the waters, there is no looking at that. The
one flow does not end in the other, but continues in it, one with it,
two clarities merged without a shadow.

All waters are one. This is a reach of the sea, flung like a net over   16
the hill, and now drawn back to the sea. And as the sea is never raised
in the earthly nets of fishermen, so the hill is never caught and pulled
down by the watery net of the sea. But always a little of it is. Each of
the gathering strands of the net carries back some of the hill melted in
it. Sometimes, as now, it carries so little that the water seems to flow
clear; sometimes it carries a lot and is brown and heavy with it. Whenever greedy or thoughtless men have lived on it, the hill has literally
flowed out of their tracks into the bottom of the sea.

There appears to be a law that when creatures have reached the   17
level of consciousness, as men have, they must become conscious of
the creation; they must learn how they fit into it and what its needs
are and what it requires of them, or else pay a terrible penalty: the
spirit of the creation will go out of them, and they will become destructive. The very earth will depart from them and go where they cannot
follow.

My mind is never empty or idle at the joinings of streams. Here   18
is the work of the world going on. The creation is felt, alive and intent
on its materials, in such places. In the angle of the meeting of the two
streams stands the steep wooded point of the ridge, like the prow of an
upturned boat — finished, as it was a thousand years ago, as it will be
in a thousand years. Its becoming is only incidental to its being. It will
be because it is. It has no aim or end except to be. By being it is growing
and wearing into what it will be. The fork of the stream lies at the foot
of the slope like hammer and chisel laid down at the foot of a finished
sculpture. But the stream is no dead tool; it is alive, it is still at its
work. Put your hand to it to learn the health of this part of the world.
It is the wrist of the hill.

Perhaps it is to prepare to hear some day the music of the spheres   19
that I am always turning my ears to the music of streams. There is
indeed a music in streams, but it is not for the hurried. It has to be
loitered by and imagined. Or imagined *toward,* for it is hardly for men

at all. Nature has a patient ear. To her the slowest funeral march sounds like a jig. She is satisfied to have the notes drawn out to the lengths of days or weeks or months. Small variations are acceptable to her, modulations as leisurely as the opening of a flower.

20   The stream is full of stops and gates. Here it has piled up rocks in its path, and pours over them into a tiny pool it has scooped at the foot of its fall. Here it has been dammed by a mat of leaves caught behind a fallen limb. Here it must force a narrow passage, here a wider one. Tomorrow the flow may increase or slacken, and the tone will shift. In an hour or a week that rock may give way, and the composition will advance by another note. Some idea of it may be got by walking slowly along and noting the changes as one passes from one little fall or rapid to another. But this is a highly simplified and diluted version of the real thing, which is too complex and widespread ever to be actually heard by us. The ear must imagine an impossible patience in order to grasp even the unimaginableness of such music.

21   But the creation is musical, and this is a part of its music, as birdsong is, or the words of poets. The music of the streams is the music of the shaping of the earth, by which the rocks are pushed and shifted downward toward the level of the sea.

22   And now I find lying in the path an empty beer can. This is the track of the ubiquitous man Friday of all our woods. In my walks I never fail to discover some sign that he has preceded me. I find his empty shotgun shells, his empty cans and bottles, his sandwich wrappings. In wooded places along roadsides one is apt to find, as well, his over-travelled bedsprings, his outcast refrigerator, and heaps of the imperishable refuse of his modern kitchen. A year ago, almost in this same place where I have found his beer can, I found a possum that he had shot dead and left lying, in celebration of his manhood. He is the true American pioneer, perfectly at rest in his assumption that he is the first and the last whose inheritance and fate this place will ever be. Going forth, as he may think, to sow, he only broadcasts his effects.

23   As I go on down the path alongside Camp Branch, I walk by the edge of croplands abandoned only within my own lifetime. On my left are south slopes where the woods are old, long undisturbed. On my right, the more fertile north slopes are covered with patches of briars and sumacs and a lot of young walnut trees. Tobacco of an extraordinary quality was once grown here, and then the soil wore thin, and these places were given up for the more accessible ridges that were not so steep, where row-cropping made better sense anyway. But now, under the thicket growth, a mat of bluegrass has grown to testify to

the good nature of this ground. It was fine dirt that lay here once, and I am far from being able to say that I could have resisted the temptation to plow it. My understanding of what is best for it is the tragic understanding of hindsight, the awareness that I have been taught what was here to be lost by the loss of it.

We have lived by the assumption that what was good for us would 24 be good for the world. And this has been based on the even flimsier assumption that we could know with any certainty what was good even for us. We have fulfilled the danger of this by making our personal pride and greed the standard of our behavior toward the world — to the incalculable disadvantage of the world and every living thing in it. And now, perhaps very close to too late, our great error has become clear. It is not only our own creativity — our own capacity for life — that is stifled by our arrogant assumption; the creation itself is stifled.

We have been wrong. We must change our lives, so that it will be 25 possible to live by the contrary assumption that what is good for the world will be good for us. And that requires that we make the effort to *know* the world and to learn what is good for it. We must learn to cooperate in its processes, and to yield to its limits. But even more important, we must learn to acknowledge that the creation is full of mystery; we will never entirely understand it. We must abandon arrogance and stand in awe. We must recover the sense of the majesty of creation, and the ability to be worshipful in its presence. For I do not doubt that it is only on the condition of humility and reverence before the world that our species will be able to remain in it.

Standing in the presence of these worn and abandoned fields, 26 where the creation has begun its healing without the hindrance or the help of man, with the voice of the stream in the air and the woods standing in silence on all the slopes around me, I am deep in the interior not only of my place in the world, but of my own life, its sources and searches and concerns. I first came into these places following the men to work when I was a child. I knew the men who took their lives from such fields as these, and their lives to a considerable extent made my life what it is. In what came to me from them there was both wealth and poverty, and I have been a long time discovering which was which.

It was in the woods here along Camp Branch that Bill White, my 27 grandfather's Negro hired hand, taught me to hunt squirrels. Bill lived in a little tin-roofed house on up nearer the head of the hollow. And this was, I suppose more than any other place, his hunting ground. It was the place of his freedom, where he could move without subservience, without considering who he was or who anybody else was. On late summer mornings, when it was too wet to work, I would follow him into the woods. As soon as we stepped in under the trees he would become silent, and absolutely attentive to the life of the place. He was a good teacher and an exacting one. The rule seemed to be that if I wanted to stay with him, I had to make it possible for him to forget I was there. I was to make no noise. If I did he would look back and make a downward emphatic gesture with his hand, as explicit as writing: Be quiet, or go home. He would see a squirrel crouched in a fork or lying along the top of a branch, and indicate with a grin and a small jerk of his head where I should look; and then wait, while I, conscious of being watched and demanded upon, searched it out for myself. He taught me to look and to listen and to be quiet. I wonder if he knew the value of such teaching or the rarity of such a teacher.

28   In the years that followed I hunted often here alone. And later in these same woods I experienced my first obscure dissatisfactions with hunting. Though I could not have put it into words then, the sense had come to me that hunting as I knew it — the eagerness to kill something I did not need to eat — was an artificial relation to the place, when what I was beginning to need, just as inarticulately then, was a relation that would be deeply natural and meaningful. That was a time of great uneasiness and restlessness for me. It would be the fall of the year, the leaves would be turning, and ahead of me would be another year of school. There would be confusions about girls and ambitions, the wordless hurried feeling that time and events and my own nature were pushing me toward what I was going to be — and I had no notion what it was, or how to prepare.

29   And then there were years when I did not come here at all — when these places and their history were in my mind, and part of me, in places thousands of miles away. And now I am here again, changed from what I was, and still changing. The future is no more certain to me now than it ever was, though its risks are clearer, and so are my own desires; I am the father of two young children whose lives are hostages given to the future. Because of them and because of events in the world, life seems more fearful and difficult to me now than ever before; but it is also more inviting, and I am constantly aware of its nearness to joy. Much of the interest and excitement that I have in my life now has come from the deepening, in the years since my return here, of my relation to this countryside that is my native place. For in spite of all that has happened to me in other places, the great change and the great possibility of change in my life has been in my sense of

this place. The major difference is perhaps only that I have grown able to be wholeheartedly present here. I am able to sit and be quiet at the foot of some tree here in this woods along Camp Branch, and feel a deep peace, both in the place and in my awareness of it, that not too long ago I was not conscious of the possibility of. This peace is partly in being free of the suspicion that pursued me for most of my life, no matter where I was, that there was perhaps another place I *should* be, or would be happier or better in; it is partly in the increasingly articulate consciousness of being here, and of the significance and importance of being here.

After more than thirty years I have at last arrived at the candor   30
necessary to stand on this part of the earth that is so full of my own history and so much damaged by it, and ask: What *is* this place? What is in it? What is its nature? How should men live in it? What must I do?

I have not found the answers, though I believe that in partial and   31
fragmentary ways they have begun to come to me. But the questions are more important than their answers. In the final sense they *have* no answers. They are like the questions — they are perhaps the same questions — that were the discipline of Job. They are part of the necessary enactment of humility, teaching a man what his importance is, what his responsibility is, and what his place is, both on the earth and in the order of things. And though the answers must always come obscurely and in fragments, the questions must be persistently asked. They are fertile questions. In their implications and effects, they are moral and esthetic and, in the best and fullest sense, practical. They promise a relationship to the world that is decent and preserving.

They are also, both in origin and effect, religious. I am uneasy   32
with the term, for such religion as has been openly practiced in this part of the world has promoted and fed upon a destructive schism between body and soul, heaven and earth. It has encouraged people to believe that the world is of no importance, and that their only obligation in it is to submit to certain churchly formulas in order to get to heaven. And so the people who might have been expected to care most selflessly for the world have had their minds turned elsewhere — to a pursuit of "salvation" that was really only another form of gluttony and self-love, the desire to perpetuate their own small lives beyond the life of the world. The heaven-bent have abused the earth thoughtlessly, by inattention, and their negligence has permitted and encouraged others to abuse it deliberately. Once the creator was removed from the creation, divinity became only a remote abstraction, a social weapon

in the hands of the religious institutions. This split in public values produced or was accompanied by, as it was bound to be, an equally artificial and ugly division in people's lives, so that a man, while pursuing heaven with the sublime appetite he thought of as his soul, could turn his heart against his neighbors and his hands against the world. For these reasons, though I know that my questions *are* religious, I dislike having to *say* that they are.

33   But when I ask them my aim is not primarily to get to heaven. Though heaven is certainly more important than the earth if all they say about it is true, it is still morally incidental to it and dependent on it, and I can only imagine it and desire it in terms of which I know of the earth. And so my questions do not aspire beyond the earth. They aspire *toward* it and *into* it. Perhaps they aspire *through* it. They are religious because they are asked at the limit of what I know; they acknowledge mystery and honor its presence in the creation; they are spoken in reverence for the order and grace that I see, and that I trust beyond my power to see.

34   The stream has led me down to an old barn built deep in the hollow to house the tobacco once grown on those abandoned fields. Now it is surrounded by the trees that have come back on every side — a relic, a fragment of another time, strayed out of its meaning. This is the last of my historical landmarks. To here, my walk has had insistent overtones of memory and history. It has been a movement of consciousness through knowledge, eroding and shaping, adding and wearing away. I have descended like the water of the stream through what I know of myself, and now that I have there is a little more to know. But here at the barn, the old roads and the cow paths — the formal connections with civilization — come to an end.

35   I stoop between the strands of a barbed wire fence, and in that movement I go out of time into timelessness. I come into a wild place. I walk along the foot of a slope that was once cut bare of trees, like all the slopes of this part of the country — but long ago; and now the woods is established again, the ground healed, the trees grown big, their trunks rising clean, free of undergrowth. The place has a serenity and dignity that one feels immediately; the creation is whole in it and unobstructed. It is free of the strivings and dissatisfactions, the partialities and imperfections of places under the mechanical dominance of men. Here, what to a housekeeper's eye might seem disorderly is nonetheless orderly and within order; what might seem arbitrary or accidental is included in the design of the whole as if by intention; what might seem evil or violent is a comfortable member of the household.

Where the creation is whole nothing is extraneous. The presence of the creation here makes this a holy place, and it is as a pilgrim that I have come — to give the homage of awe and love, to submit to mystification. It is the creation that has attracted me, its perfect interfusion of life and design. I have made myself its follower and its apprentice.

One early morning last spring, I came and found the woods floor strewn with bluebells. In the cool sunlight and the lacy shadows of the spring woods the blueness of those flowers, their elegant shape, their delicate fresh scent kept me standing and looking. I found a rich delight in them that I cannot describe and that I will never forget. Though I had been familiar for years with most of the spring woods flowers, I had never seen these and had not known they grew here. Looking at them, I felt a strange feeling of loss and sorrow that I had never seen them before. But I was also exultant that I saw them now — that they were here. 36

For me, in the thought of them will always be the sense of the joyful surprise with which I found them — the sense that came suddenly to me then that the world is blessed beyond my understanding, more abundantly than I will ever know. What lives are still ahead of me here to be discovered and exulted in, tomorrow, or in twenty years? What wonder will be found here on the morning after my death? Though as a man I inherit great evils and the possibility of great loss and suffering, I know that my life is blessed and graced by the yearly flowering of the bluebells. How perfect they are! In their presence I am humble and joyful. If I were given all the learning and all the methods of my race I could not make one of them, or even imagine one. Solomon in all his glory was not arrayed like one of these. It is the privilege and the labor of the apprentice of creation to come with his imagination into the unimaginable, and with his speech into the unspeakable. 37

_____ CONSIDERATIONS _____

1. To think of habits as paths worn in the mind is no very original idea. How does Berry make it different as he works the image into the essay?

2. In another image, the gate is a fist that has gathered thousands of passings to and fro. Is Berry doing merely decorative writing, or is the image vital to the essay's meaning?

3. Berry, like Annie Dillard (pages 137–139) and Virginia Woolf (pages 479–481), is not content with the surface of what he describes. Find three or four places where he goes beyond superficial detail. How does his description in depth fit in with the essay's theme?

4. Compare Berry's simile of the sea like a net with Woolf's net of rocks. Are these artistic ornaments, or are they essential to the authors' theses?

5. "Nature has a patient ear," Berry writes in Paragraph 19, demonstrating a figurative device called personification. Look for examples in other writers, or make up several yourself: "the blindness of the night," "the laughter of the wind," "the soul of the abandoned house." Then explain concisely the meaning of personification. Of what use is it to a writer like Berry?

6. Throughout the essay, Berry works to evoke a sense of place — that hill where he grew up and to which he now returns. Yet he also thinks of the wider scene — the state of the nation, and even of the world. Is he successful in fusing the two interests? If so, how does he manage it? If not, why not?

You could write a history of any western language by examining its translations of the Bible. In our language, one translation has not only reflected English, but has helped to create it. The King James Version, in England usually called the Authorized, is a great work of English prose, which has impressed its rhythms and its imagery on the ears of English speakers for nearly four centuries. The sounds of the King James Bible underlie most of the oratory in our past, and much of the poetry. Even today, many people find the voice of this translation the voice of beauty and authority in English prose.

In 1604, a conference of English churchmen undertook to sponsor the new translation, and fifty-four translators — scholars from Oxford and Cambridge and the Anglican center of Winchester — began work. (Some commentators say that the King James Bible is the only work of genius ever accomplished by a committee.) The scholars worked quickly, and the translation appeared in 1611, dedicated to James I of England.

Of course no translation satisfies everyone, or satisfies forever. Biblical scholarship steadily exposed mistranslations in the stately rhythms of the King James sentences. As the spoken language changed, Jacobean phrases (the diction already somewhat archaic in 1611) came to seem quaint, and finally obscure. For some preachers, the King James Version came to seem exclusive or elitist, a barrier to the clarity of God's Word. Revisions and new translations have been numerous.

The New English Bible started at another conference of churchmen, in 1946, and was finished in 1970. Committees of scholars and literary advisors met regularly to determine accuracy and regulate style. This translation was not a revision of the King James, like so many other versions, but a wholly new translation from the original languages into contemporary English. Widely applauded for its accuracy, in its style the New English Bible has pleased some readers and appalled others.

11

THE HOLY BIBLE
From **Ecclesiastes**

The King James Bible *The New English Bible*

CHAPTER ONE

1 The words of the Preacher, the son of David, king in Jerusalem.

2 Vanity of vanities, saith the Preacher; vanity of vanities, all is vanity. 3 What profit hath man of all his labor wherein he laboreth under the sun? 4 One generation goeth, and another generation cometh; but the earth abideth for ever. 5 The sun also ariseth, and the sun goeth down, and hasteth to its place where it ariseth. 6 The wind goeth toward the south, and turneth about unto the north; it turneth about continually in its course, and the wind returneth again to its circuits. 7 All the rivers run into the sea, yet the sea is not full; unto the place whither the rivers go, thither they go again. 8 All things are full of weariness; man cannot utter *it:* the eye is not satisfied with seeing, nor the ear filled with hearing. 9 That which hath been is that which shall be; and that which

The words of the Speaker, the son of David, king in Jerusalem. 1

Emptiness, emptiness, says the Speaker, emptiness, all is empty. 2 What does man gain from all his 3 labour and his toil here under the sun? Generations come and genera- 4 tions go, while the earth endures for ever.

The sun rises and the sun goes 5 down; back it returns to its place and rises there again. The wind blows 6 south, the wind blows north, round and round it goes and returns full circle. All streams run into the sea, yet 7 the sea never overflows; back to the place from which the streams ran they return to run again.

All things are wearisome; no man 8 can speak of them all. Is not the eye surfeited with seeing, and the ear sated with hearing? What has hap- 9 pened will happen again, and what has been done will be done again, and hath been done is that which shall be done: and there is no new thing under the sun. 10 Is there a thing whereof it may be said, See, this is new? it hath been long ago, in the ages which were before us. 11 There is no remembrance of the former *generations;* neither shall there be any remembrance of the latter *generations* that are to come, among those that shall come after.

12 I the Preacher was king over Israel in Jerusalem. 13 And I applied my heart to seek and to search out by wisdom concerning all that is done under heaven: it is a sore travail that God hath given to the sons of men to be exercised therewith. 14 I have seen all the works that are done under the sun; and, behold, all is vanity and a striving after wind. 15 That which is crooked cannot be made straight; and that which is wanting cannot be numbered. 16 I communed with mine own heart, saying, Lo, I have gotten me great wisdom above all that were before me in Jerusalem; yea, my heart hath had great experience of wisdom and knowledge. 17 And I applied my heart to know wisdom, and to know madness and folly: I perceived that this also was a striving after wind. 18 For in much wisdom is much grief; and he that increaseth knowledge increaseth sorrow.

there is nothing new under the sun. Is 10 there anything of which one can say, 'Look, this is new'? No, it has already existed, long ago before our time. The 11 men of old are not remembered, and those who follow will not be remembered by those who follow them.

I, the Speaker, ruled as king over 12, 13 Israel in Jerusalem; and in wisdom I applied my mind to study and explore all that is done under heaven. It is a sorry business that God has given men to busy themselves with. I have 14 seen all the deeds that are done here under the sun; they are all emptiness and chasing the wind. What is 15 crooked cannot become straight; what is not there cannot be counted. I said to myself, 'I have amassed great 16 wisdom, more than all my predecessors on the throne in Jerusalem; I have become familiar with wisdom and knowledge.' So I applied my mind 17 to understand wisdom and knowledge, madness and folly, and I came to see that this too is chasing the wind. For in much wisdom is much 18 vexation, and the more a man knows, the more he has to suffer.

CHAPTER TWO

1 I said in my heart, Come now, I will prove thee with mirth; therefore enjoy pleasure: and, behold, this also was vanity. 2 I said of laughter, It is mad; and of mirth, What doeth it? 3 I searched in my heart how to cheer

I said to myself, 'Come, I will plunge 1 into pleasures and enjoy myself'; but this too was emptiness. Of laughter I 2 said, 'It is madness!' And of pleasure, 'What is the good of that?' So I sought 3 to stimulate myself with wine, in the my flesh with wine, my heart yet guiding *me* with wisdom, and how to lay hold on folly, till I might see what it was good for the sons of men that they should do under heaven all the days of their life.

4 I made me great works; I builded me houses; I planted me vineyards; 5 I made me gardens and parks, and I planted trees in them of all kinds of fruit; 6 I made me pools of water, to water therefrom the forest where trees were reared; 7 I bought menservants and maid-servants, and had servants born in my house; also I had great possessions of herds and flocks, above all that were before me in Jerusalem; 8 I gathered me also silver and gold, and the treasure of kings and of the provinces; I gat me mensingers and women-singers, and the delights of the sons of men, musical instruments, and that of all sorts. 9 So I was great, and increased more than all that were before me in Jerusalem: also my wisdom remained with me. 10 And whatsoever mine eyes desired I kept not from them; I withheld not my heart from any joy; for my heart rejoiced because of all my labor; and this was my portion from all my labor. 11 Then I looked on all the works that my hands had wrought, and on the labor that I had labored to do; and, behold, all was vanity and a striving after wind, and there was no profit under the sun.

12 And I turned myself to behold wisdom, and madness, and folly: for what *can* the man *do* that cometh after the king? *even* that which hath been done long ago. 13 Then I saw that wisdom excelleth folly, as far as light excelleth darkness. 14 The wise man's eyes are in his head, and

hope of finding out what was good for men to do under heaven throughout the brief span of their lives. But my mind was guided by wisdom, not blinded by folly.

I undertook great works; I built 4 myself houses and planted vineyards; I made myself gardens and parks and 5 planted all kinds of fruit-trees in them; I made myself pools of water to 6 irrigate a grove of growing trees; I 7 bought slaves, male and female, and I had my home-born slaves as well; I had possessions, more cattle and flocks than any of my predecessors in Jerusalem; I amassed silver and gold 8 also, the treasure of kings and provinces; I acquired singers, men and women, and all that man delights in. I was great, greater than all my pre- 9 decessors in Jerusalem; and my wisdom stood me in good stead. Whatever my eyes coveted, I refused 10 them nothing, nor did I deny myself any pleasure. Yes indeed, I got pleasure from all my labour, and for all my labour this was my reward. Then 11 I turned and reviewed all my handiwork, all my labour and toil, and I saw that everything was emptiness and chasing the wind, of no profit under the sun.

I set myself to look at wisdom and 12 at madness and folly. Then I per- 13 ceived that wisdom is more profitable than folly, as light is more profitable than darkness: the wise man has eyes 14 in his head, but the fool walks in the dark. Yet I saw also that one and the same fate overtakes them both. So I 15 said to myself, 'I too shall suffer the fate of the fool. To what purpose have I been wise? What is the profit of it? Even this', I said to myself, 'is emptiness. The wise man is remembered no 16 the fool walketh in darkness: and yet I perceived that one event happeneth to them all.   15 Then said I in my heart, As it happeneth to the fool, so will it happen even to me; and why was I then more wise? Then said I in my heart, that this also is vanity.   16 For of the wise man, even as of the fool, there is no remembrance for ever; seeing that in the days to come all will have been long forgotten. And how doth the wise man die even as the fool!   17 So I hated life, because the work that is wrought under the sun was grievous unto me; for all is vanity and a striving after wind.

18 And I hated all my labor wherein I labored under the sun, seeing that I must leave it unto the man that shall be after me.   19 And who knoweth whether he will be a wise man or a fool? yet will he have rule over all my labor wherein I have labored, and wherein I have showed myself wise under the sun. This also is vanity. 20 Therefore I turned about to cause my heart to despair concerning all the labor wherein I had labored under the sun.   21 For there is a man whose labor is with wisdom, and with knowledge, and with skillfulness; yet to a man that hath not labored therein shall he leave it for his portion. This also is vanity and a great evil.   22 For what hath a man of all his labor, and of the striving of his heart, wherein he laboreth under the sun?   23 For all his days are *but* sorrows; and his travail is grief; yea, even in the night his heart taketh no rest. This also is vanity.

24 There is nothing better for a man *than* that he should eat and drink, and make his soul enjoy good in his labor. This also I saw, that it is from the

longer than the fool, for, as the passing days multiply, all will be forgotten. Alas, wise man and fool die the same death!' So I came to hate life, 17 since everything that was done here under the sun was a trouble to me; for all is emptiness and chasing the wind. So I came to hate all my labour and 18 toil here under the sun, since I should have to leave its fruits to my successor. What sort of a man will he be who succeeds me, who inherits what others have acquired? Who knows 19 whether he will be a wise man or a fool? Yet he will be master of all the fruits of my labour and skill here under the sun. This too is emptiness.

Then I turned and gave myself up 20 to despair, reflecting upon all my labour and toil here under the sun. For anyone who toils with wisdom, 21 knowledge, and skill must leave it all to a man who has spent no labour on it. This too is emptiness and utterly wrong. What reward has a man for all 22 his labour, his scheming, and his toil here under the sun? All his life long 23 his business is pain and vexation to him; even at night his mind knows no rest. This too is emptiness. There 24 is nothing better for a man to do than to eat and drink and enjoy himself in return for his labours. And yet I saw that this comes from the hand of God. For without him who can enjoy his 25 food, or who can be anxious? God 26 gives wisdom and knowledge and joy to the man who pleases him, while to the sinner is given the trouble of gathering and amassing wealth only to hand it over to someone else who pleases God. This too is emptiness and chasing the wind.

hand of God.   25 For who can eat, or who can have enjoyment, more than I?   26 For to the man that pleaseth him *God* giveth wisdom, and knowledge, and joy; but to the sinner he giveth travail, to gather and to heap up, that he may give to him that pleaseth God. This also is vanity and a striving after wind.

———————————— CHAPTER THREE ————————————

1 For everything there is a season, and a time for every purpose under heaven: 2 a time to be born, and a time to die; a time to plant, and a time to pluck up that which is planted;   3 a time to kill, and a time to heal; a time to break down, and a time to build up;   4 a time to weep, and a time to laugh; a time to mourn, and a time to dance;   5 a time to cast away stones, and a time to gather stones together; a time to embrace, and a time to refrain from embracing;   6 a time to seek, and a time to lose; a time to keep, and a time to cast away;   7 a time to rend, and a time to sew; a time to keep silence, and a time to speak;   8 a time to love, and a time to hate; a time for war, and a time for peace.   9 What profit hath he that worketh in that wherein he laboreth?   10 I have seen the travail which God hath given to the sons of men to be exercised therewith.   11 He hath made everything beautiful in its time: also he hath set eternity in their heart, yet so that man cannot find out the work that God hath done from the beginning even to the end. 12 I know that there is nothing better for them, than to rejoice, and to do good so long as they live.   13 And also that every man should eat and

For everything its season, and for every activity under heaven its time: 1
  a time to be born and a time to die;   2
  a time to plant and a time to
    uproot;
  a time to kill and a time to heal;   3
  a time to pull down and a time to
    build up;
  a time to weep and a time to   4
    laugh;
  a time for mourning and a time for
    dancing;
  a time to scatter stones and a time   5
    to gather them;
  a time to embrace and a time to
    refrain from embracing;
  a time to seek and a time to lose;   6
  a time to keep and a time to throw
    away;
  a time to tear and a time to mend;   7
  a time for silence and a time for
    speech;
  a time to love and a time to hate;   8
  a time for war and a time for peace.

What profit does one who works get   9
from all his labour? I have seen the   10
business that God has given men to
keep them busy. He has made every-   11
thing to suit its time; moreover he
has given men a sense of time past
and future, but no comprehension of
God's work from beginning to end. I   12
know that there is nothing good for

drink, and enjoy good in all his labor, is the gift of God.

man except to be happy and live the best life he can while he is alive. Moreover, that a man should eat and drink and enjoy himself, in return for all his labours, is a gift of God.   13

_____ CONSIDERATIONS _____

1. When we study sentence structure, we study syntax. Have the editors of the newer translation of Ecclesiastes made syntactic as well as lexical changes? Explain and illustrate.

2. List differences between the two versions of Ecclesiastes, beginning with the new version changing "Preacher" into "Speaker" and "vanity" into "emptiness." Studying your list, can you generalize about the changes?

3. Writers as diverse as James Baldwin, William Faulkner, and Abraham Lincoln — to name three collected in this book — have attributed some of their own style to the King James Bible. Such style must generate great power. By comparing the two texts here, determine specific characteristics of the style of the King James Version.

4. Many people have objected to modernized versions of the Bible. Can you reconstruct and explain their objections?

5. In what way might a philosophy of life be built on a line from Ecclesiastes? One of these might be 2:24. How true is the common saying that you can find anything you want to find in the Bible?

6. Compare closely the two versions of 3:1–9. Does the change in *form* create a major difference in *effect?* Explain.

Ambrose Bierce (1842–1914?) was born in a log cabin on Horse Cave Creek in Ohio. He educated himself by reading the books in his father's small library, and as a young man served in the army during the Civil War. Starting as a journalist in California, he made himself an elegant writer of short stories, which were often supernatural or macabre in theme. Because he was writing in the primitive West, in a country still generally primitive, his serious work went generally unrecognized. Melancholy deepened into misanthropy. The definitions in The Devil's Dictionary *(1906) are funny — but the humor is serious, and the wit is bitter.*

In 1913, Bierce put his affairs in order and went to Mexico, which was in the midst of a civil war. He wrote a friend as he left, ". . . if you hear of my being stood up against a Mexican stone wall and shot to rags please know that I think it a pretty good way to depart this life. It beats old age, disease, or falling down a flight of stairs." He was never heard from again.

12

AMBROSE BIERCE
Some Devil's Definitions

1   *Belladonna, n.* In Italian a beautiful lady; in English a deadly poison. A striking example of the essential identity of the two tongues.

2   *Bigot, n.* One who is obstinately and zealously attached to an opinion that you do not entertain.

3   *Bore, n.* A person who talks when you wish him to listen.

4   *Brute, n. See* HUSBAND.

5   *Cabbage, n.* A familiar kitchen-garden vegetable about as large and wise as a man's head.

6   *Calamity, n.* A more than commonly plain and unmistakable reminder that the affairs of this life are not of our own ordering. Calam-

ities are of two kinds: misfortune to ourselves, and good fortune to others.

Cannibal, n. A gastronome of the old school who preserves the 7 simple tastes and adheres to the natural diet of the pre-pork period.

Cannon, n. An instrument employed in the rectification of 8 national boundaries.

Cat, n. A soft, indestructible automaton provided by nature to be 9 kicked when things go wrong in the domestic circle.

Christian, n. One who believes that the New Testament is a 10 divinely inspired book admirably suited to the spiritual needs of his neighbor. One who follows the teachings of Christ in so far as they are not inconsistent with a life of sin.

Clairvoyant, n. A person, commonly a woman, who has the 11 power of seeing that which is invisible to her patron — namely, that he is a blockhead.

Commerce, n. A kind of transaction in which A plunders from B 12 the goods of C, and for compensation B picks the pocket of D of money belonging to E.

Conservative, n. A statesman who is enamored of existing evils, 13 as distinguished from the Liberal, who wishes to replace them with others.

Corsair, n. A politician of the seas. 14

Compromise, n. Such an adjustment of conflicting interests as 15 gives each adversary the satisfaction of thinking he has got what he ought not to have, and is deprived of nothing except what was justly his due.

Compulsion, n. The eloquence of power. 16

Congratulation, n. The civility of envy. 17

Consul, n. In American politics, a person who having failed to 18 secure an office from the people is given one by the Administration on condition that he leave the country.

Consult, v. t. To seek another's approval of a course already 19 decided on.

Coward, n. One who in a perilous emergency thinks with his 20 legs.

Curiosity, n. An objectionable quality of the female mind. The 21 desire to know whether or not a woman is cursed with curiosity is one of the most active and insatiable passions of the masculine soul.

Cynic, n. A blackguard whose faulty vision sees things as they 22 are, not as they ought to be. Hence the custom among the Scythians of plucking out a cynic's eyes to improve his vision.

23   *Dance, v. i.* To leap about to the sound of tittering music, preferably with arms about your neighbor's wife or daughter. There are many kinds of dances, but all those requiring the participation of the two sexes have two characteristics in common: they are conspicuously innocent, and warmly loved by the vicious.

24   *Debauchee, n.* One who has so earnestly pursued pleasure that he has had the misfortune to overtake it.

25   *Decalogue, n.* A series of commandments, ten in number — just enough to permit an intelligent selection for observance, but not enough to embarrass the choice.

26   *Defame, v. t.* To lie about another. To tell the truth about another.

27   *Dentist, n.* A prestidigitator who, putting metal into your mouth, pulls coins out of your pocket.

28   *Die, n.* The singular of "dice." We seldom hear the word, because there is a prohibitory proverb, "Never say die."

29   *Discussion, n.* A method of confirming others in their errors.

30   *Distance, n.* The only thing that the rich are willing for the poor to call theirs, and keep.

31   *Duel, n.* A formal ceremony preliminary to the reconciliation of two enemies. Great skill is necessary to its satisfactory observance; if awkwardly performed the most unexpected and deplorable consequences sometimes ensue. A long time ago a man lost his life in a duel.

32   *Eccentricity, n.* A method of distinction so cheap that fools employ it to accentuate their incapacity.

33   *Education, n.* That which discloses to the wise and disguises from the foolish their lack of understanding.

34   *Effect, n.* The second of two phenomena which always occur together in the same order. The first, called a Cause, is said to generate the other — which is no more sensible than it would be for one who has never seen a dog except in pursuit of a rabbit to declare the rabbit the cause of the dog.

35   *Edible, adj.* Good to eat, and wholesome to digest, as a worm to a toad, a toad to a snake, a snake to a pig, a pig to a man, and a man to a worm.

36   *Egotist, n.* A person of low taste, more interested in himself than in me.

37   *Erudition, n.* Dust shaken out of a book into an empty skull.

Eulogy, n. Praise of a person who has either the advantages of   38
wealth and power, or the consideration to be dead.

Female, n. One of the opposing, or unfair, sex.   39

Fib, n. A lie that has not cut its teeth. An habitual liar's nearest   40
approach to truth: the perigee of his eccentric orbit.

Fiddle, n. An instrument to tickle human ears by friction of a   41
horse's tail on the entrails of a cat.

Friendship, n. A ship big enough to carry two in fair weather, but   42
only one in foul.

Garter, n. An elastic band intended to keep a woman from com-   43
ing out of her stockings and desolating the country.

Ghost, n. The outward and visible sign of an inward fear.   44

Glutton, n. A person who escapes the evils of moderation by   45
committing dyspepsia.

Gout, n. A physician's name for the rheumatism of a rich patient.   46

Grammar, n. A system of pitfalls thoughtfully prepared for the   47
feet of the self-made man, along the path by which he advances to
distinction.

Guillotine, n. A machine which makes a Frenchman shrug his   48
shoulders with good reason.

_____ CONSIDERATIONS _____

1. To appreciate the humor in some of Bierce's definitions, you may
have to look up in your desk dictionary some of his words, such as "gastronome," "zealously," "adversary," "civility," "insatiable," "prestidigitator,"
"perigee," "dyspepsia." How do you add words to your working vocabulary?

2. *The Devil's Dictionary* was first published in 1906. Judging from the
definitions here, would you say that Bierce's book is dated? Which items strike
you as most relevant to our times? Which are least relevant? Why?

3. Do you find a consistent tone or attitude in Bierce's dictionary?
Explain and provide ample evidence.

4. George Orwell, in "Politics and the English Language" (pages 307–
319), is hard on euphemisms. Would Bierce agree with Orwell?

5. What proportion of the words defined by Bierce might be called general or abstract ("calamity" or "grammar"), not concrete ("cat" or "dance")?
What does that statistic imply about abstract words?

6. Compose a page of definitions for your own Devil's Dictionary, perhaps concentrating on words currently popular.

Caroline Bird (b. 1915) was born in New York City, attended and later taught at Vassar, and now divides her time between Manhattan and Poughkeepsie. She has been an editor and a teacher, as well as the author of Born Female *(1968),* Everything a Woman Needs to Know to Get Paid What She's Worth *(1973), and* The Case against College *(1975). She argues the case against college with a clear vigor, a committed pugnacity; only a skilled debater with good college education could dispute her.*

13

CAROLINE BIRD
Where College Fails Us

1   The case *for* college has been accepted without question for more than a generation. All high school graduates ought to go, says Conventional Wisdom and statistical evidence, because college will help them earn more money, become "better" people, and learn to be more responsible citizens than those who don't go.

2   But college has never been able to work its magic for everyone. And now that close to half our high school graduates are attending, those who don't fit the pattern are becoming more numerous, and more obvious. College graduates are selling shoes and driving taxis; college students sabotage each other's experiments and forge letters of recommendation in the intense competition for admission to graduate school. Others find no stimulation in their studies, and drop out — often encouraged by college administrators.

3   Some observers say the fault is with the young people themselves — they are spoiled, stoned, overindulged, and expecting too much. But

From *Signature Magazine*, Diners Club, Inc. © 1975. Reprinted by permission of the author.

that's mass character assassination, and doesn't explain all campus unhappiness. Others blame the state of the world, and they are partly right. We've been told that young people have to go to college because our economy can't absorb an army of untrained eighteen-year-olds. But disillusioned graduates are learning that it can no longer absorb an army of trained twenty-two-year-olds, either.

Some adventuresome educators and campus watchers have 4 openly begun to suggest that college may not be the best, the proper, the only place for every young person after the completion of high school. We may have been looking at all those surveys and statistics upside down, it seems, and through the rosy glow of our own remembered college experiences. Perhaps college doesn't make people intelligent, ambitious, happy, liberal, or quick to learn new things — maybe it's just the other way around, and intelligent, ambitious, happy, liberal, and quick-learning people are merely the ones who have been attracted to college in the first place. And perhaps all those successful college graduates would have been successful whether they had gone to college or not. This is heresy to those of us who have been brought up to believe that if a little schooling is good, more has to be much better. But contrary evidence is beginning to mount up.

The unhappiness and discontent of young people is nothing new, 5 and problems of adolescence are always painfully intense. But while traveling around the country, speaking at colleges, and interviewing students at all kinds of schools — large and small, public and private — I was overwhelmed by the prevailing sadness. It was as visible on campuses in California as in Nebraska and Massachusetts. Too many young people are in college reluctantly, because everyone told them they ought to go, and there didn't seem to be anything better to do. Their elders sell them college because it's good for them. Some never learn to like it, and talk about their time in school as if it were a sentence to be served.

Students tell us the same thing college counselors tell us — they 6 go because of pressure from parents and teachers, and stay because it seems to be an alternative to a far worse fate. It's "better" than the Army or a dead-end job, and it has to be pretty bad before it's any worse than staying at home.

College graduates say that they don't want to work "just" for the 7 money: They want work that matters. They want to help people and save the world. But the numbers are stacked against them. Not only are there not enough jobs in world-saving fields, but in the current slowdown it has become evident that there never were, and probably never will be, enough jobs requiring higher education to go around.

8   Students who tell their advisers they want to help people, for example, are often directed to psychology. This year the Department of Labor estimates that there will be 4,300 new jobs for psychologists, while colleges will award 58,430 bachelor's degrees in psychology.

9   Sociology has become a favorite major on socially conscious campuses, but graduates find that social reform is hardly a paying occupation. Male sociologists from the University of Wisconsin reported as gainfully employed a year after graduation included a legal assistant, sports editor, truck unloader, Peace Corps worker, publications director, and a stockboy — but no sociologist per se. The highest paid worked for the post office.

10   Publishing, writing, and journalism are presumably the vocational goal of a large proportion of the 104,000 majors in Communications and Letters expected to graduate in 1975. The outlook for them is grim. All of the daily newspapers in the country combined are expected to hire a total of 2,600 reporters this year. Radio and television stations may hire a total of 500 announcers, most of them in local radio stations. Nonpublishing organizations will need 1,100 technical writers, and public-relations activities another 4,400. Even if new graduates could get all these jobs (they can't, of course), over 90,000 of them will have to find something less glamorous to do.

11   Other fields most popular with college graduates are also pathetically small. Only 1,900 foresters a year will be needed during this decade, although schools of forestry are expected to continue graduating twice that many. Some will get sub-professional jobs as forestry aides. Schools of architecture are expected to turn out twice as many as will be needed, and while all sorts of people want to design things, the Department of Labor forecasts that there will be jobs for only 400 new industrial designers a year. As for anthropologists, only 400 will be needed every year in the 1970s to take care of all the college courses, public-health research, community surveys, museums, and all the archaeological digs on every continent. (For these jobs graduate work in anthropology is required.)

12   Many popular occupations may seem to be growing fast without necessarily offering employment to very many. "Recreation work" is always cited as an expanding field, but it will need relatively few workers who require more special training than life guards. "Urban planning" has exploded in the media, so the U.S. Department of Labor

doubled its estimate of the number of jobs to be filled every year in the 1970s — to a big, fat 800. A mere 200 oceanographers a year will be able to do all the exploring of "inner space" — and all that exciting underwater diving you see demonstrated on television — for the entire decade of the 1970s.

Whatever college graduates *want* to do, most of them are going   13
to wind up doing what *there is* to do. During the next few years, according to the Labor Department, the biggest demand will be for stenographers and secretaries, followed by retail-trade salesworkers, hospital attendants, bookkeepers, building custodians, registered nurses, foremen, kindergarten and elementary-school teachers, receptionists, cooks, cosmetologists, private-household workers, manufacturing inspectors, and industrial machinery repairmen. These are the jobs which will eventually absorb the surplus archaeologists, urban planners, oceanographers, sociologists, editors, and college professors.

Vocationalism is the new look on campus because of the discour-   14
aging job market faced by the generalists. Students have been opting for medicine and law in droves. If all those who check "doctor" as their career goal succeed in getting their MDs, we'll immediately have ten times the target ratio of doctors for the population of the United States. Law schools are already graduating twice as many new lawyers every year as the Department of Labor thinks we will need, and the oversupply grows annually.

Specialists often find themselves at the mercy of shifts in   15
demand, and the narrower the vocational training, the more risky the long-term prospects. Engineers are the classic example of the "Yo-Yo" effect in supply and demand. Today's shortage is apt to produce a big crop of engineering graduates after the need has crested, and teachers face the same squeeze.

Worse than that, when the specialists turn up for work, they   16
often find that they have learned a lot of things in classrooms that they will never use, that they will have to learn a lot of things on the job that they were never taught, and that most of what they have learned is less likely to "come in handy later" than to fade from memory. One disillusioned architecture student, who had already designed and built houses, said, "It's the degree you need, not everything you learn getting it."

A diploma saves the employer the cost of screening candidates   17
and gives him a predictable product: He can assume that those who have survived the four-year ordeal have learned how to manage them-

selves. They have learned how to budget their time, meet deadlines, set priorities, cope with impersonal authority, follow instructions, and stick with a task that may be tiresome without direct supervision.

18   The employer is also betting that it will be cheaper and easier to train the college graduate because he has demonstrated his ability to learn. But if the diploma serves only to identify those who are talented in the art of schoolwork, it becomes, in the words of Harvard's Christopher Jencks, "a hell of an expensive aptitude test." It is unfair to the candidates because they themselves must bear the cost of the screening — the cost of college. Candidates without the funds, the academic temperament, or the patience for the four-year obstacle race are ruled out, no matter how well they may perform on the job. But if "everyone" has a diploma, employers will have to find another way to choose employees, and it will become an empty credential.

19   (Screening by diploma may in fact already be illegal. The 1971 ruling of the Supreme Court in *Griggs* v. *Duke Power Co.* contended that an employer cannot demand a qualification which systemically excludes an entire class of applicants, unless that qualification reliably predicts success on the job. The requiring of a high school diploma was outlawed in the *Griggs* case, and this could extend to a college diploma.)

20   The bill for four years at an Ivy League college is currently climbing toward $25,000; at a state university, a degree will cost the student and his family about $10,000 (with taxpayers making up the difference).

21   Not many families can afford these sums, and when they look for financial aid, they discover that someone else will decide how much they will actually have to pay. The College Scholarship Service, which establishes a family's degree of need for most colleges, is guided by noble principles: uniformity of sacrifice, need rather than merit. But families vary in their willingness to "sacrifice" as much as the bureaucracy of the CSS thinks they ought to. This is particularly true of middle-income parents, whose children account for the bulk of the country's college students. Some have begun to rebel against this attempt to enforce the same values and priorities on all. "In some families, a college education competes with a second car, a color television, or a trip to Europe — and it's possible that college may lose," one financial-aid officer recently told me.

22   Quite so. College is worth more to some middle-income families than to others. It is chilling to consider the undercurrent of resentment

that families who "give up everything" must feel toward their college-age children, or the burden of guilt children must bear every time they goof off or receive less than top grades in their courses.

The decline in return for a college degree within the last generation has been substantial. In the 1950s, a Princeton student could pay his expenses for the school year — eating club and all — on less than $3,000. When he graduated, he entered a job market which provided a comfortable margin over the earnings of his agemates who had not been to college. To be precise, a freshman entering Princeton in 1956, the earliest year for which the Census has attempted to project lifetime earnings, could expect to realize a 12.5 percent return on his investment. A freshman entering in 1972, with the cost nearing $6,000 annually, could expect to realize only 9.3 percent, less than might be available in the money market. This calculation was made with the help of a banker and his computer, comparing college as an investment in future earnings with other investments available in the booming money market of 1974, and concluded that in strictly financial terms, college is not always the best investment a young person can make. 23

I postulated a young man (the figures are different with a young woman, but the principle is the same) whose rich uncle would give him, in cash, the total cost of four years at Princeton — $34,181. (The total includes what the young man would earn if he went to work instead of to college right after high school.) If he did not spend the money on Princeton, but put it in the savings bank at 7.5 percent interest compounded daily, he would have, at retirement age sixty-four, more than five times as much as the $199,000 extra he could expect to earn between twenty-two and sixty as a college man rather than a mere high school graduate. And with all that money accumulating in the bank, he could invest in something with a higher return than a diploma. At age twenty-eight, when his nest egg had reached $73,113, he could buy a liquor store, which would return him well over 20 percent on his investment, as long as he was willing to mind the store. He might get a bit fidgety sitting there, but he'd have to be dim-witted to lose money on a liquor store, and right now we're talking only about dollars. 24

If the young man went to a public college rather than Princeton, the investment would be lower, and the payoff higher, of course, because other people — the taxpayers — put up part of the capital for him. But the difference in return between an investment in public and private colleges is minimized because the biggest part of the investment in either case is the money a student might earn if he went to 25 work, not to college — in economic terms, his "foregone income." That he bears himself.

26   Rates of return and dollar signs on education are a fascinating brain teaser, and, obviously, there is a certain unreality to the game. But the same unreality extends to the traditional calculations that have always been used to convince taxpayers that college is a worthwhile investment.

27   The ultimate defense of college has always been that while it may not teach you anything vocationally useful, it will somehow make you a better person, able to do anything better, and those who make it through the process are initiated into the "fellowship of educated men and women." In a study intended to probe what graduates seven years out of college thought their colleges should have done for them, the Carnegie Commission found that most alumni expected the "development of my abilities to think and express myself." But if such respected educational psychologists as Bruner and Piaget are right, specific learning skills have to be acquired very early in life, perhaps even before formal schooling begins.

28   So, when pressed, liberal-arts defenders speak instead about something more encompassing, and more elusive. "College changed me inside," one graduate told us fervently. The authors of a Carnegie Commission report, who obviously struggled for a definition, concluded that one of the common threads in the perceptions of a liberal education is that it provides "an integrated view of the world which can serve as an inner guide." More simply, alumni say that college should have "helped me to formulate the values and goals of my life."

29   In theory, a student is taught to develop these values and goals himself, but in practice, it doesn't work quite that way. All but the wayward and the saintly take their sense of the good, the true, and the beautiful from the people around them. When we speak of students acquiring "values" in college, we often mean that they will acquire the values — and sometimes that means only the tastes — of their professors. The values of professors may be "higher" than many students will encounter elsewhere, but they may not be relevant to situations in which students find themselves in college and later.

30   Of all the forms in which ideas are disseminated, the college professor lecturing a class is the slowest and most expensive. You don't have to go to college to read the great books or learn about the great ideas of Western Man. Today you can find them everywhere — in paperbacks, in the public libraries, in museums, in public lectures,

in adult-education courses, in abridged, summarized, or adapted form in magazines, films, and television. The problem is no longer one of access to broadening ideas; the problem is the other way around: how to choose among the many courses of action proposed to us, how to edit the stimulations that pour into our eyes and ears every waking hour. A college experience that piles option on option and stimulation on stimulation merely adds to the contemporary nightmare.

What students and graduates say that they did learn on campus comes under the heading of personal, rather than intellectual, development. Again and again I was told that the real value of college is learning to get along with others, to practice social skills, to "sort out my head," and these have nothing to do with curriculum. 31

For whatever impact the academic experience used to have on college students, the sheer size of many undergraduate classes in the 1970s dilutes faculty-student dialogue, and, more often than not, they are taught by teachers who were hired when colleges were faced with a shortage of qualified instructors, during their years of expansion and when the big rise in academic pay attracted the mediocre and the less than dedicated. 32

On the social side, colleges are withdrawing from responsibility for feeding, housing, policing, and protecting students at a time when the environment of college may be the most important service it could render. College officials are reluctant to "intervene" in the personal lives of the students. They no longer expect to take over from parents, but often insist that students — who have, most often, never lived away from home before — take full adult responsibility for their plans, achievements, and behavior. 33

Most college students do not live in the plush, comfortable country-clublike surroundings their parents envisage, or, in some cases, remember. Open dorms, particularly when they are coeducational, are noisy, usually overcrowded, and often messy. Some students desert the institutional "zoos" (their own word for dorms) and move into run-down, overpriced apartments. Bulletin boards in student centers are littered with notices of apartments to share and the drift of conversation suggests that a lot of money is dissipated in scrounging for food and shelter. 34

Taxpayers now provide more than half of the astronomical sums that are spent on higher education. But less than half of today's high school graduates go on, raising a new question of equity: Is it fair to make all the taxpayers pay for the minority who actually go to college? 35

We decided long ago that it is fair for childless adults to pay school taxes because everyone, parents and nonparents alike, profits by a literate population. Does the same reasoning hold true for state-supported higher education? There is no conclusive evidence on either side.

36   Young people cannot be expected to go to college for the general good of mankind. They may be more altruistic than their elders, but no great numbers are going to spend four years at hard intellectual labor, let alone tens of thousands of family dollars, for "the advancement of human capability in society at large," one of the many purposes invoked by the Carnegie Commission report. Nor do any considerable number of them want to go to college to beat the Russians to Jupiter, improve the national defense, increase the Gross National Product, lower the crime rate, improve automobile safety, or create a market for the arts — all of which have been suggested at one time or other as benefits taxpayers get for supporting higher education.

37   One sociologist said that you don't have to have a reason for going to college because it's an institution. His definition of an institution is something everyone subscribed to without question. The burden of proof is not on why you should go to college, but why anyone thinks there might be a reason for not going. The implication — and some educators express it quite frankly — is that an eighteen-year-old high school graduate is still too young and confused to know what he wants to do, let alone what is good for him.

38   Mother knows best, in other words.

39   It had always been comfortable for students to believe that authorities, like Mother, or outside specialists, like educators, could determine what was best for them. However, specialists and authorities no longer enjoy the credibility former generations accorded them. Patients talk back to doctors and are not struck suddenly dead. Clients question the lawyer's bills and sometimes get them reduced. It is no longer self-evident that all adolescents must study a fixed curriculum that was constructed at a time when all educated men could agree on precisely what it was that made them educated.

40   The same with college. If high school graduates don't want to continue their education, or don't want to continue it right away, they may perceive more clearly than their elders that college is not for them.

41   College is an ideal place for those young adults who love learning for its own sake, who would rather read than eat, and who like nothing better than writing research papers. But they are a minority, even at

the prestigious colleges, which recruit and attract the intellectually oriented.

The rest of our high school graduates need to look at college more   42 closely and critically, to examine it as a consumer product, and decide if the cost in dollars, in time, in continued dependency, and in future returns, is worth the very large investment each student — and his family — must make.

_____ CONSIDERATIONS _____

1. To what extent is Bird's essay an attack on the conviction that universal education is the surest way to cure the ills and injustices of the world?

2. In her first paragraph, the author states three popular justifications for a college education. Examine her essay to see how, for the most part, it is organized around those three reasons.

3. In her final paragraph, Bird urges high school graduates to examine college "as a consumer product." Is that possible? Explain. Read about Richard Wright's struggle to educate himself ("The Library Card," pages 483–491) and try to imagine him examining that experience as "a consumer product."

4. Bird makes extensive use of statistics to prove her first proposition: that college is a poor investment. Does she cite the sources of her figures? Does she use the figures fairly? How can you tell?

5. How many of your college friends have clear ideas of their vocational or educational goals? Do you? What about friends who are not in college?

6. Bird points out, rightly enough, that "you don't have to go to college to read the great books or learn about the great ideas of Western Man." Judging from your experience with self-directed reading programs, how effective is Bird's statement as an argument?

John N. Bleibtreu (b. 1926) lives in New York City, where he works at Arica Institute, an ESP–sensitivity-training center. In The Parable of the Beast *(1968) he examines and explains many types of research on animal behavior. He explores different creatures' orientations to time, to space, and to the community in an attempt to understand mechanisms that might work in human beings as they do in animals. His prose explains with meticulous scientific accuracy, but its simple clarity allows even a layman to perceive analogies between animal and human psychology. Exposition that imparts scientific information to the general reader is particularly difficult to write, and welcome to read.*

14

JOHN N. BLEIBTREU
The Moment of Being

1   The cattle tick is a small, flat-bodied, blood-sucking insect with a curious life history. It emerges from the egg not yet fully developed, lacking a pair of legs, and sex organs. In this state it is still capable of attacking cold-blooded animals such as frogs and lizards, which it does. After shedding its skin several times, it acquires its missing organs, mates, and is then prepared to attack warm-blooded animals.

2   The eyeless female is directed to the tip of a twig on a bush by her photosensitive skin, and there she stays through darkness and light, through fair weather and foul, waiting for the moment that will fulfill her existence. In the Zoological Institute, at Rostock, prior to World War I ticks were kept on the ends of twigs, waiting for this moment for a period of eighteen years. The metabolism of the insect is sluggish to the point of being suspended entirely. The sperm she

received in the act of mating remains bundled into capsules where it, too, waits in suspension until mammalian blood reaches the stomach of the tick, at which time the capsules break, the sperm are released and they fertilize the eggs which have been reposing in the ovary, also waiting in a kind of time suspension.

The signal for which the tick waits is the scent of butyric acid, a 3 substance present in the sweat of all mammals. This is the only experience that will trigger time into existence for the tick.

The tick represents, in the conduct of its life, a kind of apotheosis 4 of subjective time perception. For a period as long as eighteen years nothing happens. The period passes as a single moment; but at any moment within this span of literally senseless existence, when the animal becomes aware of the scent of butyric acid it is thrust into a perception of time, and other signals are suddenly perceived.

The animal then hurls itself in the direction of the scent. The 5 object on which the tick lands at the end of this leap must be warm; a delicate sense of temperature is suddenly mobilized and so informs the insect. If the object is not warm, the tick will drop off and reclimb its perch. If it is warm, the tick burrows its head deeply into the skin and slowly pumps itself full of blood. Experiments made at Rostock with membranes filled with fluids other than blood proved that the tick lacks all sense of taste, and once the membrane is perforated the animal will drink any fluid, provided it is of the right temperature.

The extraordinary preparedness of this creature for that moment 6 of time during which it will re-enact the purpose of its life contrasts strikingly with probability that this moment will ever occur. There are doubtless many bushes on which ticks perch, which are never bypassed by a mammal within range of the tick's leap. As do most animals, the tick lives in an absurdly unfavorable world — at least so it would appear to the compassionate human observer. But this world is merely the environment of the animal. The world it perceives — which experimenters at Rostock called its *umwelt,* its perceptual world — is not at all unfavorable. A period of eighteen years, as measured objectively by the circuit of the earth around the sun, is meaningless to the tick. During this period, it is apparently unaware of temperature changes. Being blind, it does not see the leaves shrivel and fall and then renew themselves on the bush where it is affixed. Unaware of time it is also unaware of space, and the multitudes of forms and colors which appear in space. It waits, suspended in duration for its particular moment of time, a moment distinguished by being filled with a single, unique experience; the scent of butyric acid.

7   Though we consider ourselves far removed as humans from such a lowly insect form as this, we too are both aware and unaware of elements which comprise our environment. We are more aware than the tick of the passage of time. We are subjectively aware of the aging process; we know that we grow older, that time is shortened by each passing moment. For the tick, however, this moment that precedes its burst of volitional activity, the moment when it scents butyric acid and is thrust into purposeful movement, is close to the end of time for the tick. When it fills itself with blood, it drops from its host, lays its eggs, and dies.

_____ CONSIDERATIONS _____

1. Do any sentences or phrases in "The Moment of Being" suggest that Bleibtreu is writing a parable, not a scientific paper? In what ways might a parable qualify as exposition? Who was the most famous user of the parable as a means of explaining?

2. The author describes the life of the cattle tick mechanistically, implying that the tick's life is determined by forces over which it has no control. Look up "naturalism" in a dictionary of literary terms, and see if Bleibtreu's essay is a good illustration.

3. What does Bleibtreu mean by "a kind of apotheosis of subjective time perception"? Have you experienced "subjective time perception"? How else might you express the idea in that phrase? What other kind of time telling is there?

4. How closely can you compare the cycle of human life with that of the cattle tick? Do you find such a comparison attractive? Repellent? Humorous? Depressing? Explain.

5. It is extremely common to use animals in calling attention to traits or habits in man. Think of common expressions such as "a horse laugh," "dirty dog," "snake in the grass," "a bear of a man," "a wolf in sheep's clothing." Think, too, of Aesop's fables. How do you account for such a widespread use of animal imagery?

Peter Bogdanovich (b. 1939) is known as a film director, espe-
cially for The Last Picture Show *(1971). But he has written about*
films longer than he has directed them. Among his books are The
Cinema of Alfred Hitchcock *(1963),* Fritz Lang in America *(1967),*
and Pieces of Time: Peter Bogdanovich on the Movies *(1973). In*
the essay below he writes about Humphrey Bogart, describing
that familiar Bogart look, that attitude, that way of talking.

15

PETER BOGDANOVICH
Bogie in Excelsis

Usually he wore the trench coat unbuttoned, just tied with the   1
belt, and a slouch hat, rarely tilted. Sometimes it was a captain's cap
and a yachting jacket. Almost always his trousers were held up by a
cowboy belt. You know the kind: one an Easterner waiting for a plane
out of Phoenix buys just as a joke and then takes a liking to. Occasionally, he'd hitch up his slacks with it, and he often jabbed his thumbs
behind it, his hands ready for a fight or a dame.

Whether it was Sirocco or Casablanca, Martinique or Sahara, he   2
was the only American around (except maybe for the girl) and you
didn't ask him how he got there, and he always worked alone — except
for the fellow who thought he took care of him, the rummy, the piano
player, the one *he* took care of, the one you didn't mess with. There
was very little he couldn't do, and in a jam he could do anything:
remove a slug from a guy's arm, fix a truck that wouldn't start. He was
an excellent driver, knowing precisely how to take those curves or
how to lose a guy that was tailing him. He could smell a piece of a
broken glass and tell you right away if there'd been poison in it, or he

could walk into a room and know just where the button was that opened the secret door. At the wheel of a boat, he was beautiful.

3   His expression was usually sour and when he smiled only the lower lip moved. There was a scar on his upper lip — maybe that's what gave him the faint lisp. He would tug meditatively at his earlobe when he was trying to figure something out and every so often he had a strange little twitch — a kind of backward jerk of the sides of his mouth coupled with a slight squinting of the eyes. He held his cigarette (a Chesterfield) cupped in his hand. He looked right holding a gun.

4   Unsentimental was a good word for him. "Leave 'im where he is," he might say to a woman whose husband has just been wounded, "I don't want 'im bleeding all over my cushions." And blunt: "I don't like you. I don't like your friends and I don't like the idea of her bein' married to you." And straight: "When a man's partner is killed he's supposed to do something about it. It doesn't make any difference what you thought of him. He was your partner and you're supposed to do something about it."

5   He was tough; he could stop you with a look or a line. "Go ahead, slap *me*," he'd say, or, "That's right, *go* for it," and there was in the way he said it just the right blend of malice, gleeful anticipation and the promise of certain doom. He didn't like taking orders. Or favors. It was smart not to fool around with him too much.

6   As far as the ladies were concerned, he didn't have too much trouble with them, except maybe keeping them away. It was the girl who said if he needed anything, all he had to do was whistle; he never said that to the girl. Most of the time he'd call her "angel," and if he liked her he'd tell her she was "good, awful good."

7   Whatever he was engaged in, whether it was being a reporter, a saloon-keeper, a gangster, a detective, a fishing-boat owner, a D.A. or a lawyer, he was impeccably, if casually, a complete professional. "You take chances," someone would say. "I get paid to," was his answer. But he never took himself too seriously. What was his job, a girl would ask. Conspiratorially, he'd lean in and say with the slightest flicker of a grin, "I'm a private dick on a case." He wasn't going to be taken in by Art either; he'd been to college, but he was a bit suspicious of the intellectuals. If someone mentioned Proust, he'd ask, "Who's he?" even though he knew.

8   Finally, he was wary of Causes. He liked to get paid for taking chances. He was a man who tried very hard to be Bad because he knew it was easier to get along in the world that way. He always failed

because of an innate goodness which surely nauseated him. Almost always he went from belligerent neutrality to reluctant commitment. From: "I stick my neck out for nobody." To: "I'm no good at being noble, but it doesn't take much to see that the problems of three little people don't amount to a hill o' beans in this crazy world." At the start, if the question was, "What are your sympathies?", the answer was invariably, "Minding my own business." But by the end, if asked why he was helping, risking his life, he might say, "Maybe 'cause I like you. Maybe 'cause I don't like them." Of course it was always "maybe" because he wasn't going to be that much of a sap, wasn't making any speeches, wasn't going to be a Good guy. Probably he rationalized it: "I'm just doing my job." But we felt good inside. We knew better.

___ CONSIDERATIONS ___

1. Comparing "Bogie in Excelsis" with other selections describing people ("Winter and Summer," pages 1–6, and "Mr. Red Leg," pages 16–21), you may recognize a class of words used by Bogdanovich not used by the other writers. List these words and speculate on their appropriateness and effectiveness.

2. How much of Bogdanovich's description of Humphrey Bogart describes the "real" Bogart? How much describes the screen image of Bogart? What does that proportion do to your understanding of the essay?

3. The cult of Bogie worshippers is still alive. It supports Bogart sweatshirts, wall-sized posters, and the like. Can you nominate a well-known personality important to your own generation who might take the place of this famous actor?

4. Working with your nomination in question 3, how could you adapt your writing style to his or her personality if you wrote a sketch like Bogdanovich's?

5. Do you detect irony in this essay? If you find any, do you suspect that the author is indulging in gentle satire? Discuss.

6. Select three or four attitudes characteristic of Bogart — toward women, for instance, or toward dangerous work or righteous causes — and explain them by concocting a scene in which a group of Hollywood writers and directors deliberately fabricate the screen image of this star-to-be. Write dialogue and stage directions.

Daniel J. Boorstin (b. 1914) attended Oxford as a Rhodes scholar after graduating from Harvard, then studied law in England and in the United States. After teaching history for many years, especially at the University of Chicago, he became Librarian of Congress in 1975. His books include the cultural history The Americans, *which has three parts:* The Colonial Experience *(1958),* The National Experience *(1965), and* The Democratic Experience *(1975).*

For several decades, intellectuals have discerned a cultural gap widening between people with a sense of the past, and people with a sense of nothing but the present. Modern Americans tend to praise living in the present; Boorstin suggests that we pay a price for lacking history.

16

DANIEL J. BOORSTIN
The Prison of the Present

1   Our inventive, up-to-the-minute, wealthy democracy makes new tests of the human spirit. Our very instruments of education, of information and of "progress" make it harder every day for us to keep our bearings in the larger universe, in the stream of history and in the whole world of peoples who feel strong ties to their past. A new price of our American standard of living is our imprisonment in the present.

2   That imprisonment tempts us to a morbid preoccupation with ourselves, and so induces hypochondria. That, the dictionary tells us, is "an abnormal condition characterized by a depressed emotional state and imaginary ill health; excessive worry or talk about one's health." We think we are the beginning and the end of the world. And

as a result we get our nation and our lives, our strengths and our ailments, quite out of focus.

We will not be on the way to curing our national hypochondria 3 unless we first see ourselves in history. This requires us to accept the unfashionable possibility that many of our national ills are imaginary and that others may not be as serious as we imagine. Unless we begin to believe that we won't be dead before morning, we may not be up to the daily tasks of a healthy life. By recalling some of the premature obituaries pronounced on other nations, we may listen more skeptically to the moralists and smart alecks who pretend to have in their pocket a life-expectancy chart for nations.

Overwhelmed by the instant moment — headlined in this morn- 4 ing's newspaper and flashed on this hour's newscast — we don't see the whole real world around us. We don't see the actual condition of our long-lived body national.

In a word, we have lost our sense of history. In our schools the 5 story of our nation has been displaced by "social studies" — which is often the story only of what ails us. In our churches the effort to see man *sub specie aeternitatis*[1] has been displaced by a "social gospel" — which is a polemic against the supposed special evils of our time. Our book publishers and literary reviewers no longer seek the timeless and the durable, but spend much of their efforts in fruitless search for à la mode "social commentary" — which they pray won't be out of date when the issue goes to press in two weeks or when the manuscript becomes a book in six months. Our merchandisers frantically devise their semi-annual models which will cease to be voguish when their sequels appear a few months hence. Neither our classroom lessons nor our sermons nor our books nor the things we live with nor the houses we live in are any longer strong ties to our past. We have become a nation of short-term doomsayers.

Without the materials of historical comparison, having lost our 6 traditional respect for the wisdom of ancestors and the culture of kindred nations, we are left with little but abstractions, baseless utopias, to compare ourselves with. No wonder, then, that some of our distraught citizens libel us as the worst nation in the world, or the bane of human history. For we have wandered out of history.

We have nearly lost interest in those real examples from the 7 human past which alone can help us shape standards of the humanly

---

[1] Under the aspect of eternity. — ED.

possible. So we compare ours with a mythical Trouble-Free World, where all mankind was at peace. We talk about the war in Vietnam as if it were the first war in American history to which many Americans were opposed. We condemn our nation for not yet having attained perfect justice, and we forget that ours is the most motley and miscellaneous great nation in history — the first to use the full force of law and constitutions and to enlist the vast majority of its citizens in a strenuous quest for justice for all races and ages and religions.

8   We flagellate ourselves as "poverty-ridden" — by comparison with some mythical time when there was no bottom 20 percent in the economic scale. We sputter against the Polluted Environment — as if it had come with the age of the automobile. We compare our smoggy air not with the odor of horse dung and the plague of flies and the smells of garbage and human excrement which filled cities in the past, but with the honeysuckle perfumes of some nonexistent City Beautiful. We forget that even if the water in many cities today is not as spring-pure nor as palatable as we would like, still for most of history the water of the cities (and of the countryside) was undrinkable. We reproach ourselves for the ills of disease and malnourishment, and forget that until recently, enteritis and measles and whooping cough, diphtheria and typhoid, were killing diseases of childhood, puerperal fever plagued mothers in childbirth, polio was a summer monster.

9   Flooded by screaming headlines and televised "news" melodramas of dissent, of shrill cries for "liberation," we haunt ourselves with the illusory ideal of some "whole nation" which had a deep and outspoken "faith" in its "values."

10   We become so obsessed by where we are that we forget where we came from and how we got here. No wonder that we begin to lack the courage to confront the normal ills of modern history's most diverse, growing, burbling Nation of Nations.

11   Our national hypochondria is compounded by distinctively American characteristics. The American belief in speed, which led us to build railroads farther and faster than any other nation, to invent "quick-lunch" and self-service to save that intolerable ten-minute wait, to build automobiles and highways so we can commute at 70 miles an hour, and which made us a nation of instant cities, instant coffee, and TV dinners, has bred in us a colossal impatience. Any social problem that can't be solved instantly by money and legislation seems fatal. Our appliances and our buildings — and our very lives — seem out of date even before we know it. What can't be done right now seems hardly worth doing at all.

Some of these current attitudes are themselves the late-twen-   12
tieth-century perversions of the old American Booster Spirit, which
has had no precise parallel anywhere else. Totalitarian nations have
been marked by their obsession with "planning" — with five-year
plans and ten-year plans. But planning expresses willingness to accept
a sharp distinction between present and future, between the way
things are and the way they might be. And that distinction has never
been too popular in the U.S.A. The nineteenth-century Boosters of
Western cities defended their extravagant boasts by saying there was
no reason to wait, if you were actually bragging only about things that
were certain to happen. To them the beauties of Oleopolis or Gopher
City were not less real just because they had "not yet gone through the
formality of taking place."

This Booster-Vagueness has always made Americans wonderfully   13
unpedantic about the distinction between the present and the future.
The amiable vagueness, which once gave an optimistic nineteenth-
century America the energy and the hope to go on, still survives. But
in a hypochondriac twentieth-century America its effects can be disastrous. Now that very same extravagant vagueness leads some Americans to believe that every battle is Armageddon and that the nation is
not less dead just because the national demise also has "not yet gone
through the formality of taking place."

An immigrant nation, without an established religion and with-   14
out political dogma, has had to depend heavily on its sense of a shared
past (and a shared future). American history itself was an antidote to
dogmatism and utopianism. It proved that a nation did not need to be
altogether one thing or another. Federalism was a way of combining
local control with national government. Ethnic pluralism was a way
of allowing people to keep as much as they wanted of their Old World
langauge, religion, and cuisine — to live among themselves as much
as they wished. The immigrant was not compelled either to keep or to
abandon his Old World identity. Despite flagrant exceptions expressing prejudices of race, religion, and sex, nevertheless, in the nation as
a whole free public schools, and the American innovations of the free
high school and the public college, have tried to have standards and
yet give everybody the same commodity. The nation aimed to preserve
"free private enterprise" (freer and on a larger scale than anywhere
else) and yet to provide social security, farm price supports, and other
insurance against the free market. On a priori grounds, each and all of
these would have seemed impossible, and they were all messy, philo-
sophically speaking.

15   The best antidote, then, against ruthless absolutes and simple-minded utopias has been American history itself. But that history becomes more and more inaccessible when the technology and institutions of our time imprison us in the present. How can we escape the prison?

16   First, we must awaken our desire to escape. To do this we must abandon the prevalent belief in the superior wisdom of the ignorant. Unless we give up the voguish reverence for youth and for the "culturally deprived," unless we cease to look to the vulgar community as arbiters of our schools, of our art and literature, and of all our culture, we will never have the will to de-provincialize our minds. We must make every effort to reverse the trend in our schools and colleges — to move away from the "relevant" and toward the cosmopolitanizing, the humanizing, and the unfamiliar. Education is learning what you didn't even know you didn't know. The vogue for "Black Studies" itself grew out of the ghetto, and ironically enough, unwittingly became an effort to idealize the ways of the ghetto. The last thing the able young Negro needs is "Black Studies" — which simply reinforces the unfortunate narrowness of his experience and confines him in *his* provincial present. He does need a better, more cosmopolitan educational system, from kindergarten on up, and a freer opportunity to grasp the opportunities in the whole nation. While he has suffered more than most other Americans from imprisonment in his provincial present, ultimately we all have the same need. We need liberation, too, from the White Ghetto. We all need more ancient history, more medieval history, more of the history and culture of Asia and Africa.

17   Then, we must enlarge and widen and deepen what we mean by our history. The preoccupation with politics, which has been the bane of the history classroom, fosters unreasonable notions that today governments are the root of all good and evil. The self-righteous effort by self-styled prophets of self-vaunted new "schools" of history would make history a mere tool of contemporary polemics, and so destroy the reason for exploring our past. They would make men of all other ages into the slaves of our conceit — to be used only for our purposes. We must make our history more total by incorporating the past that people lived but that historians have not talked much about. In the United States this means an effort to make more of the history of immigrants, of the history of technology, of the history of everyday life, of business and advertising and housing and eating and drinking and clothing. Democratizing our history does not mean perverting it to the current needs of demagogic or "revolutionary" politics. It does

mean enlarging its once-pedantic scope to include the whole spectrum of the ways of life of all men and women and children.

When we allow ourselves to be imprisoned in the present, to be 18 obsessed by the "relevant," we show too little respect for ourselves and our possibilities. We assume that we can properly judge our capacities by the peculiar tests of our own day. But we must look into the whole Historical Catalogue of man's possibilities. To be really persuaded that things can be otherwise, we must see how and when and why they actually have been otherwise.

To revive our sense of history is no panacea for current ills. But it 19 surely is a palliative. It may help us discover what is now curable, may help us define the timetable of the possible, and so help us become something that we are not. If history cannot give us panaceas, it is the best possible cure of the yen for panaceas. And the only proven antidote for utopianism.

"The voice of the intellect," observed Sigmund Freud (who did 20 not underestimate the role of the irrational) in 1928, "is a soft one, but it does not rest until it has gained a hearing. Ultimately, after endlessly repeated rebuffs, it succeeds. This is one of the few points in which one may be optimistic about the future of mankind." Beneath the strident voice of the present we must try to hear the insistent whisper of reason. It does not sound "with it." It speaks only to the attentive listener. It speaks a language always unfamiliar and often archaic. It speaks the language of all past times and places, which is the language of history.

_____ CONSIDERATIONS _____

1. "We have wandered out of history," says Boorstin in Paragraph 6. Is such a wandering literally possible? What does he mean? How does he explain the statement?

2. Boorstin is one of America's foremost historians, which might strengthen his plea that we pay more attention to history, or expose him to a charge of special pleading. How do you handle such conflicting notions about an author?

3. Boorstin expresses his conviction that we are prisoners of the present in a series of generalizations — for example, the first sentences of paragraphs 6, 7, 8, 9, 10. Does he support those generalizations with enough detail to satisfy you? Compare his performance with Caroline Bird's (pages 64–73).

4. This argumentative essay breaks down into three major parts. Can you identify them? How else might the author have organized his essay?

5. Do you agree with Boorstin's definition of education? See paragraphs 16 and 17, in which he makes a number of unpopular statements about many common teaching methods.

6. Toward the end of his essay, Boorstin makes a strong plea for "the voice of the intellect." Compare this with Richard Hofstadter's comments in "Intellect and Intelligence," pages 191–196.

Truman Capote (b. 1924) became a successful writer very early: he wrote articles for Madamoiselle *when he was nineteen, was hired by* The New Yorker *when he was twenty-one, won an O. Henry Award for a short story when he was twenty-two, and published his first novel* Other Voices, Other Rooms *when he was twenty-four. More recently he has concentrated on nonfiction that uses devices, like dialogue, usually associated with fiction. Thus Capote classified as a nonfiction novel* In Cold Blood *(1965), his account of a Kansas murder and the arrest, conviction, and execution of the two murderers. In "A Ride through Spain," the reporter's eye for detail combines with the novelist's inventive imagination, observing — among other animals — train seats that "sagged like the jowls of a bulldog."*

17

TRUMAN CAPOTE
A Ride through Spain

Certainly the train was old. The seats sagged like the jowls of a   1
bulldog, windows were out and strips of adhesive held together those
that were left; in the corridor a prowling cat appeared to be hunting
mice, and it was not unreasonable to assume his search would be
rewarded.

Slowly, as though the engine were harnessed to elderly coolies,   2
we crept out of Granada. The southern sky was as white and burning
as a desert; there was one cloud, and it drifted like a traveling oasis.

We were going to Algeciras, a Spanish seaport facing the coast of   3
Africa. In our compartment there was a middle-aged Australian wear-

ing a soiled linen suit; he had tobacco-colored teeth and his fingernails were unsanitary. Presently he informed us that he was a ship's doctor. It seemed curious, there on the dry, dour plains of Spain, to meet someone connected with the sea. Seated next to him there were two women, a mother and daughter. The mother was an overstuffed, dusty woman with sluggish, disapproving eyes and a faint mustache. The focus for her disapproval fluctuated; first, she eyed me rather strongly because as the sunlight fanned brighter, waves of heat blew through the broken windows and I had removed my jacket — which she considered, perhaps rightly, discourteous. Later on, she took a dislike to the young soldier who also occupied our compartment. The soldier, and the woman's not very discreet daughter, a buxom girl with the scrappy features of a prizefighter, seemed to have agreed to flirt. Whenever the wandering cat appeared at our door, the daughter pretended to be frightened, and the soldier would gallantly shoo the cat into the corridor: this by-play gave them frequent opportunity to touch each other.

4   The young soldier was one of many on the train. With their tasseled caps set at snappy angles, they hung about in the corridors smoking sweet black cigarettes and laughing confidentially. They seemed to be enjoying themselves, which apparently was wrong of them, for whenever an officer appeared the soldiers would stare fixedly out the windows, as though enraptured by the landslides of red rock, the olive fields and stern stone mountains. Their officers were dressed for a parade, many ribbons, much brass; and some wore gleaming, improbable swords strapped to their sides. They did not mix with the soldiers, but sat together in a first-class compartment, looking bored and rather like unemployed actors. It was a blessing, I suppose, that something finally happened to give them a chance at rattling their swords.

5   The compartment directly ahead was taken over by one family: a delicate, attenuated, exceptionally elegant man with a mourning ribbon sewn around his sleeve, and traveling with him, six thin, summery girls, presumably his daughters. They were beautiful, the father and his children, all of them, and in the same way: hair that had a dark shine, lips the color of pimientos, eyes like sherry. The soldiers would glance into their compartment, then look away. It was as if they had seen straight into the sun.

6   Whenever the train stopped, the man's two youngest daughters would descend from the carriage and stroll under the shade of parasols. They enjoyed many lengthy promenades, for the train spent the great-

est part of our journey standing still. No one appeared to be exasperated by this except myself. Several passengers seemed to have friends at every station with whom they could sit around a fountain and gossip long and lazily. One old woman was met by different little groups in a dozen-odd towns — between these encounters she wept with such abandon that the Australian doctor became alarmed: why no, she said, there was nothing he could do, it was just that seeing all her relatives made her so happy.

At each stop cyclones of barefooted women and somewhat naked children ran beside the train sloshing earthen jars of water and furrily squalling *Agua! Agua!* For two pesetas you could buy a whole basket of dark runny figs, and there were trays of curious white-coated candy doughnuts that looked as though they should be eaten by young girls wearing Communion dresses. Toward noon, having collected a bottle of wine, a loaf of bread, a sausage and a cheese, we were prepared for lunch. Our companions in the compartment were hungry, too. Packages were produced, wine uncorked, and for a while there was a pleasant, almost graceful festiveness. The soldier shared a pomegranate with the girl, the Australian told an amusing story, the witch-eyed mother pulled a paper-wrapped fish from between her bosoms and ate it with a glum relish.   7

Afterward everyone was sleepy; the doctor went so solidly to sleep that a fly meandered undisturbed over his open-mouthed face. Stillness etherized the whole train; in the next compartment the lovely girls leaned loosely, like six exhausted geraniums; even the cat had ceased to prowl, and lay dreaming in the corridor. We had climbed higher, the train moseyed across a plateau of rough yellow wheat, then between the granite walls of deep ravines where wind, moving down from the mountains, quivered in strange, thorny trees. Once, at a parting in the trees, there was something I'd wanted to see, a castle on a hill, and it sat there like a crown.   8

It was a landscape for bandits. Earlier in the summer, a young Englishman I know (rather, know of) had been motoring through this part of Spain when, on the lonely side of a mountain, his car was surrounded by swarthy scoundrels. They robbed him, then tied him to a tree and tickled his throat with the blade of a knife. I was thinking of this when without preface a spatter of bullet fire strafed the dozy silence.   9

It was a machine gun. Bullets rained in the trees like the rattle of castanets, and the train, with a wounded creak, slowed to a halt. For a   10 moment there was no sound except the machine gun's cough. Then, "Bandits!" I said in a loud, dreadful voice.

11   *"Bandidos!"* screamed the daughter.

12   *"Bandidos!"* echoed her mother, and the terrible word swept through the train like something drummed on a tom-tom. The result was slapstick in a grim key. We collapsed on the floor, one cringing heap of arms and legs. Only the mother seemed to keep her head; standing up, she began systematically to stash away her treasures. She stuck a ring into the buns of her hair and without shame hiked up her skirts and dropped a pearl-studded comb into her bloomers. Like the cryings of birds at twilight, airy twitterings of distress came from the charming girls in the next compartment. In the corridor the officers bumped about yapping orders and knocking into each other.

13   Suddenly, silence. Outside, there was the murmur of wind in leaves, of voices. Just as the weight of the doctor's body was becoming too much for me, the outer door of our compartment swung open, and a young man stood there. He did not look clever enough to be a bandit.

14   *"Hay un médico en el tren?"* he said, smiling.

15   The Australian, removing the pressure of his elbow from my stomach, climbed to his feet. "I'm a doctor," he admitted, dusting himself. "Has someone been wounded?"

16   "Si, Señor. An old man. He is hurt in the head," said the Spaniard, who was not a bandit: alas, merely another passenger. Settling back in our seats, we listened, expressionless with embarrassment, to what had happened. It seemed that for the last several hours an old man had been stealing a ride by clinging to the rear of the train. Just now he'd lost his hold, and a soldier, seeing him fall, had starting firing a machine gun as a signal for the engineer to stop the train.

17   My only hope was that no one remembered who had first mentioned bandits. They did not seem to. After acquiring a clean shirt of mine which he intended to use as a bandage, the doctor went off to his patient, and the mother, turning her back with sour prudery, reclaimed her pearl comb. Her daughter and the soldier followed after us as we got out of the carriage and strolled under the trees, where many passengers had gathered to discuss the incident.

18   Two soldiers appeared carrying the old man. My shirt was wrapped around his head. They propped him under a tree and all the women clustered about vying with each other to lend him their rosary; someone brought a bottle of wine, which pleased him more. He seemed quite happy, and moaned a great deal. The children who had been on the train circled around him, giggling.

We were in a small wood that smelled of oranges. There was a   19
path, and it led to a shaded promontory; from here, one looked across
a valley where sweeping stretches of scorched golden grass shivered as
though the earth were trembling. Admiring the valley, and the shadowy changes of light on the hills beyond, the six sisters, escorted by
their elegant father, sat with their parasols raised above them like
guests at a *fête champêtre*. The soldiers moved around them in a
vague, ambitious manner; they did not quite dare to approach, though
one brash, sassy fellow went to the edge of the promontory and called,
"Yo te quiero mucho." The words returned with the hollow sub-music
of a perfect echo, and the sisters, blushing, looked more deeply into
the valley.

A cloud, somber as the rocky hills, had massed in the sky, and   20
the grass below stirred like the sea before a storm. Someone said he
thought it would rain. But no one wanted to go: not the injured man,
who was well on his way through a second bottle of wine, nor the
children who, having discovered the echo, stood happily caroling into
the valley. It was like a party, and we all drifted back to the train as
though each of us wished to be the last to leave. The old man, with
my shirt like a grand turban on his head, was put into a first-class
carriage and several eager ladies were left to attend him.

In our compartment, the dark, dusty mother sat just as we had   21
left her. She had not seen fit to join the party. She gave me a long,
glittering look. *"Bandidos,"* she said with a surly, unnecessary vigor.

The train moved away so slowly butterflies blew in and out the   22
windows.

_____ CONSIDERATIONS _____

1. Truman Capote, best known as a novelist and short story writer,
exhibits in this essay his talent for vivid, quickly drawn characters. Note the
high degree of selectivity he exercises in choosing the few details used to
describe the train, the people, the events.

2. Which passenger stirred up the alarm over "bandidos"? Why?

3. Using specific passages, characterize the author's attitude toward the
people he observed. How does he keep himself aloof from them? How does he
see himself as one of them?

4. Underline several of the figures of speech Capote uses. How do they
add information, as well as increase the pleasure of reading the account?

5. The author obviously enjoyed his ride through Spain. Imagine the

same trip reported by one who found it unpleasant. Taking this negative point of view, write a description of one of the people Capote met.

6. Why did the six sisters blush when one of the soldiers shouted from the hill, " *'Yo te quiero mucho'* "? What do you do about foreign words and expressions you meet in your reading? Why do authors use them? Would anything have been lost if Capote had had the soldier shout in English?

Frank Conroy (b. 1936) grew up in various towns along the eastern seaboard, and attended Haverford College. He writes about his early life in the only book he has published to date, Stop-Time *(1967). His prose has the qualities that make the best reminiscence: details feel exact and bright, though miniature with distance, like the landscape crafted for background to model trains.*

18

FRANK CONROY

A Yo-Yo Going Down

The common yo-yo is crudely made, with a thick shank between   1
two widely spaced wooden disks. The string is knotted or stapled to the shank. With such an instrument nothing can be done except the simple up-down movement. My yo-yo, on the other hand, was a perfectly balanced construction of hard wood, slightly weighted, flat, with only a sixteenth of an inch between the halves. The string was not attached to the shank, but looped over it in such a way as to allow the wooden part to spin freely on its own axis. The gyroscopic effect thus created kept the yo-yo stable in all attitudes.

I started at the beginning of the book and quickly mastered the   2
novice, intermediate, and advanced stages, practicing all day every day in the woods across the street from my house. Hour after hour of practice, never moving to the next trick until the one at hand was mastered.

The string was tied to my middle finger, just behind the nail. As   3
I threw — with your palm up, make a fist; throw down your hand,

fingers unfolding, as if you were casting grain — a short bit of string would tighten across the sensitive pad of flesh at the tip of my finger. That was the critical area. After a number of weeks I could interpret the condition of the string, the presence of any imperfections on the shank, but most importantly the exact amount of spin or inertial energy left in the yo-yo at any given moment — all from that bit of string on my fingertip. As the throwing motion became more and more natural I found I could make the yo-yo "sleep" for an astonishing length of time — fourteen or fifteen seconds — and still have enough spin left to bring it back to my hand. Gradually the basic moves became reflexes. Sleeping, twirling, swinging, and precise aim. Without thinking, without even looking, I could run through trick after trick involving various combinations of the elemental skills, switching from one to the other in a smooth continuous flow. On particularly good days I would hum a tune under my breath and do it all in time to the music.

4   Flicking the yo-yo expressed something. The sudden, potentially comic extension of one's arm to twice its length. The precise neatness of it, intrinsically soothing, as if relieving an inner tension too slight to be noticeable, the way a man might hitch up his pants simply to enact a reassuring gesture. It felt good. The comfortable weight in one's hand, the smooth, rapid descent down the string, ending with a barely audible snap as the yo-yo hung balanced, spinning, pregnant with force and the slave of one's fingertip. That it was vaguely masturbatory seems inescapable. I doubt that half the pubescent boys in America could have been captured by any other means, as, in the heat of the fad, half of them were. A single Loop-the-Loop might represent, in some mysterious way, the act of masturbation, but to break down the entire repertoire into the three stages of throw, trick, and return representing erection, climax, and detumescence seems immoderate.

5   The greatest pleasure in yo-yoing was an abstract pleasure — watching the dramatization of simple physical laws, and realizing they would never fail if a trick was done correctly. The geometric purity of it! The string wasn't just a string, it was a tool in the enactment of theorems. It was a line, an idea. And the top was an entirely different sort of idea, a gyroscope, capable of storing energy and of interacting with the line. I remember the first time I did a particularly lovely trick, one in which the sleeping yo-yo is swung from right to left while the string is interrupted by an extended index finger. Momentum carries the yo-yo in a circular path around the finger, but instead of completing the arc the yo-yo falls on the taut string between the performer's

hands, where it continues to spin in an upright position. My pleasure at that moment was as much from the beauty of the experiment as from pride. Snapping apart my hands I sent the yo-yo into the air above my head, bouncing it off nothing, back into my palm.

I practiced the yo-yo because it pleased me to do so, without the   6
slightest application of will power. It wasn't ambition that drove me, but the nature of yo-yoing. The yo-yo represented my first organized attempt to control the outside world. It fascinated me because I could see my progress in clearly defined stages, and because the intimacy of it, the almost spooky closeness I began to feel with the instrument in my hand, seemed to ensure that nothing irrelevant would interfere. I was, in the language of jazz, "up tight" with my yo-yo, and finally free, in one small area at least, of the paralyzing sloppiness of life in general.

The first significant problem arose in the attempt to do fifty con-   7
secutive Loop-the-Loops. After ten or fifteen the yo-yo invariably started to lean and the throws became less clean, resulting in loss of control. I almost skipped the whole thing because fifty seemed excessive. Ten made the point. But there it was, written out in the book. To qualify as an expert you had to do fifty, so fifty I would do.

It took me two days, and I wouldn't have spent a moment more.   8
All those Loop-the-Loops were hard on the strings. Time after time the shank cut them and the yo-yo went sailing off into the air. It was irritating, not only because of the expense (strings were a nickel each, and fabricating your own was unsatisfactory), but because a random element had been introduced. About the only unforeseeable disaster in yo-yoing was to have your string break, and here was a trick designed to do exactly that. Twenty-five would have been enough. If you could do twenty-five clean Loop-the-Loops you could do fifty or a hundred. I supposed they were simply trying to sell strings and went back to the more interesting tricks.

The witty nonsense of Eating Spaghetti, the surprise of The   9
Twirl, the complex neatness of Cannonball, Backwards round the World, or Halfway round the World — I could do them all, without false starts or sloppy endings. I could do every trick in the book. Perfectly.

The day was marked on the kitchen calendar (God Gave Us Blue-   10
bell Natural Bottled Gas). I got on my bike and rode into town. Pedaling along the highway I worked out with the yo-yo to break in a new string. The twins were appearing at the dime store.

I could hear the crowd before I turned the corner. Kids were com-   11 ing on bikes and on foot from every corner of town, rushing down the streets like madmen. Three or four policemen were busy keeping the street clear directly in front of the store, and in a small open space around the doors some of the more adept kids were running through their tricks, showing off to the general audience or stopping to compare notes with their peers. Standing at the edge with my yo-yo safe in my pocket, it didn't take me long to see I had them all covered. A boy in a sailor hat could do some of the harder tricks, but he missed too often to be a serious threat. I went inside.

12   As Ramos and Ricardo performed I watched their hands carefully, noticing little differences in style, and technique. Ricardo was a shade classier, I thought, although Ramos held an edge in the showy two-handed stuff. When they were through we went outside for the contest.

13   "Everybody in the alley!" Ramos shouted, his head bobbing an inch or two above the others. "Contest starting now in the alley!" A hundred excited children followed the twins into an alley beside the dime store and lined up against the wall.

14   "Attention all kids!" Ramos yelled, facing us from the middle of the street like a drill sergeant. "To qualify for contest you got to Rock the Cradle. You got to rock yo-yo in cradle four time. Four time! Okay? Three time no good. Okay. Everybody happy?" There were murmurs of disappointment and some of the kids stepped out of line. The rest of us closed ranks. Yo-yos flicked nervously as we waited. "Winner receive grand prize. Special Black Beauty Prize Yo-Yo with Diamonds," said Ramos, gesturing to his brother who smiled and held up the prize, turning it in the air so we could see the four stones set on each side. ("The crowd gasped . . ." I want to write. Of course they didn't. They didn't make a sound, but the impact of the diamond yo-yo was obvious.) We'd never seen anything like it. One imagined how the stones would gleam as it revolved, and how much prettier the tricks would be. The ultimate yo-yo! The only one in town! Who knew what feats were possible with such an instrument? All around me a fierce, nervous resolve was settling into the contestants, suddenly skittish as racehorses.

15   "Ricardo will show trick with Grand Prize Yo-Yo. Rock the Cradle four time!"

16   "One!" cried Ramos.

17   "Two!" the kids joined in.

18   "Three!" It was really beautiful. He did it so slowly you would have thought he had all the time in the world. I counted seconds under my breath to see how long he made it sleep.

"Four!" said the crowd.   19

"Thirteen," I said to myself as the yo-yo snapped back into his   20
hand. Thirteen seconds. Excellent time for that particular trick.

"Attention all kids!" Ramos announced. "Contest start now at   21
head of line."

The first boy did a sloppy job of gathering his string but managed   22
to rock the cradle quickly four times.

"Okay." Ramos tapped him on the shoulder and moved to the   23
next boy, who fumbled. "Out." Ricardo followed, doing an occasional
Loop-the-Loop with the diamond yo-yo. "Out . . . out . . . okay," said
Ramos as he worked down the line.

There was something about the man's inexorable advance that   24
unnerved me. His decisions were fast, and there was no appeal. To my
surprise I felt my palms begin to sweat. Closer and closer he came, his
voice growing louder, and then suddenly he was standing in front of
me. Amazed, I stared at him. It was as if he'd appeared out of thin air.

"What happen boy, you swarrow bubble gum?"   25

The laughter jolted me out of it. Blushing, I threw down my yo-   26
yo and executed a slow Rock the Cradle, counting the four passes and
hesitating a moment at the end so as not to appear rushed.

"Okay." He tapped my shoulder. "Good."   27

I wiped my hands on my blue jeans and watched him move down   28
the line. "Out . . . out . . . out." He had a large mole on the back of his
neck.

Seven boys qualified. Coming back, Ramos called out, "Next   29
trick Backward Round the World! Okay? Go!"

The first two boys missed, but the third was the kid in the sailor   30
hat. Glancing quickly to see that no one was behind him, he hunched
up his shoulder, threw, and just barely made the catch. There was
some loose string in his hand, but not enough to disqualify him.

Number four missed, as did number five, and it was my turn. I   31
stepped forward, threw the yo-yo almost straight up over my head, and
as it began to fall pulled very gently to add some speed. It zipped neatly
behind my legs and there was nothing more to do. My head turned to
one side, I stood absolutely still and watched the yo-yo come in over
my shoulder and slap into my hand. I added a Loop-the-Loop just to
show the tightness of the string.

"Did you see that?" I heard someone say.   32

Number seven missed, so it was between myself and the boy in   33
the sailor hat. His hair was bleached by the sun and combed up over
his forehead in a pompadour, held from behind by the white hat. He

was a year or two older than me. Blinking his blue eyes nervously, he adjusted the tension of his string.

34   "Next trick Cannonball! Cannonball! You go first this time," Ramos said to me.

35   Kids had gathered in a circle around us, those in front quiet and attentive, those in back jumping up and down to get a view. "Move back for room," Ricardo said, pushing them back. "More room, please."

36   I stepped into the center and paused, looking down at the ground. It was a difficult trick. The yo-yo had to land exactly on the string and there was a chance I'd miss the first time. I knew I wouldn't miss twice. "Can I have one practice?"

37   Ramos and Ricardo consulted in their mother tongue, and then Ramos held up his hands. "Attention all kids! Each boy have one practice before trick."

38   The crowd was silent, watching me. I took a deep breath and threw, following the fall of the yo-yo with my eyes, turning slightly, matador-fashion, as it passed me. My finger caught the string, the yo-yo came up and over, and missed. Without pausing I threw again. "Second time," I yelled, so there would be no misunderstanding. The circle had been too big. This time I made it small, sacrificing beauty for security. The yo-yo fell where it belonged and spun for a moment. (A moment I don't rush, my arms widespread, my eyes locked on the spinning toy. The Trick! There it is, brief and magic, right before your eyes! My hands are frozen in the middle of a deaf-and-dumb sentence, holding the whole airy, tenuous statement aloft for everyone to see.) With a quick snap I broke up the trick and made my catch.

39   Ramos nodded. "Okay. Very good. Now next boy."

40   Sailor-hat stepped forward, wiping his nose with the back of his hand. He threw once to clear the string.

41   "One practice," said Ramos.

42   He nodded.

43   "C'mon Bobby," someone said. "You can do it."

44   Bobby threw the yo-yo out to the side, made his move, and missed. "Damn," he whispered. (He said "dahyum.") The second time he got halfway through the trick before his yo-yo ran out of gas and fell impotently off the string. He picked it up and walked away, winding slowly.

45   Ramos came over and held my hand in the air. "The winner!" he yelled. "Grand prize Black Beauty Diamond Yo-Yo will now be awarded."

Ricardo stood in front of me. "Take off old yo-yo." I loosened the   46
knot and slipped it off. "Put out hand." I held out my hand and he
looped the new string on my finger, just behind the nail, where the
mark was. "You like Black Beauty," he said, smiling as he stepped
back. "Diamond make pretty colors in the sun."

"Thank you," I said.   47

"Very good with yo-yo. Later we have contest for whole town.   48
Winner go to Miami for State Championship. Maybe you win. Okay?"

"Okay." I nodded. "Thank you."   49

A few kids came up to look at Black Beauty. I threw it once or   50
twice to get the feel. It seemed a bit heavier than my old one. Ramos
and Ricardo were surrounded as the kids called out their favorite
tricks.

"Do Pickpocket! Pickpocket!"   51

"Do the Double Cannonball!"   52

"Ramos! Ramos! Do the Turkish Army!"   53

Smiling, waving their hands to ward off the barrage of requests,   54
the twins worked their way through the crowd toward the mouth of
the alley. I watched them moving away and was immediately struck
by a wave of fierce and irrational panic. "Wait," I yelled, pushing
through after them. "Wait!"

I caught them on the street.   55

"No more today," Ricardo said, and then paused when he saw it   56
was me. "Okay. The champ. What's wrong? Yo-yo no good?"

"No. It's fine."   57

"Good. You take care of it."   58

"I wanted to ask when the contest is. The one where you get to   59
go to Miami."

"Later. After school begins." They began to move away. "We   60
have to go home now."

"Just one more thing," I said, walking after them. "What is the   61
hardest trick you know?"

Ricardo laughed. "Hardest trick killing flies in air."   62

"No, no. I mean a real trick."   63

They stopped and looked at me. "There is a very hard trick,"   64
Ricardo said. "I don't do it, but Ramos does. Because you won the
contest he will show you. But only once, so watch carefully."

We stepped into the lobby of the Sunset Theater. Ramos cleared   65
his string. "Watch," he said, and threw. The trick started out like a
Cannonball, and then unexpectedly folded up, opened again, and as I
watched breathlessly the entire complex web spun around in the air,

propelled by Ramos' two hands making slow circles like a swimmer. The end was like the end of a Cannonball.

66   "That's beautiful," I said, genuinely awed. "What's it called?"
67   "The Universe."
68   "The Universe," I repeated.
69   "Because it goes around and around," said Ramos, "like the planets."

___ CONSIDERATIONS _____

1. List the several ways in which Conroy says one can get pleasure from the yo-yo.

2. How much of performance is play? Would you use the word performance for the work of a painter, an opera singer, a tennis star, a poet? Are professional athletes paid to play? What is the difference between work and play?

3. One respected writer says that "play is the direct opposite of seriousness," yet writers like Conroy are serious in recalling their childhood play. Can you resolve this apparent contradiction?

4. Conroy's essay might be divided into two major sections. Where would you draw the dividing line? Describe the two sections in terms of the author's intention. In the second section, the author makes constant use of dialogue; in the first, there is none. Why?

5. "I practiced the yo-yo because it pleased me to do so, without the slightest application of will power." Consider the relevance or irrelevance of will power to pleasure. Are they mutually exclusive?

6. In Paragraph 14, Conroy interrupts his narrative with a parenthetical remark about himself as the writer: "('The crowd gasped . . .' I want to write. Of course they didn't. They didn't make a sound, but the impact of the diamond yo-yo was obvious.)" Are such glimpses of the writer conscious of himself writing useful or merely distracting? Discuss.

Malcolm Cowley (b. 1898) is an editor, poet, critic, and literary journalist, whose appreciations have furthered the careers of other writers, most notably William Faulkner's. Cowley's best known work is Exile's Return, *describing American writers of the Lost Generation; it was published in 1934 and revised in 1951. A collection of newer essays called* And I Work at the Writer's Trade *appeared in 1978.*

With this essay, Cowley takes on sociology, or at least its language. In the twenty years since Cowley wrote this article, jargon has spread like a weed; thus it has been determined on the basis of subjective input assessment to accession this nacreous style description to the second edition of A Writer's Reader.

19

MALCOLM COWLEY

Sociological Habit Patterns in Linguistic Transmogrification

I have a friend who started as a poet and then decided to take a   1
postgraduate degree in sociology. For his doctoral dissertation he combined his two interests by writing on the social psychology of poets. He had visited poets by the dozen, asking each of them a graded series of questions, and his conclusions from the interviews were modest and useful, though reported in what seemed to me a barbarous jargon. After reading the dissertation I wrote and scolded him. "You have such a fine sense of the poet's craft," I said, "that you shouldn't have allowed the sociologists to seduce you into writing their professional slang — or at least that's my judgmental response to your role selection."

2   My friend didn't write to defend himself; he waited until we met again. Then, dropping his voice, he said: "I knew my dissertation was badly written, but I had to get my degree. If I had written it in English, Professor Blank" — he mentioned a rather distinguished name — "would have rejected it. He would have said it was merely belletristic."

3   From that time I began to study the verbal folkways of the sociologists. I read what they call "the literature." A few sociologists write the best English they are capable of writing, and I suspect that they are the best men in the field. There is no mystery about them. If they go wrong, their mistakes can be seen and corrected. Others, however — and a vast majority — write in a language that has to be learned almost like Esperanto. It has a private vocabulary which, in addition to strictly sociological terms, includes new words for the commonest actions, feelings, and circumstances. It has the beginnings of a new grammar and syntax, much inferior to English grammar in force and precision. So far as it has an effect on standard English, the effect is largely pernicious.

4   Sometimes it misleads the sociologists themselves, by making them think they are profoundly scientific at points where they are merely being verbose. I can illustrate by trying a simple exercise in translation, that is, by expressing an idea first in English and then seeing what it looks like in the language of sociology.

5   An example that comes to hand is the central idea of an article by Norman E. Green, printed in the February, 1956, issue of the *American Sociological Review*. In English his argument might read as follows:

6   "Rich people live in big houses set farther apart than those of poor people. By looking at an aerial photograph of any American city, we can distinguish the richer from the poorer neighborhoods."

7   I won't have to labor over a sociological expression of the same idea, because Mr. Green has saved me the trouble. Here is part of his contribution to comparative linguistics. "In effect, it was hypothesized," he says — a sociologist must never say "I assumed," much less "I guessed" — "that certain physical data categories including housing types and densities, land use characteristics, and ecological location" — not just "location," mind you, but "ecological location," which is almost equivalent to locational location — "constitute a scalable content area. This could be called a continuum of residential desirability. Likewise, it was hypothesized that several social data categories,

describing the same census tracts, and referring generally to the social stratification system of the city, would also be scalable. This scale could be called a continuum of socio-economic status. Thirdly, it was hypothesized that there would be a high positive correlation between the scale types on each continuum."

Here, after ninety-four words, Mr. Green is stating, or concealing, 8 an assumption with which most laymen would have started, that rich people live in good neighborhoods. He is now almost ready for his deduction, or snapper:

"This relationship would define certain linkages between the 9 social and physical structure of the city. It would also provide a precise definition of the commonalities among several spatial distributions. By the same token, the correlation between the residential desirability scale and the continuum of socio-economic status would provide an estimate of the predictive value of aerial photographic data relative to the social ecology of the city."

Mr. Green has used 160 words — counting "socio-economic" as 10 only one — to express an idea that a layman would have stated in thirty-three. As a matter of fact, he has used many more than 160 words, since the whole article is an elaboration of this one thesis. Whatever may be the virtues of the sociological style — or Socspeak, as George Orwell might have called it — it is not specifically designed to save ink and paper. Let us briefly examine some of its other characteristics.

A layman's first impression of sociological prose, as compared 11 with English prose, is that it contains a very large proportion of abstract words, most of them built on Greek or Latin roots. Often — as in the example just quoted — they are used to inflate or transmogrify a meaning that could be clearly expressed in shorter words surviving from King Alfred's time.

These Old English or Anglo-Saxon words are in number less than 12 one-tenth of the entries in the largest dictionaries. But they are the names of everyday objects, attributes, and actions, and they are also the pronouns, the auxiliary verbs, and most of the prepositions and conjunctions, so that they form the grammatical structure of the language. The result is that most novelists use six Anglo-Saxon words for every one derived from French, Latin, or Greek and that is probably close to the percentage that would be found in spoken English.

For comparison or contrast, I counted derivations in the passage 13 quoted from the *American Sociological Review*, which is a typical example of "the literature." No less than 49 per cent of Mr. Green's prose consists of words from foreign or classical languages. By this standard of measurement, his article is more abstruse than most textbooks of advanced chemistry and higher mathematics, which are said to contain only 40 per cent of such words.

14   In addition to being abstruse, the language of the sociologists is also rich in neologisms. Apparently they like nothing better than inventing a word, deforming a word, or using a technical word in a strange context. Among their favorite nouns are "ambit," "extensity" (for "extent"), "scapegoating," "socializee," "ethnicity," "directionality," "cathexis," "affect" (for "feeling"), "maturation" (for both "maturing" and "maturity"), and "commonalities" (for "points in common"). Among their favorite adjectives are "processual," "prestigeful," and "insightful" — which last is insightful to murder — and perhaps their favorite adverb is "minimally," which seems to mean "in some measure." Their maximal pleasure seems to lie in making new combinations of nouns and adjectives and nouns used as adjectives, until the reader feels that he is picking his way through a field of huge boulders, lost among "universalistic-specific achievement patterns" and "complementary role-expectation-sanction systems," as he struggles vainly toward "ego-integrative action orientation," guided only by "orientation to improvement of the gratification-deprivation balance of the actor" — which last is Professor Talcott Parsons's rather involved way of saying "the pleasure principle."

15   But Professor Parsons, head of the Sociology Department at Harvard, is not the only delinquent recidivist, convicted time and again of corrupting the language. Among sociologists in general there is a criminal fondness for using complicated terms when there are simple ones available. A child says "Do it again," a teacher says "Repeat the exercise," but the sociologist says "It was determined to replicate the investigation." Instead of saying two things are alike or similar as a layman would do, the sociologist describes them in being either isomorphic or homologous. Instead of saying that they are different, he calls them allotropic. Every form of leadership or influence is called a hegemony.

16   A sociologist never cuts anything in half or divides it in two like a layman. Instead he dichotomizes it, bifurcates it, subjects it to a process of binary fission, or restructures it in a dyadic conformation — around polar foci.

17   So far I have been dealing with the vocabulary of sociologists, but their private language has a grammar too, and one that should be the

subject of intensive research by the staff of a very well-endowed foundation. I have space to mention only a few of its more striking features.

The first of these is the preponderance of nouns over all the other 18 parts of speech. Nouns are used in hyphenated pairs or dyads, and sometimes in triads, tetrads, and pentads. Nouns are used as adjectives without change of form, and they are often used as verbs, with or without the suffix "ize." The sociological language is gritty with nouns, like sanded sugar.

On the other hand, it is poor in pronouns. The singular pronoun 19 of the first person has entirely disappeared, except in case histories, for the sociologist never comes forward as "I." Sometimes he refers to himself as "the author" or "the investigator," or as "many sociologists," or even as "the best sociologists," when he is advancing a debatable opinion. On rare occasions he calls himself "we," like Queen Elizabeth speaking from the throne, but he usually avoids any personal form and writes as if he were a force of nature.

The second-personal pronoun has also disappeared, for the soci- 20 ologist pretends to be speaking not to living persons but merely for the record. Masculine and feminine pronouns of the third person are used with parsimony, and most sociologists prefer to say "the subject," or "X____," or "the interviewee," where a layman would use the simple "he" or "she." As for the neuter pronoun of the third person, it survives chiefly as the impersonal subject of a passive verb. "It was hypothesized," we read, or "It was found to be the case." Found by *whom?*

The neglect and debasement of the verb is another striking fea- 21 ture of "the literature." The sociologist likes to reduce a transitive verb to an intransitive, so that he speaks of people's adapting, adjusting, transferring, relating, and identifying, with no more of a grammatical object than if they were coming or going. He seldom uses transitive verbs of action, like "break," "injure," "help," and "adore." Instead he uses verbs of relation, verbs which imply that one series of nouns and adjectives, used as the compound subject of a sentence, is larger or smaller than, dominant over, subordinate to, causative of, or resultant from another series of nouns and adjectives.

Considering this degradation of the verb, I have wondered how 22 one of Julius Caesar's boasts could be translated into Socspeak. What Caesar wrote was *"Veni, vidi, vici"* — only three words, all of them verbs. The English translation is in six words: "I came, I saw, I conquered," and three of the words are first-personal pronouns, which the sociologist is taught to avoid. I suspect that he would have to write:

"Upon the advent of the investigator, his hegemony became minimally coextensive with the areal unit rendered visible by his successive displacements in space."

23   The whole sad situation leads me to dream of a vast allegorical painting called "The Triumph of the Nouns." It would depict a chariot of victory drawn by the other conquered parts of speech — the adverbs and adjectives still robust, if yoked and harnessed; the prepositions bloated and pale; the conjunctions tortured; the pronouns reduced to sexless skeletons; the verbs dichotomized and feebly tottering — while behind them, arrogant, overfed, roseate, spilling over the triumphal car, would be the company of nouns in Roman togas and Greek chitons, adorned with laurel branches and flowering hegemonies.

_____ CONSIDERATIONS _____

1. In a final effort to ridicule sociological jargon, Cowley spins out an exaggerated dream in Paragraph 23. Compare that paragraph with H. L. Mencken's exaggerated language in his sarcastic review of Harding's inaugural address (pages 274–277).

2. Jargon invites parody — see the last sentence in Cowley's first paragraph. Try parody yourself by finding a passage of jargon in a newspaper, a textbook, a politician's speech. What are the requirements of a good parody? What can be learned about style from attempting one?

3. In Paragraph 10, Cowley alludes to something George Orwell called "Socspeak." The reference is to Orwell's famous novel *1984*, and to that author's straightfaced but highly satirical "Principles of Newspeak," printed as an appendix to the novel. If you can't spare time for the novel, read Orwell's "Politics and the English Language" (pages 306–319) to understand better Cowley's vehemence on the subject.

4. What does Cowley mean by a "neologism"? Can you find any in your favorite newspaper, magazine, or textbook, or in your own writing?

5. To understand sociological jargon, Cowley insists, we must study something other than vocabulary. What is that other element and how is it related to vocabulary?

6. Does Ambrose Bierce, in "Some Devil's Definitions" (pages 60–63), use what Cowley calls "corruptions" of the language? Why?

Clarence Darrow (1857–1938) was the most famous lawyer of his day, defender of labor leaders and radicals during the red-baiting twenties. Occasionally he undertook the cases of notorious criminals, notably Leopold and Loeb, two young men accused of murder; if he did not win acquittals he minimized sentences. In one of his most famous cases, the Scopes Monkey Trial, he defended a Tennessee schoolteacher indicted for teaching Darwinian theories of evolution in the schools, theories that were illegal because they conflicted with the narrative of Genesis. (The prosecution was conducted by William Jennings Bryan; see Walter Lippmann's essay, pages 233–241.) Darrow's agnosticism, evident during the trial, at the time seemed shocking, modern, and progressive. In this essay, the reader may catch the tone of an embattled and confident skeptic.

20

CLARENCE DARROW
Why I Am an Agnostic

An agnostic is a doubter. The word is generally applied to those 1
who doubt the verity of accepted religious creeds of faiths. Everyone is an agnostic as to the beliefs or creeds they do not accept. Catholics are agnostic to the Protestant creeds, and the Protestants are agnostic to the Catholic creed. Anyone who thinks is an agnostic about something, otherwise he must believe that he is possessed of all knowledge. And the proper place for such a person is in the madhouse or the home for the feeble-minded. In a popular way, in the western world, an agnostic is one who doubts or disbelieves the main tenets of the Christian faith.

From *Verdicts Out of Court* (New York: Quadrangle, 1963). Reprinted by permission of the Darrow family.

2   I would say that belief in at least three tenets is necessary to the faith of a Christian: a belief in God, a belief in immortality, and a belief in a supernatural book. Various Christian sects require much more, but it is difficult to imagine that one could be a Christian, under any intelligent meaning of the word, with less. Yet there are some people who claim to be Christians who do not accept the literal interpretation of all the Bible, and who give more credence to some portions of the book than to others.

3   I am an agnostic as to the question of God. I think that it is impossible for the human mind to believe in an object or thing unless it can form a mental picture of such object or thing. Since man ceased to worship openly an anthropomorphic God and talked vaguely and not intelligently about some force in the universe, higher than man, that is responsible for the existence of man and the universe, he cannot be said to believe in God. One cannot believe in a force excepting as a force that pervades matter and is not an individual entity. To believe in a thing, an image of the thing must be stamped on the mind. If one is asked if he believes in such an animal as a camel, there immediately arises in his mind an image of the camel. This image has come from experience or knowledge of the animal gathered in some way or other. No such image comes, or can come, with the idea of a God who is described as a force.

4   Man has always speculated upon the origin of the universe, including himself. I feel, with Herbert Spencer, that whether the universe had an origin — and if it had — what the origin is will never be known to man. The Christian says that the universe could not make itself; that there must have been some higher power to call it into being. Christians have been obsessed for many years by Paley's argument that if a person passing through a desert should find a watch and examine its spring, its hands, its case and its crystal, he would at once be satisfied that some intelligent being capable of design had made the watch. No doubt this is true. No civilized man would question that someone made the watch. The reason he would not doubt it is because he is familiar with watches and other appliances made by man. The savage was once unfamiliar with a watch and would have had no idea upon the subject. There are plenty of crystals and rocks of natural formation that are as intricate as a watch, but even to intelligent man they carry no implication that some intelligent power must have made them. They carry no such implication because no one has any knowledge or experience of someone having made these natural objects which everywhere abound.

To say that God made the universe gives us no explanation of the   5
beginning of things. If we are told that God made the universe, the
question immediately arises: Who made God? Did he always exist, or
was there some power back of that? Did he create matter out of nothing, or his existence coextensive with matter? The problem is still
there. What is the origin of it all? If, on the other hand, one says that
the universe was not made by God, that it always existed, he has the
same difficulty to confront. To say that the universe was here last year,
or millions of years ago, does not explain its origin. This is still a
mystery. As to the question of the origin of things, man can only
wonder and doubt and guess.

As to the existence of the soul, all people may either believe or   6
disbelieve. Everyone knows the origin of the human being. They know
that it came from a single cell in the body of the mother, and that the
cell was one out of ten thousand in the mother's body. Before gestation
the cell must have been fertilized by a spermatozoön from the body of
the father. This was one out of perhaps a billion spermatozoa that was
the capacity of the father. When the cell is fertilized a chemical process
begins. The cell divides and multiplies and increases into millions of
cells, and finally a child is born. Cells die and are born during the life
of the individual until they finally drop apart, and this is death.

If there is a soul, what is it, and where did it come from, and   7
where does it go? Can anyone who is guided by his reason possibly
imagine a soul independent of a body, or the place of its residence, or
the character of it, or anything concerning it? If man is justified in any
belief or disbelief on any subject, he is warranted in the disbelief in a
soul. Not one scrap of evidence exists to prove any such impossible
thing.

Many Christians base the belief of a soul and God upon the Bible.   8
Strictly speaking, there is no such book. To make the Bible, sixty-six
books are bound into one volume. These books are written by many
people at different times, and no one knows the time or the identity of
any author. Some of the books were written by several authors at
various times. These books contain all sorts of contradictory concepts
of life and morals and the origin of things. Between the first and last
nearly a thousand years intervened, a longer time than has passed since
the discovery of America by Columbus.

When I was a boy the theologians used to assert that the proof of   9
the divine inspiration of the Bible rested on miracles and prophecies.
But a miracle means a violation of a natural law, and there can be no
proof imagined that could be sufficient to show the violation of a

natural law; even though proof seemed to show violation, it would only show that we were not acquainted with all natural laws. One believes in the truthfulness of a man because of his long experience with the man, and because the man has always told a consistent story. But no man has told so consistent a story as nature.

10   If one should say that the sun did not rise, to use the ordinary expression, on the day before, his hearer would not believe it, even though he had slept all day and knew that his informant was a man of the strictest veracity. He would not believe it because the story is inconsistent with the conduct of the sun in all the ages past.

11   Primitive and even civilized people have grown so accustomed to believing in miracles that they often attribute the simplest manifestations of nature to agencies of which they know nothing. They do this when the belief is utterly inconsistent with knowledge and logic. They believe in old miracles and new ones. Preachers pray for rain, knowing full well that no such prayer was ever answered. When a politician is sick, they pray for God to cure him, and the politician almost invariably dies. The modern clergyman who prays for rain and for the health of the politician is no more intelligent in this matter than the primitive man who saw a separate miracle in the rising and setting of the sun, in the birth of an individual, in the growth of a plant, in the stroke of lightning, in the flood, in every manifestation of nature and life.

12   As to prophecies, intelligent writers gave them up long ago. In all prophecies facts are made to suit the prophecy, or the prophecy was made after the facts, or the events have no relation to the prophecy. Weird and strange and unreasonable interpreations are used to explain simple statements, that a prophecy may be claimed.

13   Can any rational person believe that the Bible is anything but a human document? We now know pretty well where the various books came from, and about when they were written. We know that they were written by human beings who had no knowledge of science, little knowledge of life, and were influenced by the barbarous morality of primitive times, and were grossly ignorant of most things that men know today. For instance, Genesis says that God made the earth, and he made the sun to light the day and the moon to light the night, and in one clause disposes of the stars by saying that "he made the stars also." This was plainly written by someone who had no conception of the stars. Man, by the aid of his telescope, has looked out into the heavens and found stars whose diameter is as great as the distance between the earth and the sun. We know that the universe is filled with stars and suns and planets and systems. Every new telescope

looking further into the heavens only discovers more and more worlds and suns and systems in the endless reaches of space. The men who wrote Genesis believed, of course, that this tiny speck of mud that we call the earth was the center of the universe, the only world in space, and made for man, who was the only being worth considering. These men believed that the stars were only a little way above the earth, and were set in the firmament for man to look at, and for nothing else. Everyone today knows that this conception is not true.

The origin of the human race is not as blind a subject as it once 14 was. Let alone God creating Adam out of hand, from the dust of the earth, does anyone believe that Eve was made from Adam's rib — that the snake walked and spoke in the Garden of Eden — that he tempted Eve to persuade Adam to eat an apple, and that it is on that account that the whole human race was doomed to hell — that for four thousand years there was no chance for any human to be saved, though none of them had anything whatever to do with the temptation; and that finally men were saved only through God's son dying for them, and that unless human beings believed this silly, impossible and wicked story they were doomed to hell? Can anyone with intelligence really believe that a child born today should be doomed because the snake tempted Eve and Eve tempted Adam? To believe that is not God-worship; it is devil-worship.

Can anyone call this scheme of creation and damnation moral? It 15 defies every principle of morality, as man conceives morality. Can anyone believe today that the whole world was destroyed by flood, save only Noah and his family and a male and female of each species of animal that entered the Ark? There are almost a million species of insects alone. How did Noah match these up and make sure of getting male and female to reproduce life in the world after the flood had spent its force? And why should all the lower animals have been destroyed? Were they included in the sinning of man? This is a story which could not beguile a fairly bright child of five years of age today.

Do intelligent people believe that the various languages spoken 16 by man on earth came from the confusion of tongues at the Tower of Babel, some four thousand years ago? Human languages were dispersed all over the face of the earth long before that time. Evidences of civilizations are in existence now that were old long before the date that romancers fix for the building of the Tower, and even before the date claimed for the flood.

Do Christians believe that Joshua made the sun stand still, so 17 that the day could be lengthened, that a battle might be finished? What kind of person wrote that story, and what did he know about astronomy? It is perfectly plain that the author thought that the earth was the center of the universe and stood still in the heavens, and that the sun either went around it or was pulled across its path each day, and that the stopping of the sun would lengthen the day. We know now that had the sun stopped when Joshua commanded it, and had it stood still until now, it would not have lengthened the day. We know that the day is determined by the rotation of the earth upon its axis, and not by the movement of the sun. Everyone knows that this story simply is not true, and not many even pretend to believe the childish fable.

18   What of the tale of Balaam's ass speaking to him, probably in Hebrew? Is it true, or is it a fable? Many asses have spoken, and doubtless some in Hebrew, but they have not been that breed of asses. Is salvation to depend on a belief in a monstrosity like this?

19   Above all the rest, would any human being today believe that a child was born without a father? Yet this story was not at all unreasonable in the ancient world; at least three or four miraculous births are recorded in the Bible, including John the Baptist and Samson. Immaculate conceptions were common in the Roman world at the time and at the place where Christianity really had its nativity. Women were taken to the temples to be inoculated of God so that their sons might be heroes, which meant, generally, wholesale butchers. Julius Caesar was a miraculous conception — indeed, they were common all over the world. How many miraculous-birth stories is a Christian now expected to believe?

20   In the days of the formation of the Christian religion, disease meant the possession of human beings by devils. Christ cured a sick man by casting out the devils, who ran into the swine, and the swine ran into the sea. Is there any question but what that was simply the attitude and belief of a primitive people? Does anyone believe that sickness means the possession of the body by devils, and that the devils must be cast out of the human being that he may be cured? Does anyone believe that a dead person can come to life? The miracles recorded in the Bible are not the only instances of dead men coming to life. All over the world one finds testimony of such miracles; miracles which no person is expected to believe, unless it is his kind of a miracle. Still at Lourdes today, and all over the present world, from New York to Los Angeles and up and down the lands, people believe in miraculous occurrences, and even in the return of the dead. Superstition is everywhere prevalent in the world. It has been so from the beginning, and most likely will be so unto the end.

The reasons for agnosticism are abundant and compelling. Fan- 21
tastic and foolish and impossible consequences are freely claimed for
the belief in religion. All the civilization of any period is put down as
a result of religion. All the cruelty and error and ignorance of the period
has no relation to religion. The truth is that the origin of what we call
civilization is not due to religion but to skepticism. So long as men
accepted miracles without question, so long as they believed in original sin and the road to salvation, so long as they believed in a hell
where man would be kept for eternity on account of Eve, there was no
reason whatever for civilization: life was short, and eternity was long,
and the business of life was preparation for eternity.

When every event was a miracle, when there was no order or 22
system or law, there was no occasion for studying any subject, or being
interested in anything excepting a religion which took care of the soul.
As man doubted the primitive conceptions about religion, and no
longer accepted the literal, miraculous teachings of ancient books, he
set himself to understand nature. We no longer cure disease by casting
out devils. Since that time, men have studied the human body, have
built hospitals and treated illness in a scientific way. Science is responsible for the building of railroads and bridges, of steamships, of telegraph lines, of cities, towns, large buildings and small, plumbing and
sanitation, of the food supply, and the countless thousands of useful
things that we now deem necessary to life. Without skepticism and
doubt, none of these things could have been given to the world.

The fear of God is not the beginning of wisdom. The fear of God 23
is the death of wisdom. Skepticism and doubt lead to study and investigation, and investigation is the beginning of wisdom.

_____ CONSIDERATIONS _____

1. Darrow's essay begins a controversial argument by defining terms.
What strengths and weaknesses do you detect in this strategy?

2. In Paragraph 4, Darrow refers to a famous and widely used argument
to prove the existence of God, published by William Paley in a book entitled
Natural Theology (1802) that begins with the example of the watch. Read the
first short chapter of Paley's book and check Darrow's reliability as a reporter.

3. Among other things that Darrow doubts is one particular view of the
Bible — see the second sentence of Paragraph 8. If research on the Bible interests you, begin with the note (page 53) preceding the selection from Ecclesiastes in this volume.

4. Note how many of Darrow's paragraphs begin with questions. How many of these are *real* questions asked in search of an answer? How many are rhetorical devices?

5. In Paragraph 20, Darrow refers to a time when "disease meant the possession of human beings by devils." This same idea is explored fully, if satirically, in a novel by Samuel Butler, *Erewhon*, about a utopian land where criminals are treated as we treat the sick, and the sick as we treat criminals.

6. Some of Darrow's argument is based on deduction, some on induction. Remind yourself of the difference between these two processes of thought by consulting Robert Gorham Davis, pages 115–125; then evaluate Darrow's methods of proof.

Robert Gorham Davis (b. 1908) recently retired as Professor of English at Columbia University. He has published books about John Dos Passos and C. P. Snow, successful texts, short stories, and literary essays. Not a philosopher but a literary man, he writes here about logic as we know it in daily life — or, more likely, as we do not know it well enough in daily life.

21

ROBERT GORHAM DAVIS
Logic and Logical Fallacies

Expression does not exist apart from thought, and cannot be analyzed or profitably discussed apart from thought. Just as clear and effective organization is essential to good writing, so consistent thinking and coherence of mind underlie consistent writing and coherence of style. The faults and errors which [fall] under the headings of style and structure are closely bound up with orderly thought, as the student can hardly fail to notice. But some direct suggestions on the modes of consistent thinking and of analyzing and criticizing arguments and assertions ought also to prove useful. The following pages accordingly present some notes on logic and common logical fallacies. 1

UNDEFINED TERMS

The first requirement for logical discourse is knowing what the words you use actually mean. Words are not like paper money or counters in a game. Except for technical terms in some of the sciences, they do not have a fixed face value. Their meanings are fluid and 2

From the *Harvard Handbook for English*, 4th edition. Copyright 1947, the President and Fellows of Harvard College. Copyright © 1975 by Robert Gorham Davis. Reprinted by permission of the author.

changing, influenced by many considerations of context and reference, circumstance and association. This is just as true of common words such as *fast* as it is of literary terms such as *romantic.* Moreover, if there is to be communication, words must have approximately the same meaning for the reader that they have for the writer. A speech in an unknown language means nothing to the hearer. When an adult speaks to a small child or an expert to a layman, communication may be seriously limited by lack of a mature vocabulary or ignorance of technical terms. Many arguments are meaningless because the speakers are using important words in quite different senses.

3   Because we learn most words — or guess at them — from the contexts in which we first encounter them, our sense of them is often incomplete or wrong. Readers sometimes visualize the Assyrian who comes down like the wolf on the fold as an enormous man dressed in cohorts (some kind of fancy armor, possibly) gleaming in purple and gold. "A rift in the lute" suggests vaguely a cracked mandolin. Failure to ascertain the literal meaning of figurative language is a frequent reason for mixed metaphors. We are surprised to find that the "devil" in "the devil to pay" and "the devil and the deep blue sea" is not Old Nick, but part of a ship. Unless terms mean the same thing to both writer and reader, proper understanding is impossible.

ABSTRACTIONS

4   The most serious logical difficulties occur with abstract terms. An abstraction is a word which stands for a quality found in a number of different objects or events from which it has been "abstracted" or taken away. We may, for instance, talk of the "whiteness" of paper or cotton or snow without considering qualities of cold or inflammability or usefulness which these materials happen also to possess. Usually, however, our minds carry over other qualities by association. See, for instance, the chapter called "The Whiteness of the Whale" in *Moby Dick.*

5   In much theoretic discussion the process of abstraction is carried so far that although vague associations and connotations persist, the original objects or events from which the qualities have been abstracted are lost sight of completely. Instead of thinking of words like *sincerity* and *Americanism* as symbols standing for qualities that have to be abstracted with great care from examples and test cases, we come to think of them as real things in themselves. We assume that

Americanism is Americanism just as a bicycle is a bicycle, and that everyone knows what it means. We forget that before the question, "Is Father Coughlin sincere?" can mean anything, we have to agree on the criteria of sincerity.

When we try to define such words and find examples, we discover   6
that almost no one agrees on their meaning. The word *church* may refer to anything from a building on the corner of Spring Street to the whole tradition of institutionalized Christianity. *Germany* may mean a geographical section of Europe, a people, a governing group, a cultural tradition, or a military power. Abstractions such as *freedom, courage, race, beauty, truth, justice, nature, honor, humanism, democracy,* should never be used in a theme unless their meaning is defined or indicated clearly by the context. Freedom for whom? To do what? Under what circumstances? Abstract terms have merely emotional value unless they are strictly defined by asking questions of this kind. The study of a word such as *nature* in a good unabridged dictionary will show that even the dictionary, indispensable though it is, cannot determine for us the sense in which a word is being used in any given instance. Once the student understands the importance of definition, he will no longer be betrayed into fruitless arguments over such questions as whether free verse is "poetry" or whether you can change "human nature."

NAME-CALLING

It is a common unfairness in controversy to place what the writer   7
dislikes or opposes in a generally odious category. The humanist dismisses what he dislikes by calling it *romantic;* the liberal, by calling it *fascist;* the conservative, by calling it *communistic.* These terms tell the reader nothing. What is *piety* to some will be *bigotry* to others. *Non-Catholics* would rather be called *Protestants* than *heretics.* What is *right-thinking* except a designation for those who agree with the writer? Labor leaders become *outside agitators;* industrial organizations, *forces of reaction;* the Child Labor Amendment, the *youth control bill;* prison reform, *coddling;* progressive education, *fads and frills.* Such terms are intended to block thought by an appeal to prejudice and associative habits. Three steps are necessary before such epithets have real meaning. First, they must be defined; second, it must be shown that the object to which they are applied actually possesses these qualities; third, it must be shown that the possession of such

qualities in this particular situation is necessarily undesirable. Unless a person is alert and critical both in choosing and in interpreting words, he may be alienated from ideas with which he would be in sympathy if he had not been frightened by a mere name.

GENERALIZATION

8   Similar to the abuse of abstract terms and epithets is the habit of presenting personal opinions in the guise of universal laws. The student often seems to feel that the broader the terms in which he states an opinion, the more effective he will be. Ordinarily the reverse is true. An enthusiasm for Thomas Wolfe should lead to a specific critical analysis of Wolfe's novels that will enable the writer to explain his enthusiasm to others; it should not be turned into the argument that Wolfe is "the greatest American novelist," particularly if the writer's knowledge of American novelists is somewhat limited. The same questions of *who* and *when* and *why* and under what *circumstances* which are used to check abstract terms should be applied to generalizations. Consider how contradictory proverbial wisdom is when detached from particular circumstances. "Look before you leap," but "he who hesitates is lost."

9   Superlatives and the words *right* and *wrong*, *true* and *untrue*, *never* and *always* must be used with caution in matters of opinion. When a student says flatly that X is true, he often is really saying that he or his family or the author of a book he has just been reading, persons of certain tastes and background and experience, *think* that X is true. Unless these people are identified and their reasons for thinking so explained, the assertion is worthless. Because many freshmen are taking survey courses in which they read a single work by an author or see an historical event through the eyes of a single historian whose bias they may not be able to measure, they must guard against this error.

SAMPLING

10   Assertions of a general nature are frequently open to question because they are based on insufficient evidence. Some persons are quite ready, after meeting one Armenian or reading one medieval romance, to generalize about Armenians and medieval romances. One

ought, of course, to examine objectively as many examples as possible before making a generalization, but the number is less important than the representativeness of the examples chosen. The Literary Digest Presidential Poll, sent to hundreds of thousands of people selected from telephone directories, was far less accurate than the Gallup Poll which questioned far fewer voters, but selected them carefully and proportionately from all different social groups.[1] The "typical" college student, as portrayed by moving pictures and cartoons, is very different from the "representative" college student as determined statistically. We cannot let uncontrolled experience do our sampling for us; instances and examples which impress themselves upon our minds do so usually because they are exceptional. In propaganda and arguments extreme cases are customarily treated as if they were characteristic.

If one is permitted arbitrarily to select some examples and ignore others, it is possible to find convincing evidence for almost any theory, no matter how fantastic. The fact that the mind tends naturally to remember those instances which confirm its opinions imposes a duty upon the writer, unless he wishes to encourage prejudice and superstition, to look carefully for exceptions to all generalizations which he is tempted to make. We forget the premonitions which are not followed by disaster and the times when our hunches failed to select the winner in a race. Patent medicine advertisements print the letters of those who survived their cure, and not of those who died during it. All Americans did not gamble on the stock exchange in the twenties, and all Vermonters are not thin-lipped and shrewd. Of course the search for negative examples can be carried too far. Outside of mathematics or the laboratory, few generalizations can be made airtight, and most are not intended to be. But quibbling is so easy that resort to it is very common, and the knowledge that people can and will quibble over generalizations is another reason for making assertions as limited and explicitly conditional as possible.

FALSE ANALOGY

Illustration, comparison, analogy are most valuable in making an essay clear and interesting. It must not be supposed, however, that they prove anything or have much argumentative weight. The rule

11

12

[1] On the basis of its misconducted poll, a magazine called *The Literary Digest* predicted a landslide for Landon over Roosevelt in 1936. — ED.

that what is true of one thing in one set of circumstances is not necessarily true of another thing in another set of circumstances seems almost too obvious to need stating. Yet constantly nations and businesses are discussed as if they were human beings with human habits and feelings; human bodies are discussed as if they were machines; the universe, as if it were a clock. It is assumed that what held true for seventeenth century New England or the thirteen Atlantic colonies also holds true for an industrial nation of 130,000,000 people. Carlyle dismissed the arguments for representative democracy by saying that if a captain had to take a vote among his crew every time he wanted to do something, he would never get around Cape Horn. This analogy calmly ignores the distinction between the lawmaking and the executive branches of constitutional democracies. Moreover, voters may be considered much more like the stockholders of a merchant line than its hired sailors. Such arguments introduce assumptions in a metaphorical guise in which they are not readily detected or easily criticized. In place of analysis they attempt to identify their position with some familiar symbol which will evoke a predictable, emotional response in the reader. The revival during the 1932 presidential campaign of Lincoln's remark, "Don't swap horses in the middle of the stream," was not merely a picturesque way of saying keep Hoover in the White House. It made a number of assumptions about the nature of depressions and the function of government. This propagandist technique can be seen most clearly in political cartoons.

DEGREE

13   Often differences in degree are more important than differences in kind. By legal and social standards there is more difference between an habitual drunkard and a man who drinks temperately, than between a temperate drinker and a total abstainer. In fact differences of degree produce what are regarded as differences of kind. At known temperatures ice turns to water and water boils. At an indeterminate point affection becomes love and a man who needs a shave becomes a man with a beard. The fact that no men or systems are perfect makes rejoinders and counter-accusations very easy if differences in degree are ignored. Newspapers in totalitarian states, answering American accusations of brutality and suppression, refer to lynchings and gangsterism here. Before a disinterested judge could evaluate these mutual accusations, he would have to settle the question of the degree to which

violent suppression and lynching are respectively prevalent in the countries under consideration. On the other hand, differences in degree may be merely apparent. Lincoln Steffens pointed out that newspapers can create a "crime wave" any time they wish, simply by emphasizing all the minor assaults and thefts commonly ignored or given an inch or two on a back page. The great reported increases in insanity may be due to the fact that in a more urban and institutionalized society cases of insanity more frequently come to the attention of authorities and hence are recorded in statistics.

CAUSATION

The most common way of deciding that one thing causes another   14
thing is the simple principle: *post hoc, ergo propter hoc,* "After this, therefore because of this." Rome fell after the introduction of Christianity; therefore Christianity was responsible for the fall of Rome. Such reasoning illustrates another kind of faulty generalization. But even if one could find ten cases in which a nation "fell" after the introduction of Christianity, it still would not be at all certain that Christianity caused the fall. Day, it has frequently been pointed out, follows night in every observable instance, and yet night cannot be called the cause of day. Usually a combination of causes produces a result. Sitting in a draught may cause a cold, but only given a certain physical condition in the person sitting there. In such instances one may distinguish between necessary and sufficient conditions. Air is a necessary condition for the maintenance of plant life, but air alone is not sufficient to produce plant life. And often different causes at different times may produce the same result. This relation is known as plurality of causes. If, after sitting in a stuffy theatre on Monday, and then again after eating in a stuffy restaurant on Thursday, a man suffered from headaches, he might say, generalizing, that bad air gave him headaches. But actually the headache on Monday may have been caused by eye-strain and on Thursday by indigestion. To isolate the causative factor it is necessary that all other conditions be precisely the same. Such isolation is possible, except in very simple instances, only in the laboratory or with scientific methods. If a picture falls from the wall every time a truck passes, we can quite certainly say that the truck's passing is the cause. But with anything as complex and conditional as a nation's economy or human character, the determination of cause is not easy or certain. A psychiatrist often sees a patient for an

hour daily for a year or more before he feels that he understands his psychosis.

15   Ordinarily when we speak of cause we mean the proximate or immediate cause. The plants were killed by frost; we had indigestion from eating lobster salad. But any single cause is one in an unbroken series. When a man is murdered, is his death caused by the loss of blood from the wound, or by the firing of the pistol, or by the malice aforethought of the murderer? Was the World War "caused" by the assassination at Sarajevo? Were the Navigation Acts or the ideas of John Locke more important in "causing" the American Revolution? A complete statement of cause would comprise the sum total of the conditions which preceded an event, conditions stretching back indefinitely into the past. Historical events are so interrelated that the isolation of a causative sequence is dependent chiefly on the particular preoccupations of the historian. An economic determinist can "explain" history entirely in terms of economic developments; an idealist, entirely in terms of the development of ideas.

SYLLOGISTIC REASONING

16   The formal syllogism of the type,

All men are mortal
John is a man
Therefore John is mortal,

is not so highly regarded today as in some earlier periods. It merely fixes an individual as a member of a class, and then assumes that the individual has the given characteristics of the class. Once we have decided who John is, and what "man" and "mortal" mean, and have canvassed all men, including John, to make sure that they are mortal, the conclusion naturally follows. It can be seen that the chief difficulties arise in trying to establish acceptable premises. Faults in the premises are known as "material" fallacies, and are usually more serious than the "formal" fallacies, which are logical defects in drawing a conclusion from the premises. But although directly syllogistic reasoning is not much practiced, buried syllogisms can be found in all argument, and it is often a useful clarification to outline your own or another writer's essay in syllogistic form. The two most frequent defects in the syllogism itself are the undistributed and the ambiguous

middle. The middle term is the one that appears in each of the premises and not in the conclusion. In the syllogism,

> All good citizens vote
> John votes
> Therefore John is a good citizen,

the middle term is not "good citizens," but "votes." Even though it
were true that all good citizens vote, nothing prevents bad citizens
from voting also, and John may be one of the bad citizens. To distribute
the middle term "votes" one might say (but only if that is what one
meant),

> All voters are good citizens
> John is a voter
> Therefore John is a good citizen.

The ambiguous middle term is even more common. It represents   17
a problem in definition, while the undistributed middle is a problem
in generalization. All acts which benefit others are virtuous, losing
money at poker benefits others, therefore losing at poker is a virtuous
act. Here the middle term "act which benefits others" is obviously
used very loosely and ambiguously.

NON-SEQUITUR

This phrase, meaning "it does not follow," is used to characterize   18
the kind of humor found in pictures in which the Marx Brothers perform. It is an amusing illogicality because it usually expresses, beneath
its apparent incongruity, an imaginative, associative, or personal truth.
"My ancestors came over on the Mayflower; therefore I am naturally
opposed to labor unions." It is not logically necessary that those whose
ancestors came over on the Mayflower should be opposed to unions;
but it may happen to be true as a personal fact in a given case. Contemporary psychologists have effectively shown us that there is often such
a wide difference between the true and the purported reasons for an
attitude that, in rationalizing our behavior, we are often quite unconscious of the motives that actually influence us. A fanatical antivivi-
sectionist, for instance, may have temperamental impulses toward
cruelty which he is suppressing and compensating for by a reasoned
opposition to any kind of permitted suffering. We may expect, then, to

come upon many conclusions which are psychologically interesting in themselves, but have nothing to do with the given premises.

IGNORATIO ELENCHI

19   This means, in idiomatic English, "arguing off the point," or ignoring the question at issue. A man trying to show that monarchy is the best form of government for the British Empire may devote most of his attention to the character of George V and the affection his people felt for him. In ordinary conversational argument it is almost impossible for disputants to keep to the point. Constantly turning up are tempting side-issues through which one can discomfit an opponent or force him to irrelevant admissions that seem to weaken his case.

BEGGING THE QUESTION; ARGUING IN A CIRCLE

20   The first of these terms means to assume in the premises what you are pretending to prove in the course of your argument. The function of logic is to demonstrate that because one thing or group of things is true, another must be true as a consequence. But in begging the question you simply say in varying language that what is assumed to be true is assumed to be true. An argument which asserts that we shall enjoy immortality because we have souls which are immaterial and indestructible establishes nothing, because the idea of immortality is already contained in the assumption about the soul. It is the premise which needs to be demonstrated, not the conclusion. Arguing in a circle is another form of this fallacy. It proves the premise by the conclusion and the conclusion by the premise. The conscience forbids an act because it is wrong; the act is wrong because the conscience forbids it.

ARGUMENTS AD HOMINEM AND AD POPULUM

21   It is very difficult for men to be persuaded by reason when their interest or prestige is at stake. If one wishes to preach the significance

of physiognomy, it is well to choose a hearer with a high forehead and a determined jaw. The arguments in favor of repealing the protective tariff on corn or wheat in England were more readily entertained by manufacturers than by landowners. The cotton manufacturers in New England who were doing a profitable trade with the South were the last to be moved by descriptions of the evils of slavery. Because interest and desire are so deeply seated in human nature, arguments are frequently mingled with attempts to appeal to emotion, arouse fear, play upon pride, attack the characters of proponents of an opposite view, show that their practice is inconsistent with their principles; all matters which have, strictly speaking, nothing to do with the truth or falsity, the general desirability or undesirability, of some particular measure. If men are desperate enough they will listen to arguments proper only to an insane asylum but which seem to promise them relief.

After reading these suggestions, which are largely negative, the 22 student may feel that any original assertion he can make will probably contain one or several logical faults. This assumption is not true. Even if it were, we know from reading newspapers and magazines that worldly fame is not dimmed by the constant and, one suspects, conscious practice of illogicality. But generalizations are not made only by charlatans and sophists. Intelligent and scrupulous writers also have a great many fresh and provocative observations and conclusions to express and are expressing them influentially. What is intelligence but the ability to see the connection between things, to discern causes, to relate the particular to the general, to define and discriminate and compare? Any man who thinks and feels and observes closely will not want for something to express.

And in his expression a proponent will find that a due regard for 23 logic does not limit but rather increases the force of his argument. When statements are not trite, they are usually controversial. Men arrive at truth dialectically; error is weeded out in the course of discussion, argument, attack, and counterattack. Not only can a writer who understands logic show the weaknesses of arguments he disagrees with, but also, by anticipating the kind of attack likely to be made on his own ideas, he can so arrange them, properly modified with qualifications and exceptions, that the anticipated attack is made much less effective. Thus, fortunately, we do not have to depend on the spirit of fairness and love of truth to lead men to logic; it has the strong support of argumentative necessity and of the universal desire to make ideas prevail.

——— CONSIDERATIONS ———————————————————

1. Davis's first sentence goes far toward explaining why freshman composition classes commonly include a unit on logic, which some would insist is more properly a part of Philosophy I than of English I. To learn Davis's logic in practice, apply Davis's notions about undefined terms and abstractions to the argumentative essays in this book: James Baxter, Caroline Bird, Daniel Boorstin, Clarence Darrow, Richard Hofstadter, Walter Lippmann, H. L. Mencken, George Orwell, Plato, Thomas Szasz, and Mark Twain. Do any of these writers use undefined terms or abstractions illogically?

2. Under "Generalization," in Paragraph 8, Davis defines a function of literary criticism and suggests what questions to ask to make such criticism useful to yourself and others. Try out his advice on an essay, short story, or poem in this book that has troubled or pleased you.

3. How clearly and consistently can you discriminate between matters of fact and matters of opinion? Discuss some examples found in your reading.

4. Have you ever been tempted by the *post hoc, ergo propter hoc* fallacy? (See Paragraph 14.) Can you find an example of it in the newspaper, on television, in the conversation of your friends, in any of the readings in this book, in your papers, or in your instructor's remarks?

5. Study Davis's explanation of syllogistic reasoning, Paragraph 16. Try to reduce the major argument of any of the authors noted in question 1 to a syllogism or a series of syllogisms.

6. Davis is not the only author in this book who appreciates the use of logic. After reading Davis, turn to Walter Lippmann's "Why Should the Majority Rule?" and decide whether he presents Bryan's "inescapable" conclusions fairly, despite Lippmann's obvious opposition to Bryan's position.

Emily Dickinson (1830–1886) was little known as a poet in her lifetime, and is now acknowledged among the greatest of American poets. She spent her entire life in Amherst, Massachusetts, where her family was connected with the college. Never married, she lived much of her life as a virtual recluse, but remained close to her family, and made contact with the world outside by a huge correspondence. She wrote thousands of poems. At first she tried to publish them, with small success. Later she stopped sending her poems to editors, but Emily Dickinson continued to sit alone in her room in a white house in Amherst and write great poetry. Perhaps the eccentric punctuation, and the air of haste or breathlessness, derives from her suspicion that her poems would never be read by others.

22

EMILY DICKINSON
There's a certain Slant of light

There's a certain Slant of light,
Winter Afternoons–
That oppresses, like the Heft
Of Cathedral Tunes–

Heavenly Hurt, it gives us–   5
We can find no scar,
But internal difference,
Where the Meanings, are–

Reprinted by permission of the publishers and the Trustees of Amherst College from *The Poems of Emily Dickinson,* edited by Thomas H. Johnson, Cambridge Mass.: The Belknap Press of Harvard University Press, Copyright © 1951, 1955 by the President and Fellows of Harvard College.

None may teach it—Any—
10 'Tis the Seal Despair—
An imperial affliction
Sent us of the Air—

When it comes, the Landscape listens—
Shadows—hold their breath—
15 When it goes, 'tis like the Distance
On the look of Death—

23

JOAN DIDION
On Keeping a Notebook

" 'That woman Estelle,' " the note reads, " 'is partly the reason why George Sharp and I are separated today.' *Dirty crepe-de-Chine wrapper, hotel bar, Wilmington RR, 9:45 a.m. August Monday morning.*"

Since the note is in my notebook, it presumably has some meaning to me. I study it for a long while. At first I have only the most general notion of what I was doing on an August Monday morning in the bar of the hotel across from the Pennsylvania Railroad station in Wilmington, Delaware (waiting for a train? missing one? 1960? 1961? why Wilmington?), but I do remember being there. The woman in the dirty crepe-de-Chine wrapper had come down from her room for a beer, and the bartender had heard before the reason why George Sharp and she were separated today. "Sure," he said, and went on mopping the floor. "You told me." At the other end of the bar is a girl. She is talking, pointedly, not to the man beside her but to a cat lying in the triangle of sunlight cast through the open door. She is wearing a plaid silk dress from Peck & Peck, and the hem is coming down.

3   Here is what it is: the girl has been on the Eastern Shore, and now she is going back to the city, leaving the man beside her, and all she can see ahead are the viscous summer sidewalks and the 3 A.M. long-distance calls that will make her lie awake and then sleep drugged through all the steaming mornings left in August (1960? 1961?). Because she must go directly from the train to lunch in New York, she wishes that she had a safety pin for the hem of the plaid silk dress, and she also wishes that she could forget about the hem and the lunch and stay in the cool bar that smells of disinfectant and malt and make friends with the woman in the crepe-de-Chine wrapper. She is afflicted by a little self-pity, and she wants to compare Estelles. That is what that was all about.

4   Why did I write it down? In order to remember, of course, but exactly what was it I wanted to remember? How much of it actually happened? Did any of it? Why do I keep a notebook at all? It is easy to deceive oneself on all those scores. The impulse to write things down is a peculiarly compulsive one, inexplicable to those who do not share it, useful only accidentally, only secondarily, in the way that any compulsion tries to justify itself. I suppose that it begins or does not begin in the cradle. Although I have felt compelled to write things down since I was five years old, I doubt that my daughter ever will, for she is singularly blessed and accepting child, delighted with life exactly as life presents itself to her, unafraid to go to sleep and unafraid to wake up. Keepers of private notebooks are a different breed altogether, lonely and resistant rearrangers of things, anxious malcontents, children afflicted apparently at birth with some presentiment of loss.

5   My first notebook was a Big Five tablet, given to me by my mother with the sensible suggestion that I stop whining and learn to amuse myself by writing down my thoughts. She returned the tablet to me a few years ago; the first entry is an account of a woman who believed herself to be freezing to death in the Arctic night, only to find, when day broke, that she had stumbled onto the Sahara Desert, where she would die of the heat before lunch. I have no idea what turn of a five-year-old's mind could have prompted so insistently "ironic" and exotic a story, but it does reveal a certain predilection for the extreme which has dogged me into adult life; perhaps if I were analytically inclined I would find it a truer story than any I might have told about

Donald Johnson's birthday party or the day my cousin Brenda put Kitty Litter in the aquarium.

So the point of my keeping a notebook has never been, nor is it 6 now, to have an accurate factual record of what I have been doing or thinking. That would be a different impulse entirely, an instinct for reality which I sometimes envy but do not possess. At no point have I ever been able successfully to keep a diary; my approach to daily life ranges from the grossly negligent to the merely absent, and on those few occasions when I have tried dutifully to record a day's events, boredom has so overcome me that the results are mysterious at best. What is this business about "shopping, typing piece, dinner with E, depressed"? Shopping for what? Typing what piece? Who is E? Was this "E" depressed, or was I depressed? Who cares?

In fact I have abandoned altogether that kind of pointless entry; 7 instead I tell what some would call lies. "That's simply not true," the members of my family frequently tell me when they come up against my memory of a shared event. "The party was *not* for you, the spider was *not* a black widow, *it wasn't that way at all.*" Very likely they are right, for not only have I always had trouble distinguishing between what happened and what merely might have happened, but I remain unconvinced that the distinction, for my purposes, matters. The cracked crab that I recall having for lunch the day my father came home from Detroit in 1945 must certainly be embroidery, worked into the day's pattern to lend verisimilitude; I was ten years old and would not now remember the cracked crab. The day's events did not turn on cracked crab. And yet it is precisely that fictitious crab that makes me see the afternoon all over again, a home movie run all too often, the father bearing gifts, the child weeping, an exercise in family love and guilt. Or that is what it was to me. Similarly, perhaps it never did snow that August in Vermont; perhaps there never were flurries in the night wind, and maybe no one else felt the ground hardening and summer already dead even as we pretended to bask in it, but that was how it felt to me, and it might as well have snowed, could have snowed, did snow.

How it felt to me: that is getting closer to the truth about a 8 notebook. I sometimes delude myself about why I keep a notebook, imagine that some thrifty virtue derives from preserving everything observed. See enough and write it down, I tell myself, and then some morning when the world seems drained of wonder, some day when I am only going through the motions of doing what I am supposed to do, which is write — on that bankrupt morning I will simply open my notebook and there it will all be, a forgotten account with accumulated interest, paid passage back to the world out there: dialogue overheard in hotels and elevators and at the hat-check counter in Pavillon (one middle-aged man shows his hat check to another and says, "That's my old football number"); impressions of Bettina Aptheker and Benjamin Sonnenberg and Teddy ("Mr. Acapulco") Stauffer; careful *aperçus* about tennis bums and failed fashion models and Greek shipping heiresses, one of whom taught me a significant lesson (a lesson I could have learned from F. Scott Fitzgerald, but perhaps we must meet the very rich for ourselves) by asking, when I arrived to interview her in her orchid-filled sitting room on the second day of a paralyzing New York blizzard, whether it was snowing outside.

9   I imagine, in other words, that the notebook is about other people. But of course it is not. I have no real business with what one stranger said to another at the hat-check counter in Pavillon; in fact I suspect that the line "That's my old football number" touched not my own imagination at all, but merely some memory of something once read, probably "The Eighty-Yard Run." Nor is my concern with a woman in a dirty crepe-de-Chine wrapper in a Wilmington bar. My stake is always, of course, in the unmentioned girl in the plaid silk dress. *Remember what it was to be me: that is always the point.*

10   It is a difficult point to admit. We are brought up in the ethic that others, any others, all others, are by definition more interesting than ourselves; taught to be diffident, just this side of self-effacing. ("You're the least important person in the room and don't forget it," Jessica Mitford's governess would hiss in her on the advent of any social occasion; I copied that into my notebook because it is only recently that I have been able to enter a room without hearing some such phrase in my inner ear.) Only the very young and the very old may recount their dreams at breakfast, dwell upon self, interrupt with memories of beach picnics and favorite Liberty lawn dresses and the rainbow trout in a creek near Colorado Springs. The rest of us are expected, rightly, to affect absorption in other people's favorite dresses, other people's trout.

11   And so we do. But our notebooks give us away, for however dutifully we record what we see around us, the common denominator of all we see is always, transparently, shamelessly, the implacable "I." We are not talking here about the kind of notebook that is patently for public consumption, a structural conceit for binding together a series

of graceful *pensées:* we are talking about something private, about bits of the mind's string too short to use, an indiscriminate and erratic assemblage with meaning only for its maker.

And sometimes even the maker has difficulty with the meaning. There does not seem to be, for example, any point in my knowing for the rest of my life that, during 1964, 720 tons of soot fell on every square mile of New York City, yet there it is in my notebook, labeled "FACT." Nor do I really need to remember that Ambrose Bierce liked to spell Leland Stanford's[1] name "£eland $tanford" or that "smart women almost always wear black in Cuba," a fashion hint without much potential for practical application. And does not the relevance of these notes seem marginal at best?:

> In the basement museum of the Inyo County Courthouse in Independence, California, sign pinned to a mandarin coat: "This MANDARIN COAT was often worn by Mrs. Minnie S. Brooks when giving lectures on her TEAPOT COLLECTION."

> Redhead getting out of car in front of Beverly Wilshire Hotel, chinchilla stole, Vuitton bags with tags reading:
> MRS LOU FOX
> HOTEL SAHARA
> VEGAS

Well perhaps not entirely marginal. As a matter of fact, Mrs. Minnie S. Brooks and her MANDARIN COAT pull me back into my own childhood, for although I never knew Mrs. Brooks and did not visit Inyo County until I was thirty, I grew up in just such a world, in houses cluttered with Indian relics and bits of gold ore and ambergris and the souvenirs my Aunt Mercy Farnsworth brought back from the Orient. It is a long way from that world to Mrs. Lou Fox's world, where we all live now, and is it not just as well to remember that? Might not Mrs. Minnie S. Brooks help me to remember what I am? Might not Mrs. Lou Fox help me to remember what I am not?

But sometimes the point is harder to discern. What exactly did I have in mind when I noted down that it cost the father of someone I know $650 a month to light the place on the Hudson in which he lived before the Crash? What use was I planning to make of this line by Jimmy Hoffa: "I may have my faults, but being wrong ain't one of them"? And although I think it interesting to know where the girls

[1] Railroad magnate (1834–1893) who founded the university. — ED.

who travel with the Syndicate have their hair done when they find themselves on the West Coast, will I ever make suitable use of it? Might I not be better off just passing it on to John O'Hara? What is a recipe for sauerkraut doing in my notebook? What kind of magpie keeps this notebook? *"He was born the night the Titanic went down."* That seems a nice enough line, and I even recall who said it, but is it not really a better line in life than it could ever be in fiction?

15   But of course that is exactly it: not that I should ever use the line, but that I should remember the woman who said it and the afternoon I heard it. We were on her terrace by the sea, and we were finishing the wine left from lunch, trying to get what sun there was, a California winter sun. The woman whose husband was born the night the *Titanic* went down wanted to rent her house, wanted to go back to her children in Paris. I remember wishing that I could afford the house, which cost $1,000 a month. "Someday you will," she said lazily. "Someday it all comes." There in the sun on her terrace it seemed easy to believe in someday, but later I had a low-grade afternoon hangover and ran over a black snake on the way to the supermarket and was flooded with inexplicable fear when I heard the checkout clerk explaining to the man ahead of me why she was finally divorcing her husband. "He left me no choice," she said over and over as she punched the register. "He has a little seven-month-old baby by her, he left me no choice." I would like to believe that my dread then was for the human condition, but of course it was for me, because I wanted a baby and did not then have one and because I wanted to own the house that cost $1,000 a month to rent and because I had a hangover.

16   It all comes back. Perhaps it is difficult to see the value in having one's self back in that kind of mood, but I do see it; I think we are well advised to keep on nodding terms with the people we used to be, whether we find them attractive company or not. Otherwise they turn up unannounced and surprise us, come hammering on the mind's door at 4 a.m. of a bad night and demand to know who deserted them, who betrayed them, who is going to make amends. We forget all too soon the things we thought we could never forget. We forget the loves and the betrayals alike, forget what we whispered and what we screamed, forget who we were. I have already lost touch with a couple of people I used to be; one of them, a seventeen-year-old, presents little threat, although it would be of some interest to me to know again what it feels like to sit on a river levee drinking vodka-and-orange-juice and listening to Les Paul and Mary Ford and their echoes sing "How High

the Moon" on the car radio. (You see I still have the scenes, but I no longer perceive myself among those present, no longer could even improvise the dialogue.) The other one, a twenty-three-year-old, bothers me more. She was always a good deal of trouble, and I suspect she will reappear when I least want to see her, skirts too long, shy to the point of aggravation, always the injured party, full of recriminations and little hurts and stories I do not want to hear again, at once saddening me and angering me with her vulnerability and ignorance, an apparition all the more insistent for being so long banished.

It is a good idea, then, to keep in touch, and I suppose that keeping 17 in touch is what notebooks are all about. And we are all on our own when it comes to keeping those lines open to ourselves: your notebook will never help me, nor mine you. *"So what's new in the whiskey business?"* What could that possibly mean to you? To me it means a blonde in a Pucci bathing suit sitting with a couple of fat men by the pool at the Beverly Hills Hotel. Another man approaches, and they all regard one another in silence for a while. "So what's new in the whiskey business?" one of the fat men finally says by way of welcome, and the blonde stands up, arches one foot and dips it in the pool, looking all the while at the cabaña where Baby Pignatari is talking on the telephone. That is all there is to that, except that several years later I saw the blonde coming out of Saks Fifth Avenue in New York with her California complexion and a voluminous mink coat. In the harsh wind that day she looked old and irrevocably tired to me, and even the skins in the mink coat were not worked the way they were doing them that year, not the way she would have wanted them done, and there is the point of the story. For a while after that I did not like to look in the mirror, and my eyes would skim the newspapers and pick out only the deaths, the cancer victims, the premature coronaries, the suicides, and I stopped riding the Lexington Avenue IRT because I noticed for the first time that all the strangers I had seen for years — the man with the seeing-eye dog, the spinster who read the classified pages every day, the fat girl who always got off with me at Grand Central — looked older than they once had.

It all comes back. Even that recipe for sauerkraut: even that 18 brings it back. I was on Fire Island when I first made that sauerkraut, and it was raining, and we drank a lot of bourbon and ate the sauerkraut and went to bed at ten, and I listened to the rain and the Atlantic and felt safe. I made the sauerkraut again last night and it did not make me feel any safer, but that is, as they say, another story.

—— CONSIDERATIONS ——————————————————

1. What is the difference between the selection by Didion and those by F. Scott Fitzgerald (pages 169–171), Anaïs Nin (pages 293–295) and Thomas Wolfe (pages 470–476)?

2. How far must you read in Didion's piece before you know her real reason for keeping a journal? Why does she delay that announcement so long? Might such a delay work well in one of your essays?

3. "You're the least important person in the room and don't you forget it" is a line from Didion's journal. Does she believe that statement? If not, why does she include it in her essay?

4. The randomness of a notebook is one of Didion's topics. How does she use this randomness or lack of order or purpose to bring order and purpose to her essay? Take paragraphs 14 and 15, and study the method she derives from her seeming madness.

5. In Paragraph 16, Didion says she has already "lost touch with a couple of people I used to be." Is such an awareness related to the last line of James Agee's "Knoxville: Summer 1915" (page 11)? Have you ever had similar feelings about some of the people you used to be? What significant details in your memory come to mind?

6. Like Clarence Darrow (pages 107–113), Didion asks many questions in her essay. How does her purpose in asking them differ from Darrow's?

24

ANNIE DILLARD

Strangers to Darkness

Where Tinker Creek flows under the sycamore log bridge to the
tear-shaped island, it is slow and shallow, fringed thinly in cattail
marsh. At this spot an astonishing bloom of life supports vast breeding
populations of insects, fish, reptiles, birds, and mammals. On windless
summer evenings I stalk along the creek bank or straddle the sycamore
log in absolute stillness, watching for muskrats. The night I stayed too
late I was hunched on the log staring spellbound at spreading, reflected
stains of lilac on the water. A cloud in the sky suddenly lighted as if
turned on by a switch; its reflection just as suddenly materialized on
the water upstream, flat and floating, so that I couldn't see the creek
bottom, or life in the water under the cloud. Downstream, away from
the cloud on the water, water turtles smooth as beans were gliding
down with the current in a series of easy, weightless push-offs, as men
bound on the moon. I didn't know whether to trace the progress of one

turtle I was sure of, risking sticking my face in one of the bridge's spider webs made invisible by the gathering dark, or take a chance on seeing the carp, or scan the mudbank in hope of seeing a muskrat, or follow the last of the swallows who caught at my heart and trailed it after them like streamers as they appeared from directly below, under the log, flying upstream with their tails forked, so fast.

2   But shadows spread and deepened and stayed. After thousands of years we're still strangers to darkness, fearful aliens in an enemy camp with our arms crossed over our chests. I stirred. A land turtle on the bank, startled, hissed the air from its lungs and withdrew to its shell. An uneasy pink here, an unfathomable blue there, gave great suggestion of lurking beings. Things were going on. I couldn't see whether that rustle I heard was a distant rattlesnake, slit-eyed, or a nearby sparrow kicking in the dry flood debris slung at the foot of a willow. Tremendous action roiled the water everywhere I looked, big action, inexplicable. A tremor welled up beside a gaping muskrat burrow in the bank and I caught my breath, but no muskrat appeared. The ripples continued to fan upstream with a steady, powerful thrust. Night was knitting an eyeless mask over my face, and I still sat transfixed. A distant airplane, a delta wing out of nightmare, made a gliding shadow on the creek's bottom that looked like a stingray cruising upstream. At once a black fin slit the pink cloud on the water, shearing it in two. The two halves merged together and seemed to dissolve before my eyes. Darkness pooled in the cleft of the creek and rose, as water collects in a well. Untamed, dreaming lights flickered over the sky. I saw hints of hulking underwater shadows, two pale splashes out of the water, and round ripples rolling close together from a blackened center.

3   At last I stared upstream where only the deepest violet remained of the cloud, a cloud so high its underbelly still glowed, its feeble color reflected from a hidden sky lighted in turn by a sun halfway to China. And out of that violet, a sudden enormous black body arced over the water. Head and tail, if there was a head and tail, were both submerged in cloud. I saw only one ebony fling, a headlong dive to darkness; then the waters closed, and the lights went out.

4   I walked home in a shivering daze, up hill and down. Later I lay openmouthed in bed, my arms flung wide at my sides to steady the whirling darkness. At this latitude I'm spinning 836 miles an hour round the earth's axis; I feel my sweeping fall as a breakneck arc like the dive of dolphins, and the hollow rushing of wind raises the hairs on my neck and the side of my face. In orbit around the sun I'm moving 64,800 miles an hour. The solar system as a whole, like a merry-go-

round unhinged, spins, bobs, and blinks at the speed of 43,200 miles an hour along a course set east of Hercules. Someone has piped, and we are dancing a tarantella until the sweat pours. I open my eyes and I see dark, muscled forms curl out of water, with flapping gills and flattened eyes. I close my eyes and I see stars, deep stars giving way to deeper stars, deeper stars bowing to deepest stars at the crown of an infinite cone.

____ CONSIDERATIONS ____

1. Like exposition and argument, description and narration are encountered together more often than they are encountered separately. Still, there are real differences between describing something and following a sequence of actions. To see this difference, compare and contrast Dillard's descriptive writing with a clearly narrative selection in this book: Truman Capote, Lillian Hellman, Ernest Hemingway, John McPhee, Norman Mailer, Lillian Ross, Richard Selzer, or Eudora Welty, "A Worn Path."

2. Telling what she saw that night along Tinker Creek, Dillard uses many literal and figurative images; list them and discuss their differences. In your own essays, do you use phrases that appeal to the senses?

3. Toward the end of this short selection, Dillard suddenly injects facts — the speed of the earth's rotation, for instance. How does this information contribute to her attempt to evoke wonder in us?

4. "Night was knitting an eyeless mask over my face. . . ." Many might describe such language as fancy, flowery, or indirect, and protest that the writer should "just come out and say what she means." Discuss these complaints, thinking of what Dillard intends to accomplish.

5. Dillard describes the effects of one evening on one small creek in one rural neighborhood. Why, then, does she refer to China and the solar system?

*Loren Eiseley (1907–1977) was an anthropologist who taught at
the University of Pennsylvania, and a writer of unusual ability,
author of two books of poems and numerous collections of prose
including* The Night Country *(1971) and* All the Strange Hours
*(1975). Eiseley was a scientist-poet, a human brooder over the
natural world, determined never to distort the real world by his
brooding dream, an objective anthropologist with a talent for subjective response.*

25

LOREN EISELEY

The Long Loneliness:
Man and the Porpoise

1   There is nothing more alone in the universe than man. He is
alone because he has the intellectual capacity to know that he is separated by a vast gulf of social memory and experiment from the lives
of his animal associates. He has entered into the strange world of
history, of social and intellectual change, while his brothers of the
field and forest remain subject to the invisible laws of biological evolution. Animals are molded by natural forces they do not comprehend.
To their minds there is no past and no future. There is only the ever-
lasting present of a single generation — its trails in the forest, its hidden pathways of the air and in the sea.

2   Man, by contrast, is alone with the knowledge of his history until
the day of his death. When we were children we wanted to talk to
animals and struggled to understand why this was impossible. Slowly

we gave up the attempt as we grew into the solitary world of human adulthood; the rabbit was left on the lawn, the dog was relegated to his kennel. Only in acts of inarticulate compassion, in rare and hidden moments of communion with nature, does man briefly escape his solitary destiny. Frequently in science fiction he dreams of worlds with creatures whose communicative power is the equivalent of his own.

It is with a feeling of startlement, therefore, and eager interest 3 touching the lost child in every one of us, that the public has received the recent accounts of naval research upon the intelligence of one of our brother mammals — the sea-dwelling, bottlenosed porpoise or dolphin.

These small whales who left the land millions of years ago to 4 return to the great mother element of life, the sea, are now being regarded by researchers as perhaps the most intelligent form of life on our planet next to man. Dr. John Lilly, of the Communications Research Institute in the Virgin Islands, reports that the brain of the porpoise is 40 percent larger than man's and is just as complex in its functional units. Amazed by the rapidity with which captive porpoises solved problems that even monkeys found difficult, Dr. Lilly is quoted as expressing the view that "man's position at the top of the hierarchy [of intelligence] begins to be questioned."

Dr. Lilly found that his captives communicated in a series of 5 underwater whistles and that, in addition, they showed an amazing "verbalizing" ability in copying certain sounds heard in the laboratory. The experimental animal obviously hoped to elicit by this means a reproduction of the pleasurable sensations he had been made to experience under laboratory conditions. It is reported that in spite of living in a medium different from the one that man inhabits, and therefore having quite a different throat structure, one of the porpoises even uttered in a Donald-Duckish voice a short number series it had heard spoken by one of the laboratory investigators.

The import of these discoveries is tremendous and may not be 6 adequately known for a long time. An animal from a little explored medium, which places great barriers in the way of the psychologist, has been found to have not only a strong social organization, but to show a degree of initiative in experimental communicative activity unmatched by man's closest relatives, the great apes. The porpoises reveal, moreover, a touching altruism and friendliness in their attempts to aid injured companions. Can it be, one inevitably wonders, that man is so locked in his own type of intelligence — an intelligence that is linked to a prehensile, grasping hand giving him power over his environment — that he is unable to comprehend the intellectual life of a highly endowed creature from another domain such as the sea?

7   Perhaps the water barrier has shut us away from a potentially communicative and jolly companion. Perhaps we have some things still to learn from the natural world around us before we turn to the far shores of space and whatever creatures may await us there. After all, the porpoise is a mammal. He shares with us an ancient way of birth and affectionate motherhood. His blood is warm, he breathes air as we do. We both bear in our bodies the remnants of a common skeleton torn asunder for divergent purposes far back in the dim dawn of mammalian life. The porpoise has been superficially streamlined like a fish.

8   His are not, however, the cold-blooded ways of the true fishes. Far higher on the tree of life than fishes, the dolphin's paddles are made-over paws, rather than fins. He is an ever-constant reminder of the versatility of life and its willingness to pass through strange dimensions of experience. There are environmental worlds on earth every bit as weird as what we may imagine to revolve by far-off suns. It is our superficial familiarity with this planet that inhibits our appreciation of the unknown until a porpoise, rearing from a tank to say Three-Two-Three, re-creates for us the utter wonder of childhood.

9   Unless we are specialists in the study of communication and its relation to intelligence, however, we are apt to oversimplify or define poorly what intelligence is, what communication and language are, and thus confuse and mystify both ourselves and others. The mysteries surrounding the behavior of the bottlenosed porpoise, and even of man himself, are not things to be probed simply by the dissector's scalpel. They lie deeper. They involve the whole nature of the mind and its role in the universe.

10   We are forced to ask ourselves whether native intelligence in another form than man's might be as high, or even higher than his own, yet be marked by no such material monuments as man has placed upon the earth. At first glance we are alien to this idea, because man is particularly a creature who has turned the tables on his environment so that he is now engrossed in shaping it, rather than being shaped by it. Man expresses himself upon his environment through the use of tools. We therefore tend to equate the use of tools in a one-to-one relationship with intelligence.

11   The question we must now ask ourselves, however, is whether this involves an unconsciously man-centered way of looking at intel-

ligence. Let us try for a moment to enter the dolphin's kingdom and the dolphin's body, retaining, at the same time, our human intelligence. In this imaginative act, it may be possible to divest ourselves of certain human preconceptions about our kind of intelligence and at the same time to see more clearly why mind, even advanced mind, may have manifestations other than the tools and railroad tracks and laboratories that we regard as evidence of intellect. If we are particularly adept in escaping from our own bodies, we may even learn to discount a little the kind of world of rockets and death that our type of busy human curiosity, linked to a hand noted for its ability to open assorted Pandora's boxes, has succeeded in foisting upon the world as a symbol of universal intelligence.

We have now sacrificed, in our imagination, our hands for flippers   12
and our familiar land environment for the ocean. We will go down into the deep waters as naked of possessions as when we entered life itself. We will take with us one thing alone that exists among porpoises as among men: an ingrained biological gregariousness — a sociality that in our new world will permit us to run in schools, just as early man ran in the packs that were his ancient anthropoid heritage. We will assume in the light of Dr. Lilly's researches that our native intelligence, as distinguished from our culturally transmitted habits, is very high. The waters have closed finally over us, our paws have been sacrificed for the necessary flippers with which to navigate.

The result is immediately evident and quite clear: No matter   13
how well we communicate with our fellows through the water medium we will never build drowned empires in the coral; we will never inscribe on palace walls the victorious boasts of porpoise kings. We will know only water and the wastes of water beyond the power of man to describe. We will be secret visitors in hidden canyons beneath the mouths of torrential rivers. We will survey in innocent astonishment the flotsam that pours from the veins of continents — dead men, great serpents, giant trees — or perhaps the little toy boat of a child loosed far upstream will come floating past. Bottles with winking green lights will plunge by us into the all-embracing ooze. Meaningless appearances and disappearances will comprise our philosophies. We will hear the earth's heart ticking in its thin granitic shell. Volcanic fires will growl ominously in steam-filled crevices. Vapor, bird cries and sea wrack will compose our memories. We will see death in many forms and, on occasion, the slow majestic fall of battleships through the green light that comes from beyond our domain.

Over all that region of wondrous beauty we will exercise no more   14 control than the simplest mollusc. Even the octopus with flexible arms will build little shelters that we cannot imitate. Without hands we will have only the freedom to follow the untrammeled sea winds across the planet.

15 Perhaps if those whistling sounds that porpoises make are truly symbolic and capable of manipulation in our brains, we will wonder about the world in which we find ourselves — but it will be a world not susceptible to experiment. At best we may nuzzle in curiosity a passing shipbottom and be harpooned for our pains. Our thoughts, in other words, will be as limited as those of the first men who roved in little bands in the times before fire and the writing that was to open to man the great doorway of his past.

16 Man without writing cannot long retain his history in his head. His intelligence permits him to grasp some kind of succession of generations; but without writing, the tale of the past rapidly degenerates into fumbling myth and fable. Man's greatest epic, his four long battles with the advancing ice of the great continental glaciers, has vanished from human memory without a trace. Our illiterate fathers disappeared and with them, in a few scant generations, died one of the great stories of all time. This episode has nothing to do with the biological quality of a brain as between then and now. It has to do instead with a device, an invention made possible by the hand. That invention came too late in time to record eyewitness accounts of the years of the Giant Frost.

17 Primitives of our own species, even today, are historically shallow in their knowledge of the past. Only the poet who writes speaks his message across the millennia to other hearts. Only in writing can the cry from the great cross on Golgotha still be heard in the minds of men. The thinker of perceptive insight, even if we allow him for the moment to be a porpoise rather than a man, has only his individual glimpse of the universe until such time as he can impose that insight upon unnumbered generations. In centuries of pondering, man has come upon but one answer to this problem: speech translated into writing that passes beyond human mortality.

18 Writing, and later printing, is the product of our adaptable many-purposed hands. It is thus, through writing, with no increase in genetic, inborn capacity since the last ice advance, that modern man carries in his mind the intellectual triumphs of all his predecessors who were able to inscribe their thoughts for posterity.

19 All animals which man has reason to believe are more than usually intelligent — our relatives the great apes, the elephant, the rac-

coon, the wolverine, among others — are problem solvers, and in at least a small way manipulators of their environment. Save for the instinctive calls of their species, however, they cannot communicate except by direct imitation. They cannot invent words for new situations nor get their fellows to use such words. No matter how high the individual intelligence, its private world remains a private possession locked forever within a single, perishable brain. It is this fact that finally balks our hunger to communicate even with the sensitive dog who shares our fireside.

Dr. Lilly insists, however, that the porpoises communicate in high-pitched, underwater whistles that seem to transmit their wishes and problems. The question then becomes one of ascertaining whether these sounds represent true language — in the sense of symbolic meanings, additive, learned elements — or whether they are simply the instinctive signals of a pack animal. To this there is as yet no clear answer, but the eagerness with which laboratory sounds and voices were copied by captive porpoises suggests a vocalizing ability extending perhaps to or beyond the threshold of speech. 20

Most of the intelligent land animals have prehensile, grasping organs for exploring their environment — hands in man and his anthropoid relatives, the sensitive inquiring trunk in the elephant. One of the surprising things about the porpoise is that his superior brain is unaccompanied by any type of manipulative organ. He has, however, a remarkable range-finding ability involving some sort of echo-sounding. Perhaps this acute sense — far more accurate than any man has been able to devise artificially — brings him greater knowledge of his watery surroundings than might at first seem possible. Human beings think of intelligence as geared to things. The hand and the tool are to us the unconscious symbols of our intellectual achievement. It is difficult for us to visualize another kind of lonely, almost disembodied intelligence floating in the wavering green fairyland of the sea — an intelligence possibly near or comparable to our own but without hands to build, to transmit knowledge by writing, or to alter by one hairsbreadth the planet's surface. Yet at the same time there are indications that this is a warm, friendly and eager intelligence quite capable of coming to the assistance of injured companions and striving to rescue them from drowning. Porpoises left the land when mammalian brains were still small and primitive. Without the stimulus provided by agile exploring fingers, these great sea mammals have yet taken a divergent road toward intelligence of a high order. Hidden in their sleek bodies is an impressively elaborated instrument, the reason for whose appear- 21 ance is a complete enigma. It is as though both man and porpoise were each part of some great eye which yearned to look both outward on eternity and inward to the sea's heart — that fertile entity so like the mind in its swarming and grotesque life.

22   Perhaps man has something to learn after all from fellow creatures without the ability to drive harpoons through living flesh, or poison with strontium the planetary winds. One is reminded of those watery blue vaults in which, as in some idyllic eternity, Herman Melville once saw the sperm whales nurse their young. And as Melville wrote of the sperm whale, so we might now paraphrase his words in speaking of the porpoise. "Genius in the porpoise? Has the porpoise ever written a book, spoken a speech? No, his great genius is declared in his doing nothing particular to prove it. It is declared in his pyramidical silence." If man had sacrificed his hands for flukes, the moral might run, he would still be a philosopher, but there would have been taken from him the devastating power to wreak his thought upon the body of the world. Instead he would have lived and wandered like the porpoise, homeless across currents and winds and oceans, intelligent, but forever the lonely and curious observer of unknown wreckage falling through the blue light of eternity. This role would now be a deserved penitence for man. Perhaps such a transformation would bring him once more into that mood of childhood innocence in which he talked successfully to all things living but had no power and no urge to harm. It is worth at least a wistful thought that someday the porpoise may talk to us and we to him. It would break, perhaps, the long loneliness that has made man a frequent terror and abomination even to himself.

_____ CONSIDERATIONS _____

1. Eiseley begins by saying that man "has entered into the strange world of history. . . ." Daniel Boorstin (page 81) says we have "wandered out of history." Are the two statements contradictory? Or must they be considered in relation to what the two authors say in their essays?

2. Much of Eiseley's essay depends upon the work of another scientist, John Lilly. Thus we might call Eiseley's piece a research paper. Study how Eiseley adapts Lilly's findings to his own interests to make the essay truly his, not simply a summary of Lilly's research.

3. The human need for communication is also presented, in another form, by Lewis Thomas, in "Ceti," pages 395–398. Can you make use of parts of both the Thomas and Eiseley selections in an essay on communication?

4. A naturalist, Jane van Lawick-Goodall, observed chimpanzees and reports that those animals have the ability not only to use tools but to invent them. She then suggests that her finding may force us to redefine mankind, as though it were imperative to keep mankind separate from other animals. Do you find this concern in the quote from Lilly at the end of Paragraph 4, or in Eiseley's statements in paragraphs 10 and 11? Why, in all his attempts to classify the animal kingdom, does man consistently put himself at the top of the hierarchy?

5. Is Eiseley convincing in his attempt to see the world through the porpoise's eyes? See especially Paragraph 13. Experiment by imagining the world from the viewpoint of a different being — say a mosquito, or a giraffe, or the seed of a dandelion, or a milkweed plant or an elm or a cottonwood tree.

6. Much of Eiseley's popularity among laymen as a writer on scientific subjects comes from his use of figures of speech, like those in Paragraph 13. Locate other examples.

T. S. Eliot (1888–1965) was born in St. Louis, attended Harvard, and later settled in England where he worked for a publisher and took English citizenship. The most famous poet of his time, he was an influential literary critic, and won the Nobel Prize for Literature in 1948.

This poem was printed not long after Eliot's conversion to the Church of England. The first five lines are taken from Lancelot Andrewes, theologian and bishop of the seventeenth century, arranged as verse and applied to the journey of the Wise Men — possibly to suggest that a later journey to Christ was also a difficult passage.

26

T. S. ELIOT

Journey of the Magi

"A cold coming we had of it,
Just the worst time of the year
For a journey, and such a long journey:
The ways deep and the weather sharp,
5 The very dead of winter."
And the camels galled, sore-footed, refractory,
Lying down in the melting snow.
There were times we regretted
The summer palaces on slopes, the terraces,
10 And the silken girls bringing sherbet.
Then the camel men cursing and grumbling
And running away, and wanting their liquor and women,

And the night-fires going out, and the lack of shelters,
And the cities hostile and the towns unfriendly
And the villages dirty and charging high prices: 15
A hard time we had of it.
At the end we preferred to travel all night,
Sleeping in snatches,
With the voices singing in our ears, saying
That this was all folly.   20

Then at dawn we came down to a temperate valley,
Wet, below the snow line, smelling of vegetation;
With a running stream and a water-mill beating the darkness,
And three trees on the low sky,
And an old white horse galloped away in the meadow.   25
Then we came to a tavern with vine-leaves over the lintel,
Six hands at an open door dicing for pieces of silver,
And feet kicking the empty wine-skins.
But there was no information, and so we continued
And arrived at evening, not a moment too soon   30
Finding the place; it was (you may say) satisfactory.

All this was a long time ago, I remember,
And I would do it again, but set down
This set down
This: were we led all that way for   35
Birth or Death? There was a Birth, certainly,
We had evidence and no doubt. I had seen birth and death,
But had thought they were different; this Birth was
Hard and bitter agony for us, like Death, our death.
We returned to our places, these Kingdoms,   40
But no longer at ease here, in the old dispensation,
With an alien people clutching their gods.
I should be glad of another death.

*Nora Ephron (b. 1941), daughter of two screen writers, grew up
in Hollywood wanting to come to New York and become a writer.
She did. She began by working for* Newsweek, *and soon was contributing articles to* New York *and a monthly column to* Esquire.
*Most of her writing is about women, and manages to be funny
and serious, profound and irreverent — and on occasion outra-
geous. Her latest book, on the media, is* Scribble Scribble *(1978).
She has also collected her essays in* Wallflower at the Orgy *(1970)
and* Crazy Salad *(1975), from which we take this essay on growing
up flat-chested.*

27

NORA EPHRON

A Few Words about Breasts:
Shaping Up Absurd

1   I have to begin with a few words about androgyny. In grammar
school, in the fifth and sixth grades, we were all tyrannized by a rigid
set of rules that supposedly determined whether we were boys or girls.
The episode in *Huckleberry Finn* where Huck is disguised as a girl and
gives himself away by the way he threads a needle and catches a ball
— that kind of thing. We learned that the way you sat, crossed your
legs, held a cigarette and looked at your nails, your wristwatch, the
way you did these things instinctively was absolute proof of your sex.
Now obviously most children did not take this literally, but I did. I
thought that just one slip, just one incorrect cross of my legs or flick of
an imaginary cigarette ash would turn me from whatever I was into
the other thing; that would be all it took, really. Even though I was

outwardly a girl and had many of the trappings generally associated with the field of girldom — a girl's name, for example, and dresses, my own telephone, an autograph book — I spent the early years of my adolescence absolutely certain that I might at any point gum it up. I did not feel at all like a girl. I was boyish. I was athletic, ambitious, outspoken, competitive, noisy, rambunctious. I had scabs on my knees and my socks slid into my loafers and I could throw a football. I wanted desperately not to be that way, not to be a mixture of both things but instead just one, a girl, a definite indisputable girl. As soft and as pink as a nursery. And nothing would do that for me, I felt, but breasts.

I was about six months younger than everyone in my class, and so for about six months after it began, for six months after my friends had begun to develop — that was the word we used, develop — I was not particularly worried. I would sit in the bathtub and look down at my breasts and know that any day now, any second now, they would start growing like everyone else's. They didn't. "I want to buy a bra," I said to my mother one night. "What for?" she said. My mother was really hateful about bras, and by the time my third sister had gotten to that point where she was ready to want one, my mother had worked the whole business into a comedy routine. "Why not use a Band-Aid instead?" she would say. It was a source of great pride to my mother that she had never even had to wear a brassiere until she had her fourth child, and then only because her gynecologist made her. It was incomprehensible to me that anyone would ever be proud of something like that. It was the 1950's, for God's sake. Jane Russell. Cashmere sweaters. Couldn't my mother see that? *"I am too old to wear an undershirt."* Screaming. Weeping. Shouting. "Then don't wear an undershirt," said my mother. "But I want to buy a bra." "What for?"

I suppose that for most girls, breasts, brassieres, that entire thing, has more trauma, more to do with the coming of adolescence, of becoming a woman, than anything else. Certainly more than getting your period, although that too was traumatic, symbolic. But you could *see* breasts; they were there; they were visible. Whereas a girl could claim to have her period for months before she actually got it and nobody would ever know the difference. Which is exactly what I did. All you had to do was make a great fuss over having enough nickels for the Kotex machine and walk around clutching your stomach and moaning for three to five days a month about The Curse and you could convince anybody. There is a school of thought somewhere in the women's lib/women's mag/gynecology establishment that claims that menstrual cramps are purely psychological, and I lean toward it. Not that I didn't have them finally. Agonizing cramps, heating-pad cramps, go-down-to-the-school-nurse-and-lie-on-the-cot cramps. But unlike any pain I had ever suffered, I adored the pain of cramps, welcomed it, wallowed in it, bragged about it. "I can't go. I have cramps." "I can't do that. I have cramps." And most of all, gigglingly, blushingly: "I can't swim. I have cramps." Nobody ever used the hard-core word. Menstruation. God, what an awful word. Never that. "I have cramps."

4   The morning I first got my period, I went into my mother's bedroom to tell her. And my mother, my utterly-hateful-about-bras mother, burst into tears. It was really a lovely moment, and I remember it so clearly not just because it was one of the two times I ever saw my mother cry on my account (the other was when I was caught being a six-year-old kleptomaniac), but also because the incident did not mean to me what it meant to her. Her little girl, her firstborn, had finally become a woman. That was what she was crying about. My reaction to the event, however, was that I might well be a woman in some scientific, textbook sense (and could at least stop faking every month and stop wasting all those nickels). But in another sense — in a visible sense — I was as androgynous and as liable to tip over into boyhood as ever.

5   I started with a 28AA bra. I don't think they made them any smaller in those days, although I gather that now you can buy bras for five year olds that don't have any cups whatsoever in them; trainer bras they are called. My first brassiere came from Robinson's Department Store in Beverly Hills. I went there alone, shaking, positive they would look me over and smile and tell me to come back next year. An actual fitter took me into the dressing room and stood over me while I took off my blouse and tried the first one on. The little puffs stood out on my chest. "Lean over," said the fitter (to this day I am not sure what fitters in bra departments do except to tell you to lean over). I leaned over, with the fleeting hope that my breasts would miraculously fall out of my body and into the puffs. Nothing.

6   "Don't worry about it," said my friend Libby some months later, when things had not improved. "You'll get them after you're married."

7   "What are you talking about?" I said.

8   "When you get married," Libby explained, "your husband will touch your breasts and rub them and kiss them and they'll grow."

9   That was the killer. Necking I could deal with. Intercourse I could deal with. But it had never crossed my mind that a man was going to touch my breasts, that breasts had something to do with all that, pet-

ting, my God they never mentioned petting in my little sex manual about the fertilization of the ovum. I became dizzy. For I knew instantly — as naïve as I had been only a moment before — that only part of what she was saying was true: the touching, rubbing, kissing part, not the growing part. And I knew that no one would ever want to marry me. I had no breasts. I would never have breasts.

My best friend in school was Diana Raskob. She lived a block   10
from me in a house full of wonders. English muffins, for instance. The Raskobs were the first people in Beverly Hills to have English muffins for breakfast. They also had an apricot tree in the back, and a badminton court, and a subscription to *Seventeen* magazine, and hundreds of games like Sorry and Parcheesi and Treasure Hunt and Anagrams. Diana and I spent three or four afternoons a week in their den reading and playing and eating. Diana's mother's kitchen was full of the most colossal assortment of junk food I have ever been exposed to. My house was full of apples and peaches and milk and homemade chocolate-chip cookies — which were nice, and good for you, but-not-right-before-dinner-or-you'll-spoil-your-appetite. Diana's house had nothing in it that was good for you, and what's more, you could stuff it in right up until dinner and nobody cared. Bar-B-Q potato chips (they were the first in them, too), giant bottles of ginger ale, fresh popcorn with melted butter, hot fudge sauce on Baskin-Robbins jamoca ice cream, powdered-sugar doughnuts from Van de Kamps. Diana and I had been best friends since we were seven; we were about equally popular in school (which is to say, not particularly), we had about the same success with boys (extremely intermittent) and we looked much the same. Dark. Tall. Gangly.

It is September, just before school begins. I am eleven years old,   11
about to enter the seventh grade, and Diana and I have not seen each other all summer. I have been to camp and she has been somewhere like Banff with her parents. We are meeting, as we often do, on the street midway between our two houses and we will walk back to Diana's and eat junk and talk about what has happened to each of us that summer. I am walking down Walden Drive in my jeans and my father's shirt hanging out and my old red loafers with the socks falling into them and coming toward me is . . . I take a deep breath . . . a young woman. Diana. Her hair is curled and she has a waist and hips and a bust and she is wearing a straight skirt, an article of clothing I have been repeatedly told I will be unable to wear until I have the hips to hold it up. My jaw drops, and suddenly I am crying, crying hysteri-

cally, can't catch my breath sobbing. My best friend has betrayed me. She has gone ahead without me and done it. She has shaped up.

12   Here are some things I did to help:

13   Bought a Mark Eden Bust Developer.

14   Slept on my back for four years.

15   Splashed cold water on them every night because some French actress said in *Life* magazine that that was what *she* did for her perfect bustline.

16   Ultimately, I resigned myself to a bad toss and began to wear padded bras. I think about them now, think about all those years in high school I went around in them, my three padded bras, every single one of them with different sized breasts. Each time I changed bras I changed sizes: one week nice perky but not too obtrusive breasts, the next medium-sized slightly pointed ones, the next week knockers, true knockers; all the time, whatever size I was, carrying around this rubberized appendage on my chest that occasionally crashed into a wall and was poked inward and had to be poked outward — I think about all that and wonder how anyone kept a straight face through it. My parents, who normally had no restraints about needling me — why did they say nothing as they watched my chest go up and down? My friends, who would periodically inspect my breasts for signs of growth and reassure me — why didn't they at least counsel consistency?

17   And the bathing suits. I die when I think about the bathing suits. That was the era when you could lay an uninhabited bathing suit on the beach and someone would make a pass at it. I would put one on, an absurd swimsuit with its enormous bust built into it, the bones from the suit stabbing me in the rib cage and leaving little red welts on my body, and there I would be, my chest plunging straight downward absolutely vertically from my collarbone to the top of my suit and then suddenly, wham, out came all that padding and material and wiring absolutely horizontally.

18   Buster Klepper was the first boy who ever touched them. He was my boyfriend my senior year of high school. There is a picture of him in my high-school yearbook that makes him look quite attractive in a Jewish, horn-rimmed glasses sort of way, but the picture does not show the pimples, which were air-brushed out, or the dumbness. Well, that isn't really fair. He wasn't dumb. He just wasn't terribly bright. His mother refused to accept it, refused to accept the relentlessly average report cards, refused to deal with her son's inevitable destiny in some

junior college or other. "He was tested," she would say to me, apropos of nothing, "and it came out 145. That's near-genius." Had the word underachiever been coined, she probably would have lobbed that one at me, too. Anyway, Buster was really very sweet — which is, I know, damning with faint praise, but there it is. I was the editor of the front page of the high-school newspaper and he was editor of the back page; we had to work together, side by side, in the print shop, and that was how it started. On our first date, we went to see *April Love* starring Pat Boone. Then we started going together. Buster had a green coupe, a 1950 Ford with an engine he had handchromed until it shone, dazzled, reflected the image of anyone who looked into it, anyone usually being Buster polishing it or the gas-station attendants he constantly asked to check the oil in order for them to be overwhelmed by the sparkle on the valves. The car also had a boot stretched over the back seat for reasons I never understood; hanging from the rearview mirror, as was the custom, was a pair of angora dice. A previous girl friend named Solange who was famous throughout Beverly Hills High School for having no pigment in her right eyebrow had knitted them for him. Buster and I would ride around town, the two of us seated to the left of the steering wheel. I would shift gears. It was nice.

There was necking. Terrific necking. First in the car, overlooking   19
Los Angeles from what is now the Trousdale Estates. Then on the bed of his parents' cabana at Ocean House. Incredibly wonderful, frustrating necking, I loved it, really, but no further than necking, please don't, please, because there I was absolutely terrified of the general implications of going-a-step-further with a near-dummy and also terrified of his finding out there was next to nothing there (which he knew, of course; he wasn't that dumb).

I broke up with him at one point. I think we were apart for about   20
two weeks. At the end of that time I drove down to see a friend at a boarding school in Palos Verdes Estates and a disc jockey played *April Love* on the radio four times during the trip. I took it as a sign. I drove straight back to Griffith Park to a golf tournament Buster was playing in (he was the sixth-seeded teen-age golf player in Southern California) and presented myself back to him on the green of the 18th hole. It was all very dramatic. That night we went to a drive-in and I let him get his hand under my protuberances and onto my breasts. He really didn't seem to mind at all.

"Do you want to marry my son?" the woman asked me.   21
"Yes," I said.   22

23   *I was nineteen years old, a virgin, going with this woman's son, this big strange woman who was married to a Lutheran minister in New Hampshire and pretended she was Gentile and had this son, by her first husband, this total fool of a son who ran the hero-sandwich concession at Harvard Business School and whom for one moment one December in New Hamphsire I said — as much out of politeness as anything else — that I wanted to marry.*

24   *"Fine," she said. "Now, here's what you do. Always make sure you're on top of him so you won't seem so small. My bust is very large, you see, so I always lie on my back to make it look smaller, but you'll have to be on top most of the time."*

25   *I nodded. "Thank you," I said.*

26   *"I have a book for you to read," she went on, "Take it with you when you leave. Keep it." She went to the bookshelf, found it, and gave it to me. It was a book on frigidity.*

27   *"Thank you," I said.*

28   That is a true story. Everything in this article is a true story, but I feel I have to point out that that story in particular is true. It happened on December 30, 1960. I think about it often. When it first happened, I naturally assumed that the woman's son, my boyfriend, was responsible. I invented a scenario where he had had a little heart-to-heart with his mother and had confessed that his only objection to me was that my breasts were small; his mother then took it upon herself to help out. Now I think I was wrong about the incident. The mother was acting on her own, I think: that was her way of being cruel and competitive under the guise of being helpful and maternal. You have small breasts, she was saying; therefore you will never make him as happy as I have. Or you have small breasts; therefore you will doubtless have sexual problems. Or you have small breasts; therefore you are less woman than I am. She was, as it happens, only the first of what seems to me to be a never-ending string of women who have made competitive remarks to me about breast size. "I would love to wear a dress like that," my friend Emily says to me, "but my bust is too big." Like that. Why do women say these things to me? Do I attract these remarks the way other women attract married men or alcoholics or homosexuals? This summer, for example. I am at a party in East Hampton and I am introduced to a woman from Washington. She is a minor celebrity, very pretty and Southern and blonde and outspoken and I am flattered because she has read something I have written. We are talking animatedly, we have been talking no more than five minutes, when a man comes up to join us. "Look at the two of us," the woman says to the

man, indicating me and her. "The two of us together couldn't fill an A cup." Why does she say that? It isn't even true, dammit, so why? Is she even more addled than I am on this subject? Does she honestly believe there is something wrong with her size breasts, which, it seems to me, now that I look hard at them, are just right. Do I unconsciously bring out competitiveness in women? In that form? What did I do to deserve it?

As for men.   29

There were men who minded and let me know they minded.   30
There were men who did not mind. In any case, I always minded.

And even now, now that I have been countlessly reassured that   31
my figure is a good one, now that I am grown up enough to understand that most of my feelings have very little to do with the reality of my shape, I am nonetheless obsessed by breasts. I cannot help it. I grew up in the terrible Fifties — with rigid stereotypical sex roles, the insistence that men be men and dress like men and women be women and dress like women, the intolerance of androgyny — and I cannot shake it, cannot shake my feelings of inadequacy. Well, that time is gone, right? All those exaggerated examples of breast worship are gone, right? Those women were freaks, right? I know all that. And yet, here I am, stuck with the psychological remains of it all, stuck with my own peculiar version of breast worship. You probably think I am crazy to go on like this: here I have set out to write a confession that is meant to hit you with the shock of recognition and instead you are sitting there thinking I am thoroughly warped. Well, what can I tell you? If I had had them, I would have been a completely different person. I honestly believe that.

After I went into therapy, a process that made it possible for me   32
to tell total strangers at cocktail parties that breasts were the hang-up of my life, I was often told that I was insane to have been bothered by my condition. I was also frequently told, by close friends, that I was extremely boring on the subject. And my girl friends, the ones with nice big breasts, would go on endlessly about how their lives had been far more miserable than mine. Their bra straps were snapped in class. They couldn't sleep on their stomachs. They were stared at whenever the word "mountain" cropped up in geography. And *Evangeline*, good God what they went through every time someone had to stand up and recite the Prologue to Longfellow's *Evangeline*: *". . . stand like druids of eld . . . / With beards that rest on their bosoms."* It was much worse for them, they tell me. They had a terrible time of it, they assure me. I don't know how lucky I was, they say.

33   I have thought about their remarks, tried to put myself in their place, considered their point of view. I think they are full of shit.

_____ CONSIDERATIONS _____

1. Nora Ephron's account offends some readers and attracts others for the same reason — the frank and casual exploration of a subject that generations have believed unmentionable. This problem is worth investigating: Are there, in fact, subjects that should not be discussed in the popular press? Are there words a writer must not use? Why? And who should make the list of things not to be talked about?

2. Imagine an argument about Ephron's article between a feminist and an antifeminist. What ammunition could each find in the article? Write the dialogue as you hear it.

3. Ephron reports that from a very early age she worried that she might not be "a girl, a definite indisputable girl." Is this anxiety as uncommon as she thought it was? Is worry about one's sex an exclusively female problem? Consider what James Baxter says on the subject (pages 37–39). See also what the short stories in this text can contribute to the discussion.

4. Are our ideas about masculinity and femininity changing? How are such ideas determined? How important are they in shaping personality and in channeling thoughts?

5. Ephron's article is a good example of the very informal essay. What does she do that makes it so informal? Consider both diction and sentence structure.

6. How can one smile at others' problems — or at one's own disappointments, for that matter? How can Ephron see humor now in what she thought of as tragic then?

William Faulkner (1897–1962) was a great novelist, born in Mississippi, who supported himself much of his life by screenwriting and by writing short fiction for magazines. He is another American Nobel Laureate, who receive the prize for Literature in 1950. Among his novels are The Sound and the Fury *(1929),* As I Lay Dying *(1930),* Light in August *(1932), and a comic series:* The Hamlet *(1940),* The Town *(1957), and* The Mansion *(1960). "A Rose for Emily" is expert magazine fiction, and at the same time an emblem for the disease and decease of a society.*

28

WILLIAM FAULKNER
A Rose for Emily

I

When Miss Emily Grierson died, our whole town went to her funeral: the men through a sort of respectful affection for a fallen monument, the women mostly out of curiosity to see the inside of her house, which no one save an old manservant — a combined gardener and cook — had seen in at least ten years.

It was a big, squarish frame house that had once been white, decorated with cupolas and spires and scrolled balconies in the heavily lightsome style of the seventies, set on what had once been our most select street. But garages and cotton gins had encroached and obliterated even the august names of that neighborhood; only Miss Emily's house was left, lifting its stubborn and coquettish decay above the cotton wagons and the gasoline pumps — an eyesore among eyesores. And now Miss Emily had gone to join the representatives of those august names where they lay in the cedar-bemused cemetery among the ranked and anonymous graves of Union and Confederate soldiers who fell at the battle of Jefferson.

Alive, Miss Emily had been a tradition, a duty, and a care; a sort of hereditary obligation upon the town, dating from that day in 1894 when Colonel Sartoris, the mayor — he who fathered the edict that no Negro woman should appear on the streets without an apron — remitted her taxes, the dispensation dating from the death of her father on into perpetuity. Not that Miss Emily would have accepted charity. Colonel Sartoris invented an involved tale to the effect that Miss Emily's father had loaned money to the town, which the town, as a matter of business, preferred this way of repaying. Only a man of Colonel Sartoris' generation and thought could have invented it, and only a woman could have believed it.

When the next generation, with its more modern ideas, became mayors and aldermen, this arrangement created some little dissatisfaction. On the first of the year they mailed her a tax notice. February came, and there was no reply. They wrote her a formal letter, asking her to call at the sheriff's office at her convenience. A week later the mayor wrote her himself, offering to call or to send his car for her, and received in reply a note on paper of an archaic shape, in a thin, flowing calligraphy in faded ink, to the effect that she no longer went out at all. The tax notice was also enclosed, without comment.

They called a special meeting of the Board of Aldermen. A deputation waited upon her, knocked at the door through which no visitor had passed since she ceased giving china-painting lessons eight or ten years earlier. They were admitted by the old Negro into a dim hall from which a staircase mounted into still more shadow. It smelled of dust and disuse — a close, dank smell. The Negro led them into the parlor. It was furnished in heavy, leather-covered furniture. When the Negro opened the blinds of one window, a faint dust rose sluggishly about their thighs, spinning with slow motes in the single sun-ray. On a tarnished gilt easel before the fireplace stood a crayon portrait of Miss Emily's father.

They rose when she entered — a small, fat woman in black, with a thin gold chain descending to her waist and vanishing into her belt, leaning on an ebony cane with a tarnished gold head. Her skeleton was small and spare; perhaps that was why what would have been merely plumpness in another was obesity in her. She looked bloated, like a body long submerged in motionless water, and of that pallid hue. Her eyes, lost in the fatty ridges of her face, looked like two small pieces of coal pressed into a lump of dough as they moved from one face to another while the visitors stated their errand.

She did not ask them to sit. She just stood in the door and listened quietly until the spokesman came to a stumbling halt. Then they could hear the invisible watch ticking at the end of the gold chain.

Her voice was dry and cold. "I have no taxes in Jefferson. Colonel Sartoris explained it to me. Perhaps one of you can gain access to the city records and satisfy yourselves."

"But we have. We are the city authorities, Miss Emily. Didn't you get a notice from the sheriff, signed by him?"

"I received a paper, yes," Miss Emily said. "Perhaps he considers himself the sheriff. . . . I have no taxes in Jefferson."

"But there is nothing on the books to show that, you see. We must go by the —"

"See Colonel Sartoris. I have no taxes in Jefferson."

"But, Miss Emily —"

"See Colonel Sartoris." (Colonel Sartoris had been dead almost ten years.) "I have no taxes in Jefferson. Tobe!" The Negro appeared. "Show these gentlemen out."

II

So she vanquished them, horse and foot, just as she had vanquished their fathers thirty years before about the smell. That was two years after her father's death and a short time after her sweetheart — the one we believed would marry her — had deserted her. After her father's death she went out very little; after her sweetheart went away, people hardly saw her at all. A few of the ladies had the temerity to call, but were not received, and the only sign of life about the place was the Negro man — a young man then — going in and out with a market basket.

"Just as if a man — any man — could keep a kitchen properly," the ladies said; so they were not surprised when the smell developed. It was another link between the gross, teeming world and the high and mighty Griersons.

A neighbor, a woman, complained to the mayor, Judge Stevens, eighty years old.

"But what will you have me do about it, madam?" he said.

"Why, send her word to stop it," the woman said. "Isn't there a law?"

"I'm sure that won't be necessary," Judge Stevens said. "It's probably just a snake or a rat that nigger of hers killed in the yard. I'll speak to him about it."

The next day he received two more complaints, one from a man who came in diffident deprecation. "We really must do something about it, Judge. I'd be the last one in the world to bother Miss Emily, but we've got to do something." That night the Board of Aldermen met — three gray-beards and one younger man, a member of the rising generation.

"It's simple enough," he said. "Send her word to have her place cleaned up. Give her a certain time to do it in, and if she don't . . ."

"Dammit, sir," Judge Stevens said, "will you accuse a lady to her face of smelling bad?"

So the next night, after midnight, four men crossed Miss Emily's lawn and slunk about the house like burglars, sniffing along the base of the brickwork and at the cellar openings while one of them performed a regular sowing motion with his hand out of a sack slung from his shoulder. They broke open the cellar door and sprinkled lime there, and in all the out-buildings. As they recrossed the lawn, a window that had been dark was lighted and Miss Emily sat in it, the light behind her, and her upright torso motionless as that of an idol. They crept quietly across the lawn and into the shadow of the locusts that lined the street. After a week or two the smell went away.

That was when people had begun to feel really sorry for her. People in our town remembering how old lady Wyatt, her great-aunt, had gone completely crazy at last, believed that the Griersons held themselves a little too high for what they really were. None of the young men were quite good enough for Miss Emily and such. We had long thought of them as a tableau; Miss Emily a slender figure in white in the background, her father a spraddled silhouette in the foreground, his back to her and clutching a horsewhip, the two of them framed by the back-flung front door. So when she got to be thirty and was still single, we were not pleased exactly, but vindicated; even with insanity in the family she wouldn't have turned down all of her chances if they had really materialized.

When her father died, it got about that the house was all that was left to her; and in a way, people were glad. At last they could pity Miss Emily. Being left alone, and a pauper, she had become humanized. Now she too would know the old thrill and the old despair of a penny more or less.

The day after his death all the ladies prepared to call at the house and offer condolence and aid, as is our custom. Miss Emily met them at the door, dressed as usual and with no trace of grief on her face. She told them that her father was not dead. She did that for three days, with the ministers calling on her, and the doctors, trying to persuade her to let them dispose of the body. Just as they were about to resort to law and force, she broke down, and they buried her father quickly.

We did not say she was crazy then. We believed she had to do that. We remembered all the young men her father had driven away, and we knew that with nothing left, she would have to cling to that which had robbed her, as people will.

III

She was sick for a long time. When we saw her again, her hair was cut short, making her look like a girl, with a vague resemblance to those angels in colored church windows — sort of tragic and serene.

The town had just let the contracts for paving the sidewalks, and in the summer after her father's death they began to work. The construction company came with niggers and mules and machinery, and a foreman named Homer Barron, a Yankee — a big, dark, ready man, with a big voice and eyes lighter than his face. The little boys would follow in groups to hear him cuss the niggers, and the niggers singing in time to the rise and fall of picks. Pretty soon he knew everybody in town. Whenever you heard a lot of laughing anywhere about the square, Homer Barron would be in the center of the group. Presently we began to see him and Miss Emily on Sunday afternoons driving in the yellow-wheeled buggy and the matched team of bays from the livery stable.

At first we were glad that Miss Emily would have an interest, because the ladies all said, "Of course a Grierson would not think seriously of a Northerner, a day laborer." But there were still others, older people, who said that even grief could not cause a real lady to forget *noblesse oblige* — without calling it *noblesse oblige.* They just said, "Poor Emily. Her kinsfolk should come to her." She had some kin in Alabama; but years ago her father had fallen out with them over the estate of old lady Wyatt, the crazy woman, and there was no communication between the two families. They had not even been represented at the funeral.

And as soon as the old people said, "Poor Emily," the whispering began. "Do you suppose it's really so?" they said to one another. "Of course it is. What else could . . ." This behind their hands; rustling of craned silk and satin behind jalousies closed upon the sun of Sunday afternoon as the thin, swift clop-clop-clop of the matched team passed: "Poor Emily."

She carried her head high enough — even when we believed that she was fallen. It was as if she demanded more than ever the recognition of her dignity as the last Grierson; as if it had wanted that touch of earthiness to reaffirm her imperviousness. Like when she bought the rat poison, the arsenic. That was over a year after they had begun to say "Poor Emily," and while the two female cousins were visiting her.

"I want some poison," she said to the druggist. She was over thirty then, still a slight woman, though thinner than usual, with cold, haughty black eyes in a face the flesh of which was strained across the temples and about the eyesockets as you imagine a lighthouse-keeper's face ought to look. "I want some poison," she said.

"Yes, Miss Emily. What kind? For rats and such? I'd recom — "

"I want the best you have. I don't care what kind."

The druggist named several. "They'll kill anything up to an elephant. But what you want is — "

"Arsenic," Miss Emily said. "Is that a good one?"

"Is . . . arsenic? Yes ma'am. But what you want — "

"I want arsenic."

The druggist looked down at her. She looked back at him, erect, her face like a strained flag. "Why, of course," the druggist said. "If that's what you want. But the law requires you to tell what you are going to use it for."

Miss Emily just stared at him, her head tilted back in order to look him eye for eye, until he looked away and went and got the arsenic and wrapped it up. The Negro delivery boy brought her the package; the druggist didn't come back. When she opened the package at home there was written on the box, under the skull and bones: "For rats."

IV

So the next day we all said, "She will kill herself"; and we said it would be the best thing. When she had first begun to be seen with Homer Barron, we had said, "She will marry him." Then we said, "She will persuade him yet," because Homer himself had remarked — he liked men, and it was known that he drank with the younger men in the Elk's Club — that he was not a marrying man. Later we said, "Poor Emily," behind the jalousies as they passed on Sunday afternoon in the glittering buggy, Miss Emily with her head high and Homer Barron with his hat cocked and a cigar in his teeth, reins and whip in a yellow glove.

Then some of the ladies began to say that it was a disgrace to the town and a bad example to the young people. The men did not want to interfere, but at last the ladies forced the Baptist minister — Miss Emily's people were Episcopal — to call upon her. He would never divulge what happened during that interview, but he refused to go back again. The next Sunday they again drove about the streets, and the following day the minister's wife wrote to Miss Emily's relations in Alabama.

So she had blood-kin under her roof again and we sat back to watch developments. At first nothing happened. Then we were sure that they were to be married. We learned that Miss Emily had been to the jeweler's and ordered a man's toilet set in silver, with the letters H.B. on each piece. Two days later we learned that she had bought a complete outfit of men's clothing, including a nightshirt, and we said, "They are married." We were really glad. We were glad because the two female cousins were even more Grierson than Miss Emily had ever been.

So we were surprised when Homer Barron — the streets had been finished some time since — was gone. We were a little disappointed that there was not a public blowing-off, but we believed that he had gone on to prepare for Miss Emily's coming, or to give a chance to get rid of the cousins. (By that time it was a cabal, and we were all Miss Emily's allies to help circumvent the cousins.) Sure enough, after another week they departed. And, as we had expected all along, within three days Homer Barron was back in town. A neighbor saw the Negro man admit him at the kitchen door at dusk one evening.

And that was the last we saw of Homer Barron. And of Miss Emily for some time. The Negro man went in and out with the market basket, but the front door remained closed. Now and then we would see her at a window for a moment, as the men did that night when they sprinkled the lime, but for almost six months she did not appear on the streets. Then we knew that this was to be expected too; as if that quality of her father which had thwarted her woman's life so many times had been too virulent and too furious to die.

When we next saw Miss Emily, she had grown fat and her hair was turning gray. During the next few years it grew grayer and grayer until it attained an even pepper-and-salt iron-gray, when it ceased turning. Up to the day of her death at seventy-four it was still that vigorous iron-gray, like the hair of an active man.

From that time on her front door remained closed, save for a period of six or seven years, when she was about forty, during which she gave lessons in china-painting. She fitted up a studio in one of the downstairs rooms, where the daughters and granddaughters of Colonel Sartoris' contemporaries were sent to her with the same regularity and in the same spirit that they were sent on Sundays with a twenty-five cent piece for the collection plate. Meanwhile her taxes had been remitted.

Then the newer generation became the backbone and the spirit of the town, and the painting pupils grew up and fell away and did not send their children to her with boxes of color and tedious brushes and pictures cut from the ladies' magazines. The front door closed upon the last one and remained closed for good. When the town got free postal delivery Miss Emily alone refused to let them fasten the metal numbers above her door and attach a mailbox to it. She would not listen to them.

Daily, monthly, yearly we watched the Negro grow grayer and more stooped, going in and out with the market basket. Each December we sent her a tax notice, which would be returned by the post office a week later, unclaimed. Now and then we would see her in one of the downstairs windows — she had evidently shut up the top floor of the house — like the carven torso of an idol in a niche, looking or not looking at us, we could never tell which. Thus she passed from generation to generation — dear, inescapable, impervious, tranquil, and perverse.

And so she died. Fell ill in the house filled with dust and shadows, with only a doddering Negro man to wait on her. We did not even know she was sick; we had long since given up trying to get any information from the Negro. He talked to no one, probably not even to her, for his voice had grown harsh and rusty, as if from disuse.

She died in one of the downstairs rooms, in a heavy walnut bed with a curtain, her gray head propped on a pillow yellow and moldy with age and lack of sunlight.

V

The Negro met the first of the ladies at the front door and let them in, with their hushed, sibilant voices and their quick, curious glances, and then he disappeared. He walked right through the house and out the back and was not seen again.

The two female cousins came at once. They held the funeral on the second day, with the town coming to look at Miss Emily beneath a mass of bought flowers, with the crayon face of her father musing profoundly above the bier and the ladies sibilant and macabre; and the very old men — some in their brushed Confederate uniforms — on the porch and the lawn, talking of Miss Emily as if she had been a contemporary of theirs, believing that they had danced with her and courted her perhaps, confusing time with its mathematical progression, as the old do, to whom all the past is not a diminishing road, but, instead, a huge meadow which no winter ever quite touches, divided from them now by the narrow bottleneck of the most recent decade of years.

Already we knew that there was one room in the region above stairs which no one had seen in forty years, and which would have to be forced. They waited until Miss Emily was decently in the ground before they opened it.

The violence of breaking down the door seemed to fill this room with pervading dust. A thin, acrid pall as of the tomb seemed to lie everywhere upon this room decked and furnished as for a bridal: upon the valance curtains of faded rose color, upon the rose-shaded lights, upon the dressing table, upon the delicate array of crystal and the man's toilet things backed with tarnished silver, silver so tarnished that the monogram was obscured. Among them lay a collar and tie, as if they had just been removed, which, lifted, left upon the surface a pale crescent in the dust. Upon a chair hung the suit, carefully folded; beneath it the two mute shoes and the discarded socks.

The man himself lay in the bed.

For a long while we just stood there, looking down at the profound and fleshless grin. The body had apparently once lain in the attitude of an embrace, but now the long sleep that outlasts love, that conquers even the grimace of love, had cuckolded him. What was left of him, rotted beneath what was left of the nightshirt, had become inextricable from the bed in which he lay; and upon him and upon the pillow beside him lay that even coating of the patient and biding dust.

Then we noticed that in the second pillow was the indentation of a head. One of us lifted something from it, and leaning forward, that faint and invisible dust dry and acrid in the nostrils, we saw a long strand of iron-gray hair.

____ CONSIDERATIONS _____

1. The art of narration, some say, is the successful management of a significant sequence of actions through time. But "through time" does not

necessarily imply chronological order. Identify the major events of Faulkner's story according to when they actually happened, then arrange them in the order in which they are given by the author. Try the same technique with the stories by Tillie Olsen (pages 296–303) and Eudora Welty (pages 428–439).

2. Faulkner uses the terms "Negro" and "nigger" to refer to nonwhite persons in the story. Does he intend distinction between the two words? If he were writing the story today, instead of in 1930, might he substitute the word "black"? Why? Can you think of parallel terms used to designate other minority peoples, say, Jews, Catholics, Italians, or Japanese? Of what significance is the variety of such terms?

3. In what ways, if any, is Emily Grierson presented as a sympathetic character? Why?

4. In Part III, Faulkner puts considerable emphasis on the phrase *noblesse oblige*. Look up the meaning of that phrase, then comment on the author's use of it.

5. Who is the "we" in the story? Does "we" play any significant part?

6. Obviously, death is an important feature in this story. Could Faulkner also have had in mind the death of a particular society or a way of life? Does the story invite you to think of symbols?

F. Scott Fitzgerald (1896–1940) was born in St. Paul, Minnesota, graduated from Princeton, and became a best-selling novelist with his first book, This Side of Paradise *(1920), when he was only twenty-four. He married a brilliant, disturbed woman named Zelda Sayre, and lived an extravagant life in the Europe of the twenties, supported mostly by facile short stories that he wrote for money. In 1925, despite dissipation of body and talent, Fitzgerald published his masterpiece,* The Great Gatsby. *As the twenties sank into the depressed thirties, Zelda began to spend much time in asylums, Fitzgerald drank heavily, and his writing gradually lost its public.* Tender Is the Night *(1934), a fine novel, found few readers. To support himself and his ailing wife, Fitzgerald turned to Hollywood. He was not a successful scriptwriter, and Hollywood regarded him with condescension as a has-been. Before his heart failed in 1940, he had begun a Hollywood novel,* The Last Tycoon, *published as a fragment the year after his death. It has moments of the old greatness.*

Like many writers, Fitzgerald kept notebooks. Not quite a journal, these notebooks assemble the raw material of fiction — conversations overheard, a hint of story, an observation of character, a turn of phrase, or a piece of description. These brief selections sample the notes Fitzgerald kept, his own private storehouse, to be raided for his work.

29

F. SCOTT FITZGERALD
Journal Entries

1   Family quarrels are bitter things. They don't go according to any rules. They're not like aches or wounds; they're more like splits in the skin that won't heal because there's not enough material.

2   The absent-minded gentleman on the train started to get off at the wrong station. As he walked back to his seat he assumed a mirthless smile and said aloud as though he were talking to himself: "I thought this was Great Neck."

3   "When I hear people bragging about their social position and who they are, and all that, I just sit back and laugh. Because I happen to be descended directly from Charlemagne. What do you think of that?" Josephine blushed for him.

4   Suddenly her face resumed that expression which can only come from studying moving picture magazines over and over, and only be described as one long blond wish toward something — a wish that you'd have a wedlock with the youth of Shirley Temple, the earning power of Clark Gable; the love of Clark Gable and the talent of Charles Laughton — and with a bright smile the girl was gone.

5   "The time I fell off a closet shelf."
"You what?"
"I fell off a shelf — and he put it in the paper."

From F. Scott Fitzgerald, *The Crack Up.* Copyright 1945 by New Directions Publishing Corporation. Reprinted by permission of New Directions.

"Well, what were you doing?"
"I just happened to be up a shelf and I fell off."
"Oh, don't say it."
"I've stopped giving any further explanations. Anyhow, father said it was news."

There frail dock lights glittered dimly upon innumerable fishing 6
boats heaped like shells along the beach. Farther out in the water there were other lights where a fleet of slender yachts rode the tide with slow dignity, and farther still a full ripe moon made the water bosom into a polished dancing floor.

She wanted to crawl into his pocket and be safe forever. 7

She turned her slender smile full upon Lew for a moment, and 8
then aimed it a little aside, like a pocket torch that might dazzle him.

There was once a moving picture magnate who was shipwrecked 9
on a desert island with nothing but two dozen cans of film.

Story of a man trying to live down his crazy past and encounter- 10
ing it everywhere.

Just when somebody's taken him up and making a big fuss over 11
him, he pours the soup down his hostess' back, kisses the serving maid and passes out in the dog kennel. But he's done it too often. He's run through about everybody, until there's no one left.

"She's really radiunt," she said, "really radiunt." 12

Beginning of a story, *Incorrigible.* 13
Father: Who do you admire?
Son: Andy Gump. Who do you think I admire — George Washington? Grow up!

In Virginia the Italian children say: 14
"Lincoln threw blacks out; now they're back."
"The white people fit the Yankees."
"Yankees *are* white people."
"Not I ever hear tell of."

_____ CONSIDERATIONS _____

1. Like other serious writers — Nathaniel Hawthorne, Katherine Mansfield, Albert Camus, Henry James, Cesare Pavese, Thomas Hardy, Gerard Manley Hopkins, Feodor Dostoevsky — Fitzgerald kept a running logbook of observations, ideas, phrases, questions, and notes, some of which were later developed into stories, poems, plays, or novels. Compare these excerpts from Fitzgerald's notebooks with entries by two or three other writers. Describe and discuss the differences and similarities you find.

2. Select an item from Fitzgerald's notebook and build a short essay around it. Which items seem most useful for this purpose? Why?

3. In excerpt 4, Fitzgerald describes a girl's face as "one long blond wish toward something." Explain this peculiar description of a face. Is it effective or not? Why?

4. Imagine a context in which the descriptive passage "Three frail dock lights . . ." would be appropriate. Explain.

5. In excerpt 10, Fitzgerald puts in one short sentence an idea for a story. Sketch the main elements of the story. Has it already been done? Discuss.

6. Compare and contrast the journals of Fitzgerald and Thomas Wolfe (pages 470–476). How do the two journals reveal different approaches to writing?

*Benjamin Franklin (1706–1790) invented practically every-
thing, though perhaps we go too far when we credit him with
inventing electricity. Self-educated, intellectual, practical, energetic, mischievous, he founded the American post office, he
invented the Franklin stove, he represented the colonies in
England before the Revolution, he represented the new republic in
France after the Revolution, and he fathered a number of illegiti-
mate children. A solid stylist in his writing, he undertook subjects
scientific and moral and philosophical; he wrote an autobiography, and he wrote a book about chess. When he was young he
founded a successful printing business in Philadelphia, and created Poor Richard as a font of pithy wisdom in the annual alma-
nacs he published. Here follow a brief selection of Poor Richard's
sayings, cynical and energetic and as American as their author.*

30

BENJAMIN FRANKLIN
From **Poor Richard's Almanack**

He's a Fool that makes   1
his Doctor his Heir.

A countryman between two Lawyers,   2
is like a fish between two cats.

There are no ugly loves, nor handsome Prisons.   3

Keep your eyes wide open before marriage,   4
half shut afterwards.

When there's Marriage without love,   5
There will be Love without marriage.

6   The greatest monarch on the proudest throne
    is oblig'd to sit upon his own arse.

7   Laws too gentle are seldom obeyed,
    too severe, seldom executed.

8   Lend money to an enemy, and thou'lt gain him,
    to a friend and thou'lt lose him.

9   There are three faithful friends —
    An old wife, an old dog,
    and ready money.

10 Learn of the skillful:
    He that teaches himself
    hath a fool for a master.

11 Neccessity never made a good bargain.

12 Eat to live and not live to eat.

13 Drink does not drown Care, but waters it,
    and makes it grow fast.

14 Early to bed and early to rise
    Makes a man healthy, wealthy, and wise.

15 Each year one vicious habit rooted out,
    In time might make the worst man
    good throughout.

16 Pardoning the bad is injuring the good.

17 All would live long
    but none would be old.

18 Hunger never saw bad bread.

19 Beware of meat twice boil'd.
    And of an old foe reconcil'd.

20 Fish and visitors stink in three days.

He that lives upon hope, dies farting.   21

None preaches better than the ant,   22
and she says nothing.

Who has deceiv'd thee as oft as they self?   23

Beware of him that is slow to anger: 24
He is angry for something, and will not be pleased for nothing.

Suspicion may be no great fault,   25
but showing it may be a great one.

There are three things extreamly hard,   26
steel, a diamond, and to know one's self.

Most people return small favours,   27
acknowledge middling ones,
and repay great ones with ingratitude.

Mankind are very odd creatures;   28
one half censure that they practise,
the other half practise what they censure,
the rest always say and do as they ought.

Take heed of the vinegar of sweet wine   29
and the anger of good-nature.

The wolf sheds his coat once a year,   30
his disposition never.

There was never a good knife made of bad steel.   31

Silence is not always a sign of wisdom   32
but babbling is ever a mark of folly.

When you speak to a man, look on his eyes;   33
when he speaks to thee, look on his mouth.

Strange! That a man who has wit enough   34
to write a satire
Should have folly enough to publish it.

_____ CONSIDERATIONS _____

1. Compare and contrast Poor Richard's sayings with "Some Devil's Definitions" offered by Ambrose Bierce on pages 60–63. What are some similarities and differences?

2. Poor Richard specialized in epigrams. Look up that term in a literary dictionary or handbook and read examples by other authors. What do you consider to be the attributes of a successful epigram? Try your hand at this peculiar, concentrated literary form.

3. How does the English epigram differ from the Japanese *haiku*, a fifteen-syllable poem usually written in three short lines? Are these poetic forms useful to a student of prose composition?

4. Many of Poor Richard's sayings are flat-out declarations: "Pardoning the bad is injuring the good," "There are no ugly loves, nor handsome Prisons," "There was never a good knife made of bad steel." Into what bad habits might devotion to such absolute statements lead a writer?

5. Which of Poor Richard's statements surprises you the most as coming from that grand figure, Benjamin Franklin? Why? Consider how our previous impressions of a writer influence our expectations as we read.

6. How consistent is the advice offered by Poor Richard? What about advice from similar sources, say, Aesop's fables, or anonymous, inherited folk sayings such as "Look before you leap" or "He who hesitates is lost"?

Robert Frost (1874–1963) was born in California and became the great poet of New England. He published many books of poems, won the Pulitzer Prize three times, and read a poem at President Kennedy's inauguration in 1961. A popular public figure in his lifetime, Frost was admired as a smiling, affectionate, avuncular figure given to country sayings. The private Frost was another man — guilty, jealous, bitter, miserable, sophisticated, and occasionally triumphant. Most of his best poems, like "Design," belied the public image by entertaining notions of despair or meaninglessness.

31

ROBERT FROST
Design

I found a dimpled spider, fat and white,
On a white heal-all, holding up a moth
Like a white piece of rigid satin cloth —
Assorted characters of death and blight
Mixed ready to begin the morning right,   5
Like the ingredients of a witches' broth —
A snow-drop spider, a flower like froth,
And dead wings carried like a paper kite.

What had that flower to do with being white,
The wayside blue and innocent heal-all?   10
What brought the kindred spider to that height,
Then steered the white moth thither in the night?
What but design of darkness to appall? —
If design govern in a thing so small.

_32_

LILLIAN HELLMAN
Runaway

1   It was that night that I disappeared, and that night that Fizzy said
I was disgusting mean, and Mr. Stillman said I would forever pain my
mother and father, and my father turned on both of them and said he
would handle his family affairs himself without comments from
strangers. But he said it too late. He had come home very angry with
me: the jeweler, after my father's complaints about his unreliability,
had found the lock of hair in the back of the watch. What started out
to be a mild reproof on my father's part soon turned angry when I
wouldn't explain about the hair. (My father was often angry when I

was most like him.) He was so angry that he forgot that he was attacking me in front of the Stillmans, my old rival Fizzy, and the delighted Mrs. Dreyfus, a new, rich boarder who only that afternoon had complained about my bad manners. My mother left the room when my father grew angry with me. Hannah, passing through, put up her hand as if to stop my father and then, frightened of the look he gave her, went out to the porch. I sat on the couch, astonished at the pain in my head. I tried to get up from the couch, but one ankle turned and I sat down again, knowing for the first time the rampage that could be caused in me by anger. The room began to have other forms, the people were no longer men and women, my head was not my own. I told myself that my head had gone somewhere and I have little memory of anything after my Aunt Jenny came into the room and said to my father, "Don't you remember?" I have never known what she meant, but I knew that soon after I was moving up the staircase, that I slipped and fell a few steps, that when I woke up hours later in my bed, I found a piece of angel cake — and old love, an old custom — left by my mother on my pillow. The headache was worse and I vomited out of the window. Then I dressed, took my red purse, and walked a long way down St. Charles Avenue. A St. Charles Avenue mansion had on its back lawn a famous doll's-house, an elaborate copy of the mansion itself, built years before for the small daughter of the house. As I passed this showpiece, I saw a policeman and moved swiftly back to the doll palace and crawled inside. If I had known about the fantasies of the frightened, that ridiculous small house would not have been so terrible for me. I was surrounded by ornate, carved reproductions of the mansion furniture, scaled for children, bisque figurines in miniature, a working toilet seat of gold leaf in suitable size, small draperies of damask with a sign that said "From the damask of Marie Antoinette," a miniature samovar with small bronze cups, and a tiny Madame Récamier couch on which I spent the night, my legs on the floor. I must have slept, because I woke from a nightmare and knocked over a bisque figurine. The noise frightened me, and since it was now almost light, in one of those lovely mist mornings of late spring when every flower in New Orleans seems to melt and mix with the air, I crawled out. Most of that day I spent walking, although I had a long session in the ladies' room of the railroad station. I had four dollars and two bits, but that wasn't much when you meant it to last forever and when you knew it would not be easy for a fourteen-year-old girl to find work in a city where too many people knew her. Three times I stood in line at the railroad ticket windows to ask where I could go for four dollars, but each time the question seemed too dangerous and I knew no other way of asking.

2   Toward evening, I moved to the French Quarter, feeling sad and envious as people went home to dinner. I bought a few Tootsie Rolls and a half loaf of bread and went to the St. Louis Cathedral in Jackson Square. (It was that night that I composed the prayer that was to become, in the next five years, an obsession, mumbled over and over through the days and nights: "God forgive me, Papa forgive me, Mama forgive me, Sophronia, Jenny, Hannah, and all others, through this time and that time, in life and in death." When I was nineteen, my father, who had made several attempts through the years to find out what my lip movements meant as I repeated the prayer, said, "How much would you take to stop that? Name it and you've got it." I suppose I was sick of the nonsense by that time because I said, "A leather coat and a feather fan," and the next day he bought them for me.) After my loaf of bread, I went looking for a bottle of soda pop and discovered, for the first time, the whorehouse section around Bourbon Street. The women were ranged in the doorways of the cribs, making the first early evening offers to sailors, who were the only men in the streets. I wanted to stick around and see how things like that worked, but the second or third time I circled the block, one of the girls called out to me. I couldn't understand the words, but the voice was angry enough to make me run toward the French Market.

3   The Market was empty except for two old men. One of them called to me as I went past, and I turned to see that he had opened his pants and was shaking what my circle called "his thing." I flew across the street into the coffee stand, forgetting that the owner had known me since I was a small child when my Aunt Jenny would rest from her marketing tour with a cup of fine, strong coffee.

4   He said, in the patois, *"Que faites, ma 'fant? Je suis ferme."*

5   I said, *"Rien, My tante attend"* — Could I have a doughnut?

6   He brought me two doughnuts, saying one was *lagniappe,* but I took my doughnuts outside when he said, *"Mais où est vo' tante à c' heure?"*

7   I fell asleep with my doughnuts behind a shrub in Jackson Square. The night was damp and hot and through the sleep there were many voices and, much later, there was music from somewhere near the river. When all sounds had ended, I woke, turned my head, and knew I was being watched. Two rats were sitting a few feet from me. I urinated on my dress, crawled backwards to stand up, screamed as I ran up the steps of St. Louis Cathedral and pounded on the doors. I

don't know when I stopped screaming or how I got to the railroad station, but I stood against the wall trying to tear off my dress and only knew I was doing it when two women stopped to stare at me. I began to have cramps in my stomach of a kind I had never known before. I went into the ladies' room and sat bent in a chair, whimpering with pain. After a while the cramps stopped, but I had an intimation, when I looked into the mirror, of something happening to me: my face was blotched, and there seemed to be circles and twirls I had never seen before, the straight blonde hair was damp with sweat, and a paste of green from the shrub had made lines on my jaw. I had gotten older.

Sometime during that early morning I half washed my dress, threw away my pants, put cold water on my hair. Later in the morning a cleaning woman appeared, and after a while began to ask questions that frightened me. When she put down her mop and went out of the room, I ran out of the station. I walked, I guess, for many hours, but when I saw a man on Canal Street who worked in Hannah's office, I realized that the sections of New Orleans that were known to me were dangerous for me.   8

Years before, when I was a small child, Sophronia and I would go to pick up, or try on, pretty embroidered dresses that were made for me by a colored dressmaker called Bibettera. A block up from Bibettera's there had been a large ruin of a house with a sign, ROOMS — CLEAN — CHEAP, and cheerful people seemed always to be moving in and out of the house. The door of the house was painted a bright pink. I liked that and would discuss with Sophronia why we didn't live in a house with a pink door.   9

Bibettera was long since dead, so I knew I was safe in this Negro neighborhood. I went up and down the block several times, praying that things would work and I could take my cramps to bed. I knocked on the pink door. It was answered immediately by a small young man.   10

I said, "Hello." He said nothing.   11

I said, "I would like to rent a room, please."   12

He closed the door but I waited, thinking he had gone to get the lady of the house. After a long time, a middle-aged woman put her head out of a second-floor window and said, "What you at?"   13

I said, "I would like to rent a room, please. My mama is a widow and has gone to work across the river. She gave me money and said to come here until she called for me."   14

"Who your mama?"   15

"Er. My mama."   16

"What you at? Speak out."   17

18   "I told you. I have money . . ." But as I tried to open my purse, the voice grew angry.

19   "This a nigger house. Get you off. *Vite.*"

20   I said, in a whisper, "I know. I'm part nigger."

21   The small young man opened the front door. He was laughing. "You part mischief. Get the hell out of here."

22   I said, "Please" — and then, "I'm related to Sophronia Mason. She told me to come. Ask her."

23   Sophronia and her family were respected figures in New Orleans Negro circles, and because I had some vague memory of her stately bow to somebody as she passed this house, I believed they knew her. If they told her about me I would be in trouble, but phones were not usual then in poor neighborhoods, and I had no other place to go.

24   The woman opened the door. Slowly I went into the hall.

25   I said, "I won't stay long. I have four dollars and Sophronia will give more if . . ."

26   The woman pointed up the stairs. She opened the door of a small room. "Washbasin place down the hall. Toilet place behind the kitchen. Two-fifty and no fuss, no bother."

27   I said, "Yes, ma'am, yes ma'am," but as she started to close the door, the young man appeared.

28   "Where your bag?"

29   "Bag?"

30   "Nobody put up here without no bag."

31   "Oh. You mean the bag with my clothes? It's at the station. I'll go and get it later . . ." I stopped because I knew I was about to say I'm sick, I'm in pain, I'm frightened.

32   He said, "I say you lie. I say you trouble. I say you get out."

33   I said, "And I say you shut up."

34   Years later, I was to understand why the command worked, and to be sorry that it did, but that day I was very happy when he turned and closed the door. I was asleep within minutes.

35   Toward evening, I went down the stairs, saw nobody, walked a few blocks and bought myself an oyster loaf. But the first bite made me feel sick, so I took my loaf back to the house. This time, as I climbed the steps, there were three women in the parlor, and they stopped talking when they saw me. I went back to sleep immediately, dizzy and nauseated.

36   I woke to a high, hot sun and my father standing at the foot of the bed staring at the oyster loaf.

37   He said, "Get up now and get dressed."

38   I was crying as I said, "Thank you, Papa, but I can't."

From the hall, Sophronia said, "Get along up now. *Vite*. The 39
morning is late."

My father left the room. I dressed and came into the hall carrying 40
my oyster loaf. Sophronia was standing at the head of the stairs. She
pointed out, meaning my father was on the street.

I said, "He humiliated me. He did. I won't . . ." 41

She said, "Get you going or I will never see you whenever again." 42

I ran past her to the street. I stood with my father until Sophronia 43
joined us, and then we walked slowly, without speaking, to the streetcar line. Sophronia bowed to us, but she refused my father's hand when
he attempted to help her into the car. I ran to the car meaning to ask
her to take me with her, but the car moved and she raised her hand as
if to stop me. My father and I walked again for a long time.

He pointed to a trash can sitting in front of a house. "Please put 44
that oyster loaf in the can."

At Vanalli's restaurant, he took my arm. "Hungry?" 45

I said, "No, thank you, Papa." 46

But we went through the door. It was, in those days, a New 47
Orleans custom to have an early black coffee, go to the office, and after
a few hours have a large breakfast at a restaurant. Vanalli's was
crowded, the headwaiter was so sorry, but after my father took him
aside, a very small table was put up for us — too small for my large
father, who was accommodating himself to it in a manner most unlike
him.

He said, "Jack, my rumpled daughter would like cold crayfish, a 48
nice piece of pompano, a separate bowl of Béarnaise sauce, don't ask
me why, French fried potatoes . . ."

I said, "Thank you, Papa, but I am not hungry. I don't want to be 49
here."

My father waved the waiter away and we sat in silence until the 50
crayfish came. My hand reached out instinctively and then drew back.

My father said, "Your mother and I have had an awful time." 51

I said, "I'm sorry about that. But I don't want to go home, Papa." 52

He said, angrily, "Yes, you do. But you want me to apologize first. 53
I do apologize but you should not have made me say it."

After a while I mumbled, "God forgive me, Papa forgive me, 54
Mama forgive me, Sophronia, Jenny, Hannah . . ."

"Eat your crayfish." 55

I ate everything he had ordered and then a small steak. I suppose 56
I had been mumbling throughout my breakfast.

My father said, "You're talking to yourself. I can't hear you. What 57
are you saying?"

58   "God forgive me, Papa forgive me, Mama forgive me, Sophronia, Jenny . . ."

59   My father said, "Where do we start your training as the first Jewish nun on Prytania Street?"

60   When I finished laughing, I liked him again. I said, "Papa, I'll tell you a secret. I've had very bad cramps and I am beginning to bleed. I'm changing life."

61   He stared at me for a while. Then he said, "Well, it's not the way it's usually described, but it's accurate, I guess. Let's go home now to your mother."

62   We were never, as long as my mother and father lived, to mention that time again. But it was of great importance to them and I've thought about it all my life. From that day on I knew my power over my parents. That was not to be too important: I was ashamed of it and did not abuse it too much. But I found out something more useful and more dangerous: if you are willing to take the punishment, you are halfway through the battle. That the issue may be trivial, the battle ugly, is another point.

_____ CONSIDERATIONS _____

1. Hellman's recollection of running away at fourteen is complicated by her refusal to tell it in strict chronology. Instead, she interrupts the narrative with flashbacks and episodes of later years. How can one justify such interruptions?

2. On page 182, as she is trying to talk her way into the rooming house in the black district, Hellman tells a young man to shut up and then adds, "Years later, I was to understand why the command worked, and to be sorry that it did." What did she later understand?

3. What was the "power over my parents" that Hellman learned from her runaway experience? Do you have such a power?

4. Accounts of childhood escapades often suffer as the author idealizes or glamorizes them. Does Hellman successfully resist the temptation? What is your evidence?

5. The bases the fourteen-year-old runaway touched in her flight were actually part of a familiar world: a doll's house, a cathedral, a market, a railroad station. How then does Hellman give her flight more than a touch of horror?

6. In what specific ways did her first menstrual period heighten and distort some of the things that happened — or seemed to happen — to the fourteen-year-old runaway? Discuss the ways in which physiological and psychological conditions seem to feed upon each other.

Ernest Hemingway (1899–1961) was an ambulance driver and a soldier in World War I, and made use of these experiences in his novel, A Farewell to Arms *(1929). One of the Lost Generation of expatriate American writers who lived in Paris in the twenties — a time described in his memoir,* A Moveable Feast *(1964) — he was a great prose stylist and innovator, who received a Nobel Prize for Literature in 1954. Other Hemingway novels include* The Sun Also Rises *(1926),* To Have and Have Not *(1937), and* For Whom the Bell Tolls *(1940).*

Many critics prefer Hemingway's short stories to his novels, and his early stories — "Hills Like White Elephants" among them — to his later ones. This early prose is plain, simple, and clean. In this story, pages of dialogue virtually without narrative — or description or subjective interpretation — give us two characters in the wholeness of themselves.

33

ERNEST HEMINGWAY
Hills Like White Elephants

The hills across the valley of the Ebro were long and white. On this side there was no shade and no trees and the station was between two lines of rails in the sun. Close against the side of the station there was the warm shadow of the building and a curtain, made of strings of bamboo beads, hung across the open door into the bar, to keep out flies. The American and the girl with him sat at a table in the shade, outside the building. It was very hot and the express from Barcelona would come in forty minutes. It stopped at this junction for two minutes and went on to Madrid.

"What should we drink?" the girl asked. She had taken off her hat and put it on the table.

"It's pretty hot," the man said.

"Let's drink beer."

"Dos cervezas," the man said into the curtain.

"Big ones?" a woman asked from the doorway.

"Yes. Two big ones."

The woman brought two glasses of beer and two felt pads. She put the felt pads and the beer glasses on the table and looked at the man and the girl. The girl was looking off at the line of hills. They were white in the sun and the country was brown and dry.

"They look like white elephants," she said.

"I've never seen one." The man drank his beer.

"No, you wouldn't have."

"I might have," the man said. "Just because you say I wouldn't have doesn't prove anything."

The girl looked at the bead curtain. "They've painted something on it," she said. "What does it say?"

"Anis del Toro. It's a drink."

"Could we try it?"

The man called "Listen" through the curtain.

The woman came out from the bar.

"Four reales."

"We want two Anis del Toros."

"With water?"

"Do you want it with water?"

"I don't know," the girl said. "Is it good with water?"

"It's all right."

"You want them with water?" asked the woman.

"Yes, with water."

"It tastes like licorice," the girl said and put the glass down.

"That's the way with everything."

"Yes," said the girl. "Everything tastes of licorice. Especially all the things you've waited so long for, like absinthe."

"Oh, cut it out."

"You started it," the girl said. "I was being amused. I was having a fine time."

"Well, let's try and have a fine time."

"All right. I was trying. I said the mountains looked like white elephants. Wasn't that bright?"

"That was bright."

"I wanted to try this new drink. That's all we do, isn't it — look at things and try new drinks?"

"I guess so."

The girl looked across at the hills.

"They're lovely hills," she said. "They don't really look like white elephants. I just meant the colouring of their skin through the trees."

"Should we have another drink?"

"All right."

The warm wind blew the bead curtain against the table.

"The beer's nice and cool," the man said.

"It's lovely," the girl said.

"It's really an awfully simple operation, Jig," the man said. "It's not really an operation at all."

The girl looked at the ground the table legs rested on.

"I know you wouldn't mind it, Jig. It's really not anything. It's just to let the air in."

The girl did not say anything.

"I'll go with you and I'll stay with you all the time. They just let the air in and then it's all perfectly natural."

"Then what will we do afterwards?"

"We'll be fine afterwards. Just like we were before."

"What makes you think so?"

"That's the only thing that bothers us. It's the only thing that's made us unhappy."

The girl looked at the bead curtain, put her hand out and took hold of two of the strings of beads.

"And you think then we'll be all right and be happy."

"I know we will. You don't have to be afraid. I've known lots of people that have done it."

"So have I," said the girl. "And afterward they were all so happy."

"Well," the man said, "if you don't want to you don't have to. I wouldn't have you do it if you didn't want to. But I know it's perfectly simple."

"And you really want to?"

"I think it's the best thing to do. But I don't want you to do it if you don't really want to."

"And if I do it you'll be happy and things will be like they were and you'll love me?"

"I love you now. You know I love you."

"I know. But if I do it, then it will be nice again if I say things are like white elephants, and you'll like it?"

"I'll love it. I love it now but I just can't think about it. You know how I get when I worry."

"If I do it you won't ever worry?"

"I won't worry about that because it's perfectly simple."

"Then I'll do it. Because I don't care about me."

"What do you mean?"

"I don't care about me."

"Well, I care about you."

"Oh, yes. But I don't care about me. And I'll do it and then everything will be fine."

"I don't want you to do it if you feel that way."

The girl stood up and walked to the end of the station. Across, on the other side, were fields of grain and trees along the banks of the Ebro. Far away, beyond the river, were mountains. The shadow of a cloud moved across the field of grain and she saw the river through the trees.

"And we could have all this," she said. "And we could have everything and every day we make it more impossible."

"What did you say?"

"I said we could have everything."

"We can have everything."

"No, we can't,"

"We can have the whole world."

"No, we can't."

"We can go everywhere."

"No, we can't. It isn't ours any more."

"It's ours."

"No, it isn't. And once they take it away, you never get it back."

"But they haven't taken it away."

"We'll wait and see."

"Come on back in the shade," he said. "You mustn't feel that way."

"I don't feel any way," the girl said. "I just know things."

"I don't want you to do anything that you don't want to do — "

"Nor that isn't good for me," she said. "I know. Could we have another beer?"

"All right. But you've got to realize — "

"I realize," the girl said. "Can't we maybe stop talking?"

They sat down at the table and the girl looked across at the hills on the dry side of the valley and the man looked at her and at the table.

"You've got to realize," he said, "that I don't want you to do it if you don't want to. I'm perfectly willing to go through with it if it means anything to you."

"Doesn't it mean anything to you? We could get along."

"Of course it does. But I don't want anybody but you. I don't want anyone else. And I know it's perfectly simple."

"Yes, you know it's perfectly simple."

"It's all right for you to say that, but I do know it."

"Would you do something for me now?"

"I'd do anything for you."

"Would you please please please please please please please stop talking?"

He did not say anything but looked at the bags against the wall of the station. There were labels on them from all the hotels where they had spent nights.

"But I don't want you to," he said, "I don't care anything about it."

"I'll scream," the girl said.

The woman came out through the curtains with two glasses of beer and put them down on the damp felt pads. "The train comes in five minutes," she said.

"What did she say?" asked the girl.

"That the train is coming in five minutes."

The girl smiled brightly at the woman, to thank her.

"I'd better take the bags over to the other side of the station," the man said. She smiled at him.

"All right. Then come back and we'll finish the beer."

He picked up the two heavy bags and carried them around the station to the other tracks. He looked up the tracks but could not see the train. Coming back, he walked through the bar-room, where people waiting for the train were drinking. He drank an Anis at the bar and looked at the people. They were all waiting reasonably for the train. He went out through the bead curtain. She was sitting at the table and smiled at him.

"Do you feel better?" he asked.

"I feel fine," she said. "There's nothing wrong with me. I feel fine."

_____ CONSIDERATIONS _____

1. Nearly all of Hemingway's story is dialogue, often without identifying phrases such as "he said" or "she said." Does the lack of these phrases make it difficult to decide which character is speaking? What, if anything, does Hemingway do to make up for missing dialogue tags? Compare his practice with the way other short story writers in this book handle dialogue.

2. If you have ever questioned the common statement that writers must pay careful attention to *every* word they use, spend a little time examining the way Hemingway uses "it," beginning where the couple start talking about the operation. Try to determine the various possible antecedents for that neutral pronoun in each context where it occurs. Such an effort may help you discover one reason why Hemingway's spare, almost skeletal, style is so powerful.

3. Try to put the central conflict of this story in your own words. Imagine yourself the writer suddenly getting the idea for this story and quickly writing a sentence or two to record the idea in your journal. See F. Scott Fitzgerald's journal, pages 169–171, for an example.

4. Why is Hemingway *not* explicit about the kind of operation the two characters are discussing? Is he simply trying to mystify the reader? Does understanding this help you understand other stories or poems that seem difficult at first?

5. Does the place itself (as represented in brief descriptive passages) contribute to the point of the story?

6. Why does Hemingway refuse to describe the two characters? From what the story offers, what do you know about them?

7. Hemingway's story was written in the 1920s. Have the questions he raises about the operation been resolved since then?

*Richard Hofstadter (1916–1970) was a historian who taught at
Columbia University. In 1956 he won a Pulitzer Prize for his book,*
The Age of Reform; *in 1964 he won another for* Anti-Intellectual-
ism in American Life, *from which we take this essay. Behind
Hofstadter's reasoning, behind the clear objectivity of definitions,
this writing defends a choice of life with passionate conviction.*

34

RICHARD HOFSTADTER
Intellect and Intelligence

Before attempting to estimate the qualities in our society that   1
make intellect unpopular, it seems necessary to say something about
what intellect is usually understood to be. When one hopes to understand a common prejudice, common usage provides a good place to
begin. Anyone who scans popular American writing with this interest
in mind will be struck by the manifest difference between the idea of
intellect and the idea of intelligence. The first is frequently used as a
kind of epithet, the second never. No one questions the value of intelligence; as an abstract quality it is universally esteemed, and individuals who seem to have it in exceptional degree are highly regarded.
The man of intelligence is always praised; the man of intellect is sometimes also praised, especially when it is believed that intellect involves
intelligence, but he is also often looked upon with resentment or suspicion. It is he, and not the intelligent man, who may be called unre-

liable, superfluous, immoral, or subversive; sometimes he is even said to be, for all his intellect, unintelligent.[1]

2   Although the difference between the qualities of intelligence and intellect is more often assumed than defined, the context of popular usage makes it possible to extract the nub of the distinction, which seems to be almost universally understood: intelligence is an excellence of mind that is employed within a fairly narrow, immediate, and predictable range; it is a manipulative, adjustive, unfailingly practical quality — one of the most eminent and endearing of the animal virtues. Intelligence works within the framework of limited but clearly stated goals, and may be quick to shear away questions of thought that do not seem to help in reaching them. Finally, it is of such universal use that it can daily be seen at work and admired alike by simple or complex minds.

3   Intellect, on the other hand, is the critical, creative, and contemplative side of mind. Whereas intelligence seeks to grasp, manipulate, reorder, adjust, intellect examines, ponders, wonders, theorizes, criticizes, imagines. Intelligence will seize the immediate meaning in a situation and evaluate it. Intellect evaluates evaluations, and looks for the meanings of situations as a whole. Intelligence can be praised as a quality in animals; intellect, being a unique manifestation of human dignity, is both praised and assailed as a quality in men. When the difference is so defined, it becomes easier to understand why we sometimes say that a mind of admittedly penetrating intelligence is relatively unintellectual; and why, by the same token, we see among minds that are unmistakably intellectual a considerable range of intelligence.

4   This distinction may seem excessively abstract, but it is frequently illustrated in American culture. In our education, for example, it has never been doubted that the selection and development of intelligence is a goal of central importance; but the extent to which education should foster intellect has been a matter of the most heated controversy, and the opponents of intellect in most spheres of public education have exercised preponderant power. But perhaps the most

[1] I do not want to suggest that this distinction is made only in the United States, since it seems to be common wherever there is a class that finds intellectuals a nuisance and yet does not want to throw overboard its own claims to intelligence. Thus, in France, after the intellectuals had emerged as a kind of social force, one finds Maurice Barrès writing in 1902: "I'd rather be intelligent than an intellectual." Victor Brombert: *The Intellectual Hero: Studies in the French Novel, 1880–1955* (Philadelphia, 1961), p. 25.

impressive illustration arises from a comparison of the American regard for inventive skill as opposed to skill in pure science. Our greatest inventive genius, Thomas A. Edison, was all but canonized by the American public, and a legend has been built around him. One cannot, I suppose, expect that achievements in pure science would receive the same public applause that came to inventions as spectacular and as directly influential on ordinary life as Edison's, But one might have expected that our greatest genius in pure science, Josiah Willard Gibbs, who laid the theoretical foundations for modern physical chemistry, would have been a figure of some comparable acclaim among the educated public. Yet Gibbs, whose work was celebrated in Europe, lived out his life in public and even professional obscurity at Yale, where he taught for thirty-two years. Yale, which led American universities in its scientific achievements during the nineteenth century, was unable in those thirty-two years to provide him with more than a half dozen or so graduate students who could understand his work, and never took the trouble to award him an honorary degree.[2]

A special difficulty arises when we speak of the fate of intellect 5 in society; this difficulty stems from the fact that we are compelled to speak of intellect in vocational terms, though we may recognize that intellect is not simply a matter of vocation. Intellect is considered in general usage to be an attribute of certain professions and vocations; we speak of the intellectual as being a writer or a critic, a professor or a scientist, an editor, journalist, lawyer, clergyman, or the like. As Jacques Barzun has said, the intellectual is a man who carries a brief case. It is hardly possible to dispense with this convenience; the status and the role of intellectuals are bound up with the aggregate of the brief-case-carrying professions. But few of us believe that a member of a profession, even a learned profession, is necessarily an intellectual in any discriminating or demanding sense of the word. In most professions intellect may help, but intelligence will serve well enough without it. We know, for instance, that all academic men are not intellectuals; we often lament this fact. We know that there is something about intellect, as opposed to professionally trained intelligence, which does not adhere to whole vocations but only to persons. And when we are troubled about the position of intellect and the intellec-

[2] The situation of Gibbs is often mentioned as a consequence of American attitudes. For the general situation it symbolized, see Richard H. Shryock: "American Indifference to Basic Science during the Nineteenth Century," *Archives Internationales d'Histoire des Sciences*, No. 5 (1948), pp. 50–65.

tual class in our society, it is not only the status of certain vocational groups which we have in mind, but the value attached to a certain mental quality.

6   A great deal of what might be called the journeyman's work of our culture — the work of lawyers, editors, engineers, doctors, indeed of some writers and of most professors — though vitally dependent upon ideas, is not distinctively intellectual. A man in any of the learned or quasi-learned professions must have command of a substantial store of frozen ideas to do his work; he must, if he does it well, use them intelligently; but in his professional capacity he uses them mainly as instruments. The heart of the matter — to borrow a distinction made by Max Weber about politics — is that the professional man lives *off* ideas, not *for* them. His professional role, his professional skills, do not make him an intellectual. He is a mental worker, a technician. He may *happen* to be an intellectual as well, but if he is, it is because he brings to his profession a distinctive feeling about ideas which is not required by his job. As a professional, he has acquired a stock of mental skills that are for sale. The skills are highly developed, but we do not think of him as being an intellectual if certain qualities are missing from his work — disinterested intelligence, generalizing power, free speculation, fresh observation, creative novelty, radical criticism. At home he may happen to be an intellectual, but at his job he is a hired mental technician who uses his mind for the pursuit of externally determined ends. It is this element — the fact that ends are set from some interest or vantage point outside the intellectual process itself — which characterizes both the zealot, who lives obsessively for a single idea, and the mental technician, whose mind is used not for free speculation but for a salable end. The goal here is external and not self-determined, whereas the intellectual life has a certain spontaneous character and inner determination. It has also a peculiar poise of its own, which I believe is established by a balance between two basic qualities in the intellectual's attitude toward ideas — qualities that may be designated as playfulness and piety.

7   To define what is distinctively intellectual it is necessary to be able to determine what differentiates, say, a professor or a lawyer who is an intellectual from one who is not; or perhaps more properly, what enables us to say that at one moment a professor or a lawyer is acting in a purely routine professional fashion and at another moment as an intellectual. The difference is not in the character of the ideas with which he works but in his attitude toward them. I have suggested that in some sense he lives for ideas — which means that he has a sense of

dedication to the life of the mind which is very much like a religious commitment. This is not surprising, for in a very important way the role of the intellectual is inherited from the office of the cleric: it implies a special sense of the ultimate value in existence of the act of comprehension. Socrates, when he said that the unexamined life is not worth living, struck the essence of it. We can hear the voice of various intellectuals in history repeating their awareness of this feeling, in accents suitable to time, place, and culture. "The proper function of the human race, taken in the aggregate," wrote Dante in *De Monar-chia,* "is to actualize continually the entire capacity possible to the intellect, primarily in speculation, then through its extension and for its sake, secondarily in action." The noblest thing, and the closest possible to divinity, is thus the act of knowing. It is only a somewhat more secular and activist version of the same commitments which we hear in the first sentence of Locke's *Essay Concerning Human Under-standing:* "It is the *Understanding* that sets man above the rest of sensible beings, and gives him all the advantage and dominion which he has over them." Hawthorne, in a passage near the end of *The Blithedale Romance,* observes that Nature's highest purpose for man is "that of conscious intellectual life and sensibility." Finally, in our own time André Malraux puts the question in one of his novels: "How can one make the best of one's life?" and answers: "By converting as wide a range of experience as possible into conscious thought."

Intellectualism, though by no means confined to doubters, is   8 often the sole piety of the skeptic. Some years ago a colleague asked me to read a brief essay he had written for students going on to do advanced work in his field. Its ostensible purpose was to show how the life of the mind could be cultivated within the framework of his own discipline, but its effect was to give an intensely personal expression to his dedication to intellectual work. Although it was written by a corrosively skeptical mind, I felt that I was reading a piece of devotional literature in some ways comparable to Richard Steele's *The Tradesman's Calling* or Cotton Mather's *Essays to Do Good,* for in it the intellectual task had been conceived as *calling,* much in the fashion of the old Protestant writers. His work was undertaken as a kind of devotional exercise, a personal discipline, and to think of it in this fashion was possible because it was more than merely workmanlike and professional: it was work at thinking, work done supposedly in the service of truth. The intellectual life has here taken on a kind of primary moral significance. It is this aspect of the intellectual's feeling about ideas that I call his piety. The intellectual is *engagé* — he is pledged, committed, enlisted. What everyone else is willing to admit, namely that ideas and abstractions are of signal importance in human life, he imperatively feels.

9   Of course what is involved is more than a purely personal discipline and more than the life of contemplation and understanding itself. For the life of thought, even though it may be regarded as the highest form of human activity, is also a medium through which other values are refined, reasserted, and realized in the human community. Collectively, intellectuals have often tried to serve as the moral antennae of the race, anticipating and if possible clarifying fundamental moral issues before these have forced themselves upon the public consciousness. The thinker feels that he ought to be the special custodian of values like reason and justice which are related to his own search for truth, and at times he strikes out passionately as a public figure because his very identity seems to be threatened by some gross abuse. One thinks here of Voltaire defending the Calas family, of Zola speaking out for Dreyfus, of the American intellectuals outraged at the trial of Sacco and Vanzetti.

10   It would be unfortunate if intellectuals were alone in their concern for these values, and it is true that their enthusiasm has at times miscarried. But it is also true that intellectuals are properly more responsive to such values than others; and it is the historic glory of the intellectual class of the West in modern times that, of all the classes which could be called in any sense privileged, it has shown the largest and most consistent concern for the well-being of the classes which lie below it in the social scale. Behind the intellectual's feeling of commitment is the belief that in some measure the world should be made responsive to his capacity for rationality, his passion for justice and order: out of this conviction arises much of his value to mankind and, equally, much of his ability to do mischief.

___ CONSIDERATIONS _____

1. In his opening paragraphs, Hofstadter seems to follow the advice of Robert Gorham Davis by defining his terms (see pages 115–125). By the end of Paragraph 3, has Hofstadter succeeded in distinguishing between the two words?

2. Would Loren Eiseley (pages 140–146) agree with Hofstadter on the nature of intelligence?

3. Some commentators on our society have described the 1960s and 1970s as a period of neoromanticism that depreciates the intellect in favor of

the emotions. If you were neoromantic, how would you answer the authorities cited by Hofstadter in Paragraph 7?

4. The author says that an intellectual "has a sense of dedication to the life of the mind which is very much like a religious commitment." Is there a contradiction built into that statement? A paradox? An irony?

5. Does Hofstadter acknowledge negative as well as positive characteristics of intellectuals. Should he?

35

LANGSTON HUGHES
Salvation

1   I was saved from sin when I was going on thirteen. But not really saved. It happened like this. There was a big revival at my Auntie Reed's church. Every night for weeks there had been much preaching, singing, praying, and shouting, and some very hardened sinners had been brought to Christ, and the membership of the church had grown by leaps and bounds. Then just before the revival ended, they held a special meeting for children, "to bring the young lambs to the fold." My aunt spoke of it for days ahead. That night I was escorted to the front row and placed on the mourners' bench with all the other young sinners, who had not yet been brought to Jesus.

2   My aunt told me that when you were saved you saw a light, and something happened to you inside! And Jesus came into your life! And God was with you from then on! She said you could see and hear and feel Jesus in your soul. I believed her. I had heard a great many old people say the same thing and it seemed to me they ought to know. So

I sat there calmly in the hot, crowded church, waiting for Jesus to come to me.

The preacher preached a wonderful rhythmical sermon, all moans and shouts and lonely cries and dire pictures of hell, and then he sang a song about the ninety and nine safe in the fold, but one little lamb was left out in the cold. Then he said: "Won't you come? Won't you come to Jesus? Young lambs, won't you come?" And he held out his arms to all us young sinners there on the mourners' bench. And the little girls cried. And some of them jumped up and went to Jesus right away. But most of us just sat there.   3

A great many old people came and knelt around us and prayed, old women with jet-black faces and braided hair, old men with work-gnarled hands. And the church sang a song about the lower lights are burning, some poor sinners to be saved. And the whole building rocked with prayer and song.   4

Still I kept waiting to *see* Jesus.   5

Finally all the young people had gone to the altar and were saved, but one boy and me. He was a rounder's son named Westley. Westley and I were surrounded by sisters and deacons praying. It was very hot in the church, and getting late now. Finally Westley said to me in a whisper: "God damn! I'm tired o' sitting here. Let's get up and be saved." So he got up and was saved.   6

Then I was left all alone on the mourners' bench. My aunt came and knelt at my knees and cried, while prayers and songs swirled all around me in the little church. The whole congregation prayed for me alone, in a mighty wail of moans and voices. And I kept waiting serenely for Jesus, waiting, waiting — but he didn't come. I wanted to see him, but nothing happened to me. Nothing! I wanted something to happen to me, but nothing happened.   7

I heard the songs and the minister saying: "Why don't you come? My dear child, why don't you come to Jesus? Jesus is waiting for you. He wants you. Why don't you come? Sister Reed, what is this child's name?"   8

"Langston," my aunt sobbed.   9

"Langston, why don't you come? Why don't you come and be saved? Oh, Lamb of God! Why don't you come?"   10

Now it was really getting late. I began to be ashamed of myself, holding everything up so long. I began to wonder what God thought about Westley, who certainly hadn't seen Jesus either, but who was now sitting proudly on the platform, swinging his knickerbockered legs and grinning down at me, surrounded by deacons and old women   11 on their knees praying. God had not struck Westley dead for taking his name in vain or for lying in the temple. So I decided that maybe to save further trouble, I'd better lie, too, and say that Jesus had come, and get up and be saved.

12   So I got up.

13   Suddenly the whole room broke into a sea of shouting, as they saw me rise. Waves of rejoicing swept the place. Women leaped in the air. My aunt threw her arms around me. The minister took me by the hand and led me to the platform.

14   When things quieted down, in a hushed silence, punctuated by a few ecstatic "Amens," all the new young lambs were blessed in the name of God. Then joyous singing filled the room.

15   That night, for the last time in my life but one — for I was a big boy twelve years old — I cried. I cried, in bed alone, and couldn't stop. I buried my head under the quilts, but my aunt heard me. She woke up and told my uncle I was crying because the Holy Ghost had come into my life, and because I had seen Jesus. But I was really crying because I couldn't bear to tell her that I had lied, that I had deceived everybody in the church, and I hadn't seen Jesus, and that now I didn't believe there was a Jesus any more, since he didn't come to help me.

_____ **CONSIDERATIONS** _____

1. Hughes tells this critical episode of his childhood in a simple, straightforward, unelaborated fashion, almost as though he were still a child telling the story as it happened. Why is it necessary to say *"almost* as though he were still a child"? Compare this account with Walter White's version of an equally important event in his childhood (pages 449–454). Do the two writers remember differently? How would you go about recounting a critical moment in your own childhood? Where does simple childhood memory stop and adult judgment take over?

2. Hughes's disillusionment is an example of what people call "an initiation story." Compare it with the Ernest Hemingway short story (pages 185–189), or John Updike's story (pages 419–427), or the autobiographical essay by Lillian Hellman (pages 178–184). Discuss the *degrees* of awareness noticeable among these varied characters.

3. Why was it so important to the congregation of Auntie Reed's church that everyone, children included, acknowledge that they were saved?

4. Why did Westley finally proclaim that he had been saved?

5. In his final paragraph, Hughes writes, "That night, for the last time in my life but one . . . I cried." He does not tell us, in this account, what that other time was. Read a little more of his life, or simply use your imagination, and write a brief account of the other time.

Aldous Huxley (1894–1963) was an English novelist, essayist, and poet, the grandson of Thomas Henry Huxley (Victorian biologist and writer, leading public advocate of Darwin's theory of evolution), grandnephew of Matthew Arnold (see page 22), and brother of Julian Huxley (another distinguished scientist and essayist.) He is best known for his novels, Point Counter Point *(1928) and* Brave New World, *an anti-utopia published in 1932. He lived in California the last twenty-five years of his life, where he pursued an interest in mysticism, and in hallucinogens like peyote and mescaline. He died on November 22, 1963 — with the result that few Americans read his obituary.*

When he was younger, Huxley was acquainted with D. H. Lawrence — and was Lawrence's opposite. Superbly educated, possessed by knowledge and intellect, at his best Huxley organized his historical intelligence into brilliant essays like this one.

36

ALDOUS HUXLEY
Comfort

NOVELTY OF THE PHENOMENON

French hotel-keepers call it *Le confort moderne,* and they are   1
right. For comfort is a thing of recent growth, younger than steam, a
child when telegraphy was born, only a generation older than radio.
The invention of the means of being comfortable and the pursuit of
comfort as a desirable end — one of the most desirable that human
beings can propose to themselves — are modern phenomena, unparal-
leled in history since the time of the Romans. Like all phenomena

with which we are extremely familiar, we take them for granted, as a fish takes the water in which it lives, not realizing the oddity and novelty of them, not bothering to consider their significance. The padded chair, the well-sprung bed, the sofa, central heating, and the regular hot bath — these and a host of other comforts enter into the daily lives of even the most moderately prosperous of the Anglo-Saxon bourgeoisie. Three hundred years ago they were unknown to the greatest kings. This is a curious fact which deserves to be examined and analyzed.

2   The first thing that strikes one about the discomfort in which our ancestors lived is that it was mainly voluntary. Some of the apparatus of modern comfort is of purely modern invention; people could not put rubber tyres on their carriages before the discovery of South America and the rubber plant. But for the most part there is nothing new about the material basis of our comfort. Men could have made sofas and smoking-room chairs, could have installed bathrooms and central heating and sanitary plumbing any time during the last three or four thousand years. And as a matter of fact, at certain periods they did indulge themselves in these comforts. Two thousand years before Christ, the inhabitants of Cnossos were familiar with sanitary plumbing. The Romans had invented an elaborate system of hot-air heating, and the bathing facilities in a smart Roman villa were luxurious and complete beyond the dreams of the modern man. There were sweating-rooms, massage-rooms, cold plunges, tepid drying-rooms with (if we may believe Sidonius Apollinaris) improper frescoes on the walls and comfortable couches where you could lie and get dry and talk to your friends. As for the public baths they were almost inconceivably luxurious. "To such a height of luxury have we reached," said Seneca, "that we are dissatisfied if, in our baths, we do not tread on gems." The size and completeness of the thermae was proportionable to their splendour. A single room of the baths of Diocletian has been transformed into a large church.

3   It would be possible to adduce many other examples showing what could be done with the limited means at our ancestors' disposal in the way of making life comfortable. They show sufficiently clearly that if the men of the Middle Ages and early modern epoch lived in filth and discomfort, it was not for any lack or ability to change their mode of life; it was because they chose to live in this way, because filth and discomfort fitted in with their principles and prejudices, political, moral, and religious.

COMFORT AND THE SPIRITUAL LIFE

What have comfort and cleanliness to do with politics, morals, 4
and religion? At a first glance one would say that there was and could
be no causal connection between armchairs and democracies, sofas
and the relaxation of the family system, hot baths and the decay of
Christian orthodoxy. But look more closely and you will discover that
there exists the closest connection between the recent growth of comfort and the recent history of ideas. I hope in this essay to make that
connection manifest, to show why it was not possible (not materially,
but psychologically impossible) for the Italian princes of the quatro-
cento, for the Elizabethan, even for Louis xiv to live in what the
Romans would have called common cleanliness and decency, or enjoy
what would be to us indispensable comforts.

Let us begin with the consideration of armchairs and central heat- 5
ing. These, I propose to show, only became possible with the breakdown of monarchical and feudal power and the decay of the old family
and social hierarchies. Smoking-room chairs and sofas exist to be lolled
in. In a well-made modern armchair you cannot do anything but loll.
Now, lolling is neither dignified nor respectful. When we wish to
appear impressive, when we have to administer a rebuke to an inferior,
we do not lie in a deep chair with our feet on the mantel-piece; we sit
up and try to look majestical. Similarly, when we wish to be polite to
a lady or show respect to the old or eminent, we cease to loll; we stand,
or at least we straighten ourselves up. Now, in the past human society
was a hierarchy in which every man was always engaged in being
impressive towards his inferiors or respectful to those above him. Lolling in such societies was utterly impossible. It was as much out of the
question for Louis xiv to loll in the presence of his courtiers as it was
for them to loll in the presence of their king. It was only when he
attended a session of the Parlement that the King of France ever lolled
in public. On these occasions he reclined in the Bed of Justice, while
princes sat, the great officers of the crown stood, and the smaller fry
knelt. Comfort was proclaimed as the appanage of royalty. Only the
king might stretch his legs. We may feel sure, however, that he
stretched them in a very majestic manner. The lolling was purely
ceremonial and accompanied by no loss of dignity. At ordinary times
the king was seated, it is true, but seated in a dignified and upright
position; the appearance of majesty had to be kept up. (For, after all,
majesty is mainly a question of majestical appearance.) The courtiers,

meanwhile, kept up the appearances of deference, either standing, or else, if their rank was very high and their blood peculiarly blue, sitting, even in the royal presence, on stools. What was true of the king's court was true of the nobleman's household; and the squire was to his dependents, the merchant was to his apprentices and servants, what the monarch was to his courtiers. In all cases the superior had to express his superiority by being dignified, the inferior his inferiority by being deferential; there could be no lolling. Even in the intimacies of family life it was the same: the parents ruled like popes and princes, by divine right; the children were their subjects. Our fathers took the fifth commandment very seriously — how seriously may be judged from the fact that during the great Calvin's theocratic rule of Geneva a child was publicly decapitated for having ventured to strike its parents. Lolling on the part of children, though not perhaps a capital offence, would have been regarded as an act of the grossest disrespect, punishable by much flagellation, starving, and confinement. For a slighter insult — neglect to touch his cap — Vespasiano Gonzaga kicked his only son to death; one shudders to think what he might have been provoked to do if the boy had lolled. If the children might not loll in the presence of their parents, neither might the parents loll in the presence of their children, for fear of demeaning themselves in the eyes of those whose duty it was to honour them. Thus we see that in the European society of two or three hundred years ago it was impossible for any one — from the Holy Roman Emperor and the King of France down to the poorest beggar, from the bearded patriarch to the baby — to loll in the presence of any one else. Old furniture reflects the physical habits of the hierarchical society for which it was made. It was in the power of mediaeval and renaissance craftsmen to create armchairs and sofas that might have rivalled in comfort those of to-day. But society being what, in fact, it was, they did nothing of the kind. It was not, indeed, until the sixteenth century that chairs became at all common. Before that time a chair was a symbol of authority. Committee-men now loll. Members of Parliament are comfortably seated, but authority still belongs to a Chairman, still issues from a symbolical Chair. In the Middle Ages only the great had chairs. When a great man travelled, he took his chair with him, so that he might never be seen detached from the outward and visible sign of his authority. To this day the Throne no less than the Crown is the symbol of royalty. In mediaeval times the vulgar sat, whenever it was permissible for them to sit, on benches, stools, and settles. With the rise, during the Renaissance period, of a rich and independent bourgeoisie, chairs began to be more freely used.

Those who could afford chairs sat in them, but sat with dignity and discomfort; for the chairs of the sixteenth century were still very throne-like, and imposed upon those who sat in them a painfully majestic attitude. It was only in the eighteenth century, when the old hierarchies were seriously breaking up, that furniture began to be comfortable. And even then there was no real lolling. Armchairs and sofas on which men (and, later, women) might indecorously sprawl, were not made until democracy was firmly established, the middle classes enlarged to gigantic proportions, good manners lost from out of the world, women emancipated, and family restraints dissolved.

CENTRAL HEATING
AND THE FEUDAL SYSTEM

Another essential component of modern comfort — the adequate   6
heating of houses — was made impossible, at least for the great ones
of the earth, by the political structure of ancient societies. Plebeians
were more fortunate in this respect than nobles. Living in small
houses, they were able to keep warm. But the nobleman, the prince,
the king, and the cardinal inhabited palaces of a grandeur corresponding with their social position. In order to prove that they were greater
than other men, they had to live in surroundings considerably more
than life-size. They received their guests in vast halls like roller-skat-
ing rinks; they marched in solemn processions along galleries as long
and as draughty as Alpine tunnels, up and down triumphal staircases
that looked like the cataracts of the Nile frozen into marble. Being
what he was, a great man in those days had to spend a great deal of his
time in performing solemn symbolical charades and pompous ballets
— performances which required a lot of room to accommodate the
numerous actors and spectators. This explains the enormous dimensions of royal and princely palaces, even of the houses of ordinary
landed gentlemen. They owed it to their position to live, as though
they were giants, in rooms a hundred feet long and thirty high. How
splendid, how magnificent! But oh, how bleak! In our days the self-
made great are not expected to keep up their position in the splendid
style of those who were great by divine right. Sacrificing grandiosity to
comfort, they live in rooms small enough to be heated. (And so, when
they were off duty, did the great in the past; most old palaces contain
a series of tiny apartments to which their owners retired when the
charades of state were over. But the charades were long-drawn affairs,

and the unhappy princes of old days had to spend a great deal of time being magnificent in icy audience-chambers and among the whistling draughts of interminable galleries.) Driving in the environs of Chicago, I was shown the house of a man who was reputed to be one of the richest and most influential of the city. It was a medium-sized house of perhaps fifteen or twenty smallish rooms. I looked at it in astonishment, thinking of the vast palaces in which I myself have lived in Italy (for considerably less rent than one would have to pay for garaging a Ford in Chicago). I remembered the rows of bedrooms as big as ordinary ballrooms, the drawing-rooms like railway stations, the staircase on which you could drive a couple of limousines abreast. Noble *palazzi,* where one has room to feel oneself a superman! But remembering also those terrible winds that blow in February from the Apennines, I was inclined to think that the rich man of Chicago had done well in sacrificing the magnificences on which his counterpart in another age and country would have spent his riches.

BATHS AND MORALS

7   It is to the decay of monarchy, aristocracy, and ancient social hierarchy that we owe the two components of modern comfort hitherto discussed; the third great component — the bath — must, I think, be attributed, at any rate in part, to the decay of Christian morals. There are still on the continent of Europe, and for all I know, elsewhere, convent schools in which young ladies are brought up to believe that human bodies are objects of so impure and obscene a character that it is sinful for them to see, not merely other people's nakedness, but even their own. Baths, when they are permitted to take them (every alternate Saturday) must be taken in a chemise descending well below the knees. And they are even taught a special technique of dressing which guarantees them from catching so much as a glimpse of their own skin. These schools are now, happily, exceptional, but there was a time, not so long ago, when they were the rule. Theirs is the great Christian ascetic tradition which has flowed on in majestic continuity from the time of St. Anthony and the unwashed, underfed, sex-starved monks of the Thebaid, through the centuries, almost to the present day. It is to the weakening of that tradition that women at any rate owe the luxury of frequent bathing.

8   The early Christians were by no means enthusiastic bathers; but it is fair to point out that Christian ascetic tradition has not at all

times been hostile to baths as such. That the Early Fathers should have found the promiscuity of Roman bathing shocking is only natural. But the more moderate of them were prepared to allow a limited amount of washing, provided that the business was done with decency. The final decay of the great Roman baths was as much due to the destructiveness of the Barbarians as to Christian ascetic objections. During the Ages of Faith there was actually a revival of bathing. The Crusaders came back from the East, bringing with them the oriental vapour bath, which seems to have had a considerable popularity all over Europe. For reasons which it is difficult to understand, its popularity gradually waned, and the men and women of the late sixteenth and early seventeenth centuries seem to have been almost as dirty as their barbarous ancestors. Medical theory and court fashions may have had something to do with these fluctuations.

The ascetic tradition was always strongest where women were   9 concerned. The Goncourts record in their diary the opinion, which seems to have been current in respectable circles during the Second Empire, that female immodesty and immorality had increased with the growth of the bath habit. "Girls should wash less," was the obvious corollary. Young ladies who enjoy their bath owe a debt of gratitude to Voltaire for his mockeries, to the nineteenth-century scientists for their materialism. If these men had never lived to undermine the convent school tradition, our girls might still be as modest and as dirty as their ancestresses.

COMFORT AND MEDICINE

It is, however, to the doctors that the bath-lovers owe their great- 10 est debt. The discovery of microbic infection has put a premium on cleanliness. We wash now with religious fervour, like the Hindus. Our baths have become something like magic rites to protect us from the powers of evil, embodied in the dirt-loving germ. We may venture to prophesy that this medical religion will go still further in undermining the Christian ascetic tradition. Since the discovery of the beneficial effects of sunlight, too much clothing has become, medically speaking, a sin. Immodesty is now a virtue. It is quite likely that the doctors, whose prestige among us is almost equal to that of the medicine men among their savages, will have us stark naked before very long. That will be the last stage in the process of making clothes more comfortable. It is a process which has been going on for some time — first among men, later among women — and among its determining causes are the decay of hierarchic formalism and of Christian morality. In his lively little pamphlet describing Gladstone's visit to Oxford shortly before his death, Mr. Fletcher has recorded the Grand Old Man's comments on the dress of the undergraduates. Mr. Gladstone, it appears, was distressed by the informality and the cheapness of the students' clothes. In his day, he said, young men went about with a hundred pounds worth of clothes and jewellery on their persons, and every self-respecting youth had at least one pair of trousers in which he never sat down for fear of spoiling its shape. Mr. Gladstone visited Oxford at a time when undergraduates still wore very high starched collars and bowler hats. One wonders what he would have said of the open shirts, the gaudily coloured sweaters, the loose flannel trousers of the present generation. Dignified appearances have never been less assiduously kept up than they are at present; informality has reached an unprecedented pitch. On all but the most solemn occasions a man, whatever his rank or position, may wear what he finds comfortable.

11   The obstacles in the way of women's comforts were moral as well as political. Women were compelled not merely to keep up social appearances, but also to conform to a tradition of Christian ascetic morality. Long after men had abandoned their uncomfortable formal clothes, women were still submitting to extraordinary inconveniences in the name of modesty. It was the war which liberated them from their bondage. When women began to do war work, they found that the traditional modesty in dress was not compatible with efficiency. They preferred to be efficient. Having discovered the advantages of immodesty, they have remained immodest ever since, to the great improvement of their health and increase of their personal comfort. Modern fashions are the most comfortable that women have ever worn. Even the ancient Greeks were probably less comfortable. Their under-tunic, it is true, was as rational a garment as you could wish for; but their outer robe was simply a piece of stuff wound round the body like an Indian *sari*, and fastened with safety-pins. No woman whose appearance depended on safety-pins can ever have felt really comfortable.

COMFORT AS AN END IN ITSELF

12   Made possible by changes in the traditional philosophy of life, comfort is now one of the causes of its own further spread. For comfort

has now become a physical habit, a fashion, an ideal to be pursued for its own sake. The more comfort is brought into the world, the more it is likely to be valued. To those who have known comfort, discomfort is a real torture. And the fashion which now decrees the worship of comfort is quite as imperious as any other fashion. Moreover, enormous material interests are bound up with the supply of the means of comfort. The manufacturers of furniture, of heating apparatus, of plumbing fixtures, cannot afford to let the love of comfort die. In modern advertisement they have means for compelling it to live and grow.

Having now briefly traced the spiritual origins of modern comfort, I must say a few words about its effects. One can never have something for nothing, and the achievement of comfort has been accompanied by a compensating loss of other equally, or perhaps more, valuable things. A man of means who builds a house to-day is in general concerned primarily with the comfort of his future residence. He will spend a great deal of money (for comfort is very expensive: in America they talk of giving away the house with the plumbing) on bathrooms, heating apparatus, padded furnishings, and the like; and having spent it, he will regard his house as perfect. His counterpart in an earlier age would have been primarily concerned with the impressiveness and magnificence of his dwelling — with beauty, in a word, rather than comfort. The money our contemporary would spend on baths and central heating would have been spent in the past on marble staircases, a grand façade, frescoes, huge suites of gilded rooms, pictures, statues. Sixteenth-century popes lived in a discomfort that a modern bank manager would consider unbearable; but they had Raphael's frescoes, they had the Sistine chapel, they had their galleries of ancient sculpture. Must we pity them for the absence from the Vatican of bathrooms, central heating, and smoking-room chairs? I am inclined to think that our present passion for comfort is a little exaggerated. Though I personally enjoy comfort, I have lived very happily in houses devoid of almost everything that Anglo-Saxons deem indispensable. Orientals and even South Europeans, who know not comfort and live very much as our ancestors lived centuries ago, seem to get on very well without our elaborate and costly apparatus of padded luxury. I am old-fashioned enough to believe in higher and lower things, and can see no point in material progress except in so far as it subserves thought. I like labour-saving devices, because they economize time and energy which may be devoted to mental labour. (But then I enjoy mental labour; there are plenty of people who detest it, and who feel as much enthusiasm for thought-saving devices as for

13

automatic dishwashers and sewing-machines.) I like rapid and easy transport, because by enlarging the world in which men can live it enlarges their minds. Comfort for me has a similar justification: it facilitates mental life. Discomfort handicaps thought; it is difficult when the body is cold and aching to use the mind. Comfort is a means to an end. The modern world seems to regard it as an end in itself, an absolute good. One day, perhaps, the earth will have been turned into one vast feather-bed, with man's body dozing on top of it and his mind underneath, like Desdemona, smothered.

_____ CONSIDERATIONS _____

1. Some of the most provocative ideas of Huxley's essay are buried in improbable places. For example, in his lengthy Paragraph 5, Huxley slips in the quizzical notion that "majesty is mainly a question of majestical appearance." Is this idea really the extraneous afterthought the parentheses represents it to be?

2. Huxley's essay consists of conclusions drawn from his study of social history, and details used to reinforce or illustrate those conclusions. He covers great stretches of time and many different cultures. Those facts about the whole essay may explain the pains he takes in his opening to let the reader know precisely what he is going to do and how he hopes to do it. Would such an introduction be suitable for a 500-word essay? What other ways are there to begin this essay?

3. What connection does Huxley make between politics and the easy chair?

4. How does Huxley use his personal experience to underline a historical point about comfort?

5. Huxley's interest in the largely anonymous history of what we regard as commonplace things — furniture, the bathroom, industrial machinery — is greatly amplified in a fascinating book, *Mechanization Takes Command*, by Sigmund Gideon, who spent many years studying the evolution of household appliances. Look at Gideon's book, and find further evidence supporting Huxley's essay.

6. What evidence do you see around you — in the mass media, in the pursuits of your friends, in the changing values of society — that comfort has become, as Huxley puts it, "a physical habit, a fashion, an ideal to be pursued for its own sake"? Do you detect any reaction against such a pursuit?

Thomas Jefferson (1743–1826) was the third president of the United States, and perhaps more truly the Father of his Country than George Washington was; or maybe we would only like to think so, for such paternity flatters the offspring. Jefferson was a politician, philosopher, architect, inventor, and writer. With an energy equal to his curiosity, he acted to improve the world: he wrote the Declaration of Independence; he wrote a life of Jesus; and he founded the University of Virginia, whose original buildings he designed. An arch-republican, fearful of Alexander Hamilton's monarchical reverence for authority, Jefferson withheld support from the Constitution until he saw the Bill of Rights added to it.

We take this text from Garry Wills's Inventing America *(1978) (from which we print an excerpt on pages 458–469); by juxtaposition, Wills demonstrates the revision of a classic.*

37

THOMAS JEFFERSON

The Declarations of Jefferson and of the Congress

I will state the form of the declaration as originally reported. The parts struck out by Congress shall be distinguished by a black line drawn under them; & those inserted by them shall be placed in the margin or in a concurrent column:

1   A Declaration by the representatives of the United states of America, in [General] Congress assembled.

2   When in the course of human events it becomes necessary for one people to dissolve the political bands which have connected

Taken from Jefferson's Notes and Proceedings — *Papers*, 1:315–319.

them with another, and to assume among the powers of the earth the separate & equal station to which the laws of nature and of nature's god entitle them, a decent respect to the opinions of mankind requires that they should declare the causes which impel them to the separation.

We hold these truths to be self evident: that all men are created ∧ certain equal; that they are endowed by their creator with ∧ [inherent and] inalienable rights; that among these are life, liberty & the pursuit of happiness: that to secure these rights, governments are instituted among men, deriving their just powers from the consent of the governed; that whenever any form of government becomes destructive of these ends, it is the right of the people to alter or to abolish it, & to institute new government, laying it's foundation on such principles, & organising it's powers in such form, as to them shall seem most likely to effect their safety & happiness. Prudence indeed will dictate that governments long established should not be changed for light & transient causes; and accordingly all experience hath shewn that mankind are more disposed to suffer while evils are sufferable than to right themselves by abolishing the forms to which they are accustomed. But when a long train of abuses & usurpations [begun at a distinguished period and] pursuing invariably the same object, evinces a design to reduce them under absolute despotism it is their right, it is their duty to throw off such government, & to provide new guards for their future security. Such has been the patient sufferance of these colonies; & ∧ alter such is now the necessity which constrains them to ∧ [expunge] their former systems of government. The history of the present ∧ repeated king of Great Britain is a history of ∧ [unremitting] injuries & usurpations, [among which appears no solitary fact to contradict ∧ all having the uniform tenor of the rest but all have] ∧ in direct object the establishment of an absolute tyranny over these states. To prove this let facts be submitted to a candid world [for the truth of which we pledge a faith yet unsullied by falsehood.]

He has refused his assent to laws the most wholesome & necessary for the public good.

He has forbidden his governors to pass laws of immediate & pressing importance, unless suspended in their operation till his assent should be obtained; & when so suspended, he has utterly neglected to attend to them.

He has refused to pass other laws for the accommodation of large districts of people, unless those people would relinquish the right of representation in the legislature, a right inestimable to them, & formidable to tyrants only.

He has called together legislative bodies at places unusual, uncomfortable, and distant from the depository of their public rec-

3

4

5

6

7

ords, for the sole purpose of fatiguing them into compliance with his measures.

8   He has dissolved representative houses repeatedly [& continually] for opposing with manly firmness his invasions on the rights of the people.

9   He has refused for a long time after such dissolutions to cause others to be elected, whereby the legislative powers, incapable of annihilation, have returned to the people at large for their exercise, the state remaining in the mean time exposed to all the dangers of invasion from without & convulsions within.

10   He has endeavored to prevent the population of these states; for that purpose obstructing the laws for naturalization of foreigners, refusing to pass others to encourage their migrations hither, & raising the conditions of new appropriations of lands.

11   He has ∧ [suffered] the administration of justice [totally to cease in some of these states] ∧ refusing his assent to laws for establishing judiciary powers.   ∧ obstructed ∧ by

12   He has made [our] judges dependant on his will alone, for the tenure of their offices, & the amount & paiment of their salaries.

13   He has erected a multitude of new offices [by a self assumed power] and sent hither swarms of new officers to harrass our people and eat out their substance.

14   He has kept among us in times of peace standing armies [and ships of war] without the consent of our legislatures.

15   He has affected to render the military independant of, & superior to the civil power.

16   He has combined with others to subject us to a jurisdiction foreign to our constitutions & unacknoleged by our laws, giving his assent to their acts of pretended legislation for quartering large bodies of armed troops among us; for protecting them by a mock-trial from punishment for any murders which they should commit on the inhabitants of these states; for cutting off our trade with all parts of the world; for imposing taxes on us without our consent; for depriving us ∧ of the benefits of trial by jury; for transporting us beyond seas to be tried for pretended offences; for abolishing the free system of English laws in a neighboring province, establishing therein an arbitrary government, and enlarging it's boundaries, so as to render it at once an example and fit instrument for introducing the same absolute rule into these ∧ [states]; for taking away our charters, abolishing our most valuable laws, and altering fundamentally the forms of our governments; for suspending our own legislatures, & declaring themselves invested with power to legislate for us in all cases whatsoever.   ∧ in many cases   ∧ colonies

17   He has abdicated government here ∧ [withdrawing his governors, and declaring us out of his allegiance & protection.]   ∧ by declaring us out of his protection & waging war against us.

He has plundered our seas, ravaged our coasts, burnt our towns, & destroyed the lives of our people. 18

He is at this time transporting large armies of foreign merce- 19 naries to compleat the works of death, desolation & tyranny already begun with circumstances of cruelty and perfidy ∧ unworthy the head of a civilized nation.

∧ scarcely paralleled in the most barbarous ages, & totally

He has constrained our fellow citizens taken captive on the high 20 seas to bear arms against their country, to become the executioners of their friends & brethren, or to fall themselves by their hands.

He has ∧ endeavored to bring on the inhabitants of our frontiers 21 the merciless Indian savages, whose known rule of warfare is an undistinguished destruction of all ages, sexes, & conditions [of existence.]

∧ excited domestic insurrections amongst us, & has

[He has incited treasonable insurrections of our fellow-citizens, 22 with the allurements of forfeiture & confiscation of our property.

He has waged cruel war against human nature itself, violating 23 it's most sacred rights of life and liberty in the persons of a distant people who never offended him, captivating & carrying them into slavery in another hemisphere or to incur miserable death in their transportation thither. This piratical warfare, the opprobrium of *infidel* powers, is the warfare of the *Christian* king of Great Britain. Determined to keep open a market where *Men* should be bought & sold, he has prostituted his negative for suppressing every legislative attempt to prohibit or to restrain this execrable commerce. And that this assemblage of horrors might want no fact of distinguished die, he is now exciting those very people to rise in arms among us, and to purchase that liberty of which he has deprived them, by murdering the people on whom he also obtruded them: thus paying off former crimes committed against the *Liberties* of one people, with crimes which he urges them to commit against the *lives* of another.]

In every stage of these oppressions we have petitioned for redress 24 in the most humble terms: our repeated petitions have been answered only by repeated injuries. A prince whose character is thus marked by every act which may define a tyrant is unfit to be the ruler of a ∧ people [who mean to be free. Future ages will scarcely believe that the hardiness of one man adventured, within the short compass of twelve years only, to lay a foundation so broad & so undisguised for tyranny over a people fostered & fixed in principles of freedom.]

∧ free

Nor have we been wanting in attentions to our British brethren. 25 We have warned them from time to time of attempts by their legislature to extend ∧ [a] jurisdiction over ∧ [these our states.] We have reminded them of the circumstances of our emigration & settlement here, [no one of which could warrant so strange a pre-

∧ an unwarrantable   ∧ us

tension: that these were effected at the expence of our own blood & treasure, unassisted by the wealth or the strength of Great Britain: that in constituting indeed our several forms of government, we had adopted one common king, thereby laying a foundation for perpetual league & amity with them: but that submission to their parliament was no part of our constitution, nor ever in idea, if history may be credited: and,] we ∧ appealed to their native justice ∧ have
and magnanimity ∧ [as well as to] the ties of our common kindred ∧ and we have conjured them
to disavow these usurpations which ∧ [were likely to] interrupt our by
connection and correspondence. They too have been deaf to the
voice of justice & of consanguinity, [and when occasions have been ∧ would inevitably
given them, by the regular course of their laws, of removing from
their councils the disturbers of our harmony, they have, by their
free election, re-established them in power. At this very time too
they are permitting their chief magistrate to send over not only
souldiers of our common blood, but Scotch & foreign mercenaries
to invade & destroy us. These facts have given the last stab to
agonizing affection, and manly spirit bids us to renounce for ever
these unfeeling brethren. We must endeavor to forget our former
love for them, and to hold them as we hold the rest of mankind
enemies in war, in peace friends. We might have been a free and a
great people together; but a communication of grandeur & of freedom it seems is below their dignity. Be it so, since they will have
it. The road to happiness & to glory is open to us too. We will tread
it apart from them, and] ∧ acquiesce in the necessity which ∧ we must therefore
denounces our [eternal] separation ∧ ! ∧ and hold them
as we hold the
rest of mankind,
enemies in war,
in peace friends.

26   We therefore the representatives of the United states of America in General Congress assembled do in the name, & by the authority of the good people of these [states reject & renounce all allegiance & subjection to the kings of Great Britain & all others who may hereafter claim by, through or under them: we utterly dissolve all political connection which may heretofore have subsisted between us & the people or parliament of Great Britain: & finally we do assert & declare these colonies to be free & independant states,] & that as free

We therefore the representatives of the United states of America in General Congress assembled, appealing to the supreme judge of the world for the rectitude of our intentions, do in the name, & by the authority of the good people of these colonies, solemnly publish & declare that these United colonies are & of right ought to be free & independant states; that they are absolved from all allegiance to the British crown, and that all political connection between them & the state of Great Britain is, & ought to be, totally dissolved; & that as free

& independant states, they have full power to levy war, conclude peace, contract alliances, establish commerce, & to do all other acts & things which independant states may of right do.

27 And for the support of this declaration we mutually pledge to each other our lives, our fortunes & our sacred honour.

& independant states they have full power to levy war, conclude peace, contract alliances, establish commerce & to do all other acts & things which independant states may of right do.

And for the support of this declaration, with a firm reliance on the protection of divine providence we mutually pledge to each other our lives, our fortunes & our sacred honour.

_____ CONSIDERATIONS _____

1. What part of the original declaration deleted by Congress most surprises you? Why?

2. Make a careful study of the first eight or ten changes imposed by Congress on Jefferson's original declaration. Why do you think each was made? Would any of them have made good examples for George Orwell to use in his "Politics and the English Language"?

3. Garry Wills writes (page 459) that the declaration is easy to misunderstand because it "is written in the lost language of the Enlightenment." What was the Enlightenment? Can you find an example to clarify what Wills means by this lost language? Perhaps the declaration should be rewritten in modern English. Compare the two versions of Ecclesiastes (pages 53–59) before you come to a conclusion.

4. If you conclude that the declaration should be rewritten, try your hand at it. Try, say, rewriting the famous third paragraph: "We hold these truths . . ." Can you be sure you're not writing a parody?

5. How is the declaration organized? Does it break down into distinct parts? If so, what is the function of those parts?

6. For a more thorough exploration of the before-and-after versions of the declaration and of the political and literary motives for the changes, see Carl Becker's *The Declaration of Independence*.

Etheridge Knight (b. 1933) was born in Mississippi and fought in Korea. He has said of himself, "I died in Korea from a shrapnel wound and narcotics resurrected me. I died in 1960 from a prison sentence and poetry brought me back to life." He began writing poems in Indiana State Prison — where his method of supporting his addiction landed him — from which he was released in 1968. In the same year he published his first book, Poems from Prison, *which includes this poem. Knight has since taught at universities and free workshops all over the country. In 1973, he published* Belly Song.

38

ETHERIDGE KNIGHT
The Idea of Ancestry

I

Taped to the wall of my cell are 47 pictures: 47 black
faces: my father, mother, grandmothers (1 dead), grand
fathers (both dead), brothers, sisters, uncles, aunts,
cousins (1st & 2nd), nieces, and nephews. They stare
across the space at me sprawling on my bunk. I know   5
their dark eyes, they know mine. I know their style,
they know mine. I am all of them, they are all of me;
they are farmers, I am a thief, I am me, they are thee.

I have at one time or another been in love with my mother,
1 grandmother, 2 sisters, 2 aunts (1 went to the asylum),   10
and 5 cousins. I am now in love with a 7 yr old niece

(she sends me letters written in large block print, and
her picture is the only one that smiles at me).

I have the same name as 1 grandfather, 3 cousins, 3 nephews,
15   and 1 uncle. The uncle disappeared when he was 15, just took
off and caught a freight (they say). He's discussed each year
when the family has a reunion, he causes uneasiness in
the clan, he is an empty space. My father's mother, who is 93
and who keeps the Family Bible with everybody's birth dates
20   (and death dates) in it, always mentions him. There is no
place in her Bible for 'whereabouts unknown'.

II

Each Fall the graves of my grandfathers call me, the brown
hills and red gullies of mississippi send out their electric
messages, galvanizing my genes. Last yr/like a salmon
       quitting
25   the cold ocean — leaping and bucking up his birthstream/I
hitchhiked my way from L.A. with 16 caps in my pocket and a
monkey on my back. and I almost kicked it with the kinfolks.
I walked barefooted in my grandmother's backyard/I smelled
       the old
land and the woods/I sipped cornwhiskey from fruit jars
       with the men/
30   I flirted with the women/I had a ball till the caps ran out
and my habit came down. That night I looked at my grand-
       mother
and split/my guts were screaming for junk/but I was almost
contented/I had almost caught up with me.
(The next day in Memphis I cracked a croaker's crib for a fix.)

This yr there is a gray stone wall damming my stream, and
35   when
the falling leaves stir my genes, I pace my cell or flop on my
       bunk
and stare at 47 black faces across the space. I am all of them,
they are all of me, I am me, they are thee, and I have no sons
to float in the space between.

D. H. Lawrence (1885–1930) was born in Nottinghamshire, in England, son of a coal-miner father brutalized by work and poverty, and a schoolteacher mother who encouraged his writing. The family was poor and Lawrence was sickly, but he studied to become certified as a teacher, and wrote poetry and fiction when he could. In 1911 he published his first novel, The White Peacock, *and quit his post as a teacher. The next year, he met Frieda von Richtofen Weekley, German wife of a Professor Weekley, and cousin of the Baron Manfred von Richtofen who was to become the Red Baron of World War I. Lawrence and Frieda fell in love, and Frieda left her husband and children to run away with Lawrence; they remained together, tempestuous and difficult and devoted, until his death.*

His first book of poems appeared in 1913, as did the first of his great novels, Sons and Lovers. *Lawrence and Frieda, who were able to marry in 1914, traveled in Germany and Italy, and settled in England when the war started.* The Prussian Officer, *a book of stories, appeared in 1914, followed by* The Rainbow *(1915). That novel's second half,* Women in Love, *was not published until 1920 because publishers feared the response to its relative explicitness about sexual feeling.*

Living by his wits, Lawrence published innumerable stories, essays, novels, poems, criticism, and travel books. He and Frieda traveled continually. After World War I, they took off for Italy; two of his travel books are about that country. A journey to Australia resulted in a novel called Kangaroo *(1923). In the New World, he delighted in Mexico (*The Plumed Serpent, *1926) and New Mexico. During the last years before his death from tuberculosis, he wrote* Lady Chatterly's Lover, *which was suppressed, and his best poetry.*

*In his poems and novels, in his essays on literature (*Studies in Classic American Literature, *1923, is itself classic), in his philosophical psychology (*Psychoanalysis of the Unconscious, *1921;* Fantasia of the Unconscious, *1922) Lawrence pursues a single theme. Modern man (to a lesser extent modern woman) lacks sexual and spiritual energy, which has been sapped by industrial society. The contemporary reader of this fifty-year-old essay must substitute new examples for old ones, but the problem Lawrence speaks of has grown more intense. The tracks continue in the same direction, because it is no longer true that "Science hasn't even learned how to wash dishes for us." If he were alive now, Lawrence would still warn us in his shrill, urgent, serious voice to "get your bodies back."*

39

D. H. LAWRENCE

Men Must Work and Women As Well

1   Supposing that circumstances go on pretty much in the same way they're going on in now, then men and women will go on pretty much in the same way they are now going on in. There is always an element of change, we know. But change is of two sorts: the next step, or a jump in another direction. The next step is called progress. If our society continues its course of gay progress along the given lines, then men and women will do the same: always along the given lines.

2   So what is important in that case is not so much men and women, but the given lines. The railway train doesn't matter particularly in itself. What matters is where it is going to. If I want to go to Crewe, then a train to Bedford is supremely uninteresting to me, no matter how full it may be. It will only arouse a secondary and temporal interest if it happens to have an accident.

3   And there you are with men and women today. They are not particularly interesting, and they are not, in themselves, particularly important. All the thousands and millions of bowler hats and neat handbags that go bobbing to business every day may represent so many immortal souls, but somehow we feel that is not for us to say. The clergyman is paid to tickle our vanity in these matters. What all the bowler hats and neat handbags represent to you and me and to each other is business, my dear, and a job.

4   So that, granted the present stream of progress towards better business and better jobs continues, the point is, not to consider the

men and women bobbing in the stream, any more than you consider the drops of water in the Thames — but where the stream is flowing. Where is the stream flowing, indeed, the stream of progress? Everybody hopes, of course, it is flowing towards bigger business and better jobs. And what does that mean, again, to the man under the bowler hat and the woman who clutches the satchel?

It means, of course, more money, more congenial labours, and   5
fewer hours. It means freedom from all irksome tasks. It means, apart from the few necessary hours of highly paid and congenial labour, that men and women shall have nothing to do except enjoy themselves. No beastly housework for the women, no beastly homework for the men. Free! free to enjoy themselves. More films, more motor-cars, more dances, more golf, more tennis and more getting completely away from yourself. And the goal of life is enjoyment.

Now if men and women want these things with sufficient inten-   6
sity, they may really get them, and go on getting them. While the game is worth the candle, men and women will go on playing the game. And it seems today as if the motor-car, the film, the radio and the jazz were worth the candle. This being so, progress will continue from business to bigger business, and from job to better job. This is, in very simple terms, the plan of the universe laid down by the great magnates of industry like Mr. Ford. And they know what they are talking about.

But — and the "but" is a very big one — it is not easy to turn   7
business into bigger business, and it is sometimes *impossible* to turn uncongenial jobs into congenial ones. This is where science really leaves us in the lurch, and calculation collapses. Perhaps in Mr. Ford's super-factory of motor-cars all jobs may be made abstract and conge-nial. But the woman whose cook falls foul of the kitchen range, heated with coal, every day, hates that coal range herself even more darkly than the cook hates it. Yet many housewives can't afford electric cook-ing. And if everyone could, it still doesn't make housework entirely congenial. All the inventions of modern science fail to make house-work anything but uncongenial to the modern woman, be she mistress or servant-maid. Now the only decent way to get something done is to get it done by somebody who quite likes doing it. In the past, cooks really enjoyed cooking and housemaids enjoyed scrubbing. Those days are over; like master, like man, and still more so, like mistress, like maid. Mistress loathes scrubbing; in two generations, maid loathes scrubbing. But scrubbing must be done. At what price? — raise the price. The price is raised, the scrubbing goes a little better. But after a

while, the loathing of scrubbing becomes again paramount in the kitchen-maid's breast, and then ensues a general state of tension, and a general outcry: Is it worth it? Is it really worth it?

8   What applies to scrubbing applies to all labour that cannot be mechanized or abstracted. A girl will slave over shorthand and typing for a pittance because it is not muscular work. A girl will not do housework well, not for a good wage. Why? Because, for some mysterious or obvious reason, the modern woman and the modern man hate physical work. Ask your husband to peel the potatoes, and earn his deep resentment. Ask your wife to wash your socks, and earn the same. There is still a certain thrill about "mental" and purely mechanical work like attending a machine. But actual labour has become to us, with our education, abhorrent.

9   And it is here that science has not kept pace with human demand. It is here that progress is fatally threatened. There is an enormous, insistent demand on the part of the human being that mere labour, such as scrubbing, hewing and loading coal, navvying, the crude work that is the basis of all labour, shall be done away with. Even washing dishes. Science hasn't even learned how to wash dishes for us yet. The mistress who feels so intensely bitter about her maid who will not wash the dishes properly does so because she herself so loathes washing them. Science has rather left us in the lurch in these humble but basic matters. Before babies are conveniently bred in bottles, let the scientist find a *hey presto!* trick for turning dirty teacups into clean ones; since it is upon science we depend for our continued progress.

10   Progress, then, which proceeds so smoothly, and depends on science, does not proceed as rapidly as human feelings change. Beef-steaks are beef-steaks still, though all except the eating is horrible to us. A great deal must be done about a beef-steak besides the eating of it. And this great deal is done, we have to face the fact, unwillingly. When the mistress loathes trimming and grilling a beef-steak, or paring potatoes, or wringing the washing, the maid will likewise loathe these things, and do them at last unwillingly, and with a certain amount of resentment.

11   The one thing we don't sufficiently consider, in considering the march of human progress, is also the very dangerous march of human feeling that goes on at the same time, and not always parallel. The change in human feeling! And one of the greatest changes that has ever taken place in man and woman is this revulsion from physical effort, physical labour and physical contact, which has taken place within the last thirty years. This change hits woman even harder than man,

for she has always had to keep the immediate physical side going. And now it is repellent to her — just as nearly all physical activity is repellent to modern man. The film, the radio, the gramophone were all invented because physical effort and physical contact have become repulsive to man and woman alike. The aim is to abstract as far as possible. And science is our only help. And science still can't wash the dinner-things or darn socks, or even mend the fire. Electric heaters or central heating, of course! But that's not all.

What, then, is the result? In the abstract we sail ahead to bigger 12 business and better jobs and babies bred in bottles and food in tabloid form. But meanwhile science hasn't rescued us from beef-steaks and dish-washing, heavy labour and howling babies. There is a great hitch. And owing to the great hitch, a great menace to progress. Because every day mankind hates the business of beef-steaks and dish-washing, heavy labour and howling babies more bitterly.

The housewife is full of resentment — she can't help it. The 13 young husband is full of resentment — he can't help it, when he has to plant potatoes to eke out the family income. The housemaid is full of resentment, the navvy is full of resentment, the collier is full of resentment, and the collier's wife is full of resentment, because her man can't earn a proper wage. Resentment grows as the strange fastidiousness of modern men and woman increases. Resentment, resentment, resentment — because the basis of life is still brutally physical, and that has become repulsive to us. Mr. Ford, being in his own way a genius, has realized that what the modern workman wants, just like the modern gentleman, is abstraction. The modern workman doesn't *want* to be "interested" in his job. He wants to be as little interested, as nearly perfectly mechanical, as possible. This is the great will of the people, and there is no gainsaying it. It is precisely the same in woman as in man. Woman demands an electric cooker because it makes no call on her attention or her "interest" at all. It is almost a pure abstraction, a few switches, and no physical contact, no *dirt,* which is the inevitable result of physical contact, at all. If only we could make housework a real abstraction, a matter of turning switches and guiding a machine, the housewife would again be more or less content. But it can't quite be done, even in America.

And the resentment is enormous. The resentment against *eating,* 14 in the breast of modern woman who has to prepare food, is profound. Why all this work and bother about *mere eating?* Why, indeed? Because neither science nor evolution has kept up with the change in human feeling, and beef-steaks are beef-steaks still, no matter how detestable they may have become to the people who have to prepare them. The loathsome fuss of food continues, and will continue, in spite of all talk about tabloids. The loathsome digging of coal out of the earth, by half-naked men, continues, deep underneath Mr. Ford's super-factories. There it is, and there it will be, and you can't get away from it. While men quite enjoyed hewing coal, which they did, and while women really enjoyed cooking, even with a coal range, which they did — then all was well. But suppose society *en bloc* comes to hate the thought of sweating cooking over a hot range, or sweating hacking at a coal-seam, then what are you to do? You have to ask, or to demand, that a large section of society shall do something they have come to hate doing, and which you would hate to do yourself. What then? Resentment and ill-feeling!

15   Social life means all classes of people living more or less harmoniously together. And private life means men and women, man and woman living together more or less congenially. If there is serious discord between the social classes, then society is threatened with confusion. If there is serious discord between man and woman, then the individual, and that means practically everybody, is threatened with internal confusion and unhappiness.

16   Now it is quite easy to keep the working classes in harmonious working order, so long as you don't ask them to do work they simply do not want to do. The Board-schools, however, did the fatal deed. They said to the boys: Work is noble, but what you want is to *get on*, you don't want to stick down a coal-mine all your life. Rise up, and do *clean* work! become a school teacher or a clerk, not a common collier.

17   This is sound Board-school education, and is in keeping with all the noblest social ideals of the last century. Unfortunately it entirely overlooks the unpleasant effect of such teaching on those who *cannot* get on, and who must perforce stick down a coal-mine all their lives. And these, in the Board-school of a mining district, are at least 90 per cent of the boys; it must be so. So that 90 per cent of these Board-school scholars are deliberately taught, at school, to be malcontents, taught to despise themselves for not having "got on," for not having "got out of the pit," for sticking down all their lives doing "dirty work" and being "common colliers." Naturally, every collier, doomed himself, wants to get his boys out of the pit, to be gentlemen. And since this again is *impossible* in 90 per cent of the cases, the number of "gentlemen," or clerks and school teachers, being strictly proportionate to the number of colliers, there comes again the sour disillusion. So that by the third generation you have exactly what you've got today,

the young malcontent collier. He has been deliberately produced by modern education coupled with modern conditions, and is logically, inevitably and naturally what he is: a malcontent collier. According to all the accepted teaching, he ought to have risen and bettered himself: equal opportunity, you know. And he hasn't risen and bettered himself. Therefore he is more or less a failure in his own eyes even. He is doomed to do dirty work. He is a malcontent. Now even Mr. Ford can't make coal-mines clean and shiny and abstract. Coal won't be abstracted. Even a Soviet can't do it. A coal-mine remains a hole in the black earth, where blackened men hew and shovel and sweat. You can't abstract it, or make it an affair of pulling levers, and, what is even worse, you can't abandon it, you can't do away with it. There it is, and it has got to be. Mr. Ford forgets that his clean and pure and harmonious super-factory, where men only pull shining levers or turn bright handles, has all had to be grossly mined and smelted before it could come into existence, Mr. Ford's is one of the various heavens of industry. But these heavens rest on various hells of labour, always did and always will. Science rather leaves us in the lurch in these matters. Science is supposed to remove these hells for us. And — it doesn't. Not at all!

If you had never taught the blackened men down in the various 18
hells that they *were* in hell, and made them despise themselves for being there — a *common* collier, a *low* labourer — the mischief could never have developed so rapidly. But now we have it, all society resting on a labour basis of smouldering resentment. And the collier's question: How would *you* like to be a collier? — is unanswerable. We know perfectly well we should dislike it intensely. — At the same time, my father, who never went to a Board-school, quite liked it. But he has been improved on. Progress! Human feeling has changed, changed rapidly and radically. And science has not changed conditions to fit.

What is to be done? We all loathe brute physical labour. We all 19
think it is horrible to have to do it. We consider those that actually do it low and vile, and we have told them so, for fifty years, urging them to get away from it and "better themselves," which would be very nice, if everybody *could* get on, and brute labour could be abandoned, as scientifically, it ought to be. But actually, not at all. We are forced to go on forcing a very large proportion of society to remain "unbettered," "low and common," "common colliers, common labourers," since a very large portion of humanity must still spend its life labouring, now and in the future, science having let us down in this respect. You can't teach mankind to "better himself" unless you'll better the

gross earth to fit him. And the gross earth remains what it was, and man its slave. For neither science nor evolution shows any signs of saving us from our gross necessities. The labouring masses are and will be, even if all else is swept away: because they must be. They represent the gross necessity of man, which science has failed to save us from.

20   So then, what? The only thing that remains to be done is to make labour as likeable as possible, and try to teach the labouring masses to like it: which, given the trend of modern feeling, not only sounds, but is, fatuous. Mankind *en bloc* gets more fastidious and more "nice" every day. Every day it loathes dirty work more deeply. And every day the whole pressure of social consciousness works towards making everybody more fastidious, more "nice," more refined, and more unfit for dirty work. Before you make all humanity unfit for dirty work, you should first remove the necessity for dirty work.

21   But such being the condition of men and women with regard to work — a condition of repulsion in the breasts of men and women for the work that has got to be done — what about private life, the relation between man and woman? How does the new fastidiousness and nicety of mankind affect this?

22   Profoundly! The revulsion from physical labour, physical effort, physical contact has struck a death-blow at marriage and home-life. In the great trend of the times, a woman cannot save herself from the universal dislike of housework, housekeeping, rearing children and keeping a home going. Women make the most unselfish efforts in this direction, because it is generally expected of them. But this cannot remove the *instinctive* dislike of preparing meals and scouring sauce-pans, cleaning baby's bottles or darning the man's underwear, which a large majority of women feel today. It is something which there is no denying, a real physical dislike of doing these things. Many women school themselves and are excellent housewives, physically disliking it all the time. And this, though admirable, is wearing. It is an exhaus-tive process, with many ill results.

23   Can it be possible that women actually ever did like scouring saucepans and cleaning the range? — I believe some few women still do. I believe that twenty years ago, even, the majority of women en-joyed it. But what, then, has happened? Can human instincts really change?

24   They can, and in the most amazing fashion. And this is the great problem for the sociologist: the violent change in human instinct, especially in women. Woman's instinct used to be all for home, shel-ter, the protection of the man, and the happiness of running her own

house. Now it is all against. Woman *thinks* she wants a lovely little home of her own, but her instinct is all against it, when it means matrimony. She *thinks* she wants a man of her own, but her instinct is dead against having him around all the time. She would like him on a long string, that she can let out or pull in, as she feels inclined. But she just doesn't want him inevitably and insidiously there all the time — not even every evening — not even for week-ends, if it's got to be a fixture. She wants him to be merely intermittent in her landscape, even if he is always present in her soul, and she writes him the most intimate letters every day. All well and good! But her instinct is against him, against his permanent and perpetual physical presence. She doesn't want to feel his presence as something material, unavoidable, and permanent. It goes dead against her grain, it upsets her instinct. She loves him, she loves, even, being faithful to him. But she doesn't want him substantially around. She doesn't want his actual physical presence — except in snatches. What she *really* loves is the thought of him, the idea of him, the *distant* communion with him — varied with snatches of actually being together, like little festivals, which we are more or less glad when they are over.

Now a great many modern girls feel like this, even when they 25 force themselves to behave in the conventional side-by-side fashion. And a great many men feel the same — though perhaps not so acutely as the women. Young couples may force themselves to be conventional husbands and wives, but the strain is often cruel, and the result often disastrous.

Now then we see the trend of our civilization, in terms of human 26 feeling and human relation. It is, and there is no denying it, towards a greater and greater abstraction from the physical, towards a further and further physical separateness between men and women, and between individual and individual. Young men and women today are together all the time, it will be argued. Yes, but they are together as good sports, good chaps, in strange independence of one another, intimate one moment, strangers the next, hands-off! all the time, and as little connected as the bits in a kaleidoscope.

The young have the fastidiousness, the nicety, the revulsion from 27 the physical, intensified. To the girl of today, a man whose physical presence she is aware of, especially a bit *heavily* aware of, is or becomes really abhorrent. She wants to fly away from him to the uttermost ends of the earth. And as soon as women or girls get a bit female physical, young men's nerves go all to pieces. The sexes can't stand one another. They adore one another as spiritual or personal creatures, all talk and wit and back-chat, or jazz and motor-cars and machines, or tennis and swimming — even sitting in bathing-suits all day on a beach. But this is all peculiarly non-physical, a flaunting of the body in its non-physical, merely optical aspect. So much nudity, fifty years ago, would have made man and woman quiver through and through. Now, not at all! People flaunt their bodies to show how unphysical they are. The more the girls are not desired, the more they uncover themselves.

28   And this means, when we analyse it out, repulsion. The young are, in a subtle way, physically repulsive to one another, the girl to the man and the man to the girl. And they rather enjoy the feeling of repulsion, it is a sort of contest. It is as if the young girl said to the young man today: I rather like you, you know. You are so thrillingly repulsive to me. — And as if the young man replied: Same here! — There may be, of course, an intense bodiless sort of affection between young men and women. But as soon as either becomes a positive physical presence to the other, immediately there is repulsion.

29   And marriage based on the thrill of physical repulsion, as so many are today, even when coupled with mental "adoring" or real wistful, bodiless affection, are in the long run — not so very long, either — catastrophic. There you have it, the great "spirituality," the great "betterment" or refinement; the great fastidiousness; the great "niceness" of feeling; when a girl must be a flat, thin, bodiless stick, and a boy a correct manikin, each of them abstracted towards real caricature. What does it all amount to? What is its motive force?

30   What it amounts to, really, is physical repulsion. The great spirituality of our age means that we are all physically repulsive to one another. The great advance in refinement of feeling and squeamish fastidiousness means that we hate the *physical* existence of anybody and everybody, even ourselves. The amazing move into abstraction on the part of the whole of humanity — the film, the radio, the gramophone — means that we loathe the physical element in our amusements, we don't *want* the physical contact, we want to get away from it. We don't *want* to look at flesh and blood people — we want to watch their shadows on a screen. We don't *want* to hear their actual voices: only transmitted through a machine. We must get away from the physical.

31   The vast mass of the lower classes — and this is most extraordinary — are even more grossly abstracted, if we may use the term, than the educated classes. The uglier sort of working man today truly has no body and no real feelings at all. He eats the most wretched food,

because taste has left him, he only *sees* his meal, he never *really* eats it. He drinks his beer by idea, he no longer tastes it at all. This must be so, or the food and beer could not be as bad as they are. And as for his relation to his women — his poor women — they are pegs to hang clothes on, and there's an end of them. It is a horrible state of feelings depravity, atrophy of the senses.

But under it all, as ever, as everywhere, vibrates the one great   32
impulse of our civilization, physical recoil from every other being and from every form of physical existence. Recoil, recoil, recoil. Revulsion, revulsion, revulsion. Repulsion, repulsion, repulsion. This is the rhythm that underlies our social activity, everywhere, with regard to physical existence.

Now we are all basically and permanently physical. So is the   33
earth, so even is the air. What then is going to be the result of all this recoil and repulsion, which our civilization has deliberately fostered?

The result is really only one and the same: some form of collec-   34
tive social madness. Russia, being a very physical country, was in a frantic state of physical recoil and "spirituality" twenty years ago. We can look on the revolution, really, as nothing but a great outburst of anti-physical insanity; we can look on Soviet Russia as nothing but a logical state of society established in anti-physical insanity. — Physical and material are, of course, not the same; in fact, they are subtly opposite. The machine is absolutely material, and absolutely anti-physical — as even our fingers know. And the Soviet is established on the image of the machine, "pure" materialism. The Soviet hates the real physical body far more deeply than it hates Capital. It mixes it up with the bourgeois. But it sees very little danger in it, since all western civilization is now mechanized, materialized and ready for an outburst of insanity which shall throw us all into some purely machine-driven unity of lunatics.

What about it, then? What about it, men and women? The only   35
thing to do is to get your bodies back, men and women. A great part of society is irreparably lost: abstracted into non-physical, mechanical entities whose motive power is still recoil, revulsion, repulsion, hate, and, ultimately, blind destruction. The driving force *underneath* our society remains the same: recoil, revulsion, hate. And let this force once run out of hand, and we know what to expect. It is not only in the working class. The well-to-do classes are just as full of the driving force of recoil, revulsion, which ultimately becomes hate. The force is universal in our spiritual civilization. Let it once run out of hand, and then — —

36   It only remains for some men and women, individuals, to try to get back their bodies and preserve the other flow of warmth, affection and physical unison. There is nothing else to do.

_____ CONSIDERATIONS _____

1. Lawrence's essay, originally published in England in 1929, may strike Americans in this decade as remote in time and place. Isolate examples. Does the essay overcome or counterbalance these characteristics?

2. *Listening to* (as well as *reading*) Lawrence's essay, can provide an opportunity to study the difference between spoken and written English. Explain why, using examples from the essay.

3. Even the professional writer occasionally lapses. Look carefully through paragraphs 6, 7, and 8 to find clichés. Rewrite these phrases and be prepared to justify your changes.

4. In paragraphs 5 and 7, Lawrence uses the word "congenial" (and its negative form) frequently. At first glance, his choice might seem inexact. Use your dictionary to determine the rightness of the author's diction in those passages.

5. Early in his essay, Lawrence says, "In the past, cooks really enjoyed cooking and housemaids enjoyed scrubbing," but in Paragraph 21, he talks about a woman's "instinctive dislike" of housework. Does he escape this apparent contradiction?

6. Trace the major steps of Lawrence's argument, which concludes with his final statement in Paragraph 35. Does any of the argument correlate with Aldous Huxley's exposition of comfort, on pages 201–210?

Abraham Lincoln (1809–1865) was our sixteenth president, and a consensus of historians ranks him our greatest president — a ranking generally supported by the American people. He grew up self-educated, nurturing his mind on five special books: the King James Version of the Bible, Shakespeare, Parson Weems's Life of Washington, *John Bunyan's* Pilgrim's Progress, *and Daniel Defoe's* Robinson Crusoe. *His speeches and letters are models of a formal, rhythmic, studied English prose. (See Garry Wills's remarks on Lincoln — his style and his mind — on pages 459–463.) None of his utterances is so known — so parodied, so quoted, so misquoted — as the speech he gave at Gettysburg.*

40

ABRAHAM LINCOLN
The Gettysburg Address

Four score and seven years ago our fathers brought forth on this 1
continent, a new nation, conceived in Liberty, and dedicated to the
proposition that all men are created equal.

Now we are engaged in a great civil war, testing whether that 2
nation, or any nation so conceived and so dedicated, can long endure.
We are met on a great battle-field of that war. We have come to dedicate a portion of that field, as a final resting place for those who here
gave their lives that that nation might live. It is altogether fitting and
proper that we should do this.

But, in a larger sense, we can not dedicate — we can not conse- 3
crate — we can not hallow — this ground. The brave men, living and
dead, who struggled here, have consecrated it, far above our poor power
to add or detract. The world will little note, nor long remember what
we say here, but it can never forget what they did here. It is for us the
living, rather, to be dedicated here to the unfinished work which they
who fought here have thus far so nobly advanced. It is rather for us to

be here dedicated to the great task remaining before us — that from these honored dead we take increased devotion to that cause for which they gave the last full measure of devotion — that we here highly resolve that these dead shall not have died in vain — that this nation, under God, shall have a new birth of freedom — and that government of the people, by the people, for the people, shall not perish from the earth.

_____ CONSIDERATIONS _____

1. Lincoln's Gettysburg Address was not subjected to the intense study, criticism, and revision that Congress gave Thomas Jefferson's Declaration of Independence (pages 211–216), but neither did Lincoln give his short speech off the top of his head. He reworked the composition before he delivered it. One of the changes occurred in the last sentence of Paragraph 2, which in an earlier version read, "This we may, in all propriety do." What do you think of his decision to change that sentence?

2. Commentators have noted that Lincoln made telling use of repeated sentence structure. Locate a good example in the address, then compose two sentences of your own, on any subject, but built in the same way.

3. Shortly after Lincoln delivered the address, the *Chicago Times* criticized his phrase, "a new birth of freedom" and called it a misrepresentation of the motives of the men slain at Gettysburg. The *Times* argued that the soldiers had died to maintain the government, the Constitution, and the union — not to advance Lincoln's "odious abolition doctrines." Can an objective reading of the address help you determine whether the *Times* attack had any substance?

4. Note how Lincoln's first reference to place is the word "continent"; his second is to "nation"; his third to "battle-field"; and his fourth to "a portion of that field." What do you make of this progressive narrowing of the field of vision? Can you see a use for such a device in your own writing?

5. Lincoln begins Paragraph 3 with a sentence in which he moves from "dedicate" to "consecrate" to "hallow." Are these words synonyms? If so, why does he say the same thing three times? If they have different meanings, is there any significance in the order in which Lincoln arranges them? Consult a good dictionary or collection of synonyms.

Walter Lippmann (1889–1974) was an editor and a political thinker, author of many books including Public Opinion *(1922) and* A Preface to Morals *(1929). His newspaper column appeared from 1931 until 1966, when he stopped writing in disgust over the Vietnam War. Lippmann was an articulate and thoughtful citizen, who did not panic, who took the long view, who defended democracy by criticizing it. This essay begins by referring to the Scopes Monkey Trial of 1925 — mentioned earlier in connection with Clarence Darrow, who took the side opposite William Jennings Bryan. Bryan, populist leader of the Democrats, and erstwhile candidate for the presidency, argued for the right of the state of Tennessee to forbid the teaching of evolution.*

41

WALTER LIPPMANN
Why Should the Majority Rule?

During the Dayton trial there was much discussion about what had happened to Mr. Bryan. How had a progressive democrat become so illiberal? How did it happen that the leader of the hosts of progress in 1896 was the leader of the hosts of darkness in 1925? 1

It was said that he had grown old. It was said that he was running for President. It was said that he had the ambition to lead an uprising of fundamentalists and prohibitionists. It was said that he was a beaten orator who had found his last applauding audience in the backwoods. And it was said that he had undergone a passionate religious conversion. 2

No matter whether the comment was charitable or malicious, it was always an explanation. There was always the assumption that Mr. 3

Bryan had changed and, that in changing, he had departed from the cardinal tenets of his political faith. Mr. Bryan vehemently denied this and, on reflection, I am now inclined to think he was right. We were too hasty. Mr. Bryan's career was more logical and of a piece than it looked. There was no such contradiction, as most of us assumed, in the spectacle of the Great Commoner fighting for the legal suppression of scientific teaching.

4   He had argued that a majority of the voters in Tennessee had the right to decide what should be taught in their schools. He had always argued that a majority had the right to decide. He had insisted on their right to decide on war and peace, on their right to make and unmake laws and lawmakers. He had fought to extend the suffrage so that the largest possible majority might help to decide; he had fought for the direct election of senators, for the initiative and referendum and direct primary, and for every other device which would permit the people to rule. He had always insisted that the people should rule. And he had never qualified this faith by saying what they should rule and how. It was no great transformation of thought, and certainly it was not for him an abandonment of principle to say that, if a majority in Tennessee was fundamentalist, then the public schools in Tennessee should be conducted on fundamentalist principles.

5   To question this right of the majority would have seemed to him as heretical as to question the fundamentalist creed. Mr. Bryan was as true to his political as he was to his religious faith. He had always believed in the sanctity of the text of the Bible. He had always believed that a majority of the people should rule. Here in Tennessee was a majority which believed in the sanctity of the text. To lead this majority was the logical climax of his career, and he died fighting for a cause in which the two great dogmas of his life were both at stake.

6   Given his two premises, I do not see how it is possible to escape his conclusions. If every word of the first chapter of Genesis is directly inspired by an omniscient and omnipotent God, then there is no honest way of accepting what scientists teach about the origin of man. And if the doctrine of majority rule is based on the eternal and inherent rights of man, then it is the only true basis of government, and there can be no fair objections to the moral basis of a law made by a fundamentalist majority in Tennessee. It is no answer to Mr. Bryan to say that the law is absurd, obscurantist, and reactionary. It follows from his premises, and it can be attacked radically only by attacking his premises.

7   This first premise: that the text of the Bible was written, as John

Donne put it, by the Secretaries of the Holy Ghost, I shall not attempt to discuss here. There exists a vast literature of criticism. I am interested in his second premise: that the majority is of right sovereign in all things. And here the position is quite different. There is a literature of dissent and of satire and denunciation. But there exists no carefully worked-out higher criticism of a dogma which, in theory at least, constitutes the fundamental principle of nearly every government in the western world. On the contrary, the main effort of political thinkers during the last few generations has been devoted to vindicating the rights of masses of men against the vested rights of clerics and kings and nobles and men of property. There has been a running counter attack from those who distrusted the people, or had some interest in opposing their enfranchisement, but I do not know of any serious attempt to reach a clear understanding of where and when the majority principle applies.

Mr. Bryan applied it absolutely at Dayton, and thereby did a service to democratic thinking. For he reduced to absurdity a dogma which had been held carelessly but almost universally, and thus demonstrated that it was time to reconsider the premises of the democratic faith. Those who believed in democracy have always assumed that the majority should rule. They have assumed that, even if the majority is not wise, it is on the road to wisdom, and that with sufficient education the people would learn how to rule. But in Tennessee the people used their power to prevent their own children from learning, not merely the doctrine of evolution, but the spirit and method by which learning is possible. They had used their right to rule in order to weaken the agency which they had set up in order that they might learn how to rule. They had used the prerogatives of democracy to destroy the hopes of democracy. 8

After this demonstration in Tennessee it was no longer possible to doubt that the dogma of majority rule contains within it some sort of deep and destructive confusion. 9

In exploring this dogma it will be best to begin at the very beginning with the primitive intuition from which the whole democratic view of life is derived. It is a feeling of ultimate equality and fellowship with all other creatures. 10

There is no worldly sense in this feeling, for it is reasoned from the heart: "there you are, sir, and there is your neighbor. You are better born than he, you are richer, you are stronger, you are handsomer, nay, you are better, wiser, kinder, more likable; you have given more to 11 your fellowmen and taken less than he. By any and every test of intelligence, of virtue, of usefulness, you are demonstrably a better man than he, and yet — absurd as it sounds — these differences do not matter, for the last part of him is untouchable and incomparable and unique and universal." Either you feel this or you do not; when you do not feel it the superiorities that the world acknowledges seem like mountainous waves at sea; when you do feel it they are slight and impermanent ripples upon a vast ocean. Men were possessed by this feeling long before they had imagined the possibility of democratic government. They spoke of it in many ways but the essential quality of feeling is the same from Buddha to St. Francis to Whitman.

12   There is no way of proving the doctrine that all souls are precious in the eyes of God, or, as Dean Inge recently put it, that "the personality of every man and woman is sacred and inviolable." The doctrine proceeds from a mystical intuition. There is felt to be a spiritual reality behind and independent of the visible character and behavior of a man. We have no scientific evidence that this exists. But we know each of us, in a way too certain for doubting, that, after all the weighing and comparing and judging of us is done, there is something left over which is the heart of the matter. Hence our conviction when we ourselves are judged that mercy is more just than justice. When we know the facts as we can know only the facts about ourselves, there is something too coarse in all the concepts of the intelligence and something too rough in all the standards of morality. The judgments of men fall upon behavior. They may be necessary judgments, but we do not believe they are final. There is something else, which is inadmissable, perhaps, as evidence in this world, which would weigh mightily before divine justice.

13   Each of us knows that of himself, and some attribute the same reserved value to others. Some natures with a genius for sympathy extend it to everyone they know and can imagine; others can barely project it to their wives and children. But even though few really have this sympathy with all men, there is enough of it abroad, reinforced perhaps with each man's dread of his fate in the unknown, to establish the doctrine rather generally. So we execute the murderer, but out of respect for an inviolable part of him we allow him the consolation of a priest and we bury him respectfully when he is dead. For we believe that, however terrible was his conduct, there is in him, nevertheless, though no human mind can detect it, a final quality which makes him part of our own destiny in the universe.

14   I can think of no inherent reason why men should entertain this mystical respect for other men. But it is easy to show how much that

we find best in the world would be lost if the sense of equality and fellowship were lost. If we judged and were judged by our visible behavior alone, the inner defenses of civility and friendship and enduring love would be reached. Outward conduct is not good enough to endure a cold and steady analysis. Only an animal affection become habitual and reflected in mystical respect can blind people sufficiently to our faults. They would not like us enough to pardon us if all they had to go on was a strict behaviorist account of our conduct. They must reach deeper, blindly and confidently, to something which they know is likable although they do not know why. Otherwise the inequalities of men would be intolerable. The strong, the clever, the beautiful, the competent, and the good, would make life miserable for their neighbors. They would be unbearable with their superiorities, and they would find unbearable the sense of inferiority they implanted in others. There would be no term upon the arrogance of the successful and the envy of the defeated. For without the mystic sense of equality the obvious inequalities would seem unalterable.

These temporal differences are seen in perspective by the doctrine 15 that in the light of eternity there are no differences at all.

It is not possible for most of us, however, to consider anything 16 very clearly or steadily in the light of eternity. The doctrine of ultimate human equality cannot be tested in human experience; it rests on a faith which transcends experience. That is why those who understood the doctrine have always been ascetic; they ignored or renounced worldly goods and worldly standards. These things belonged to Caesar. The mystical democrat did not say that they should not belong to Caesar; he said that they would be of no use to Caesar ultimately, and that, therefore, they were not to be taken seriously now.

But in the reception of this subtle argument the essential reser- 17 vation was soon obscured. The mystics were preaching equality only to those men who had renounced their carnal appetites; they were welcomed as preachers of equality in this world. Thus the doctrine that I am as good as you in eternity because all the standards of goodness are finite and temporary, was converted into the doctrine that I am as good as you are in this world by this world's standards. The mystics had attained a sense of equality by transcending and renouncing all the standards by which we measure inequality. The populace retained its appetites and its standards and then sought to deny the inequalities which they produced and revealed.

The mystical democrat had said, "Gold and precious stones are 18 of no account"; the literal democrat understood him to say that everybody ought to have gold and precious stones. The mystical democrat had said, "Beauty is only skin deep"; and the literal democrat preened himself and said, "I always suspected I was as handsome as you." Reason, intelligence, learning, wisdom, dealt for the mystic only with passing events in a temporal world and could help men little to fathom the ultimate meaning of creation; to the literal democrat this incapacity of reason was evidence that one man's notion was intrinsically as good as another's.

19   Thus the primitive intuition of democracy became the animus of a philosophy which denied that there could be an order of values among men. Any opinion, any taste, any action was intrinsically as good as any other. Each stands on its own bottom and guarantees itself. If I feel strongly about it, it is right; there is no other test. It is right not only as against your opinion, but against my own opinions, about which I no longer feel so strongly. There is no arbitrament by which the relative value of opinions is determined. They are all free, they are all equal, all have the same rights and powers.

20   Since no value can be placed upon an opinion, there is no way in this philosophy of deciding between opinions except to count them. Thus the mystical sense of equality was translated to mean in practice that two minds are better than one mind and two souls better than one soul. Your true mystic would be horrified at the notion that you can add up souls and that the greater number is superior to the lesser. To him souls are imponderable and incommensurable; that is the only sense in which they are truly equal. And yet in the name of that sense of equality which he attains by denying that the worth of a soul can be measured, the worldly democrats have made the mere counting of souls the final arbiter of all worth. It is a curious misunderstanding; Mr. Bryan brought it into high relief during the Tennessee case. The spiritual doctrine that all men will stand at last equal before the throne of God meant to him that all men are equally good biologists before the ballotbox of Tennessee. That kind of democracy is quite evidently a gross materialization of an idea that in essence cannot be materialized. It is a confusing interchange of two worlds that are not interchangeable.

21   Although the principle of majority rule derives a certain sanctity from the mystical sense of equality; it is really quite unrelated to it. There is nothing in the teachings of Jesus or St. Francis which justifies us in thinking that the opinions of fifty-one per cent of a group are

better than the opinions of forty-nine per cent. The mystical doctrine of equality ignores the standards of the world and recognizes each soul as unique; the principle of majority rule is a device for establishing the standards of action in this world by the crude and obvious device of adding up voters. Yet owing to a confusion between the two; the mystical doctrine has been brutalized and made absurd, and the principle of majority rule has acquired an unction that protects it from criticism. A mere political expedient, worth using only when it is necessary or demonstrably useful to the conduct of affairs, has been hallowed by an altogether adventitious sanctity due to an association of ideas with a religious hope of salvation.

Once we succeed in disentangling this confusion of ideas, it be- 22 comes apparent that the principle of majority rule is wholly alien to what the humane mystic feels. The rule of the majority is the rule of force. For while nobody can seriously maintain that the greatest number must have the greatest wisdom or the greatest virtue, there is no denying that under modern social conditions they are likely to have the most power. I say likely to have, for we are reminded by the recent history of Russia and of Italy that organized and armed minorities can under certain circumstances disfranchise the majority. Nevertheless, it is a good working premise that in the long run the greater force resides in the greater number, and what we call a democratic society might be defined for certain purposes as one in which the majority is always prepared to put down a revolutionary minority.

The apologists of democracy have done their best to dissemble 23 the true nature of majority rule. They have argued that by some mysterious process the opinion to which a majority subscribes is true and righteous. They have even attempted to endow the sovereign majority with the inspiration of an infallible church and of kings by the grace of God. It was a natural mistake. Although they saw clearly enough that the utterances of the church were the decisions of the ruling clergy, and that the divine guidance of the king was exercised by his courtiers, they were not prepared to admit that the new sovereign was a purely temporal ruler. They felt certain they must ascribe to the majority of the voters the same supernatural excellence which had always adhered to the traditional rulers. Throughout the Nineteenth Century, therefore, the people were flattered and mystified by hearing that deep within a fixed percentage of them there lay the same divine inspiration and the same gifts of revelation which men had attributed previously to the established authorities.

And then just as in the past men had invented a mythical ances- 24 try for their king, tracing his line back to David or Aeneas or Zeus himself, so the minnesingers of democracy have invented their own account of the rise of popular government. The classic legend is to be found in the theory of the Social Contract, and a few naïve democrats are without traces of belief in this legend. They imagine that somehow "the people" got together and established nations and governments and institutions. Yet the historic record plainly shows that the progress of democracy has consisted in an increasing participation of an increasing number of people in the management of institutions they neither created nor willed. And the record shows, too, that new numbers were allowed to participate when they were powerful enough to force their way in; they were enfranchised not because "society" sought the benefits of their wisdom, and not because "society" wished them to have power; they were enfranchised because they had power, and giving them the vote was the least disturbing way of letting them exercise their power. For the principle of majority rule is the mildest form in which the force of numbers can be exercised. It is a pacific substitute for civil war in which the opposing armies are counted and the victory is awarded to the larger before any blood is shed.

25   Except in the sacred tests of democracy and in the incantations of the orators, we hardly take the trouble to pretend that the rule of the majority is not at bottom a rule of force. What other virtue can there be in fifty-one per cent except the brute fact that fifty-one is more than forty-nine? The rule of fifty-one per cent is a convenience, it is for certain matters a satisfactory political device, it is for others the lesser of two evils, and for still others it is acceptable because we do not know any less troublesome method of obtaining a political decision. But it may easily become an absurd tyranny if we regard it worshipfully, as though it were more than a political device. We have lost all sense of its true meaning when we imagine that the opinion of fifty-one per cent is in some high fashion the true opinion of the whole hundred per cent, or indulge in the sophistry that the rule of a majority is based upon the ultimate equality of man.

26   At Dayton Mr. Bryan contended that in schools supported by the state the majority of the voters had a right to determine what should be taught. If my analysis is correct, there is no fact from which that right can be derived except the fact that the majority is stronger than the minority. It cannot be argued that the majority in Tennessee represented the whole people of Tennessee; nor that fifty-one Tennesseans are better than forty-nine Tennesseans; nor that they were

better biologists, or better Christians, or better parents, or better Americans. It cannot be said they are necessarily more in tune with the ultimate judgments of God. All that can be said for them is that there are more of them, and that in a world ruled by force it may be necessary to defer to the force they exercise.

When the majority exercises that force to destroy the public   27
schools, the minority may have to yield for a time to this force but there is no reason why they should accept the result. For the votes of a majority have no intrinsic bearing on the conduct of a school. They are external facts to be taken into consideration like the weather or the hazard of fire. Guudance for a school can come ultimately only from educators, and the question of what shall be taught as biology can be determined only by biologists. The votes of a majority do not settle anything here and they are entitled to no respect whatever. They may be right or they may be wrong; there is nothing in the majority principle which will make them either right or wrong. In the conduct of schools, and especially as to the details of the curriculum, the majority principle is an obvious irrelevance. It is not even a convenient device, as it is in the determination, say, of who shall pay the taxes.

But what good is it to deny the competence of the majority when   28
you have admitted that it has the power to enforce its decisions? I enter this denial myself because I prefer clarity to confusion, and the ascriptions of wisdom to fifty-one per cent seems to me a pernicious confusion. But I do it also because I have some hope that the exorcising of the superstition which has become attached to majority rule will weaken its hold upon the popular imagination, and tend therefore to keep it within convenient limits. Mr. Bryan would not have won the logical victory he won at Dayton if educated people had not been caught in a tangle of ideas which made it seem as if the acknowledgment of the absolutism of the majority was necessary to faith in the final value of the human soul. It seems to me that a rigorous untangling of this confusion may help to arm the minority for a more effective resistance in the future.

_____ CONSIDERATIONS _____

1. Lippmann begins his essay by discussing Bryan's position in the Scopes trial in terms of formal logic: first premise, second premise, and conclusions derived from those premises. Refresh your memory of syllogistic reason-

ing by reading pages 122–123 of Robert Gorham Davis's essay on logic and logical fallacy. Construct the syllogism that Lippmann considers the basis of Bryan's position. Do you agree with Lippmann?

2. In Paragraph 8, Lippmann states one conviction of those who believe in democracy: that "with sufficient education the people would learn how to rule." Does this conviction run parallel or counter to Caroline Bird's arguments in her negative evaluation of American college education (pages 64–73)?

3. Lippmann asserts that the idea of majority rule derives ultimately, not from reasoned argument but from feeling. Does his explanation help explain Thomas Jefferson's statement in the Declaration of Independence that all men are created equal? Or do you prefer Garry Wills's explanation of the same statement in his essay on the declaration (pages 458–469)? Does Lippmann's statement make him a Romantic in Wills's eyes?

4. How would you have to change your life, according to Lippmann, if you were to be a true believer in democracy? See paragraphs 12, 13, 14, and 15.

5. Lippmann argues that, "Although the principle of majority rule derives a certain sanctity from the mystical sense of equality, it is really quite unrelated to it." How does he support or clarify that argument?

6. Lippmann's essay is a discussion of abstractions. Study the ways in which he attempts to pin down those abstractions to concrete reality. Are they adequate? Relevant? Fairly chosen?

John McPhee (b. 1931) was born in Princeton, New Jersey, where he graduated from college, and where he still lives. His writing, largely for The New Yorker, *has taken him far afield, to Florida for a book about oranges, to Maine for a book about birchbark canoes, and all over the country for encounters with the American wilderness. In 1977 he published a report on Alaska called* Coming into the Country.

He can also write about tennis, with a command of detail, precise and fascinating, which almost obscures the skill of his sentences, his transitions, and his paragraph structure.

42

JOHN McPHEE

Ashe and Graebner

Ashe returns serve with a solid forehand, down the line. Graebner, lunging, picks it up with a backhand half-volley. The ball floats back to Ashe. He takes a three-hundred-degree roundhouse swing and drives the ball crosscourt so fast that Graebner, who is within close reach of it, cannot react quickly enough to get his racquet on it. Hopefully, Graebner whips his head around to see where the ball lands. It lands on the line — a liner, in the language of the game. "There's Ashe getting lucky again." 1

Ashe does a deep knee bend to remind himself to stay low. Graebner hits a big serve wide, and a second serve that ticks the cord and skips away. Double fault. Carole pats the air. Calm down, Clark. Graebner can consider himself half broken. The score is love-thiry. Ashe thinks, "You're in trouble, Clark. Deep trouble." 2

3   "I'll bet a hundred to one I pull out of it," Graebner tells himself. Crunch. His serve is blocked back, and he punches a volley to Ashe's backhand. Ashe now has two principal alternatives: to return the ball conservatively and safely, adding to the pressure that is already heavy on Graebner, or to cut loose the one-in-ten shot, going for the overwhelming advantage of a love-forty score by the method of the fast kill. Ashe seems to have no difficulty making the choice. He blasts. He misses. Fifteen-thirty.

4   Graebner serves, attacks the net, volleys, rises high for an overhead — he goes up like a basketball player for a rebound — and smashes the ball away. Thirty-all.

5   Now the thought crosses Graebner's mind that Ashe has not missed a service return in this game. The thought unnerves him a little. He hits a big one four feet too deep, then bloops his second serve with terrible placement right into the center of the service court. He now becomes the mouse, Ashe the cat. With soft, perfectly placed shots, Ashe jerks him around the forecourt, then closes off the point with a shot to remember. It is a forehand, with top spin, sent crosscourt so lightly that the ball appears to be flung rather than hit. Its angle to the net is less than ten degrees — a difficult, brilliant stroke, and Ashe hit it with such nonchalance that he appeared to be thinking of something else. Graebner feels the implications of this. Ashe is now obviously loose. Loose equals dangerous. When a player is loose, he serves and volleys at his best level. His general shotmaking ability is optimum. He will try anything. "Look at the way he hit that ball, gave it the casual play," Graebner says to himself. "Instead of trying a silly shot and missing it, he tries a silly shot and makes it." If Ashe wins the next point, he will have broken Graebner, and the match will be, in effect, even.

6   Again Graebner misses his first serve. Ashe, waiting for the second, says to himself, "Come on. Move in. Move in. I should get it now." When Ashe really feels he has a chance for a break, the index of his desire is that he moves in a couple of steps on second serves. He takes his usual position, about a foot behind the baseline, until Graebner lifts the ball. Then he moves quickly about a yard forward and stops, motionless, as if he were participating in a game of kick-the-can and Graebner were It. Graebner's second serve spins in, and bounces high to Ashe's backhand. Ashe strokes it with underspin. Graebner hits a deep approach shot to Ashe's backhand. Ashe hits a deft, appropriate lob. Graebner wants this point just as much as Ashe does.

Scrambling backward, he reaches up and behind him and picks out of the sun an overhead that becomes an almost perfect drop shot, surprising Ashe and drawing him toward the net. At a dead run, Ashe reaches for the ball and more or less shovels it over the net. Graebner has been moving forward, too, and he has stopped for half a second, legs apart, poised, to see what will happen. The ball moves toward his backhand. He moves to the ball and drives it past Ashe, down the line. Graebner is still unbroken. But the game is at deuce. It is only the second time Ashe has extended him that far.

After this game, new balls will be coming in — all the more reason for Ashe to try to break Graebner now. Tennis balls are used for nine games (warm-up counts for two), and over that span they get fluffier and fluffier. When they are new and the nap is flat, wind resistance is minimal and they come through fast and heavy. Newies, or freshies, as the tennis players call them, are a considerable advantage to the server — something like a supply of bullets. Graebner meanwhile serves wide to Ashe's forehand, and Ashe hits the return with at least equal velocity. Graebner is caught on his heels, and hits a defensive backhand down the middle. It bounces in no man's land. Ashe, taking it on his backhand, has plenty of time. His racquet is far back and ready. Graebner makes a blind rush for the net, preferring to be caught in motion than helpless on the baseline. But Ashe's shot is too hard, too fast, too tough, too accurate, skidding off the turf in the last square foot of Graebner's forehand corner. Advantage Ashe. 7

"Look at that shot. That's ridiculous," Graebner tells himself. He glances at Carole, who has both fists in the air. Pull yourself together, Clark. This is a big point. Graebner takes off his glasses and wipes them on his dental towel. "Stalling," Ashe mumbles. While he is waiting, he raises his left index finger and slowly pushes his glasses into place across the bridge of his nose. "Just one point, Arthur." Graebner misses his first serve again. Ashe moves in. He hits sharply crosscourt. Graebner dives for it, catches it with a volley, then springs up, ready, at the net. Ashe lobs into the sun, thinking, "That was a good get on that volley. I didn't think he'd get that." Graebner reaches for the overhead and smashes it directly at Ashe. Ashe, swinging desperately, belts it right back at him. Graebner punches the ball away with a forehand volley. Deuce. Ashe is rattling the gates, but Graebner will not let him in. Carole has her hand on the top of her head. Unbelievable. 8

Graebner serves, moves up, and volleys. Ashe, running, smacks 9 an all-or-nothing backhand that hums past Graebner and lands a few inches inside the line. Graebner says to himself, "He's hitting the lines, the lucky bastard. The odds are ten to one against him and he makes the shot. That bugs me." Advantage Ashe.

10   Jack Kramer, broadcasting the match, says that this is the best game not only of this match but of the entire tournament so far. Again Ashe needs just one point and he will be leading four games to two. Graebner serves. Ashe returns. Graebner half-volleys. Ashe throws a lob into the sun. Graebner nearly loses it there. He can only hit it weakly — a kind of overhead tap that drops softly at Ashe's feet. This is it. Ashe swings — a big backhand — for the kill. The ball lands two feet out. Graebner inhales about seven quarts of air, and slowly releases six. It is deuce again.

11   Donald Dell, the captain of the Davis Cup Team, is sitting in the Marquee. He says, "Arthur has hit five winners and he hasn't won the game. He looks perturbed." Dell knows Ashe so well that he can often tell by the way Ashe walks or stands what is going on behind the noncommittal face. But Ashe is under control. He is telling himself, "If you tend to your knitting, you will get the job done." Graebner's first serve, which has misfired seven times in this game, does not misfire now. Ashe reacts, swings, hits it hard — a hundredth of a second too late. The shot, off his backhand, fails by a few inches to come in to the sideline. Advantage Graebner.

12   Carole's fists are up. Clark adjusts his glasses, wipes off his right hand, and bounces the ball. He serves hard to Ashe's forehand. The ball, blasted, comes back. Disappointment races through Graebner's mind. "I'm serving to his forehand. His forehand is his weakest shot. If the guy returns his weakest shot all the time, he's just too good." Graebner tries a drop shot, then goes to his right on the sheer gamble that Ashe's response will take that direction. It does. Graebner, with full power, drives an apparent putaway down the line. But Ashe gets to it and blocks the ball, effecting what under the circumstances is a remarkably good lob. Graebner leaps, whips his racquet overhead, and connects. The ball hits the turf on Ashe's backhand and bounces wide. Ashe plunges for it, swings with both feet off the ground, and hits the ball so hard down the line that Graebner cannot get near it. Graebner can be pardoned if he cannot believe it. For the fourth time, the game is at deuce.

13   "Arthur is just seeing the ball better, or something," Graebner tells himself. But Graebner sees the ball, too, and he hits a big-crunch unplayable serve. Advantage Graebner.

Serve, return, volley — Ashe hits a forehand into the tape. Ashe   14
has not been able to get out from under. Games are three-all, second
set.

_____ CONSIDERATIONS _____

1. An unusual feature of McPhee's account is that it is told in the present tense. Flip quickly through this book to see if you can find any other pieces
in the present tense. How does this use of tense contribute to the effect of
McPhee's account? Why don't more authors use the present tense?

2. From whose point of view does McPhee give us this story: his own,
Ashe's, Graebner's, or some combination of all three? Is it difficult to decide?

3. McPhee often uses sentence fragments, as in paragraphs 2, 3, 4, and 5.
Since most professional writers routinely avoid fragments, what reason can
you produce for McPhee's use of them?

4. Select one sentence that seems particularly effective in giving the
impression of action. Study its construction. Try to reproduce that structure
by composing a sentence, identical in syntactical construction, on a different
subject.

5. Tennis, like many other sports, has developed its own special vocabulary, a jargon that sometimes excludes the general public. What use does
McPhee make of tennis jargon, and how does he avoid mystifying the reader
who may not know a tennis racquet from a handsaw? What, for example, do
you make of "That was a good get" in Paragraph 8?

6. Is there any point in ending his account halfway through the second
set with the games tied up?

Norman Mailer (b. 1923) grew up in Brooklyn and went to Harvard. As an undergraduate he was already publishing short stories, and his first book was a novel about World War II called The Naked and the Dead *(1948). He has published four novels since —* Barbary Shore *(1951),* The Deer Park *(1955),* An American Dream *(1965), and* Why Are We in Vietnam? *(1967) — but more and more of his writing has been nonfiction, and he is an eminent practitioner of the New Journalism, nonfiction that employs many devices we used to associate only with fiction — lively description, dialogue, subjective exposition of character, and a tone that combines informality with energy. Early essays appeared in* Advertisements for Myself *(1959), along with stories and parts of abandoned novels. In* The Presidential Papers *(1963) he began to go more fully into politics, a subject that returned in* Cannibals and Christians *(1966) and books about the protest movement (*The Armies of the Night, *1968) and about the political campaigns of 1968 and 1972 (*Miami and the Siege of Chicago, *1968;* St. George and the Godfather, *1972). More recently, he is author of books about Marilyn Monroe and Muhammad Ali.*

Perhaps the best of his nonfiction books is Of a Fire on the Moon *(1971), his account of the first journey to the moon. This book uses some observation and personal experience; Mailer interviewed Werner Von Braun, he watched the Apollo take off. He has used much diligent research in engineering and the sciences, perhaps drawing on memories of his studies for the Bachelor of Science degree in aeronautical engineering that he took at Harvard in 1943. But Mailer's personal style often disguises Mailer's hard work. His novelist's ear for language allows him to describe with brilliance such matters as the difficulty of wedging a bulky space suit through a narrow hatch. Here, he narrates and explains the moments of man's first steps on the moon.*

43

NORMAN MAILER

A Walk on the Moon

It was not until nine-forty at night, Houston time, that they got   1
the hatch open at last. In the heat of running almost two hours late,
ensconced in the armor of a man-sized spaceship, could they still have
felt an instant of awe as they looked out that open hatch at a panorama
of theater: the sky is black, but the ground is brightly lit, bright as
footlights on the floor of a dark theater. A black and midnight sky, yet
on the moon ground, "you could almost go out in your shirt-sleeves
and get a suntan," Aldrin would say. "I remember thinking, 'Gee, if I
didn't know where I was, I could believe that somebody had created
this environment somewhere out in the West and given us another
simulation to work in.' " Everywhere on that pitted flat were shadows
dark as the sky above, shadows dark as mine shafts.

What a struggle to push out from that congested cabin, now twice   2
congested in their bulky-wham suits, no feeling of obstacle against
their flesh, their sense of touch dead and numb, spaceman body manip-
ulated out into the moon world like an upright piano turned by movers
on the corner of the stairs.

"You're lined up on the platform. Put your left foot to the right a   3
little bit. Okay, that's good. Roll left."

Armstrong was finally on the porch. Could it be with any sense   4
of an alien atmosphere receiving the fifteen-layer encapsulations of the
pack and suit on his back? Slowly, he climbed down the ladder. Archetypal, he must have felt, a boy descending the rungs in the wall of an
abandoned well, or was it Jack down the stalk? And there he was on
the bottom, on the footpad of the leg of the Lem, a metal plate perhaps
three feet across. Inches away was the soil of the moon. But first he

jumped up again to the lowest rung of the ladder. A couple of hours later, at the end of the EVA, conceivably exhausted, the jump from the ground to the rung, three feet up, might be difficult in that stiff and heavy space suit, so he tested it now. "It takes," said Armstrong, "a pretty good little jump."

5   Now, with television working, and some fraction of the world peering at the murky image of this instant, poised between the end of one history and the beginning of another, he said quietly, "I'm at the foot of the ladder. The Lem footpads are only depressed in the surface about one or two inches, although the surface appears to be very very fine-grained as you get close to it. It's almost like a powder." One of Armstrong's rare confessions of uneasiness is focused later on this moment. "I don't recall any particular emotion or feeling other than a little caution, a desire to be sure it was safe to put my weight on that surface outside Eagle's footpad."

6   Did his foot tingle in the heavy lunar overshoe? "I'm going to step off the Lem now."

7   Did something in him shudder at the touch of the new ground? Or did he draw a sweet strength from the balls of his feet? Nobody was necessarily going ever to know.

8   "That's one small step for a man," said Armstrong, "one giant leap for mankind." He had joined the ranks of the forever quoted. Patrick Henry, Henry Stanley and Admiral Dewey moved over for him.

9   Now he was out there, one foot on the moon, then the other foot on the moon, the powder like velvet underfoot. With one hand still on the ladder, he comments, "The surface is fine and powdery. I can . . . I can pick it up loosely with my toe." And as he releases his catch, the grains fall back slowly to the soil, a fan of feathers gliding to the floor. "It does adhere in fine layers like powdered charcoal to the sole and sides of my boots. I only go in a small fraction of an inch. Maybe an eighth of an inch. But I can see the footprints of my boots and the treads in the fine sand particles."

10   Capcom: "Neil, this is Houston. We're copying."

11   Yes, they would copy. He was like a man who goes into a wrecked building to defuse a new kind of bomb. He talks into a microphone as he works, for if a mistake is made, and the bomb goes off, it will be easier for the next man if every detail of his activities has been mentioned as he performed them. Now, he released his grip on the ladder and pushed off for a few steps on the moon, odd loping steps, almost thrust into motion like a horse trotting up a steep slope. It could have

been a moment equivalent to the first steps he took as an infant for there was nothing to hold onto and he did not dare to fall — the ground was too hot, the rocks might tear his suit. Yet if he stumbled, he could easily go over for he could not raise his arms above his head nor reach to his knees, his arms in the pressure bladder stood out before him like sausages; so, if he tottered, the weight of the pack could twist him around, or drop him. They had tried to shape up simulations of lunar gravity while weighted in scuba suits at the bottom of a pool, but water was not a vacuum through which to move; so they had also flown in planes carrying two hundred pounds of equipment on their backs. The pilot would take the plane through a parabolic trajectory. There would be a period of twenty-two seconds at the top of the curve when a simulation of one-sixth gravity would be present, and the two hundred pounds of equipment would weigh no more than on the moon, no more than thirty-plus pounds, and one could take loping steps down the aisle of the plane, staggering through unforeseen wobbles or turbulence. Then the parabolic trajectory was done, the plane was diving, and it would have to pull out of the dive. That created the reverse of one-sixth gravity — it multiplied gravity by two and a half times. The two hundred pounds of equipment now weighed five hundred pounds and the astronauts had to be supported by other men straining to help them bear the weight. So simulations gave them time for hardly more than a clue before heavy punishment was upon them. But now he was out in the open endless lunar gravity, his body and the reflexes of his life obliged to adopt a new rhythm and schedule of effort, a new disclosure of grace.

Still, he seemed pleased after the first few steps. "There seems to 12 be no difficulty in moving around as we suspected. It's even perhaps easier than the simulations . . ." He would run a few steps and stop, run a few steps and stop. Perhaps it was not unlike directing the Lem when it hovered over the ground. One moved faster than on earth and with less effort, but it was harder to stop — one had to pick the place to halt from several yards ahead. Yes, it was easier once moving, but awkward at the beginning and the end because of the obdurate plastic bendings of the suit. And once standing at rest, the sense of the vertical was sly. One could be leaning further forward than one knew. Or leaning backward. Like a needle on a dial one would have to oscillate from side to side of the vertical to find position. Conceivably the sensation was not unlike skiing with a child on one's back.

It was time for Aldrin to descend the ladder from the Lem to the 13 ground, and Armstrong's turn to give directions: "The shoes are about to come over the sill. Okay, now drop your PLSS down. There you go. You're clear. . . . About an inch clearance on top of your PLSS.''

14 Aldrin spoke for future astronauts: "Okay, you need a little bit of arching of the back to come down . . .''

15 When he reached the ground, Aldrin took a big and exuberant leap up the ladder again, as if to taste the pleasures of one-sixth gravity all at once. "Beautiful, beautiful,'' he exclaimed.

16 Armstrong: "Isn't that something. Magnificent sight out here.''

17 Aldrin: "Magnificent desolation.''

18 They were looking at a terrain which lived in a clarity of focus unlike anything they had ever seen on earth. There was no air, of course, and so no wind, nor clouds, nor dust, nor even the finest scattering of light from the smallest dispersal of microscopic particles on a clear day on earth, no, nothing visible or invisible moved in the vacuum before them. All light was pure. No haze was present, not even the invisible haze of the finest day — therefore objects did not go out of focus as they receded into the distance. If one's eyes were good enough, an object at a hundred yards was as distinct as a rock at a few feet. And their eyes were good enough. Just as one could not determine one's altitude above the moon, not from fifty miles up nor five, so now along the ground before them no distance was real, for all distances had the faculty to appear equally near if one peered at them through blinders and could not see the intervening details. Again the sense of being on a stage or on the lighted floor of a room so large one could not see where the dark ceiling began must have come upon them, for there were no hints of gathering evanescence in ridge beyond ridge; rather each outline was as severe as the one in front of it, and since the ground was filled with small craters of every size, from antholes to potholes to empty pools, and the horizon was near, four times nearer than on earth and sharp as the line drawn by a pencil, the moon ground seemed to slope and drop in all directions "like swimming in an ocean with six-foot or eight-foot swells and waves,'' Armstrong said later. "In that condition, you never can see very far away from where you are.'' But what they could see, they could see entirely — to the depth of their field of view at any instant their focus was complete. And as they swayed from side to side, so a sense of the vertical kept eluding them, the slopes of the craters about them seeming to tilt a few degrees to one side of the horizontal, then the other. On earth, one had only to incline one's body an inch or two and a sense of the vertical was gone, but on the moon they could lean over, then further over, lean considerably further over without beginning to fall. So verticals slid and oscillated. Rolling from side to side, they could as well have been on

water, indeed their sense of the vertical was probably equal to the subtle uncertainty of the body when a ship is rolling on a quiet sea. "I say," said Aldrin, "the rocks are rather slippery."

They were discovering the powder of the moon soil was curious   19
indeed, comparable in firmness and traction to some matter between sand and snow. While the Lem looked light as a kite, for its pads hardly rested on the ground and it appeared ready to lift off and blow away, yet their own feet sometimes sank for two or three inches into the soft powder on the slope of very small craters, and their soles would slip as the powder gave way under their boots. In other places the ground was firm and harder than sand, yet all of these variations were to be found in an area not a hundred feet out from the legs of the Lem. As he explored his footing, Aldrin sent back comments to Mission Control, reporting in the rapt professional tones of a coach instructing his team on the conditions of the turf in a new plastic football field.

Meanwhile Armstrong was transporting the television camera   20
away from the Lem to a position where it could cover most of their activities. Once properly installed, he revolved it through a full panorama of their view in order that audiences on earth might have a clue to what he saw. But in fact the transmission was too rudimentary to give any sense of what was about them, that desert sea of rocks, rubble, small boulders, and crater lips.

Aldrin was now working to set up the solar wind experiment, a   21
sheet of aluminum foil hung on a stand. For the next hour and a half, the foil would be exposed to the solar wind, an invisible, unfelt, but high-velocity flow of noble gases from the sun like argon, krypton, neon and helium. For the astronauts, it was the simplest of procedures, no more difficult than setting up a piece of sheet music on a music stand. At the end of the EVA, however, the aluminum foil would be rolled up, inserted in the rock box, and delivered eventually to a laboratory in Switzerland uniquely equipped for the purpose. There any noble gases which had been trapped in the atomic lattice of the aluminum would be baked out in virtuoso procedures of quantitative analysis, and a closer knowledge of the components of the solar wind would be gained. Since the solar wind, it may be recalled, was diverted by the magnetosphere away from the earth it had not hitherto been available for casual study.

That was the simplest experiment to set up; the other two would   22
be deployed about an hour later. One was a passive seismometer to measure erratic disturbances and any periodic vibrations, as well as moonquakes, and the impact of meteors in the weeks and months to follow; it was equipped to radio this information to earth, the energy

for transmission derived from solar panels which extended out to either side, and thereby gave it the look of one of those spaceships of the future with thin extended paperlike wings which one sees in science fiction drawings. In any case it was so sensitive that the steps of the astronauts were recorded as they walked by. Finally there was a Laser Ranging Retro-Reflector, an LRRR (or LRQ, or L R-cubed), and that was a mirror whose face was a hundred quartz crystals, black as coal, cut to a precision never obtained before in glass — one-third of an arc/sec. Since each quartz crystal was a corner of a rectangle, any ray of light striking one of the three faces in each crystal would bounce off the other two in such a way that the light would return in exactly the same direction it had been received. A laser beam sent up from earth would therefore reflect back to the place from which it was sent. The time it required to travel this half-million miles from earth to moon round trip, a journey of less than three seconds, could be measured so accurately that physicists might then discern whether the moon was drifting away from the earth a few centimeters a year, or (by using two lasers) whether Europe and America might be drifting apart some comparable distance, or even if the Pacific Ocean were contracting. These measurements could then be entered into the caverns of Einstein's General Theory of Relativity, and new proof or disproof of the great thesis could be obtained.

23   We may be certain the equipment was remarkable. Still, its packaging and its ease of deployment had probably done as much to advance its presence on the ship as any clear priority over other scientific equipment; the beauty of these items from the point of view of NASA was that the astronauts could set them up in a few minutes while working in their space suits, even set them up with inflated gloves so insensitive that special silicone pads had to be inserted at the fingertips in order to leave the astronauts not altogether numb-fingered in their manipulations. Yet these marvels of measurement would soon be installed on the moon with less effort than it takes to remove a vacuum cleaner from its carton and get it operating.

24   It was at this point that patriotism, the corporation, and the national taste all came to occupy the same head of a pin, for the astronauts next proceeded to set up the flag. But that operation, as always, presented its exquisite problems. There was, we remind ourselves, no atmosphere for the flag to wave in. Any flag made of cloth would droop, indeed it would dangle. Therefore, a species of starched plastic flag had to be employed, a flag which would stand out, there, out to the nonexistent breeze, flat as a slab of plywood. No, that would not

do either. The flag was better crinkled and curled. Waves and billows were bent into it, and a full corkscrew of a curl at the end. There it stands for posterity, photographed in the twists of a high gale on the windless moon, curled up tin flag, numb as a pickled pepper.

Aldrin would hardly agree. "Being able to salute that flag was one   25
of the more humble yet proud experiences I've ever had. To be able to look at the American flag and know how much so many people had put of themselves and their work into getting it where it was. We sensed — we really did — this almost mystical identification of all the people in the world at that instant."

Two minutes after the flag was up, the President of the United   26
States put in his phone call. Let us listen one more time:

"Because of what you have done," said Nixon, "the heavens have   27
become a part of man's world. And as you talk to us from the Sea of Tranquility, it inspires us to redouble our efforts to bring peace and tranquility to earth . . ."

"Thank you, Mr. President. It's a great honor and privilege for us   28
to be here representing not only the United States, but men of peace of all nations . . ."

In such piety is the schizophrenia of the ages.   29

Immediately afterward, Aldrin practiced kicking moon dust, but   30
he was somewhat broken up. Either reception was garbled, or Aldrin was temporarily incoherent. "They seem to leave," he said to the Capcom, referring to the particles, "and most of them have about the same angle of departure and velocity. From where I stand, a large portion of them will impact at a certain distance out. Several — the percentage is, of course, that will impact . . ."

Capcom: "Buzz, this is Houston. You're cutting out on the end of   31
your transmissions. Can you speak a little more forward into your microphone. Over."

Aldrin: "Roger. I'll try that."   32

Capcom: "Beautiful."   33

Aldrin: "Now I had that one inside my mouth that time."   34

Capcom: "It sounded a little wet."   35

And on earth, a handful of young scientists were screaming, "Stop   36
wasting time with flags and presidents — collect some rocks!"

_____ CONSIDERATIONS _____

1. Mailer's task — to narrate what the moon-walkers experienced — is complicated by the necessity to describe technical operations, equipment, and

navigational procedures. Is Mailer successful in keeping human experience uppermost? Explain.

2. Look closely at Mailer's account of setting up the American flag on the moon and at the remarks immediately following by Aldrin, President Nixon, and Mailer himself. "In such piety is the schizophrenia of the ages," says Mailer. Is this straight reporting? Is it loaded? If so, can you justify it?

3. What are some differences between the astronauts' moon exploration and the travels of others in this book, such as Lillian Hellman (pages 178–184) and N. Scott Momaday (pages 279–285).

4. "If it were spelled 'mune,' " wrote Jack Spicer, the American poet, "it would not cause madness." The moon has been surrounded by worlds of mythology, superstition, and fond fantasy. Will exact information about the moon affect our way of thinking of or responding to "moon"? Does knowledge affect belief?

5. Discuss the remote control of moon exploration, like the way in which a man in Houston tells a man on the moon when to put his left foot down.

Andrew Marvell (1621–1678) lived during a time of turmoil in England — during Cromwell's revolution, the beheading of a king, and the restoration of the monarchy. He was a political man, a member of Parliament, and at different times espoused different sides, without ever turning hypocrite. Some of his poems are political; the best are not, unless "To His Coy Mistress' is a manifesto of sexual politics. Many readers find it less concerned with sexuality than with mortality.

44

ANDREW MARVELL
To His Coy Mistress

Had we but world enough, and time,
This coyness, lady, were no crime.
We would sit down, and think which way
To walk, and pass our long love's day.
Thou by the Indian Ganges' side   5
Shoudst rubies find; I by the tide
Of Humber would complain. I would
Love you ten years before the flood,
And you should, if you please, refuse
Till the conversion of the Jews.   10
My vegetable love should grow
Vaster than empires and more slow;
An hundred years should go to praise
Thine eyes, and on thy forehead gaze;
Two hundred to adore each breast,   15
But thirty thousand to the rest;
An age at least to every part,
And the last age should show your heart.

For, lady, you deserve this state,
20 Nor would I love at lower rate
      But at my back I always hear
    Time's wingéd chariot hurrying near;
    And yonder all before us lie
    Deserts of vast eternity.
25 Thy beauty shall no more be found;
    Nor, in thy marble vault, shall sound
    My echoing song; then worms shall try
    That long-preserved virginity,
    And your quaint honor turn to dust,
30 And into ashes all my lust:
    The grave's a fine and private place,
    But none, I think, do there embrace.
      Now therefore, while the youthful hue
    Sits on thy skin like morning dew,
35 And while thy willing soul transpires
    At every pore with instant fires,
    Now let us sport us while we may,
    And now, like amorous birds of prey,
    Rather at once our time devour
40 Than languish in his slow-chapped power.
    Let us roll all our strength and all
    Our sweetness up into one ball,
    And tear our pleasures with rough strife
    Thorough the iron gates of life:
45 Thus, though we cannot make our sun
    Stand still, yet we will make him run.

Margaret Mead (1901–1978) was a psychologist and an anthropologist. She grew up in Philadelphia, and by 1925 was doing field work studying adolescent girls in Samoa. Her first book, Coming of Age in Samoa *(1928), was solid anthropology, and became a best seller as well. Later she wrote* Growing up in New Guinea *(1930),* Sex and Temperament in Three Primitive Societies *(1935), and books coming from studies of Polynesia and India.* Male and Female *in 1949 applied the discoveries of anthropology to her own western culture.*

Margaret Mead became a popular figure — writing in the magazine Redbook *— without sacrificing intellectual integrity. She remained a strong feminist. In 1972 she published an autobiography of her earlier years,* Blackberry Winter, *which was by one count her twenty-second book. Other counts, that include collaborations and editions, approach forty.*

In this essay she discusses her great predecessor Ruth Benedict. By quoting from Benedict and then adding her own comments, Mead almost engages Benedict in dialogue, and makes of her article an encounter between two exemplary minds. We learn about anthropology; we learn of a female struggle against an entrenched patriarchy; we learn about one remarkable woman from the admiring words of another.

45

MARGARET MEAD
On Ruth Benedict

1   Ruth Fulton Benedict was one of the first women to attain major stature as a social scientist. When she entered anthropology in 1919, it was still an esoteric science. By 1948, when she died, an awareness of the relativity of cultural values and some grasp of the significance of the study of cultures, primitive and modern, extended far beyond anthropology. She herself played a decisive part in bringing about this transformation.

2   *Patterns of Culture* is her best known work.[1] For more than a generation it has served not only as an introduction to anthropology but also as a guide to students in many fields who have sought for an approach to an unfolding world. Now, forty years after the book's publication, it is as alive as when it was written, for in it Ruth Benedict addressed herself to a problem that is poignantly contemporary: How is the diversity of the human search for meaning to be understood? Her exposition, scholarly in depth and infused with aesthetic appreciation in the best tradition of English literature, broke through the formal boundaries of a single social science to clarify our understanding of the human estate.

3   As a young woman, long before she discovered anthropology, Ruth Benedict wrote in her journal:

> The trouble with life isn't that there is no answer, it's that there are so many answers. There's the answer of Christ and of Buddha,

From Margaret Mead, *Ruth Benedict,* New York: Columbia University Press, 1974, by permission of the publishers and the author. Contains quoted material from *An Anthropologist at Work* by Margaret Mead. Copyright © 1959 by Margaret Mead. Reprinted by permission of Houghton Mifflin Company.
[1] Published in 1934, *Patterns of Culture* has been translated into twelve other languages and, in English alone, has sold some 1.6 million copies.

of Thomas à Kempis and of Elbert Hubbard, of Browning, Keats and of Spinoza, of Thoreau and of Walt Whitman, of Kant and of Theodore Roosevelt. By turns their answers fit my needs. And yet, because I am I and not any one of them, they can none of them be completely mine. (*AAW*: 126)[2]

This theme of her own personal search for meaning and for an 4
understanding of the individual's place within his own culture and society illuminates all of Ruth Benedict's writings, from her earliest extant journal and her sketch of the life of Mary Wollstonecraft ([1917] *AAW*: 491–519). At the end of this short biography she wrote:

> In the National Portrait Gallery hangs a picture of Mary Woll-stonecraft, a picture of her as she was a few scant months before her death. I remember the child I was when I saw it first, haunted by the terror of youth before experience. I wanted so desperately to know how other women had saved their souls alive. And the woman in the little frame arrested me, this woman with the auburn hair, and the sad, steady, light-brown eyes, and the gallant poise of the head. She had saved her soul alive; it looked out from her steady eyes unafraid. The price, too, that life had demanded of her was written ineradicably there. But to me, then, standing before her picture, even that costly payment was a guarantee, a promise. For I knew that in those days when she sat for that picture, she was content. And in the light of that content, I still spell out her life. (*AAW*: 519)

I met Ruth Benedict in the autumn of 1922, when I was a senior 5
at Barnard College. She had just completed her graduate studies under Franz Boas at Columbia University and, as his assistant at Barnard College for one year, she was taking groups of us to the American Museum of Natural History.

At this time her beauty, which had been conspicuous in her girl- 6
hood and was to become legendary in later years, was completely in eclipse. We saw her as a very shy, almost distrait, middle-aged woman whose fine, mouse-colored hair never stayed quite pinned up. Week after week she wore a very prosaic hat and the same drab dress. Men wore the same clothes every day, she said. Why shouldn't a woman, also? She stammered a little when she talked with us and sometimes blushed scarlet. On one occasion when she was speaking about Plains Indian cultures, as we were gathered around a miniature model of the

[2] Published in *An Anthropologist at Work: Writings of Ruth Benedict,* by Margaret Mead (1959). For the sake of brevity this work will be referred to here as *AAW*.

Sun Dance, I asked a detailed question. She replied hurriedly, in a manner which I at first perceived as brushing me aside, that she would give me something later. What troubled her was diffidence about mentioning her own work, as I realized when the next week she gave me the small, bright blue reprint of her first publication, "The Vision in Plains Culture" (1922).

7   In spite of her shyness, Ruth Benedict's enthusiasm for the anthropological world she had so recently entered and her delight in the detail of primitive ritual and poetry — which I soon discovered was joined with a deep interest in modern poetry — captivated all of us. The intensity of her interest, combined with the magnificent clarity of Boas' teaching, made anthropology, as such, something of a revelation to me. I was the child of social scientists and the basic ideas of the independence of race, language, and culture, as well as the importance of the comparative method, were already familiar to me. What was new to me was the emphasis on the intricate details of primitive cultures, a kind of detail of which there was no hint in the work of the comparative socioeconomists — Veblen, Paton, and Caseby — who had been my parents' teachers. Following Ruth Benedict's suggestions I spent long evenings when I was baby-sitting memorizing Australian and Toda kinship systems or copying out Northwest Coast designs until I had the feel of those marvelously dissected sharks and eagles in my fingertips.

8   She brought home to us also the desperate urgency of doing anthropological field work before the last precious and irretrievable memories of traditional American Indian cultures were carried to the grave. She herself had done her first field work in the summer of 1922, among the Morongo Valley Serrano, one of the Shoshonean groups of southern California. This was the situation she found, as she described it in "A Brief Sketch of Serrano Culture" (1924):

> Such information as may be gathered among the Serrano today is almost entirely exoteric. No old shaman (*hümtc*) or priest (*paha*) survives. The annual fiesta is still kept up in a modified form, and until a few years ago the Morongo Reservation Serrano depended on a shaman of the desert Cahuilla for some of the old dances and shamanistic performances. A great deal of the old meaning, both in social organization and in religious practices, is undoubtedly lost. It is largely by guesswork that they can give the meaning of any of the ceremonial songs; and any religious connotation in such practices as rock-painting, for instance, is now unknown. It must

therefore remain an open question in many cases, as for instance the universal animal designations of all local groups, whether the absence of any esoteric interpretations today is the reflection of an old Serrano trait, or is due to a fading of the old traditions. (pp. 366–68)

Much of what working within a vanishing culture meant to a field-worker was conveyed only very inarticulately to students like ourselves, who knew almost nothing about what field work might consist of or how it was carried out. Yet Ruth Benedict made the old men and women who were her informants very real to us and endowed them with the same poignancy that, many years later, came through so clearly in her evocation of the figure of speech used by a chief of the Digger Indians: 9

> "In the beginning," he said, "God gave to every people a cup, a cup of clay, and from this cup they drank their life." I do not know whether the figure occurred in some traditional ritual of his people that I never found, or whether it was his own imagery. . . . At any rate, in the mind of this humble Indian the figure of speech was clear and full of meaning. "They all dipped in the water," he continued, "but their cups were different. Our cup is broken now. It has passed away." ([*Patterns of Culture,*] 21–22)

As she talked with us, she made the breakdown and disappearance of the traditional culture vivid and irreparable. But she was not sentimental about the possibility of preserving Indian societies or romantic about Indians who had been disinherited. She was protected from sentimentality by her own maturity and this, in turn, protected us.

THE EARLY YEARS

She was born Ruth Fulton, on June 5, 1887, in a farming community in the Shenango Valley in northern New York State, where both her paternal and her maternal grandparents lived. Her mother, Beatrice Shattuck, had studied at Vassar College. Her father, Frederick S. Fulton, was a brilliant young surgeon with a promising career in research in New York. While Ruth was still a baby, her father fell ill of an obscure, undiagnosed disease. The young family returned to live on the Shattuck farm where Ruth's only sister, Margery, was born a few weeks before their father's death in March 1889. 10

11   Ruth grew up with her maternal grandfather's farm as the background of her life. When she was five, her mother — who was unusually independent for her day — began teaching in the nearby town of Norwich and soon thereafter took the two children to live first in St. Joseph, Missouri, then in Owatonna, Minnesota, and finally in Buffalo, New York, in order to make her living as a teacher and later as a librarian. But the Shattuck farm, to which they returned each summer and where a favorite spinster aunt lived in later years, remained home to Ruth for all her life.

12   Her memories of her childhood as she wrote about them, in 1935, in a fragmentary autobiography stress her sense of alienation. "Happiness," she wrote, "was a world I lived in all by myself, and for precious moments" (*AAW:* 100). She was repelled by her mother's persistent, grieving widowhood and she herself was given to violent, seizure-like tantrums which she traced back to a traumatic scene beside her father's coffin, where her mother passionately adjured her to remember her father's face. Very early in life she was partially deafened by illness, but for a long time this was not recognized and she was chided for being unresponsive — in contrast to her sunny-tempered, pretty, and less complicated younger sister, Margery.

13   She remembered the world at the farm with deep joy in the landscape, which she had peopled with imaginary companions. But in later years she often spoke of how she had come to feel, very early, that there was little in common between the beliefs of her family and neighbors and her own passionate wondering about life, which she soon learned to keep to herself. The Bible, rigidly adhered to by her firmly fundamentalist relatives, became the background of her daydreams, but her feeling about it was so different from that of her family that her delight in the Bible was still another source of alienation. In this way she laid the basis of an inner life that could be her own as long as she never told anyone about it. Long afterward she commented to a friend: "This is a dangerous thing for a child to learn." For years her inner life found expression only in the journals she kept intermittently and, later, in poetry, which she began to publish under various pseudonyms of which one, Anne Singleton, eventually became known. The two aspects of her life — her private, inner life and the part she acknowledged to others — began to merge only when at last she came into anthropology and met anthropologists who were also interested in poetry.

14   Although the years while she and her sister were growing up were difficult because of the stringent economies necessary to make ends

meet, she herself was indifferent to material possessions. However, her early experience of deprivation — in Buffalo this meant being poorer than any of her classmates — made her keenly sympathetic with the plight of her students in the Depression years, when she gave every penny she could spare from a meager salary to eke out the miserable funds available for writing up their field work. But, in fact, the financial deprivation of her childhood came about through her father's premature death. It was deprivation against a solid background of family security — on the farm with her grandfather, whom she deeply trusted, and in relation to aunts and uncles and cousins, all of whom were moderately well off.

Her accounts of the years in Minnesota and Buffalo before she   15
and Margery went to Vassar, in 1905, centered on her early struggles to understand the life around her, to master her uncontrollable tantrums, to maintain a cool and tearless exterior while experiencing intense inner turmoil, and to seek for moments of delight in maple buds "scarlet on the sky." In high school she began to write. This she regarded as in some way a compensation for the fact that, unlike her sister, she was not handy and found housework and making her own clothes "terribly trying." Later in life she did all chores quickly and competently, but absentmindedly and with the conviction that *not* everything that was worth doing was worth doing well.

At college, where she majored in English literature, she was still   16
solitary and strangely attractive to other lonely people. When she graduated in 1909, she was invited to accompany two of her classmates on a carefully chaperoned trip to Europe. Then after a year during which she lived with her mother in Buffalo and worked for the Charity Organization Society, she left home — as her mother had — to begin teaching. For one year, 1911–1912, she taught in the Westlake School for Girls in Los Angeles and for the next two years, 1912–1914, in the Orton School for Girls in Pasadena. Here she was near Margery, who had married Robert Freeman, a young, progressive minister. In the childless years to come it was Margery's home, full of children, that gave Ruth a sense of having a family. And it was in making baby clothes for Margery's children that she developed pleasure in doing occasional pieces of fine needlework.

This period of teaching in girls' schools was the time when she   17
came face to face with her life as a woman. Although she had met the man she later married — he was the brother of a Vassar classmate — she had no idea then that she would marry him. Life in a girls' school, with its endless round of chaperoning students and supervising their

study hours, depressed her, and she was preoccupied by her feeling that women primarily want to love and be loved. In October 1912, she wrote in her journal:

> So much of the trouble is because I am a woman. To me it seems a very terrible thing to be a woman. There is one crown which perhaps is worth it all — a great love, a quiet home, and children. We all know that is all that is worth while, and yet we must peg away, showing off our wares on the market if we have money, or manufacturing careers for ourselves if we haven't. We have not the motive to prepare ourselves for a "life-work" of teaching, of social work — we know that we would lay it down with hallelujah in the height of our success, to make a home for the right man.
>
> And all the time in the background of our consciousness rings the warning that perhaps the right man will never come. A great love is given to a very few. Perhaps this make-shift time filler of a job is our life work after all. (*AAW:* 120)

18   The thought of the future, an unchanging future, obsessed her, and she wrote: "Perhaps my trouble comes from thinking of the end as my *present* self, not as a possible and very different future self" (*AAW:* 122). And watching the spinsters around her, she felt that for many women finding a "great love" was unlikely. She daydreamed of exchanging teaching for "a garden of hollyhocks and pansies against the old apple trees and lilacs" at her grandfather's farm (*AAW:* 127).

19   At the end of the school year she talked about her doubts with the headmistress of the Orton School, who told her: " 'We narrow our interests until we grow fossilized, as — as I am. And then we have to make our teaching fill our lives. We have to, to live. I want you to have many interests. You have much to expect of life' " (*AAW:* 128). Temporarily reassured, she agreed to come back to the school for another year.

20   But within weeks of her return to the Shattuck farm for the summer, she wrote in her journal:

> Yes, I am coming back to the farm. I'll make something off the garden and the orchard — perhaps in time it will be a prosperous business. And except for my four months' vacation in the winter, I shall not need much money. I'm coming primarily because I want to — because I can't believe that joyless life is significant life. (*AAW:* 128)

21   The idea of farming tasks presented no difficulties. She was a tall, strong woman with large, capable hands. She enjoyed physical activi-

ties — walking and vigorous swimming — and sometimes sought catharsis in chopping up logs for firewood.

Yet for her, farming — like teaching — was only a means. What 22 was essential, she wrote, was something else:

> to find a way of living not utterly incongruous with certain passionate ideals: to attain to a zest for life, an enthusiasm for the adventure which will forever deliver me from my shame of cowardice, to master an attitude toward life which will somehow bind together these episodes of experience into something that may conceivably be called life. (*AAW:* 128–29)

The farm would give her "the out-door life I love, the leisure, the 23 home-life" (*AAW:* 129). Still she worried:

> There is only one argument that troubles me. It is the fear of being a quitter, of having run away from the fight for my own private enjoyment. The faith this world needs is the faith that can hold its own in the rub and irritating contact of the world. I plan large work among the farmers and their children to salve my conscience. But I do not know —— . (*AAW:* 129)

A month after this decision, in August 1913, she fell in love with 24 Stanley Benedict and promised to marry him. Then she wrote in her journal:

> And so the whole world changed. Is it not awesome — wonderful beyond expression? Every day I have grown surer, happier. Nothing in all my life would be worth setting over against our Sunday afternoon drive through Lyon Brook or our last afternoon together on the towpath.
>
> We turn in our sleep and groan because we are parasites — we women — because we produce nothing, say nothing, find our whole world in the love of a man. — For shame! We are become the veriest Philistines — in this matter of woman's sphere. I suppose it is too soon to expect us to achieve perspective on the problem of woman's rights — but surely there is no other problem of human existence where we would be childish enough to believe in the finality of our little mathematical calculations of "done" or "not done." But here in the one supremely complicated relation of man and woman which involves the perpetual interchange of all that is most difficult to be reckoned — here we thrust in "the world's coarse thumb and finger," here we say "to the eyes of the public shalt thou justify thy existence." — Oh no! do we care whether Beatrice formed clubs, or wrote a sonnet? In the quiet

self-fulfilling love of Wordsworth's home, do we ask that Mary
Wordsworth should have achieved individual self-expression? In
general — a woman has one supreme power — to love. If we are to
arrive at any blythness in facing life, we must have faith to believe
that it is in exercising this gift, in living it out to its fullest that
she achieves herself, that she "justifies her existence." (*AAW:* 130)

25   Ruth Fulton was speaking here as a woman newly in love. But
her words have a premonitory ring. Essentially she was expressing
what so many young people of both sexes half a century later have
come to believe — that life is justified by the intensity of immediate
experience and love.

26   In the autumn she returned, after all, to California and taught one
more year at the Orton School. Then, in the summer of 1914, she
married Stanley Benedict. At this time he was beginning a long and
distinguished career as a biochemist at Cornell Medical College in
New York City. During the first years of their marriage they lived in
the Long Island suburb of Douglas Manor. By 1922 she came to think
of suburban life as worse than the worst slums, more stultifying and
soul-destroying. But describing it to me, she quickly added, "Not that
I am in favor of slums!"

27   At first, however, she gloried in her newfound leisure. She wrote:
"The winter is before me to accomplish anything I wish. I have difficulty only in concentrating on something. . . ." (*AAW:* 132). "For
amusement" she thought of writing "chemical detective" stories for
which Stanley would supply the plots and "social work" stories based
on her year's work in Buffalo. She wanted to read Shakespeare and
Goethe. She wanted to "keep a book full of notes." But her pet scheme
was to

> steep myself in the lives of restless and highly enslaved women of
> past generations and write a series of biographical papers from the
> standpoint of the "new woman." My conclusion so far as I see it
> now is that there is nothing "new" about the whole thing except
> the phraseology and the more independent economic standing of
> recent times — that the restlessness and groping are inherent in
> the nature of women and this generation can outdo the others long
> since past only in the frankness with which it acts upon these; that
> nature lays a compelling and very distressing hand upon woman,
> and she struggles in vain who tries to deny it or escape it — life
> loves the little irony of proving it upon the very woman who has
> denied it; she can only hope for success by working according to
> Nature's preconceptions of her make-up — not against them.
> (*AAW:* 132–33)

This was a far cry from her later theoretical understanding of the   28
myriad ways in which culture modifies human demands on men and
women, while still presenting difficulties to those born in a particular
culture, whose temperament — rather than whose sex — provides an
intractable obstacle to the achievement of their aspirations.

In 1915 war was raging in Europe. But what gripped Ruth Bene-   29
dict at this time was the intensity of her own inner turmoil. She longed
for the child that did not come, but she also realized that having a
child would not wholly meet her urgent need. She wrote in her journal:

> There is no one of our radiant faiths that seems more surely
> planted and reared in us by a mocking Master of the Revels than
> that which shines out from all of us in our radiant faith in "our
> children." — The dreams that slipped from us like the sand in the
> hour glass, the task we laid aside to give them birth and rearing —
> all this they shall carve in the enduring stone of their achieve-
> ments — The master stroke of the irony, the stabbing hurt of it, is
> that it is all so noble and self-less a dream; it is truly, "that last
> infirmity of noble minds." (*AAW:* 133)

And she wondered: 30

> And surely the world has need of my vision as well as of Charity
> Committees; it is better to grow straight than to twist myself into
> a doubtfully useful footstool; it is better to make the most of that
> deepest cry of my heart: "Oh God let me be awake — awake in my
> lifetime." (*AAW:* 135)

In her search for intellectual bearings — her effort to find herself   31
as a person — she wrote, dissociating herself from Stanley:

> I must have my world too, my outlet, my chance to put forth my
> effort.
> And never did desires dovetail more neatly — for I don't want a
> "position," heaven forbid! nor a committee chairmanship — All I
> want I can do here at home in my ready-to-hand leisure. The only
> necessity is that I should realize my purposes seriously enough and
> work at writing with sufficient slavishness.
> — If I had children or were expecting one, it would call a truce
> to these promptings, I suppose. But surely it would be only a truce
> — it would sign no permanent terms of peace with them. . . .

> There is no misreading of life that avenges itself so piteously on
> men and women as the notion that in their children they can bring
> to fruition their own seedling dreams. And it is just as unjust to
> the child, to be born and reared as the "creation" of his parents. He

is *himself,* and it is within reason that he may be the very antith-
esis of them both. — No, it is wisdom in motherhood as in wife-
hood to have one's own individual world of effort and creation.
(*AAW:* 136)

32   Throughout this difficult period she was working on the first of
her projected biographies of "restless and highly enslaved women of
past generations," the life of Mary Wollstonecraft. But a year later, in
October 1916, she wrote in discouragement:

> Again another winter. It is hard for me to look with any satisfac-
> tion on the two winters that are passed — and now another. "Mary
> Wollstonecraft" I do believe in — but will she ever be published? I
> doubt it, and more and more I know that I want publication. (*AAW:*
> 135)

33   That December she and Stanley went up to their house on Lake
Winnepesaukee, where they spent every vacation. There, where she
felt "strong and eager and in love with life," she tried again to make a
viable plan:

> The particular problem of this winter is how I may cut through
> the . . . entanglements of our order of life and make good in my
> writing. I would like to simplify our living . . . — cut away the
> incubus of a house and coal fires and course dinners. (*AAW:* 137–
> 38)

34   On Christmas Day — "snowbound at the Lake" — she seemed to
have reached a turning point:

> I've pledged my word to a "business in life" now. Last night
> Stanley and I talked. . . .
> I said that for the sake of our love — our friendship, rather — I
> must pay my way in a job of my own. I would not, would not drift
> into the boredom, the pitiableness of lives like —— or ——. He
> said that, whatever the job, it would not hold me; nothing ever
> had, social work or teaching. Children might for a year or two, no
> more. . . .
> I told him he should see. My past list of jobs proved nothing:
> until I loved him nothing had ever seemed to me worth the effort
> of attaining. I could lay hold of no motive. Now I understood; I
> cared and cared deeply. . . . I should prove that I was no rolling
> stone. I should prove too that whatever I could achieve in my own
> life was something added to our relationship with each other.
> — And now I must prove my word. I must bind it to me till it is
> closer than breathing, nearer than hands and feet. It means that for

the first time in my life, I have committed myself to the endeavor for *success* — success in writing. It means that before summer I shall have completed "Adventures in Womanhood" — and found a publisher for them. It means that what I can do to get them into the magazines, I will do. It means that with all the force within me, I will write, this winter. (*AAW:* 138–39)

In May 1917, however, she reported that all her plans had gone 35
awry. Instead of writing she had spent the winter organizing day nurseries. "In a sense," she wrote, "I'm satisfied with the job. I've called
an organization into being that's doing good work, and needed work.
. . . A dozen other women are working well who otherwise wouldn't
have had a niche to work in" (*AAW:* 142). But the dilemma remained:

> The other day when I was getting up an open meeting and spending
> the day at the telephone, I wept because I came across a jumbled
> untouched verse manuscript. Yet I suppose I'd reverse the cause of
> tears if I were to pin my next decade to writing alone. And yet oh,
> I long to prove myself by writing! The best seems to die in me
> when I give it up. It is the self I love — not this efficient, philan-
> thropic self. And isn't that the test? (*AAW:* 142)

She did, in fact, finish "Mary Wollstonecraft" in 1917, but the 36
manuscript was rejected by Houghton Mifflin. Forty-one years later
the same publisher brought it out in *An Anthropologist at Work*
(1959). But this Ruth Benedict never knew.

During the whole decade beginning in 1911, when she succes- 37
sively tried social work and teaching and then put so much hope into
her marriage to Stanley, her desperate need was to find herself — to
commit herself to a way of life that had meaning for her and that drew
on all her talents. Again and again, during these years her journals
record her struggles and her maturing sense of what the issues were for
the women of her generation who, like herself, were struggling to
break the bonds of their traditional identifications. Later, when she
had already found her own direction, she tried again to formulate the
issues:

> In the progress of feminism the issues have been drawn usually
> on some variation of parasitism vs. labor — Mrs. Gilman claimed
> it for the sake of woman's economic independence, Olive Schreiner
> for the sake of her self-fulfillment. I think conditions are rapidly
> falsifying these issues: the vast majority have the right to labor
> now — wartimes have seen to that — in the great war-game no one
> is exempted. And it is a necessary emancipation; without it there

would be no further step. But it is only initial. Our factories are filled with women and girls, and their experience is as nothing — nothing — in their development. They get from it no sense of the dignity of associated labor, no sense of the contributive value of their product, no experience in organized self-government. It is along these lines, through trades organizations, that this pointless labor must be made a factor in the onward march of women.

Practically all the "labor" open to the majority of women is open to the same objection; something must be done to it before it can have any value. That value can be gained quite as surely off a pay roll as on it. No, I do not believe that the modern conditions require any longer the issue of labor — paid labor vs. parasitism. . . .

What is it then? Initiative to go after the big things of life — not freedom *from* somewhat; initiative *for* somewhat. Now for some women the big things of life include political activity and it is abundantly right that they should seek their place there. For the great majority of women, however, the big things of life are love, children, social activity according to their abilities. And in the matter of love and children there is no initiative, liberty of conscience, permitted. But it is necessary that we have some voice in the conditions under which these big things of our lives shall be realized, that we have the freedom for their achievement. The emotional part of woman's life — that part which makes her a woman — must be brought up out of the dark and allowed to put forth its best. (*AAW:* 145–46)

38   But in 1917 she had not yet found her direction. During the war years Stanley worked on problems of the biochemistry of poison gas and was himself badly gassed. This accentuated his need for isolation and his desire to spend long summers at the lake in New Hampshire. Ruth could no longer bear the trivialities of life in Douglas Manor. But after living for a year in New York, they moved even further from the city, to Bedford Hills. In this period Ruth experimented with rhythmic dancing, in which she took great pleasure. She also spent another year doing social work for the State Charities Aid Association. After that her strong sense of social responsibility took other forms.

39   The decisive turning point in her life came in 1919, when she went to the New School for Social Research, where she attended lectures for two years. At first this was one more attempt to fill time intelligently, for she still kept alive the hope of having a child. But during this period she finally learned that she could not have a child without undergoing a very problematic operation for which Stanley refused to give his consent. Facing empty years in a childless marriage,

she recognized that she must commit herself to her "own individual world of effort and creation." Then, as she listened to the very contrasting lectures given by Alexander Goldenweiser and Elsie Clews Parsons, she discovered anthropology. Here, in this new science, was substance she could respect. Here she could use all her talents and also perhaps find answers to her most pressing personal questions: Why did she feel herself to be a stranger in contemporary America? What, for her, was ultimately worth doing?

_____ CONSIDERATIONS _____

1. Margaret Mead's account of Ruth Benedict's life offers an opportunity to study a sustained essay, based on research, in which the author makes heavy use of quoted material. Ignoring the technical aspects of documentation (footnotes, etc.), concentrate on the way in which Mead blends the source material into her own commentary.

2. Who were Mary Wollstonecraft and Olive Schreiner, and how do these allusions contribute to an understanding of Ruth Benedict?

3. "So much of the trouble is because I am a woman," Benedict wrote in her journal in 1912. Trace the changes in her attitude about her sex from her childhood to her entry into anthropology, the field in which she achieved international recognition. What events were important in that evolution?

4. What prevented her from remaining permanently on the farm?

5. James Baldwin declares, on page 30, that "the only real concern of the artist" is "to recreate out of the disorder of life that order which is art." Can you trace a similar concern or impulse in Ruth Benedict as she struggles to find a meaning in her life and cries out, "Oh God, let me be awake — awake in my lifetime"?

6. Why didn't Ruth Benedict have any children? From what you can learn in this account, what do you think of her marriage to Stanley Benedict?

H. L. Mencken (1880–1956) was the dominant editor of his day, for the magazines Smart Set *and* American Mercury, *and wrote funny, intelligent, cantankerous, irascible, mocking essays about American political, artistic, and social mores. He collected the best of his periodical writing in six books of* Prejudices *(1919, 1920, 1922, 1924, 1926, 1927) and in a* Book of Prefaces *(1917). (See Richard Wright's reminiscence of reading Mencken, on pages 483–491.) His* American Language *(1919) and its two* Supplements *(1945, 1948) looked at the difference between American and English, and argued the vitality of the American language. Later in life he wrote an autobiography in three volumes,* Happy Days *(1940),* Newspaper Days *(1941) and* Heathen Days *(1943).*

"Gamalielese" shows Mencken's talents as a social critic, as a debunker of popular idiocy. It also demonstrates his tight observation of the American language, and his humor. Warren Gamaliel Harding was twenty-ninth president of the United States. On the question of President Harding's intellectual qualifications for office, history has been as unkind as Harding's contemporary.

46

H. L. MENCKEN
Gamalielese

1   On the question of the logical content of Dr. Harding's harangue of last Friday I do not presume to have views. The matter has been debated at great length by the editorial writers of the Republic, all of them experts in logic; moreover, I confess to being prejudiced. When a man arises publicly to argue that the United States entered the late

"Gamalielese," by H.L. Mencken from the *Baltimore Sun*, March 7, 1921. Reprinted by permission of the *Baltimore Sun*.

war because of a "concern for preserved civilization," I can only snicker in a superior way and wonder why he isn't holding down the chair of history in some American university. When he says that the U.S. has "never sought territorial aggrandizement through force," the snicker rises to the virulence of a chuckle, and I turn to the first volume of General Grant's memoirs. And when, gaining momentum, he gravely informs the boobery that "ours is a constitutional freedom where the popular will is supreme, and minorities are sacredly protected," than I abandon myself to a mirth that transcends, perhaps, the seemly, and send picture postcards of A. Mitchell Palmer,[1] and the Atlanta Penitentiary to all of my enemies who happen to be Socialists.

But when it comes to the style of a great man's discourse, I can   2
speak with a great deal less prejudice, and maybe with somewhat more competence, for I have earned most of my livelihood for twenty years past by translating the bad English of a multitude of authors into measurably better English. Thus qualified professionally, I rise to pay my small tribute to Dr. Harding. Setting aside a college professor or two and half a dozen dipsomaniacal newspaper reporters, he takes the first place in my Valhall of literati. That is to say, he writes the worst English that I have ever encountered. It reminds me of a string of wet sponges; it reminds me of tattered washing on the line; it reminds me of a stale bean-soup, of college yells, of dogs barking idiotically through endless nights. It is so bad that a sort of grandeur creeps into it. It drags itself out of the dark abysm (I was about to write abscess!) of pish, and crawls insanely up the topmost pinnacle of posh. It is rumble and bumble. It is flap and doodle. It is balder and dash.

But I grow lyrical. More scientifically, what is the matter with it?   3
Why does it seem so flabby, so banal, so confused and childish, so stupidly at war with sense? If you first read the inaugural address and then heard it intoned, as I did (at least in part), then you will perhaps arrive at an answer. That answer is very simple. When Dr. Harding prepares a speech he does not think it out in terms of an educated reader locked up in jail, but in terms of a great horde of stoneheads gathered around a stand. That is to say, the thing is always a stump speech; it is conceived as a stump speech and written as a stump speech. More, it is a stump speech addressed primarily to the sort of audience that the speaker has been used to all his life, to wit, an

---

[1] Seventh U.S. attorney general, who ordered arrests in the red scare of 1919 and 1920. — ED.

audience of small town yokels, of low political serfs, or morons scarcely able to understand a word of more than two syllables, and wholly unable to pursue a logical idea for more than two centimeters.

4   Such imbeciles do not want ideas — that is, new ideas, ideas that are unfamiliar, ideas that challenge their attention. What they want is simply a gaudy series of platitudes, of threadbare phrases terrifically repeated, of sonorous nonsense driven home with gestures. As I say, they can't understand many words of more than two syllables, but that is not saying that they do not esteem such words. On the contrary, they like them and demand them. The roll of incomprehensible polysyllables enchants them. They like phrases which thunder like salvos of artillery. Let that thunder sound, and they take all the rest on trust. If a sentence begins furiously and then peters out into fatuity, they are still satisfied. If a phrase has a punch in it, they do not ask that it also have a meaning. If a word slides off the tongue like a ship going down the ways, they are content and applaud it and wait for the next.

5   Brought up amid such hinds, trained by long practice to engage and delight them, Dr. Harding carries over his stump manner into everything he writes. He is, perhaps, too old to learn a better way. He is, more likely, too discreet to experiment. The stump speech, put into cold type, maketh the judicious to grieve. But roared from an actual stump, with arms flying and eyes flashing and the old flag overhead, it is certainly and brilliantly effective. Read the inaugural address, and it will gag you. But hear it recited through a sound-magnifier, with grand gestures to ram home its periods, and you will begin to understand it.

6   Let us turn to a specific example. I exhume a sentence from the latter half of the eminent orator's discourse:

7   "I would like government to do all it can to mitigate; then, in understanding, in mutuality of interest, in concern for the common good, our tasks will be solved."

8   I assume that you have read it. I also assume that you set it down as idiotic — a series of words without sense. You are quite right; it is. But now imagine it intoned as it was designed to be intoned. Imagine the slow tempo of a public speech. Imagine the stately unrolling of the first clause, the delicate pause upon the word "then" — and then the loud discharge of the phrases "in understanding," "in mutuality of interest," "in concern for the common good," each with its attendant glare and roll of the eyes, each with its sublime heave, each with its gesture of a blacksmith bringing down his sledge upon an egg — imagine all this, and then ask yourself where you have got. You have got, in brief, to a point where you don't know what it is all about. You hear

and applaud the phrases, but their connection has already escaped you. And so, when in violation of all sequence and logic, the final phrase, "our tasks will be solved," assaults you, you do not notice its disharmony — all you notice is that, if this or that, already forgotten, is done, "our tasks will be solved." Whereupon, glad of the assurance and thrilled by the vast gestures that drive it home, you give a cheer.

9   That is, if you are the sort of man who goes to political meetings, which is to say, if you are the sort of man that Dr. Harding is used to talking to, which is to say, if you are a jackass.

10   The whole inaugural address reeked with just such nonsense. The thing started off with an error in English in its very first sentence — the confusion of pronouns in the *one-he* combination, so beloved of bad newspaper reporters. It bristled with words misused: *civic* for *civil*, *luring* for *alluring*, *womanhood* for *women*, *referendum* for *reference*, even *task* for *problem*. "The *task* is to be *solved*" — what could be worse? Yet I find it twice. "The expressed views of world opinion" — what irritating tautology! "The expressed conscience of progress" — what on earth does it mean? "This is not selfishness, it is sanctity" — what intelligible idea do you get out of that? "I know that Congress and the administration will favor every wise government policy to aid the resumption and encourage continued progress" — the resumption of what? "Service is the supreme *commitment* of life" — *ach, du heiliger!*

11   But is such bosh out of place in a stump speech? Obviously not. It is precisely and thoroughly in place in a stump speech. A tight fabric of ideas would weary and exasperate the audience; what it wants is simply a loud burble of words, a procession of phrases that roar, a series of whoops. This is what it got in the inaugural address of the Hon. Warren Gamaliel Harding. And this is what it will get for four long years — unless God sends a miracle and the corruptible puts on incorruption . . . Almost I long for the sweeter song, the rubber-stamps of more familiar design, the gentler and more seemly bosh of the late Woodrow.

_____CONSIDERATIONS_____

1. In his first sentence, Mencken denies having opinions about "the logical content" in Harding's address, promising instead to concentrate on Harding's style. How successful is he in avoiding comment on the content of the Harding speech? What is the relationship between content and style?

2. Can you find two or three phrases that suggest Mencken's irony? What do his ironic twists and turns contribute to his essay?

3. Mencken wrote his review of Harding's address at least twenty years before George Orwell published his "Politics and the English Language" (pages 306–319). Would Orwell applaud or criticize Mencken's treatment of the president?

4. Study the variety of Mencken's words, perhaps setting up two columns, one to list words like "pish" and "posh," and the other for words or phrases like "incomprehensible polysyllables." Do such extremes of diction confuse the reader, enliven the writer's argument, both, or neither?

5. Is Mencken himself guilty of any sins that he attributes to Harding? Explain, with examples.

6. How does Mencken's style support his opinionated view of politicians and political language?

N. Scott Momaday (b. 1934) was born in Oklahoma, and attended schools on Navaho, Apache, and Pueblo reservations. After graduating from the University of New Mexico, he took a Ph.D. at Stanford and now teaches there. He won the Pulitzer Prize in 1969 for his novel House Made of Dawn, *and in 1976 collected his poems in* The Gourd Dancer.*

Momaday's father is a pure-blooded Kiowa, a teacher and an artist. His mother, also a teacher, and author of books for older children, is part English, part French, and part Cherokee. Momaday spent summers as a child with his Kiowa grandmother, and has continually turned to his Indian ancestry as a source for writing. The essay below introduces* The Way to Rainy Mountain *(1969), in which Momaday collected Kiowa legends.*

American writers continually dwell upon the return to origins — the farm in the country, the village in Sicily, the ghetto in Poland. Many of us can tell a story of going backward in time, on a journey to grandmother's house. Momaday's journey takes him further, and he takes us with him by the force of his language, to an America inside America, all but invisible to most Americans.

47

N. SCOTT MOMADAY
The Way to Rainy Mountain

A single knoll rises out of the plain in Oklahoma, north and west 1
of the Wichita Range. For my people, the Kiowas, it is an old landmark, and they gave it the name Rainy Mountain. The hardest weather in the world is there. Winter brings blizzards, hot tornadic winds arise in the spring, and in summer the prairie is an anvil's edge. The grass turns brittle and brown, and it cracks beneath your feet. There are green

First published in *The Reporter*, January 26, 1967. Reprinted from *The Way to Rainy Mountain*, copyright 1969, The University of New Mexico Press.

belts along the rivers and creeks, linear groves of hickory and pecan, willow and witch hazel. At a distance in July or August the steaming foliage seems almost to writhe in fire. Great green and yellow grass-hoppers are everywhere in the tall grass, popping up like corn to sting the flesh, and tortoises crawl about on the red earth, going nowhere in the plenty of time. Loneliness is an aspect of the land. All things in the plain are isolate; there is no confusion of objects in the eye, but *one* hill or *one* tree or *one* man. To look upon that landscape in the early morning, with the sun at your back, is to lose the sense of proportion. Your imagination comes to life, and this, you think, is where Creation was begun.

2   I returned to Rainy Mountain in July. My grandmother had died in the spring, and I wanted to be at her grave. She had lived to be very old and at last infirm. Her only living daughter was with her when she died, and I was told that in death her face was that of a child.

3   I like to think of her as a child. When she was born, the Kiowas were living the last great moment of their history. For more than a hundred years they had controlled the open range from the Smoky Hill River to the Red, from the headwaters of the Canadian to the fork of the Arkansas and Cimarron. In alliance with the Comanches, they had ruled the whole of the southern Plains. War was their sacred business, and they were among the finest horsemen the world has ever known. But warfare for the Kiowas was preeminently a matter of disposition rather than of survival, and they never understood the grim, unrelenting advance of the U.S. Cavalry. When at last, divided and ill-provisioned, they were driven onto the Staked Plains in the cold rains of autumn, they fell into panic. In Palo Duro Canyon they abandoned their crucial stores to pillage and had nothing then but their lives. In order to save themselves, they surrendered to the soldiers at Fort Sill and were imprisoned in the old stone corral that now stands as a military museum. My grandmother was spared the humiliation of those high gray walls by eight or ten years, but she must have known from birth the affliction of defeat, the dark brooding of old warriors.

4   Her name was Aho, and she belonged to the last culture to evolve in North America. Her forebears came down from the high country in western Montana nearly three centuries ago. They were a mountain people, a mysterious tribe of hunters whose language has never been positively classified in any major group. In the late seventeenth century they began a long migration to the south and east. It was a journey toward the dawn, and it led to a golden age. Along the way the Kiowas were befriended by the Crows, who gave them the culture and religion

of the Plains. They acquired horses, and their ancient nomadic spirit was suddenly free of the ground. They acquired Tai-me, the sacred Sun Dance doll, from that moment the object and symbol of their worship, and so shared in the divinity of the sun. Not least, they acquired the sense of destiny, therefore courage and pride. When they entered upon the southern Plains they had been transformed. No longer were they slaves to the simple necessity of survival; they were a lordly and dangerous society of fighters and thieves, hunters and priests of the sun. According to their origin myth, they entered the world through a hollow log. From one point of view, their migration was the fruit of an old prophecy, for indeed they emerged from a sunless world.

Although my grandmother lived out her long life in the shadow 5 of Rainy Mountain, the immense landscape of the continental interior lay like memory in her blood. She could tell of the Crows, whom she had never seen, and of the Black Hills, where she had never been. I wanted to see in reality what she had seen more perfectly in the mind's eye, and traveled fifteen hundred miles to begin my pilgrimage.

Yellowstone, it seemed to me, was the top of the world, a region 6 of deep lakes and dark timber, canyons and waterfalls. But, beautiful as it is, one might have the sense of confinement there. The skyline in all directions is close at hand, the high wall of the woods and deep cleavages of shade. There is a perfect freedom in the mountains, but it belongs to the eagle and the elk, the badger and the bear. The Kiowas reckoned their stature by the distance they could see, and they were bent and blind in the wilderness.

Descending eastward, the highland meadows are a stairway to 7 the plain. In July the inland slope of the Rockies is luxuriant with flax and buckwheat, stonecrop and larkspur. The earth unfolds and the limit of the land recedes. Clusters of trees, and animals grazing far in the distance, cause the vision to reach away and wonder to build upon the mind. The sun follows a longer course in the day, and the sky is immense beyond all comparison. The great billowing clouds that sail upon it are shadows that move upon the grain like water, dividing light. Farther down, in the land of the Crows and Blackfeet, the plain is yellow. Sweet clover takes hold of the hills and bends upon itself to cover and seal the soil. There the Kiowas paused on their way; they had come to the place where they must change their lives. The sun is at home on the plains. Precisely there does it have the certain character of a god. When the Kiowas came to the land of the Crows, they could see the dark lees of the hills at dawn across the Bighorn River, the profusion of light on the grain shelves, the oldest deity ranging after the solstices. Not yet would they veer southward to the caldron of the land that lay below; they must wean their blood from the northern winter and hold the mountains a while longer in their view. They bore Tai-me in procession to the east.

8   A dark mist lay over the Black Hills, and the land was like iron. At the top of a ridge I caught sight of Devil's Tower upthrust against the gray sky as if in the birth of time the core of the earth had broken through its crust and the motion of the world was begun. There are things in nature that engender an awful quiet in the heart of man; Devil's Tower is one of them. Two centuries ago, because they could not do otherwise, the Kiowas made a legend at the base of the rock. My grandmother said:

> Eight children were there at play, seven sisters and their brother. Suddenly the boy was struck dumb; he trembled and began to run upon his hands and feet. His fingers became claws, and his body was covered with fur. Directly there was a bear where the boy had been. The sisters were terrified; they ran, and the bear after them. They came to the stump of a great tree, and the tree spoke to them. It bade them climb upon it, and as they did so it began to rise into the air. The bear came to kill them, but they were just beyond its reach. It reared against the tree and scored the bark all around with its claws. The seven sisters were borne into the sky, and they became the stars of the Big Dipper.

From that moment, and so long as the legend lives, the Kiowas have kinsmen in the night sky. Whatever they were in the mountains, they could be no more. However tenuous their well-being, however much they had suffered and would suffer again, they had found a way out of the wilderness.

9   My grandmother had a reverence for the sun, a holy regard that now is all but gone out of mankind. There was a wariness in her, and an ancient awe. She was a Christian in her later years, but she had come a long way about, and she never forgot her birthright. As a child she had been to the Sun Dances; she had taken part in those annual rites, and by them she had learned the restoration of her people in the presence of Tai-me. She was about seven when the last Kiowa Sun Dance was held in 1887 on the Washita River above Rainy Mountain Creek. The buffalo were gone. In order to consummate the ancient sacrifice — to impale the head of a buffalo bull upon the medicine tree — a delegation of old men journeyed into Texas, there to beg and barter for an animal from the Goodnight herd. She was ten when the Kiowas came together for the last time as a living Sun Dance culture. They

could find no buffalo; they had to hang an old hide from the sacred tree. Before the dance could begin, a company of soldiers rode out from Fort Sill under orders to disperse the tribe. Forbidden without cause the essential act of their faith, having seen the wild herds slaughtered and left to rot upon the ground, the Kiowas backed away forever from the medicine tree. That was July 20, 1890, at the great bend of the Washita. My grandmother was there. Without bitterness, and for as long as she lived, she bore a vision of deicide.

Now that I can have her only in memory, I see my grandmother   10
in the several postures that were peculiar to her: standing at the wood stove on a winter morning and turning meat in a great iron skillet; sitting at the south window, bent above her beadwork, and afterwards, when her vision failed, looking down for a long time into the fold of her hands; going out upon a cane, very slowly as she did when the weight of age came upon her; praying. I remember her most often at prayer. She made long, rambling prayers out of suffering and hope, having seen many things. I was never sure that I had the right to hear, so exclusive were they of all mere custom and company. The last time I saw her she prayed standing by the side of her bed at night, naked to the waist, the light of a kerosene lamp moving upon her dark skin. Her long, black hair, always drawn and braided in the day, lay upon her shoulders and against her breasts like a shawl. I do not speak Kiowa, and I never understood her prayers, but there was something inherently sad in the sound, some merest hesitation upon the syllables of sorrow. She began in a high and descending pitch, exhausting her breath to silence; then again and again — and always the same intensity of effort, of something that is, and is not, like urgency in the human voice. Transported so in the dancing light among the shadows of her room, she seemed beyond the reach of time. But that was illusion; I think I knew then that I should not see her again.

Houses are like sentinels in the plain, old keepers of the weather   11
watch. There, in a very little while, wood takes on the appearance of great age. All colors wear soon away in the wind and rain, and then the wood is burned gray and the grain appears and the nails turn red with rust. The windowpanes are black and opaque; you imagine there is nothing within, and indeed there are many ghosts, bones given up to the land. They stand here and there against the sky, and you approach them for a longer time than you expect. They belong in the distance; it is their domain.

Once there was a lot of sound in my grandmother's house, a lot   12
of coming and going, feasting and talk. The summers there were full of

excitement and reunion. The Kiowas are a summer people; they abide the cold and keep to themselves, but when the season turns and the land becomes warm and vital they cannot hold still; an old love of going returns upon them. The aged visitors who came to my grandmother's house when I was a child were made of lean and leather, and they bore themselves upright. They wore great black hats and bright ample shirts that shook in the wind. They rubbed fat upon their hair and wound their braids with strips of colored cloth. Some of them painted their faces and carried the scars of old and cherished enmities. They were an old council of warlords, come to remind and be reminded of who they were. Their wives and daughters served them well. The women might indulge themselves; gossip was at once the mark and compensation of their servitude. They made loud and elaborate talk among themselves, full of jest and gesture, fright and false alarm. They went abroad in fringed and flowered shawls, bright beadwork and German silver. They were at home in the kitchen, and they prepared meals that were banquets.

13   There were frequent prayer meetings, and great nocturnal feasts. When I was a child I played with my cousins outside, where the lamplight fell upon the ground and the singing of the old people rose up around us and carried away into the darkness. There were a lot of good things to eat, a lot of laughter and surprise. And afterwards, when the quiet returned, I lay down with my grandmother and could hear the frogs away by the river and feel the motion of the air.

14   Now there is a funeral silence in the rooms, the endless wake of some final word. The walls have closed in upon my grandmother's house. When I returned to it in mourning, I saw for the first time in my life how small it was. It was late at night, and there was a white moon, nearly full. I sat for a long time on the stone steps by the kitchen door. From there I could see out across the land; I could see the long row of trees by the creek, the low light upon the rolling plains, and the stars of the Big Dipper. Once I looked at the moon and caught sight of a strange thing. A cricket had perched upon the handrail, only a few inches away from me. My line of vision was such that the creature filled the moon like a fossil. It had gone there, I thought, to live and die, for there, of all places, was its small definition made whole and eternal. A warm wind rose up and purled like the longing within me.

15   The next morning I awoke at dawn and went out on the dirt road to Rainy Mountain. It was already hot, and the grasshoppers began to fill the air. Still, it was early in the morning, and the birds sang out of the shadows. The long yellow grass on the mountain shone in the

bright light, and a scissortail hied above the land. There, where it ought to be, at the end of a long and legendary way, was my grandmother's grave. Here and there on the dark stones were ancestral names. Looking back once, I saw the mountain and came away.

_____ CONSIDERATIONS _____

1. Momaday attempts a large, general topic — the quest and migrations of a people, the Kiowas — yet he concentrates on one person, his grandmother. Why? A beginning writer may find an important guiding principle in this answer.

2. Momaday's essay is studded with names of native plants, such as hickory, pecan, willow, witch hazel, flax, buckwheat, stonecrop, larkspur. What do particulars do for an account like this?

3. Momaday writes that according to their origin myth, the Kiowas entered the world "through a hollow log." Why do people preserve such myths? Are you aware of any comparable myths in our culture of supermarkets, freeways, and television? Or do you believe, with some social historians, that twentieth-century Americans are a mythless people?

4. The sense of place seems to be important to human consciousness and identity. Compare Momaday's treatment of place with Wendell Berry's in "A Native Hill," on pages 41–51.

5. After reading Momaday, read Daniel Boorstin's "Prison of the Present," pages 80–85. Might Boorstin describe Momaday as a man trying to wander *back* into his history?

6. Do you *see* the image that Momaday wants us to see, when he describes the cricket against the moon in his next to last paragraph? Why does the image belong in that paragraph? If you have read Norman Mailer's account of moon exploration (pages 248–255), invent a similar image — some little object held up by one of the astronauts against the pale earth a quarter million miles away.

*Wright Morris (b. 1910) won the National Book Award in 1956
for his novel* The Field of Vision. *Altogether, he has published
more than twenty volumes of prose, most of it fiction, most of it
set in the Nebraska where he grew up.*

*In much of his writing, Morris specializes in viewing things
with the strange clarity of a Martian visitor. People have written
about sports from a variety of points of view; rarely, we believe,
have they kept their eye on the ball.*

48

WRIGHT MORRIS

Odd Balls

1   Most games that involve the use of a ball can be described, but
seldom explained. Consider the ball itself.

2   We begin with the golf ball, white until soiled, hard as a rock, the
surface uniformly pitted with mini-craters, in size about that of a
meatball. This ball is stroked with a slender, wandlike shaft, about the
length of a cane, the bottom end tipped with a blade, variously tilted,
or a fistlike wooden knob. A mystical belief that the club, not the
player, directs the ball, and the ball, not the player, determines its
direction, is common among most players. With their needs in mind,
a ball is promised that will correct the mistakes made by the club. A
ball could more easily be drawn to the hole by a magnet, but the
excitement generated among the spectators is based on the role in the
game that chance plays. No thrill equals the sight of a peerless player
missing a nine-inch putt. Golf balls not stroked are often given to
babies, found in car seats, stored in raincoat pockets, or left where they
can be stepped on.

Golf is played in the open, preferably on grass, over a course   3
cunningly strewn with obstructions. Bunkers, sand traps, trees,
streams, ponds, and spectators, along with rain, sleet, cold, and lightning, make the game of golf what it is. What it is was not known to
many golfers until they saw the game on TV. The mock-ups used by
the commentators made clear a fact that many golfers found puzzling.
What they were doing was walking up and down, back and forth. Most
ball games seem to have in common the going back and forth, rather
than going any place.

The very smallness of the ball may substantially contribute to   4
the high moral tone of the game. What is there to fight over? Each
player has several balls of his own. Although equipped with sticks that
would make good clubs, the golf player refrains from striking his opponents, making loud slurring remarks, or coughing or hissing when
another player is putting. It is not at all unusual to hear another player
described as a great gentleman.

In this game alone the opinion of an official is accepted in a   5
depressed, sportsmanlike manner. The player does not scream and
curse, as in baseball, or stage riots, as in football, but accepts without
comment or demonstration the fickle finger of fate. Law and order
prevail on the links, if viewed on prime time. The game was once
played for the health of it, by amateurs (a term currently applied to
unemployed track stars); now the lonely, single golfer is burdened with
the knowledge that he does for nothing what others are paid for. This
condition is technically described as a handicap.

Some players hit the ball and stand, dejected, waiting for it to   6
land; others turn away and leave it up to the caddy. Some enjoy the
pain they give to others, some like to torture themselves. Although
the physical challenge is substantial — miles and miles of walking,
hours of waiting, the possibility of heatstroke or of being struck by
lightning — the crucial element is mental. If not in a seizure of tor-
ment and self-doubt, the player must pass hole after hole daydreaming,
or wondering why he has so many clubs to choose from. A loss of
concentration on the easy holes will invariably cost him the hard ones.
In summary we can say that the smallness of the ball is no measure of
the effort it takes to stroke it or of the reward it brings.

Between the small golf ball and the palm-sized baseball is the   7
billiard or pool ball. Even those ignorant of the game know what it is
to be behind the eight ball. The game is played on an oblong table in a
smoke-filled room, off bounds to growing boys and women. The ball is

stroked with a long, tapering cue, first rolled on the table to see if the table is flat. If it is not flat, you use a warped cue. The way the chalk is applied to the cue's leather tip, and the green chalk dust is then blown from the fingers, distinguishes men from boys. Pocket billiards is best under lights hung low over the table, in such a manner that one sees only the hands of the players. If smoke conceals the balls, one can hear them rebound on the cushions, click when they collide, or drop into a pocket and rattle down the chute. Without billiards, small boys in YMCA lobbies would have had no cause to grow up and be men.

8   The game is rich in ceremony, symbolic objects, stroking, fondling, thrusting, chalking, cursing, shot-calling, with the dramatic dimness of light necessary to a monastic order. Once identified with masculine odors and pursuits, pool halls, YMCAs, vice dens, conclaves of sleeve-rolled toughs and ward politicians, brazenly sexist, the game will surely interest the new liberated woman. Billiard balls are also used to roll across tile floors, crush the skull of an opponent, or serve as a knob on the sportier type of gearshift. The meaning of being *in front* of the eight ball remains to be explored.

9   Once relatively rare, hidden away in drawers with flannel trousers, like a huge mothball, the snow-white, cotton-fuzzy tennis ball with the visible seams is now commonplace.

10   The aura of breeding and snobbery, so important to tennis, a game played and observed by royalty, is now on the wane as the masses have puzzled out the scoring system. If both players know how to keep score, it comes down to how to psych the opponent. This can be done by hissing at him openly, wearing unmatched socks, varying the bounce of the ball before serving, pretending to sulk, screaming at the linesmen, or delaying the game by blowing softly on the fingers of one hand. These strategies were poorly observed in the past but are now intimately revealed on the TV screen. Many players seem blinded by their own long hair, but this might well be tactical cunning.

11   Nor has tennis stood still, living in the shadow of bygone times and grass-stained balls; it has kept pace with the times with the introduction of the two-handed backhand. Theories vary, but anyone who has played the game badly has experienced the irresistible urge to club the ball with both hands. To everyone's surprise there was nothing in the rules to prevent it. Both ladies and gentlemen whack the ball in this manner, using racquets of wood and metal. Metal racquets are not new: they were used by players in the madcap twenties, one known to me personally, the steel strings noted for their length of life and the

fuzz they removed from the balls. In those days matches were observed by eight or ten girls, seated in Scripps-Booth roadsters, holding the players' sweaters and their racquet presses. Any player with a racquet *and* a press was sure to have a good girl.

In other ball games, the frenzy and enthusiasm of the spectators 12 stimulates the player to greater efforts, but in tennis absolute silence testifies to the moments of crisis. The bong of the ball, the twang of the net cord, the voice of the umpire are all that is heard, unless one of the maverick hot-blooded types is involved in a dispute. This is well known to be bad for tennis, but great for higher receipts.

Team tennis, which may puzzle some observers, is for those who 13 dislike tennis but like to bet on winners and identify with places.

The baseball is small enough to be thrown and caught by a boy 14 but large enough to be seen from the bleachers by a grownup. The use of a round bat to hit a round ball testifies to native inventive genius. Balls were once made of the materials found under beds, and became lopsided when batted, or split at the seams. Official balls were once made of miles and miles of string wound into a tight ball and covered with horsehide. God knows what they use now. Sensible players are afraid to look.

The big games are played in cities that have a ball park. The field 15 is shaped like a large wedge of pie, straight along the sides, curved at the back. There are official positions for nine players, but once the ball is batted they run about wildly. Collisions are common.

The rules of the game lull some into feeling that the object of the 16 game is the scoring of runs. *Quelle bêtise!*[1] Observe how one player, crouched as in prayer, holds the bat across his knee in a ceremonial manner. He is calm and assured. His appointed task, surely, is to crouch and wait. Another walks to the box reserved for the batter, his manner both insolent and indecisive. He steps in, then he steps back, he soils his hands with dirt, then he wipes them, he looks to see if the bat is his own, or another's, if it has the proper length, heft, and roundness; if he is assured of all these points, he re-enters the box. With his spikes he paws his own hole to stand in; straddle-legged he threatens the pitcher with his bat. No words are spoken. Both know this is the moment of truth. See how the pitcher rubs, turns, fondles, and conceals the ball; see how he stoops for the resin, note how he discards it, fingers the bill of his cap, strokes away perspiration, glances slantwise

---

[1] What stupidity! — ED.

down his cheeks at a potential runner; how he begins and stops, how he delays and stares, how he may rudely turn his back on the batter, actions designed to arouse, to incite, to distract the man at the plate from hitting the ball. In spite of these precautions it sometimes happens, to the relief and consternation of the players. Some may have dozed off, or have thoughts on their minds.

17   There are players, as well as the idly curious, who ask why the game is called "the national pastime." For one thing, if nothing else, time *passes:* sometimes the better part of an afternoon or evening, if you allow two hours or more for the game and at least an hour getting to and from the ball park. In the old days games were called off because of darkness, but in the new days they might go on forever, under the lights. Somebody has to win. That's what it says in the rules.

18   The football is oval in shape, usually thrown in a spiral, and when kicked end over end may prove difficult to catch. If not caught on the fly it bounces around erratically.

19   The apparent intent of the game is to deposit the ball across the opponent's goal line. Any child with a ball of its own might do it, six days a week and most of Sunday morning, but the rules of the game specify it must be done with members of both teams present and on the field. Owing to large-scale substitutions this is often difficult.

20   In the old days people went crazy trying to follow the ball. The players still do, but the viewing public, who are watching the game on TV, can relax and wait for the replay. If anything happens, that's where you'll see it. The disentanglement of bodies on the goal line is one of the finer visual moments available to sports fans. The tight knot bursts open, the arms and legs miraculously return to the point of rest, before the ball was snapped. Some find it unsettling. Is this what it means to be born again?

21   All ball games feature hitting and socking, chopping and slicing, smashing, slamming, stroking, and whacking, but only in football are these blows diverted from the ball to the opponent. And the more the players are helped or carried from the field, the more attendance soars. This truly male game is also enjoyed by women who find group therapy less rewarding. The sacking of the passer by the front four is especially gratifying. Charges that a criminal element threatens the game are a characteristic, but hopeful, exaggeration. What to do with big, mean, boyish-hearted men, long accustomed to horsing around in good clean dormitories, unaccustomed to the rigors of life in the Alaska oilfields, was, until football, a serious national dilemma.

All games are peculiar, one to the other, and defy the comprehen- 22
sion of nonplayers, but none is so bizarre as the game of dunking the
ball through the basket. Until basketball, boys seven feet tall ran off
and hid in the woods or joined a circus. Now the woods are combed in
search of them. If they can dribble and dunk a ball, they've got it made.
Rules are rules, and all the rules say is that the ball has to enter the
basket at the top. The tall boys dunk it. There's nothing against it,
according to the rules.

It may surprise people to learn that basketball was once played 23
by normal, flat-chested boys who shot the ball with two hands. The
show-off who shot the ball with one hand was hooted off the court.
The first change in the game was the one-hand shooter, several known
to me personally. The next change in the game was the dunk shot. The
normal thing to do would be to raise the basket and let the seven-foot
boys mull around beneath it, but what is normal about basketball?
People who watch the game understand this problem, but people who
play it think they're normal. They think of six-foot, long-winded, flat-
chested boys as being handicapped.

The importance of drafting basketball players early is to keep 24
them from playing anything but soccer. If they want to play soccer
they have personal problems they need to work out. Most athletes
have nothing to fear but fear itself, and that's how they feel. When
they run off the field at the half, or between innings, some observers
have the feeling that they won't come back. Why should they, if it's
raining and they're losing? They come back, not because they are paid
to, as you might think, but because of what it says in the rules. Hard
and fast rules are hard to come by, as you may know. When a player
runs off the field and tries to hide in the shower room, he's a free man,
and that scares him. Whose side is he on? Where does he play? Without
his Bank of America or American Express card, who is going to recognize him? Most of the games people play just go on and on without
time-outs, vacations, or free ambulance service, but ball games have a
beginning and an ending. It says so in the rules. In case you've often
wondered, that may account for their strange appeal.

_____ CONSIDERATIONS _____

1. How far do you have to read before you suspect that Morris is not
taking his sports very seriously? What are the surest clues to his attitude?

2. What does Morris imply with the final clause of the third sentence of Paragraph 5? Why? How important are the implications to Morris's essay?

3. To what extent are ritual and ceremony important in sports? Collect the several comments Morris makes on this question, add your own observations, and state your conclusion.

4. How does Morris's article differ from McPhee's account of a tennis match (pages 243–247)? Consider the difference in voice and tone, using specific examples of each in the two essays.

5. Which of the sports does Morris see as the most bizarre? Does he like one sport more than the others? Using the *Reader's Guide to Periodical Literature,* locate magazine articles on Morris and read them to find out whether he himself is a sportsman of any kind.

6. In what way are the terms "sports," "recreation," and "play" synonymous? How are they different? If an amateur becomes a professional, must he then call his activity work? How do you distinguish between play and work? Or do you see them as part of the same thing?

Anaïs Nin (1903–1977) was born in Paris. When her father, a Spanish musician and composer, left her mother in 1914, the family sailed to New York. She adored her father and began a diary addressed to him, hoping that some day she would send it to him, and by its excellence win his approval. She continued writing the diary — more than sixty-five volumes — throughout her life. At the age of fifteen she began to support her mother and her brothers, first as a model, and later as a Spanish dancer. For decades her writings were unpublished but attained a reputation among other writers, who read portions privately. She was a friend and confidant of Henry Miller, author of Tropic of Cancer *and other novels. In 1939 she printed her novel* Winter of Artifice *herself, on a foot-powered printing press, and enlarged her reputation among a small but powerful élite. Later in the forties, a New York publisher attempted to distribute several of her novels, but without commercial success. In the 1960s, the Swallow Press reissued her novels, and her reputation widened. The publication of her diaries, in six volumes to date, greatly increased her audience.*

Many of the entries in the diaries of Anaïs Nin mean little detached from the body of the text, so closely related are the references. Here we print a brief excerpt about her premature delivery of a dead child. It begins in the hospital delivery room after four difficult hours of labor. Images with the fantastic intensity of dream ("Will the ice come . . . ? At the end of the dark tunnel, a knife gleams") are common in Anaïs Nin's writing.

49

ANAÏS NIN
Journal Entry

1   The nurses begin to talk again. I say, "Let me alone." I place my two hands on my stomach and very slowly, very softly, with the tips of my fingers I drum, drum, drum on my stomach, in circles. Round and round, softly, with eyes open in great serenity. The doctor comes near and looks with amazement. The nurses are silent. Drum drum drum drum drum in soft circles, in soft quiet circles. "Like a savage," they whisper. The mystery.

2   Eyes open, nerves quiet, I drum gently on my stomach for a long while. The nerves begin to quiver. A mysterious agitation runs through them. I hear the ticking of the clock. It ticks inexorably, separately. The little nerves awaken, stir. I say, "I can push now!" and I push violently. They are shouting, "A little more! Just a little more!"

3   Will the ice come, and the darkness, before I am through? At the end of the dark tunnel, a knife gleams. I hear the clock and my heart. I say, "Stop!" The doctor holds the instrument, and he is leaning over. I sit up and shout at him. He is afraid again. "Let me alone, all of you!"

4   I lie back so quietly. I hear the ticking. Softly I drum, drum, drum. I feel my womb stirring, dilating. My hands are so weary, they will fall off. They will fall off, and I will lie there in darkness. The womb is stirring and dilating. Drum drum drum drum drum. "I am ready!" The nurse puts her knee on my stomach. There is blood in my eyes. A tunnel. I push into this tunnel. I bite my lips and push. There is fire, flesh ripping and no air. Out of the tunnel! All my blood is spilling out. "Push! Push! It is coming! It is coming!" I feel the slipperiness, the sudden deliverance, the weight is gone. Darkness.

I hear voices. I open my eyes. I hear them saying, "It was a little   5
girl. Better not show it to her." All my strength is coming back. I sit
up. The doctor shouts, "For God's sake, don't sit up, don't move!"

"Show me the child," I say.   6

"Don't show it," says the nurse, "it will be bad for her."   7

The nurses try to make me lie down. My heart is beating so   8
loudly I can hardly hear myself repeating, "Show it to me!" The doctor
holds it up. It looks dark, and small, like a diminutive man. But it is a
little girl. It has long eyelashes on its closed eyes, it is perfectly made,
and all glistening with the waters of the womb. It was like a doll, or
like a miniature Indian, about one foot long, skin on bones, no flesh.
But completely formed. The doctor told me afterwards that it had
hands and feet exactly like mine. The head was bigger than average.
As I looked at the dead child, for a moment I hated it for all the pain it
had caused me, and it was only later that this flare of anger turned into
great sadness.

_____CONSIDERATIONS_____

1. A surprisingly little-used grammatical technique adds to the tension
of the narrative. The same characteristic was used by John McPhee in his
account of the Ashe-Graebner tennis match (pages 243–247). What is it? How
does it add to the drama? Why is it so rarely used by writers?

2. "At the end of the dark tunnel, a knife gleams." What tunnel?

3. In the first paragraph, Nin describes herself as serene; in the third, "I
sit up and shout at him." How do you account for this apparent contradiction?

4. Notice how repetition raises suspense in this short narrative. How
does Nin adapt her style to make the most of the repetition in the fourth
paragraph? Do you hear that repetition echoed in Paragraph 5?

5. Take a dramatic moment from your own experience and write a short
account of it, imitating Nin's style.

6. How might those either for or against natural childbirth methods
make use of Nin's experience?

Tillie Olsen (b. 1913) was born in Nebraska, and has lived most of her life in San Francisco. Mother of four children, she found it impossible to write when she was young. Later she recalled herself "so nearly remaining mute and having let writing die over and over again in me," but the hope of writing, she said, became "the air I breathed."

It was not until 1962 that she published her first book, Tell Me a Riddle, *which contained four stories, including this one, a monologue that begins with an image and builds the character of the speaker stroke by stroke as the iron moves across the fabric.*

50

TILLIE OLSEN

I Stand Here Ironing

I stand here ironing, and what you asked me moves tormented back and forth with the iron.

"I wish you would manage the time to come in and talk with me about your daughter. I'm sure you can help me understand her. She's a youngster who needs help and whom I'm deeply interested in helping."

"Who needs help." Even if I came, what good would it do? You think because I am her mother I have a key, or that in some way you could use me as a key? She has lived for nineteen years. There is all that life that has happened outside of me, beyond me.

And when is there time to remember, to sift, to weigh, to estimate, to total? I will start and there will be an interruption and I will have to gather it all together again. Or I will become engulfed with all I did or did not do, with what should have been and what cannot be helped.

She was a beautiful baby. The first and only one of our five that was beautiful at birth. You do not guess how new and uneasy her tenancy in her now-loveliness. You did not know her all those years she was thought homely, or see her poring over her baby pictures, making me tell her over and over how beautiful she had been — and would be, I would tell her — and was now, to the seeing eye. But the seeing eyes were few or non-existent. Including mine.

I nursed her. They feel that's important nowadays. I nursed all the children, but with her, with all the fierce rigidity of first motherhood, I did like the books then said. Though her cries battered me to trembling and my breasts ached with swollenness, I waited till the clock decreed.

Why do I put that first? I do not even know if it matters, or if it explains anything.

She was a beautiful baby. She blew shining bubbles of sound. She loved motion, loved light, loved color and music and textures. She would lie on the floor in her blue overalls patting the surface so hard in ecstasy her hands and feet would blur. She was a miracle to me, but when she was eight months old I had to leave her daytimes with the woman downstairs to whom she was no miracle at all, for I worked or looked for work and for Emily's father, who "could no longer endure" (he wrote in his good-bye note) "sharing want with us."

I was nineteen. It was the pre-relief, pre-WPA world of the depression. I would start running as soon as I got off the streetcar, running up the stairs, the place smelling sour, and awake or asleep to startle awake, when she saw me she would break into a clogged weeping that could not be comforted, a weeping I can hear yet.

After a while I found a job hashing at night so I could be with her days, and it was better. But it came to where I had to bring her to his family and leave her.

It took a long time to raise the money for her fare back. Then she got chicken pox and I had to wait longer. When she finally came, I hardly knew her, walking quick and nervous like her father, looking like her father, thin, and dressed in a shoddy red that yellowed her skin and glared at the pockmarks. All the baby loveliness gone.

She was two. Old enough for nursery school they said, and I did not know then what I know now — the fatigue of the long day, and the lacerations of group life in the kinds of nurseries that are only parking places for children.

Except that it would have made no difference if I had known. It was the only place there was. It was the only way we could be together, the only way I could hold a job.

And even without knowing, I knew. I knew the teacher that was evil because all these years it has curdled into my memory, the little boy hunched in the corner, her rasp, "why aren't you outside, because Alvin hits you? that's no reason, go out, scaredy." I knew Emily hated it even if she did not clutch and implore "don't go Mommy" like the other children, mornings.

She always had a reason why we should stay home. Momma, you look sick, Momma. I feel sick. Momma, the teachers aren't there today, they're sick. Momma, we can't go, there was a fire there last night. Momma, it's a holiday today, no school, they told me.

But never a direct protest, never rebellion. I think of our others in their three-, four-year-oldness — the explosions, the tempers, the denunciations, the demands — and I feel suddenly ill. I put the iron down. What in me demanded that goodness in her? And what was the cost, the cost to her of such goodness?

The old man living in the back once said in his gentle way: "You should smile at Emily more when you look at her." What *was* in my face when I looked at her? I loved her. There were all the acts of love.

It was only with the others I remembered what he said, and it was the face of joy, and not of care or tightness or worry I turned to them — too late for Emily. She does not smile easily, let alone almost always as her brothers and sisters do. Her face is closed and sombre, but when she wants, how fluid. You must have seen it in her pantomimes, you spoke of her rare gift for comedy on the stage that rouses a laughter out of the audience so dear they applaud and applaud and do not want to let her go.

Where does it come from, that comedy? There was none of it in her when she came back to me that second time, after I had had to send her away again. She had a new daddy now to learn to love, and I think perhaps it was a better time.

Except when we left her alone nights, telling ourselves she was old enough.

"Can't you go some other time, Mommy, like tomorrow?" she would ask. "Will it be just a little while you'll be gone? Do you promise?"

The time we came back, the front door open, the clock on the floor in the hall. She rigid awake. "It wasn't just a little while. I didn't cry. Three times I called you, just three times, and then I ran downstairs to open the door so you could come faster. The clock talked loud. I threw it away, it scared me what it talked."

She said the clock talked loud again that night I went to the hospital to have Susan. She was delirious with the fever that comes before red measles, but she was fully conscious all the week I was gone and the week after we were home when she could not come near the new baby or me.

She did not get well. She stayed skeleton thin, not wanting to eat, and night after night she had nightmares. She would call for me, and I would rouse from exhaustion to sleepily call back: "You're all right, darling, go to sleep, it's just a dream," and if she still called, in a sterner voice, "now go to sleep, Emily, there's nothing to hurt you." Twice, only twice, when I had to get up for Susan anyhow, I went in to sit with her.

Now when it is too late (as if she would let me hold and comfort her like I do the others) I get up and go to her at once at her moan or restless stirring. "Are you awake, Emily? Can I get you something?" And the answer is always the same: "No, I'm all right, go back to sleep, Mother."

They persuaded me at the clinic to send her away to a convalescent home in the country where "she can have the kind of food and care you can't manage for her, and you'll be free to concentrate on the new baby." They still send children to that place. I see pictures on the society page of sleek young women planning affairs to raise money for it, or dancing at the affairs, or decorating Easter eggs or filling Christmas stockings for the children.

They never have a picture of the children so I do not know if the girls still wear those gigantic red bows and the ravaged looks on the every other Sunday when parents can come to visit "unless otherwise notified" — as we were notified the first six weeks.

Oh it is a handsome place, green lawns and tall trees and fluted flower beds. High up on the balconies of each cottage the children stand, the girls in their red bows and white dresses, the boys in white suits and giant red ties. The parents stand below shrieking up to be heard and the children shriek down to be heard, and between them the invisible wall "Not To Be Contaminated by Parental Germs or Physical Affection."

There was a tiny girl who always stood hand in hand with Emily. Her parents never came. One visit she was gone. "They moved her to Rose Cottage," Emily shouted in explanation. "They don't like you to love anybody here."

She wrote once a week, the labored writing of a seven-year-old. "I am fine. How is the baby. If I write my leter nicly I will have a star. Love." There never was a star. We wrote every other day, letters she could never hold or keep but only hear read — once. "We simply do not have room for children to keep any personal possessions," they patiently explained when we pieced one Sunday's shrieking together to plead how much it would mean to Emily, who loved so to keep things, to be allowed to keep her letters and cards.

Each visit she looked frailer. "She isn't eating," they told us.

(They had runny eggs for breakfast or mush with lumps, Emily said later, I'd hold it in my mouth and not swallow. Nothing ever tasted good, just when they had chicken.)

It took us eight months to get her released home, and only the fact that she gained back so little of her seven lost pounds convinced the social worker.

I used to try to hold and love her after she came back, but her body would lay stiff, and after a while she'd push away. She ate little. Food sickened her, and I think much of life too. Oh she had physical lightness and brightness, twinkling by on skates, bouncing like a ball up and down up and down over the jump rope, skimming over the hill; but these were momentary.

She fretted about her appearance, thin and dark and foreign-looking at a time when every little girl was supposed to look or thought she should look a chubby blonde replica of Shirley Temple. The doorbell sometimes rang for her, but no one seemed to come and play in the house or be a best friend. Maybe because we moved so much.

There was a boy she loved painfully through two school semesters. Months later she told me how she had taken pennies from my purse to buy him candy. "Licorice was his favorite and I brought him some every day, but he still liked Jennifer better'n me. Why, Mommy?" The kind of question for which there is no answer.

School was a worry to her. She was not glib or quick in a world where glibness and quickness were easily confused with ability to learn. To her overworked and exasperated teachers she was an overconscientious "slow learner" who kept trying to catch up and was absent entirely too often.

I let her be absent, though sometimes the illness was imaginary. How different from my now-strictness about attendance with the others. I wasn't working. We had a new baby, I was home anyhow. Sometimes, after Susan grew old enough, I would keep her home from school, too, to have them all together.

Mostly Emily had asthma, and her breathing, harsh and labored, would fill the house with a curiously tranquil sound. I would bring the two old dresser mirrors and her boxes of collections to her bed. She would select beads and single earrings, bottle tops and shells, dried flowers and pebbles, old postcards and scraps, all sorts of oddments; then she and Susan would play Kingdom, setting up landscapes and furniture, peopling them with action.

Those were the only times of peaceful companionship between her and Susan. I have edged away from it, that poisonous feeling between them, that terrible balancing of hurts and needs I had to do between the two, and did so badly, those earlier years.

Oh there are conflicts between the others too, each one human, needing, demanding, hurting, taking — but only between Emily and Susan, no, Emily toward Susan that corroding resentment. It seems so obvious on the surface, yet it is not obvious. Susan, the second child, Susan, golden- and curly-haired and chubby, quick and articulate and assured, everything in appearance and manner Emily was not; Susan, not able to resist Emily's precious things, losing or sometimes clumsily breaking them; Susan telling jokes and riddles to company for applause while Emily sat silent (to say to me later: that was *my* riddle, Mother, I told it to Susan); Susan, who for all the five years' difference in age was just a year behind Emily in developing physically.

I am glad for that slow physical development that widened the difference between her and her contemporaries, though she suffered over it. She was too vulnerable for that terrible world of youthful competition, of preening and parading, of constant measuring of yourself against every other, of envy, "If I had that copper hair," "If I had that skin. . . ." She tormented herself enough about not looking like the others, there was enough of the unsureness, the having to be conscious of words before you speak, the constant caring — what are they thinking of me? without having it all magnified by the merciless physical drives.

Ronnie is calling. He is wet and I change him. It is rare there is such a cry now. That time of motherhood is almost behind me when the ear is not one's own but must always be racked and listening for the child cry, the child call. We sit for a while and I hold him, looking out over the city spread in charcoal with its soft aisles of light. *"Shoogily,"* he breathes and curls closer. I carry him back to bed, asleep. *Shoogily.* A funny word, a family word, inherited from Emily, invented by her to say: *comfort.*

In this and other ways she leaves her seal, I say aloud. And startle at my saying it. What do I mean? What did I start to gather together, to try and make coherent? I was at the terrible, growing years. War years. I do not remember them well. I was working, there were four smaller ones now, there was not time for her. She had to help be a mother, and housekeeper, and shopper. She had to set her seal. Mornings of crisis and near hysteria trying to get lunches packed, hair combed, coats and shoes found, everyone to school or Child Care on time, the baby ready for transportation. And always the paper scribbled on by a smaller one, the book looked at by Susan then mislaid, the homework not done. Running out to that huge school where she was one, she was lost, she was a drop; suffering over the unpreparedness, stammering and unsure in her classes.

There was so little time left at night after the kids were bedded down. She would struggle over books, always eating (it was in those years she developed her enormous appetite that is legendary in our family) and I would be ironing, or preparing food for the next day, or writing V-mail to Bill, or tending the baby. Sometimes, to make me laugh, or out of her despair, she would imitate happenings or types at school.

I think I said once: "Why don't you do something like this in the school amateur show?" One morning she phoned me at work, hardly understandable through the weeping: "Mother, I did it. I won, I won; they gave me first prize; they clapped and clapped and wouldn't let me go."

Now suddenly she was Somebody, and as imprisoned in her difference as she had been in her anonymity.

She began to be asked to perform at other high schools, even in colleges, then at city and statewide affairs. The first one we went to, I only recognized her that first moment when thin, shy, she almost drowned herself into the curtains. Then: Was this Emily? The control, the command, the convulsing and deadly clowning, the spell, then the roaring, stamping audience, unwilling to let this rare and precious laughter out of their lives.

Afterwards: You ought to do something about her with a gift like that — but without money or knowing how, what does one do? We have left it all to her, and the gift has as often eddied inside, clogged and clotted, as been used and growing.

She is coming. She runs up the stairs two at a time with her light graceful step, and I know she is happy tonight. Whatever it was that occasioned your call did not happen today.

"Aren't you ever going to finish the ironing, Mother? Whistler painted his mother in a rocker. I'd have to paint mine standing over an ironing board." This is one of her communicative nights and she tells me everything and nothing as she fixes herself a plate of food out of the icebox.

She is so lovely. Why did you want me to come in at all? Why were you concerned? She will find her way.

She starts up the stairs to bed. "Don't get me up with the rest in the morning." "But I thought you were having midterms." "Oh, those," she comes back in, kisses me, and says quite lightly, "in a couple of years when we'll all be atom-dead they won't matter a bit."

She has said it before. She *believes* it. But because I have been dredging the past, and all that compounds a human being is so heavy and meaningful in me, I cannot endure it tonight.

I will never total it all. I will never come in to say: She was a child seldom smiled at. Her father left me before she was a year old. I had to work her first six years when there was work, or I sent her home and to his relatives. There were years she had care she hated. She was dark and thin and foreign-looking in a world where the prestige went to blondeness and curly hair and dimples, she was slow where glibness was prized. She was a child of anxious, not proud, love. We were poor and I could not afford for her the soil of easy growth. I was a young mother, I was a distracted mother. There were the other children pushing up, demanding. Her younger sister seemed all that she was not. There were years she did not want me to touch her. She kept too much in herself, her life was such she had to keep too much in herself. My wisdom came too late. She has much to her and probably little will come of it. She is a child of her age, of depression, of war, of fear.

Let her be. So all that is in her will not bloom — but in how many does it? There is still enough left to live by. Only help her to know — help make it so there is cause for her to know — that she is more than this dress on the ironing board, helpless before the iron.

_____ **CONSIDERATIONS** _____

1. How does Olsen keep away from the sentimentality that spoils so many stories about children? Or do you feel that she too is caught by that snare? Explain: where? how?

2. The speaker in Olsen's story deals with more than simple past or present time. Mark where she changes from one tense to another. Explain why she does it.

3. Who is the "you" addressed in the first sentence and in the last two paragraphs? How does this unnamed person figure in the story?

4. On page 301, Olsen's character uses the word "shoogily," explaining that it is a family word. Do you recall any of your own family words or phrases? How could such a word become important in one's memories of home? See the use Lillian Hellman makes of a childhood one-sentence prayer (pages 178–184).

5. How much of the story depends on the work the mother does? What are the kinds of work?

6. Would Olsen's story be useful in a book for prospective parents?

7. How many years of Emily's life are covered in this story? How old is she at the time the story is told? What difference does that make?

Gregory Orr (b. 1947) spent his childhood in upstate New York, graduated from Antioch College, and did graduate work in creative writing at Columbia University. His two collections of poems are Burning the Empty Nests *(1973) and* Gathering the Bones Together *(1975). He is an obsessive poet, returning again and again to certain images as compelling as dreams, making brief poems that resonate for a long time.*

51

GREGORY ORR

Washing My Face

Last night's dreams disappear.
They are like the sink draining:
a transparent rose swallowed by its stem.

George Orwell (1903–1950) was the pen name of Eric Blair, who was born in India of English parents, attended Eton on a scholarship, and returned to the East as a member of the Imperial Police. He quit his position after five years because he wanted to write, and because he came to feel that imperialism was "very largely a racket." For eight years he wrote with small success and in considerable poverty. His first book, Down and Out in Paris and London (1933), described those years. Further memoirs and novels followed, including Burmese Days (1935) and Keep the Aspidistra Flying (1938). His last books were the political fable Animal Farm (1945) and his great anti-utopia 1984, which appeared in 1949, shortly before his death. He died of tuberculosis, his health first afflicted when he was a policeman in Burma, undermined by years of poverty, and further worsened by a wound he received during the civil war in Spain.

Best known for his fiction, Orwell was essentially an essayist, and even his novels are essays. He made his living most of his adult life by writing reviews and articles for English weeklies. His collected essays, reviews, and letters form an impressive four volumes. Politics is at the center of his work — a personal politics. After his disaffection from imperialism, he became a leftist, and fought on the Loyalist side against Franco in Spain. (Homage to Catalonia comes out of this time.) But his experience of Communist duplicity there, and his early understanding of the paranoid totalitarianism of Stalin, turned him anti-Communist. He could swear allegiance to no party. His anti-Communism made him in no way conservative; he considered himself a socialist until his death, but other socialists would have nothing to do with him. He found politics shabby and politicians dishonest. With an empirical, English turn of mind, he looked skeptically at all saviors and panaceas. In this famous essay, he attacks the rhetoric of politics. He largely attacks the left — because his audience was an English intellectual class that was largely leftist.

52

GEORGE ORWELL
Politics and
the English Language

Most people who bother with the matter at all would admit that 1
the English language is in a bad way, but it is generally assumed that
we cannot by conscious action do anything about it. Our civilization
is decadent and our language — so the argument runs — must inevitably share in the general collapse. It follows that any struggle against
the abuse of language is a sentimental archaism, like preferring candles
to electric light or hansom cabs to aeroplanes. Underneath this lies the
half-conscious belief that language is a natural growth and not an
instrument which we shape for our own purposes.

Now, it is clear that the decline of a language must ultimately 2
have political and economic causes: it is not due simply to the bad
influence of this or that individual writer. But an effect can become a
cause, reinforcing the original cause and producing the same effect in
an intensified form, and so on indefinitely. A man may take to drink
because he feels himself to be a failure, and then fail all the more
completely because he drinks. It is rather the same thing that is happening to the English language. It becomes ugly and inaccurate because
our thoughts are foolish, but the slovenliness of our language makes it
easier for us to have foolish thoughts. The point is that the process is
reversible. Modern English, especially written English, is full of bad
habits which spread by imitation and which can be avoided if one is
willing to take the necessary trouble. If one gets rid of these habits one

can think more clearly, and to think clearly is a necessary first step towards political regeneration: so that the fight against bad English is not frivolous and is not the exclusive concern of professional writers. I will come back to this presently, and I hope that by that time the meaning of what I have said here will have become clearer. Meanwhile, here are five specimens of the English language as it is now habitually written.

3   These five passages have not been picked out because they are especially bad — I could have quoted far worse if I had chosen — but because they illustrate various of the mental vices from which we now suffer. They are a little below the average, but are fairly representative samples. I number them so that I can refer back to them when necessary:

> (1) I am not, indeed, sure whether it is not true to say that the Milton who once seemed not unlike a seventeenth-century Shelley had not become, out of an experience ever more bitter in each year, more alien [sic] to the founder of that Jesuit sect which nothing could induce him to tolerate.
>
> Professor Harold Laski
> (Essay in *Freedom of Expression*).

> (2) Above all, we cannot play ducks and drakes with a native battery of idioms which prescribes such egregious collocations of vocables as the Basic *put up with* for *tolerate* or *put at a loss* for *bewilder*.
>
> Professor Lancelot Hogben (*Interglossa*).

> (3) On the one side we have the free personality: by definition it is not neurotic, for it has neither conflict nor dream. Its desires, such as they are, are transparent, for they are just what institutional approval keeps in the forefront of consciousness; another institutional pattern would alter their number and intensity, there is little in them that is natural, irreducible, or culturally dangerous. But *on the other side,* the social bond itself is nothing but the mutual reflection of these self-secure integrities. Recall the definition of love. Is not this the very picture of a small academic? Where is there a place in this hall of mirrors for either personality or fraternity?
>
> Essay on psychology in *Politics* (New York).

> (4) All the "best people" from the gentlemen's clubs, and all the frantic fascist captains, united in common hatred of Socialism and bestial horror of the rising tide of the mass revolutionary movement, have turned to acts of provocation, to foul incendiarism, to

medieval legends of poisoned wells, to legalize their own destruction of proletarian organizations, and rouse the agitated petty-bourgeoisie to chauvinistic fervor on behalf of the fight against the revolutionary way out of the crisis.

Communist pamphlet.

(5) If a new spirit is to be infused into this old country, there is one thorny and contentious reform which must be tackled, and that is the humanization and galvanization of the B.B.C. Timidity here will bespeak canker and atrophy of the soul. The heart of Britain may be sound and of strong beat, for instance, but the British lion's roar at present is like that of Bottom in Shakespeare's *Midsummer Night's Dream* — as gentle as any sucking dove. A virile new Britain cannot continue indefinitely to be traduced in the eyes, or rather ears, of the world by the effete languors of Langham Place, brazenly masquerading as "standard English." When the Voice of Britain is heard at nine o'clock, better far and infinitely less ludicrous to hear aitches honestly dropped than the present priggish, inflated, inhibited, school-ma'amish arch braying of blameless bashful mewing maidens!

Letter in *Tribune.*

Each of these passages has faults of its own, but, quite apart from avoidable ugliness, two qualities are common to all of them. The first is staleness of imagery; the other is lack of precision. The writer either has a meaning and cannot express it, or he inadvertently says something else, or he is almost indifferent as to whether his words mean anything or not. This mixture of vagueness and sheer incompetence is the most marked characteristic of modern English prose, and especially of any kind of political writing. As soon as certain topics are raised, the concrete melts into the abstract and no one seems able to think of turns of speech that are not hackneyed: prose consists less and less of *words* chosen for the sake of their meaning, and more and more of *phrases* tacked together like the sections of a prefabricated hen-house. I list below, with notes and examples, various of the tricks by means of which the work of prose-construction is habitually dodged:

DYING METAPHORS

A newly invented metaphor assists thought by evoking a visual image, while on the other hand a metaphor which is technically "dead" (e.g. *iron resolution*) has in effect reverted to being an ordinary word and can generally be used without loss of vividness. But in between these two classes there is a huge dump of worn-out metaphors which have lost all evocative power and are merely used because they save people the trouble of inventing phrases for themselves. Examples are: *Ring the changes on, take up the cudgels for, toe the line, ride roughshod over, stand shoulder to shoulder with, play into the hands of, no axe to grind, grist to the mill, fishing in troubled waters, on the order of the day, Achilles' heel, swan song, hotbed.* Many of these are used without knowledge of their meaning (what is a "rift," for instance?), and incompatible metaphors are frequently mixed, a sure sign that the writer is not interested in what he is saying. Some metaphors now current have been twisted out of their original meaning without those who use them even being aware of the fact. For example, *toe the line* is sometimes written *tow the line.* Another example is *the hammer and the anvil,* now always used with the implication that the anvil gets the worst of it. In real life it is always the anvil that breaks the hammer, never the other way about: a writer who stopped to think what he was saying would be aware of this, and would avoid perverting the original phrase.

OPERATORS OR VERBAL FALSE LIMBS

6   These save the trouble of picking out appropriate verbs and nouns, and at the same time pad each sentence with extra syllables which give it an appearance of symmetry. Characteristic phrases are *render inoperative, militate against, make contact with, be subjected to, give rise to, give grounds for, have the effect of, play a leading part (role) in, make itself felt, take effect, exhibit a tendency to, serve the purpose of,* etc., etc. The keynote is the elimination of simple verbs. Instead of being a single word, such as *break, stop, spoil, mend, kill* a verb becomes a *phrase,* made up of a noun or adjective tacked on to some general-purpose verb such as *prove, serve, form, play, render.* In addition, the passive voice is wherever possible used in preference to the active, and noun constructions are used instead of gerunds (*by examination of* instead of *by examining*). The range of verbs is further cut down by means of the *-ize* and *de-* formations, and the banal statements are given an appearance of profundity by means of the *not un-* formation. Simple conjunctions and prepositions are replaced by such phrases as *with respect to, having regard to, the fact that, by dint of,*

in view of, in the interests of, on the hypothesis that; and the ends of sentences are saved from anticlimax by such resounding commonplaces as *greatly to be desired, cannot be left out of account, a development to be expected in the near future, deserving of serious consideration, brought to a satisfactory conclusion* and so on and so forth.

PRETENTIOUS DICTION

Words like *phenomenon, element, individual* (as noun), *objective, categorical, effective, virtual, basic, primary, promote, constitute, exhibit, exploit, utilize, eliminate, liquidate,* are used to dress up simple statements and give an air of scientific impartiality to biased judgments. Adjectives like *epoch-making, epic, historic, unforgettable, triumphant, age-old, inevitable, inexorable, veritable,* are used to dignify the sordid processes of international politics, while writing that aims at glorifying war usually takes on an archaic color, its characteristic words being: *realm, throne, chariot, mailed fist, trident, sword, shield, buckler, banner, jackboot, clarion.* Foreign words and expressions such as *cul de sac, ancien régime, deus ex machina, mutatis mutandis, status quo, gleichschaltung, weltanschauung,* are used to give an air of culture and elegance. Except for the useful abbreviations *i.e., e.g.,* and *etc.,* there is no real need for any of the hundreds of foreign phrases now current in English. Bad writers, and especially scientific, political and sociological writers, are nearly always haunted by the notion that Latin or Greek words are grander than Saxon ones, and unnecessary words like *expedite, ameliorate, predict, extraneous, deracinated, clandestine, subaqueous* and hundreds of others constantly gain ground from their Anglo-Saxon opposite numbers.[1] The jargon peculiar to Marxist writing (*hyena, hangman, cannibal, petty bourgeois, these gentry, lacquey, flunkey, mad dog, White Guard,* etc.) consists largely of words and phrases translated from Russian, German or French; but the normal way of coining a new word is to use a Latin or Greek root with the appropriate affix and, where necessary, the *-ize* formation. It is often easier to make up words of this kind (*deregionalize, impermissible, extramarital, non-fragmentary* and so forth) than

7

---

[1] An interesting illustration of this is the way in which the English flower names which were in use till very recently are being ousted by Greek ones, *snapdragon* becoming *antirrhinum, forget-me-not* becoming *myosotis,* etc. It is hard to see any practical reason for this change of fashion: it is probably due to an instinctive turning-away from the more homely word and a vague feeling that the Greek is scientific.

to think up the English words that will cover one's meaning. The result, in general, is an increase in slovenliness and vagueness.

MEANINGLESS WORDS

8   In certain kinds of writing, particularly in art criticism and literary criticism, it is normal to come across long passages which are almost completely lacking in meaning.[2] Words like *romantic, plastic, values, human, dead, sentimental, natural, vitality,* as used in art criticism, are strictly meaningless, in the sense that they not only do not point to any discoverable object, but are hardly ever expected to do so by the reader. When one critic writes, "The outstanding feature of Mr. X's work is its living quality," while another writes, "The immediately striking thing about Mr. X's work is its peculiar deadness," the reader accepts this as a simple difference of opinion. If words like *black* and *white* were involved, instead of the jargon words *dead* and *living,* he would see at once that language was being used in an improper way. Many political words are similarly abused. The word *Fascism* has now no meaning except in so far as it signifies "something not desirable." The words *democracy, socialism, freedom, patriotic, realistic, justice,* have each of them several different meanings which cannot be reconciled with one another. In the case of a word like *democracy,* not only is there no agreed definition, but the attempt to make one is resisted from all sides. It is almost universally felt that when we call a country democratic we are praising it: consequently the defenders of every kind of régime claim that it is a democracy, and fear that they might have to stop using the word if it were tied down to any one meaning. Words of this kind are often used in a consciously dishonest way. That is, the person who uses them has his own private definition, but allows his hearer to think he means something quite different. Statements like *Marshal Pétain was a true patriot, The Soviet Press is the freest in the world, The Catholic Church is opposed to persecution,* are almost always made with intent to deceive. Other words used in variable meanings, in most cases more or less dishon-

[2] Example: "Comfort's catholicity of perception and image, strangely Whitmanesque in range, almost the exact opposite in aesthetic compulsion, continues to evoke that trembling atmospheric accumulative hinting at a cruel, an inexorably serene timelessness. . . . Wrey Gardiner scores by aiming at simple bull's-eyes with precision. Only they are not so simple, and through his contented sadness runs more than the surface bitter-sweet of resignation." (Poetry Quarterly.)

estly, are: *class, totalitarian, science, progressive, reactionary, bourgeois, equality.*

Now that I have made this catalogue of swindles and perversions, 9
let me give another example of the kind of writing that they lead to.
This time it must of its nature be an imaginary one. I am going to
translate a passage of good English into modern English of the worst
sort. Here is a well-known verse from *Ecclesiastes:*

> I returned and saw under the sun, that the race is not to the
> swift, nor the battle to the strong, neither yet bread to the wise,
> nor yet riches to men of understanding, nor yet favour to men of
> skill; but time and chance happeneth to them all.

Here it is in modern English: 10

> Objective consideration of contemporary phenomena compels
> the conclusion that success or failure in competitive activities ex-
> hibits no tendency to be commensurate with innate capacity, but
> that a considerable element of the unpredictable must invariably
> be taken into account.

This is a parody, but not a very gross one. Exhibit (3), above, for 11
instance, contains several patches of the same kind of English. It will
be seen that I have not made a full translation. The beginning and
ending of the sentence follow the original meaning fairly closely, but
in the middle the concrete illustrations — race, battle, bread — dissolve into the vague phrase "success or failure in competitive activities." This had to be so, because no modern writer of the kind I am
discussing — no one capable of using phrases like "objective consideration of contemporary phenomena" — would ever tabulate his
thoughts in that precise and detailed way. The whole tendency of
modern prose is away from concreteness. Now analyse these two sentences a little more closely. The first contains forty-nine words but
only sixty syllables, and all its words are those of everyday life. The
second contains thirty-eight words of ninety syllables: eighteen of its
words are from Latin roots, and one from Greek. The first sentence
contains six vivid images, and only one phrase ("time and chance")
that could be called vague. The second contains not a single fresh,
arresting phrase, and in spite of its ninety syllables it gives only a
shortened version of the meaning contained in the first. Yet without a
doubt it is the second kind of sentence that is gaining ground in modern English. I do not want to exaggerate. This kind of writing is not yet
universal, and outcrops of simplicity will occur here and there in the
worst-written page. Still, if you or I were told to write a few lines on

the uncertainty of human fortunes, we should probably come much nearer to my imaginary sentence than to the one from *Ecclesiastes.*

12   As I have tried to show, modern writing at its worst does not consist in picking out words for the sake of their meaning and inventing images in order to make the meaning clearer. It consists in gumming together long strips of words which have already been set in order by someone else, and making the results presentable by sheer humbug. The attraction of this way of writing is that it is easy. It is easier — even quicker, once you have the habit — to say *In my opinion it is not an unjustifiable assumption that* than to say *I think.* If you use ready-made phrases, you not only don't have to hunt about for words; you also don't have to bother with the rhythms of your sentences, since these phrases are generally so arranged as to be more or less euphonious. When you are composing in a hurry — when you are dictating to a stenographer, for instance, or making a public speech — it is natural to fall into a pretentious, Latinized style. Tags like *a consideration which we should do well to bear in mind* or *a conclusion to which all of us would readily assent* will save many a sentence from coming down with a bump. By using stale metaphors, similes and idioms, you save much mental effort, at the cost of leaving your meaning vague, not only for your reader but for yourself. This is the significance of mixed metaphors. The sole aim of a metaphor is to call up a visual image. When these images clash — as in *The Fascist octopus has sung its swan song, the jackboot is thrown into the melting pot* — it can be taken as certain that the writer is not seeing a mental image of the objects he is naming; in other words he is not really thinking. Look again at the examples I gave at the beginning of this essay. Professor Laski (1) uses five negatives in fifty-three words. One of these is superfluous, making nonsense of the whole passage, and in addition there is the slip *alien* for *akin,* making further nonsense, and several avoidable pieces of clumsiness which increase the general vagueness. Professor Hogben (2) plays ducks and drakes with a battery which is able to write prescriptions, and, while disapproving of the everyday phrase *put up with,* is unwilling to look *egregious* up in the dictionary and see what it means; (3), if one takes an uncharitable attitude towards it, is simply meaningless: probably one could work out its intended meaning by reading the whole of the article in which it occurs. In (4), the writer knows more or less what he wants to say, but an accumulation of stale phrases chokes him, like tea leaves blocking a sink. In (5), words and meaning have almost parted company. People who write in this manner usually have a general emotional

meaning — they dislike one thing and want to express solidarity with another — but they are not interested in the detail of what they are saying. A scrupulous writer, in every sentence that he writes, will ask himself at least four questions, thus: What am I trying to say? What words will express it? What image or idiom will make it clearer? Is this image fresh enough to have an effect? And he will probably ask himself two more: Could I put it more shortly? Have I said anything that is avoidably ugly? But you are not obliged to go to all this trouble. You can shirk it by simply throwing your mind open and letting the ready-made phrases come crowding in. They will construct your sentences for you — even think your thoughts for you, to a certain extent — and at need they will perform the important service of partially concealing your meaning even from yourself. It is at this point that the special connection between politics and the debasement of language becomes clear.

In our time it is broadly true that political writing is bad writing. 13 Where it is not true, it will generally be found that the writer is some kind of rebel, expressing his private opinions and not a "party line." Orthodoxy, of whatever color, seems to demand a lifeless, imitative style. The political dialects to be found in pamphlets, leading articles, manifestos, White Papers and the speeches of undersecretaries do, of course, vary from party to party, but they are all alike in that one almost never finds in them a fresh, vivid, home-made turn of speech. When one watches some tired hack on the platform mechanically repeating the familiar phrases — *bestial atrocities, iron heel, blood-stained tyranny, free peoples of the world, stand shoulder to shoulder* — one often has a curious feeling that one is not watching a live human being but some kind of dummy: a feeling which suddenly becomes stronger at moments when the light catches the speaker's spectacles and turns them into blank discs which seem to have no eyes behind them. And this is not altogether fanciful. A speaker who uses that kind of phraseology has gone some distance towards turning himself into a machine. The appropriate noises are coming out of his larynx, but his brain is not involved as it would be if he were choosing his words for himself. If the speech he is making is one that he is accustomed to make over and over again, he may be almost unconscious of what he is saying, as one is when one utters the responses in church. And this reduced state of consciousness, if not indispensable, is at any rate favorable to political conformity.

In our time, political speech and writing are largely the defence 14 of the indefensible. Things like the continuance of British rule in India, the Russian purges and deportations, the dropping of the atom bombs on Japan, can indeed be defended, but only by arguments which are too brutal for most people to face, and which do not square with the professed aims of political parties. Thus political language has to consist largely of euphemism, question-begging and sheer cloudy vagueness. Defenceless villages are bombarded from the air, the inhabitants driven out into the countryside, the cattle machine-gunned, the huts set on fire with incendiary bullets: this is called *pacification*. Millions of peasants are robbed of their farms and sent trudging along the roads with no more than they can carry: this is called *transfer of population* or *rectification of frontiers*. People are imprisoned for years without trial, or shot in the back of the neck or sent to die of scurvy in Arctic lumber camps; this is called *elimination of unreliable elements*. Such phraseology is needed if one wants to name things without calling up mental pictures of them. Consider for instance some comfortable English professor defending Russian totalitarianism. He cannot say outright, "I believe in killing off your opponents when you can get good results by doing so." Probably, therefore, he will say something like this:

15   "While freely conceding that the Soviet régime exhibits certain features which the humanitarian may be inclined to deplore, we must, I think, agree that a certain curtailment of the right to political opposition is an unavoidable concomitant of transitional periods, and that the rigors which the Russian people have been called upon to undergo have been amply justified in the sphere of concrete achievement."

16   The inflated style is itself a kind of euphemism. A mass of Latin words falls upon the facts like soft snow, blurring the outlines and covering up all the details. The great enemy of clear language is insincerity. When there is a gap between one's real and one's declared aims, one turns as it were instinctively to long words and exhausted idioms, like a cuttlefish squirting out ink. In our age there is no such thing as "keeping out of politics." All issues are political issues, and politics itself is a mass of lies, evasions, folly, hatred and schizophrenia. When the general atmosphere is bad, language must suffer. I should expect to find — this is a guess which I have not sufficient knowledge to verify — that the German, Russian and Italian languages have all deteriorated in the last ten or fifteen years, as a result of dictatorship.

17   But if thought corrupts language, language can also corrupt thought. A bad usage can spread by tradition and imitation, even among people who should and do know better. The debased language that I have been discussing is in some ways very convenient. Phrases

like *a not unjustifiable assumption, leaves much to be desired, would serve no good purpose. a consideration which we should do well to bear in mind,* are a continuous temptation, a packet of aspirins always at one's elbow. Look back through this essay, and for certain you will find that I have again and again committed the very faults I am protesting against. By this morning's post I have received a pamphlet dealing with conditions in Germany. The author tells me that he "felt impelled" to write it. I open it at random, and here is almost the first sentence that I see: "[The Allies] have an opportunity not only of achieving a radical transformation of Germany's social and political structure in such a way as to avoid a nationalistic reaction in Germany itself, but at the same time of laying the foundations of a co-operative and unified Europe." You see, he "feels impelled" to write — feels, presumably, that he has something new to say — and yet his words, like cavalry horses answering the bugle, group themselves automatically into the familiar dreary pattern. This invasion of one's mind by ready-made phrases (*lay the foundations, achieve a radical transformation*) can only be prevented if one is constantly on guard against them, and every such phrase anaesthetizes a portion of one's brain.

I said earlier that the decadence of our language is probably curable. Those who deny this would argue, if they produced an argument at all, that language merely reflects existing social conditions, and that we cannot influence its development by any direct tinkering with words and constructions. So far as the general tone or spirit of a language goes, this may be true, but it is not true in detail. Silly words and expressions have often disappeared, not through any evolutionary process but owing to the conscious action of a minority. Two recent examples were *explore every avenue* and *leave no stone unturned,* which were killed by the jeers of a few journalists. There is a long list of flyblown metaphors which could similarly be got rid of if enough people would interest themselves in the job; and it should also be possible to laugh the *not un-* formation out of existence,[3] to reduce the amount of Latin and Greek in the average sentence, to drive out foreign phrases and strayed scientific words, and, in general, to make pretentiousness unfashionable. But all these are minor points. The defence of the English language implies more than this, and perhaps it is best to start by saying what it does *not* imply. 18

To begin with it has nothing to do with archaism, with the sal- 19

---

[3] One can cure oneself of the *not un-* formation by memorizing this sentence: *A not unblack dog was chasing a not unsmall rabbit across a not ungreen field.*

vaging of obsolete words and turns of speech, or with the setting up of a "standard English" which must never be departed from. On the contrary, it is especially concerned with the scrapping of every word or idiom which has outworn its usefulness. It has nothing to do with correct grammar and syntax, which are of no importance so long as one makes one's meaning clear, or with the avoidance of Americanisms, or with having what is called a "good prose style." On the other hand it is not concerned with fake simplicity and the attempt to make written English colloquial. Nor does it even imply in every case preferring the Saxon word to the Latin one, though it does imply using the fewest and shortest words that will cover one's meaning. What is above all needed is to let the meaning choose the word, and not the other way about. In prose, the worst thing one can do with words is to surrender to them. When you think of a concrete object, you think wordlessly, and then, if you want to describe the thing you have been visualizing you probably hunt about till you find the exact words that seem to fit it. When you think of something abstract you are more inclined to use words from the start, and unless you make a conscious effort to prevent it, the existing dialect will come rushing in and do the job for you, at the expense of blurring or even changing your meaning. Probably it is better to put off using words as long as possible and get one's meaning as clear as one can through pictures or sensations. Afterwards one can choose — not simply *accept* — the phrases that will best cover the meaning, and then switch round and decide what impression one's words are likely to make on another person. This last effort of the mind cuts out all stale or mixed images, all prefabricated phrases, needless repetitions, and humbug and vagueness generally. But one can often be in doubt about the effect of a word or a phrase, and one needs rules that one can rely on when instinct fails. I think the following rules will cover most cases:

(i) Never use a metaphor, simile or other figure of speech which you are used to seeing in print.
(ii) Never use a long word where a short one will do.
(iii) If it is possible to cut a word out, always cut it out.
(iv) Never use the passive where you can use the active.
(v) Never use a foreign phrase, a scientific word or a jargon word if you can think of an everyday English equivalent.
(vi) Break any of these rules sooner than say anything outright barbarous.

These rules sound elementary, and so they are, but they demand a deep change of attitude in anyone who has grown used to writing in the style now fashionable. One could keep all of them and still write bad English, but one could not write the kind of stuff that I quoted in those five specimens at the beginning of this article.

I have not here been considering the literary use of language, but   20 merely language as an instrument for expressing and not for concealing or preventing thought. Stuart Chase and others have come near to claiming that all abstract words are meaningless, and have used this as a pretext for advocating a kind of political quietism. Since you don't know what Fascism is, how can you struggle against Fascism? One need not swallow such absurdities as this, but one ought to recognize that the present political chaos is connected with the decay of language, and that one can probably bring about some improvement by starting at the verbal end. If you simplify your English, you are freed from the worst follies of orthodoxy. You cannot speak any of the necessary dialects, and when you make a stupid remark its stupidity will be obvious, even to yourself. Political language — and with variations this is true of all political parties, from Conservatives to Anarchists — is designed to make lies sound truthful and murder respectable, and to give an appearance of solidity to pure wind. One cannot change this all in a moment, but one can at least change one's own habits, and from time to time one can even, if one jeers loudly enough, send some worn-out and useless phrase — some *jackboot, Achilles' heel, hotbed, melting pot, acid test, veritable inferno* or other lump of verbal refuse — into the dustbin where it belongs.

—— CONSIDERATIONS ——————————————————————————

1. "Style is the man himself." How well, and in what ways, does Orwell's essay illustrate Buffon's aphorism?
2. Orwell's second paragraph might be compressed into a syllogism:
Major premise: All men are mortal.
Minor premise: Socrates is a man.
Conclusion: Socrates is mortal.
Working back from Orwell's conclusion "that the fight against bad English is not frivolous and is not the exclusive concern of professional writers," reconstruct the major and minor premises of his syllogism. For more discussion of syllogistic reasoning, see Robert Gorham Davis, pages 115–125.
3. Orwell documents his argument by quoting five passages by writers who wrote in the forties. From comparable sources, assemble a gallery of current specimens to help confirm or refute his contention "that the English language is in a bad way."
4. Orwell concludes with six rules. From the rest of his essay, how do you think he would define "anything outright barbarous" (in rule vi)?

5. Has Orwell broken some of his own rules? Point out and explain any examples you find.

6. In Paragraph 16, Orwell asserts that "The inflated style is itself a kind of euphemism." Look up the meaning of "euphemism" and compile examples from your local newspaper. Do you agree with Orwell that they are "swindles and perversions"? Note how Ambrose Bierce counts on our understanding of euphemisms in his Devil's Dictionary (pages 60–63).

John A. Parrish (b. 1939) came from Kentucky, took his B.A. from Duke and his M.D. from Yale, was a resident at the University of Michigan Hospital, and now teaches at Harvard Medical School and practices dermatology on the staff of Massachusetts General Hospital. Between Michigan and Harvard, he served in Vietnam, and later wrote 12, 20 & 5: A Doctor's Year in Vietnam *(1972). In 1973 he tried out briefly — and comically — for the Pittsburgh Pirates, and wrote about his experiences in* Playing Around *(1974).*

53

JOHN A. PARRISH
Welcome to Vietnam

We introduced ourselves and stated our home states and places of   1
training. Any special training beyond internship was listed beneath
our names on the blackboard. There were four doctors straight from
internship, one anesthesiologist, one general surgeon, and two partially trained internists. The four without specialty training were
immediately assigned to infantry battalions, three of which were out
in the field on maneuvers. The remaining four of us were assigned to
the hospital company in Phu Bai.

Captain Street walked with us to the hospital compound to show   2
us our new place of work. He was in no hurry. He had spent his entire
tour of duty in Phu Bai except when in Da Nang on business. He was
going home in eighty more days, and anything that would take up a
few hours, or even minutes, was welcome. We were his most recent
time passers.

From *12, 20 & 5: A Doctor's Year in Vietnam* by John A. Parrish. Copyright ©
1972 by John A. Parrish. Reprinted by permission of the publishers, E.P. Dutton, and
Gerard McCauley.

3   The hospital company was on the edge of the compound situated next to the airstrip. The location not only made it easy to receive casualties, but also placed the hospital directly adjacent to the prime target for enemy mortars or rockets. The airstrip was always an early target during any kind of enemy attack.

4   The building farthest from the airstrip was a single, wooden "hooch" with a large, mobile refrigeration unit attached to the rear of the building. Three layers of sandbags protected each side. The sign on the front read, "Graves Registration."

5   Street did not even slow down as we passed. "This is Graves," he said, as we walked by the front of the building. "This is the only part of the hospital company completely staffed by marines. From the field, the dead come directly here where they are washed down, identified, and put in the freezer until the next flight south. They are embalmed in Da Nang or Saigon before shipment back to the States. The marines who staff this place are 'grunts' (foot soldiers) who volunteer for this duty, usually because they are cowards. Some are being punished. Others may be mentally ill or may want to be embalmers someday. On a hot, busy day this place smells terrible." Street seemed disgusted not only with the marines who worked in Graves, but also with anybody who would be stupid or inconsiderate enough to get killed on a hot and busy day.

6   We passed two large portable units that looked like large inflated tubes. "These are the MUST (Medical Unit Self-Contained Transportable) units; one is used as a medical ward, and the other as a surgery ward. The smaller units are attached to the main building. They house our operating rooms. We have six O.R.'s and an X-ray unit. Helicopters land here on the edge of the airstrip, and the casualties go directly to the main casualty sorting area called triage."

7   As Captain Street was talking, a helicopter settled down beyond us. Several marines ran out from the main building to meet the craft. They were handed a stretcher with a wounded marine, and the helicopter was gone. The stretcher bearers ran past us carrying a big Negro kid. He was completely nude. His M16 hung over the stretcher handle, and his boots rode between his legs. He was so black that the mud on his skin was light by comparison. He was long and muscular, and his spidery fingers curled tightly around the sides of the bouncing litter. His whole body was glistening with sweat that reflected highlights of the bright morning sun. The sweat on his forehead did not drip. It remained like tiny drops of oil and glue fastened tightly to his skin.

His eyelids were forced widely apart, and his stare was straight 8
ahead into nowhere, seeing nothing, having seen too much. He threw
back his head, and his white teeth parted as if he were trying to speak,
to curse, to cry. A spasm of intolerable pain wrenched the muscles of
his face into a mask that hid a grinning skeleton beneath. His chest
heaved rapidly. The muscles of his steel arms bulged as he grasped the
muddy stretcher. A small hole in his rigid abdomen permitted a steady
snake of red and brown to spill onto the litter. The fluids created red
blacks and brown purples on the green canvas. His left knee was flexed,
and his long, uncircumsized penis lay over on his right upper thigh.
His left foot arched as his toes grasped for the litter.

As he passed by, he raised his head almost involuntarily. It 9
seemed as if the contracting straps of his neck muscles would tear off
his jaw should his head not rise. His neck veins swelled in protest. His
mouth began to open, at first for air, but then as a silent plea for help.
He extended his dirty hand directly toward me, and I turned to follow
him into triage.

Captain Street had not noticed him go by. He was still talking 10
about the compound — something about the marines putting the
retaining wall in the wrong place. He was ready to show us triage.

It was a large, open room measuring fifteen by twenty meters. 11
Reinforced on the outside with sandbags, the walls protected floor-to-
ceiling shelves filled with bandages, first-aid gear, and bottles of intravenous fluids. An unprotected tin roof was supported by four-by-fours.
At the time, there were six men lined up on stretchers supported at
either end by two lightweight metal sawhorses. Several doctors and
corpsmen were quickly, but unexcitedly, working over the wounded.
Captain Street was still talking, but I couldn't listen any longer.

On the first stretcher lay a boy whom, earlier in the day, any 12
coach would have wanted as a tackle or a defensive end. But now, as
he lay on his back, his left thigh pointed skyward and ended in a red
brown, meaty mass of twisted ligaments, jellylike muscle, blood clots,
and long bony splinters. There was no knee, and parts of the lower leg
hung loosely by skin strips and fascial strings. A tourniquet had been
placed around his thigh, and a corpsman was cutting through the strips
of tissue with shears to remove the unviable dangling calf. Lying separately on the stretcher was a boot from which the lower leg still
protruded.

In the second position a sweating doctor was administering 13
closed cardiac massage on a flaccid, pale, thin boy with multiple

wounds. A second doctor was bag breathing the boy. The vigorous chest compression seemed to be producing only the audible cracking of ribs.

14   In position three was the boy who minutes earlier had been carried past us. He already had intravenous fluids running into his arm, and a bandage was in place over his abdomen. He was vigorously protesting efforts to turn him over in order to examine his back. Positions four and five were occupied by two nude bodies quietly awaiting treatment. Their wounds were not serious. The next few positions for litters were empty. Off in the corner (position ten) lay a young man with his head wrapped tightly in blood-soaked, white bandages. No part of his body moved except for the slow, unsteady respiratory efforts of his chest. He had an endotracheal tube emerging from his nose, and each respiration made a grunting snort. No one was paying any attention to this man — a hopelessly damaged brain was awaiting death.

15   Captain Street never looked directly at any of the casualties. He showed us the rest of the hospital compound and left us with the hospital commander, a general surgeon who proved to be an intolerable, immature, egotistical, Napoleonic SOB, and an excellent surgeon. I liked him from the very first.

16   "Welcome to Vietnam," he said.

____ CONSIDERATIONS _____

1. Narrative essays most often proceed chronologically, as Parrish's does. But another organizing principle is here. It is most apparent in the first two pages. Identify it and discuss how naturally it works with the chronological sequence.

2. Study the three paragraphs on the wounded black marine carried on a stretcher. Identify the separate sentences as description or narration. By what criteria do you make this distinction?

3. List the technical jargon in Parrish's account — MUST, O.R., and the rest. Why is such terminology so common in military and governmental language. What are the uses of such words? The abuses?

4. Parrish's account of his stint in Vietnam seems straightforward and objective, but we can sense his attitudes toward people and events. How? Point out several examples. Is he consistent in these attitudes?

5. At the end of Paragraph 6, Captain Street uses the word "triage." You might have to consult more than one dictionary to find the word, but the hunt is worth the effort. The meaning of the word opens up moral questions. Discuss

Joyce Peseroff (b. 1948) lives in Massachusetts, where she coedits a poetry magazine called Green House. *She grew up in the Bronx, studied in California, and spent three years as a Junior Fellow in the Michigan Society of Fellows. In 1977, her first book of poems used this as its title poem. Note how a course in geology can turn into a poem.*

54

JOYCE PESEROFF
The Hardness Scale

Diamonds are forever so I gave you quartz
which is #7 on the hardness scale
and it's hard enough to get to know anybody these days
if only to scratch the surface
and quartz will scratch six other mineral surfaces: 5
it will scratch glass
it will scratch gold
it will even
scratch your eyes out one morning — you can't be
too careful.   10
Diamonds are industrial so I bought
a ring of topaz
which is #8 on the hardness scale.
I wear it on my right hand, the way it was
supposed to be, right? No tears and fewer regrets   15
for reasons smooth and clear as glass. Topaz will
        scratch glass,

it will scratch your quartz,
and all your radio crystals. You'll have to be silent
the rest of your days
20 not to mention your nights. Not to mention
the night you ran away very drunk very
very drunk and you tried to cross the border
but couldn't make it across the lake.
Stirring up geysers with the oars you drove the red canoe
25 in circles, tried to pole it but
your left hand didn't know
what the right hand was doing.
You fell asleep
and let everyone know it when you woke up.
30 In a gin-soaked morning (hair of the dog) you went
hunting for geese,
shot three lake trout in violation of the game laws,
told me to clean them and that
my eyes were bright as sapphires
35 which is #9 on the hardness scale.
A sapphire will cut a pearl
it will cut stainless steel
it will cut vinyl and mylar and will probably
cut a record this fall
40 to be released on an obscure label known only to aficionados.
I will buy a copy.
I may buy you a copy
depending on how your tastes have changed.
I will buy copies for my friends
45 we'll get a new needle,
a diamond needle,
which is #10 on the hardness scale
and will cut anything.
It will cut wood and mortar,
50 plaster and iron,
it will cut the sapphires in my eyes and I will bleed
blind as 4 A.M. in the subways when even degenerates
are dreaming, blind as the time
you shot up the room with a new hunting rifle
55 blind drunk
as you were.

You were #11 on the hardness scale
later that night
apologetic as
you worked your way up   60
slowly from the knees
and you worked your way down
from the open-throated blouse.
Diamonds are forever so I give you softer things.

Robert M. Pirsig (b. 1928), in his book Zen and the Art of Motor-cycle Maintenance *(1974), describes a motorcycle journey he takes with his young son, and among passages of narrative and description, explains and argues ideas about education, technology, and thought. Pirsig also reminisces about the past. Especially he remembers the thoughts of one "Phaedrus" — the "he" of this essay — who is Pirsig's earlier self, before a mental breakdown and shock treatments altered his personality. Here, he remembers Phaedrus's Church of Reason lecture to his composition course students in a western university. The lecture argues the distinction between the university as we know it and the ideal university, starting with analogy and moving on to contrast. See how Pirsig uses analogy to analyze, to suggest the separation of material and ideal.*

55

ROBERT M. PIRSIG
The Church of Reason

1   That night, for the next day's lecture, he wrote out his defense of what he was doing. This was the Church of Reason lecture, which, in contrast to his usual sketchy lecture notes, was very long and very carefully elaborated.

2   It begins with reference to a newspaper article about a country church building with an electric beer sign hanging right over the front entrance. The building had been sold and was being used as a bar. One can guess that some classroom laughter started at this point. The college was well-known for drunken partying and the image vaguely fit. The article said a number of people had complained to the church

officials about it. It had been a Catholic church, and the priest who had been delegated to respond to the criticism had sounded quite irritated about the whole thing. To him it had revealed an incredible ignorance of what a church really was. Did they think that bricks and boards and glass constituted a church? Or the shape of the roof? Here, posing as piety, was an example of the very materialism the church opposed. The building in question was not holy ground. It had been desanctified. That was the end of it. The beer sign resided over a bar, not a church, and those who couldn't tell the difference were simply revealing something about themselves.

Phaedrus said the same confusion existed about the University 3 and that was why loss of accreditation was hard to understand. The real University is not a material object. It is not a group of buildings that can be defended by police. He explained that when a college lost its accreditation, nobody came and shut down the school. There were no legal penalties, no fines, no jail sentences. Classes did not stop. Everything went on just as before. Students got the same education they would if the school didn't lose its accreditation. All that would happen, Phaedrus said, would simply be an official recognition of a condition that already existed. It would be similar to excommunication. What would happen is that the *real* University, which no legislature can dictate to and which can never be identified by any location of bricks or boards or glass, would simply declare that this place was no longer "holy ground." The real University would vanish from it, and all that would be left was the bricks and the books and the material manifestation.

It must have been a strange concept to all of the students, and I 4 can imagine him waiting for a long time for it to sink in, and perhaps then waiting for the question, What do you think the real University is?

His notes, in response to his question, state the following: 5

The real University, he said, has no specific location. It owns no 6 property, pays no salaries and receives no material dues. The real University is a state of mind. It is that great heritage of rational thought that has been brought down to us through the centuries and which does not exist at any specific location. It's a state of mind which is regenerated throughout the centuries by a body of people who traditionally carry the title of professor, but even that title is not part of the real University. The real University is nothing less than the continuing body of reason itself.

In addition to this state of mind, "reason," there's a legal entity 7 which is unfortunately called by the same name but which is quite another thing. This is a nonprofit corporation, a branch of the state with a specific address. It owns property, is capable of paying salaries, of receiving money and of responding to legislative pressures in the process.

8   But this second university, the legal corporation, cannot teach, does not generate new knowledge or evaluate ideas. It is not the real University at all. It is just a church building, the setting, the location at which conditions have been made favorable for the real church to exist.

9   Confusion continually occurs in people who fail to see this difference, he said, and think that control of the church buildings implies control of the church. They see professors as employees of the second university who should abandon reason when told to and take orders with no backtalk, the same way employees do in other corporations.

10   They see the second university, but fail to see the first.

____ CONSIDERATIONS _____

1. What are the telltale signs that the "real University" is present or absent on your campus?

2. What happens when a school loses its accreditation? How is accreditation maintained? Why?

3. Pirsig's definition of the "real University" puts a great deal of weight on rational thought. Do you agree with that emphasis?

4. Can you think of institutions other than the church and the university whose essence might be explained as in Pirsig's essay?

5. What techniques does Pirsig use that differ from those employed in other argumentative essays?

6. Is Pirsig's "church of reason" what Daniel Boorstin urges us to seek in his essay (pages 80–85)?

Plato (427?–347 B.C.) was the pupil of Socrates, whom he quotes or alleges to quote, and the teacher of Aristotle. Together these philosophers pull the troika of classical thought. In this selection, Plato attributes a speech to Socrates, who has been injustly condemned to death for misleading the young, and who explains why he chooses death as less demeaning than its alternatives. According to Plato, shortly after delivering these words, Socrates swallowed the poisonous hemlock.

56

PLATO

Socrates to His Accusers

Not much time will be gained, O Athenians, in return for the evil   1
name which you will get from the detractors of the city, who will say
that you killed Socrates, a wise man; for they will call me wise even
though I am not wise when they want to reproach you. If you had
waited a little while, your desire would have been fulfilled in the
course of nature. For I am far advanced in years, as you may perceive
and not far from death. I am speaking now only to those of you who
have condemned me to death. And I have another thing to say to them:
You think that I was convicted through deficiency of words — I mean,
that if I had thought fit to leave nothing undone, nothing unsaid, I
might have gained an acquittal. Not so; the deficiency which led to
my conviction was not of words — certainly not. But I had not the
boldness or impudence of inclination to address you as you would have
liked me to address you, weeping and wailing and lamenting, and saying and doing many things which you have been accustomed to hear
from others, and which, as I say, are unworthy of me. But I thought
that I ought not to do anything common or mean in the hour of danger:
nor do I now repent of the manner of my defence, and I would rather

die having spoken after my manner, than speak in your manner and live. For neither in war nor yet at law ought any man to use every way of escaping death. For often in battle there is no doubt that if a man will throw away his arms, and fall on his knees before his pursuers, he may escape death; and in other dangers there are other ways of escaping death, if a man is willing to say and do anything. The difficulty, my friends, is not in avoiding death, but in avoiding unrighteousness; for that runs faster than death. I am old and move slowly, and the slower runner has overtaken me, and my accusers are keen and quick, and the faster runner, who is unrighteousness, has overtaken them. And now I depart hence condemned by you to suffer the penalty of death, and they, too, go their ways condemned by the truth to suffer the penalty of villainy and wrong; and I must abide by my award — let them abide by theirs. I suppose that these things may be regarded as fated — and I think that they are well.

2   And now, O men who have condemned me, I would fain prophesy to you; for I am about to die, and that is the hour in which men are gifted with prophetic power. And I prophesy to you who are my murderers, that immediately after my death punishment far heavier than you have inflicted on me will surely await you. Me you have killed because you wanted to escape the accuser, and not to give an account of your lives. But that will not be as you suppose: far otherwise. For I say that there will be more accusers of you than there are now; accusers whom hitherto I have restrained: and as they are younger they will be more severe with you, and you will be more offended at them. For if you think that by killing men you can avoid the accuser censuring your lives, you are mistaken; that is not a way of escape which is either possible or honorable; the easiest and noblest way is not to be crushing others, but to be improving yourselves. This is the prophecy which I utter before my departure, to the judges who have condemned me.

3   Friends, who would have acquitted me, I would like also to talk with you about this thing which has happened, while the magistrates are busy, and before I go to the place at which I must die. Stay then awhile, for we may as well talk with one another while there is time. You are my friends, and I should like to show you the meaning of this event which has happened to me. O my judges — for you I may truly call judges — I should like to tell you of a wonderful circumstance. Hitherto the familiar oracle within me has constantly been in the habit of opposing me even about trifles, if I was going to make a slip or error about anything; and now as you see there has come upon me that which may be thought, and is generally believed to be, the last and

worst evil. But the oracle made no sign of opposition, either as I was leaving my house and going out in the morning, or when I was going up into this court, or while I was speaking, at anything which I was going to say; and yet I have often been stopped in the middle of a speech; but now in nothing I either said or did touching this matter has the oracle opposed me. What do I take to be the explanation of this? I will tell you. I regard this as a proof that what has happened to me is a good, and that those of us who think that death is an evil are in error. This is a great proof to me of what I am saying, for the customary sign would surely have opposed me had I been going to evil and not to good.

Let us reflect in another way, and we shall see that there is great reason to hope that death is a good, for one of two things: either death is a state of nothingness and utter unconsciousness, or, as men say, there is a change and migration of the soul from this world to another. Now if you suppose that there is no consciousness, but a sleep like the sleep of him who is undisturbed even by the sight of dreams, death will be an unspeakable gain. For if a person were to select the night in which his sleep was undisturbed even by dreams, and were to compare with this the other days and nights of his life, and then were to tell us how many days and nights he had passed in the course of his life better and more pleasantly than this one, I think that any man, I will not say a private man, but even the great king, will not find many such days or nights, when compared with the others. Now if death is like this, I say that to die, is gain; for eternity is then only a single night. But if death is the journey to another place, and there, as men say, all the dead are, what good, O my friends and judges, can be greater than this? If indeed when the pilgrim arrives in the world below, he is delivered from the professors of justice in this world, and finds the true judges who are said to give judgment there, Minos and Rhadamanthus and Æacus and Triptolemus, and other sons of God who were righteous in their own life, that pilgrimage will be worth making. What would not a man give if he might converse with Orpheus and Musæus and Hesiod and Homer? Nay, if this be true, let me die again and again. I, too, shall have a wonderful interest in a place where I can converse with Palamedes, and Ajax the son of Telamon, and other heroes of old, who have suffered death through an unjust judgment; and there will be no small pleasure, as I think, in comparing my own sufferings with theirs. Above all, I shall be able to continue my search into true and false knowledge; as in this world, so also in that; I shall find out who is wise, and who pretends to be wise, and is not. What would not a man give, O judges, to be able to examine the leader of the great Trojan expedition; or Odysseus or Sisyphus, or numberless others, men and women too! What infinite delight would there be in conversing with them and asking them questions! For in that world they do not put a man to death for this; certainly not. For besides being happier in that world than in this, they will be immortal, if what is said is true.

5   Wherefore, O judges, be of good cheer about death, and know this of a truth — that no evil can happen to a good man, either in life or after death. He and his are not neglected by the gods; nor has my own approaching end happened by mere chance. But I see clearly that to die and be released was better for me; and therefore the oracle gave no sign. For which reason also, I am not angry with my accusers, or my condemners; they have done me no harm, although neither of them meant to do me any good; and for this I may gently blame them.

6   Still I have a favor to ask of them. When my sons are grown up, I would ask you, O my friends, to punish them; and I would have you trouble them, as I have troubled you, if they seem to care about riches, or anything, more than about virtue; or if they pretend to be something when they are really nothing — then reprove them, as I have reproved you, for not caring about that for which they ought to care, and thinking that they are something when they are really nothing. And if you do this, I and my sons will have received justice at your hands.

7   The hour of departure has arrived, and we go our ways — I to die, and you to live. Which is better, God only knows.

_____ CONSIDERATIONS _____

1. Judging by his opening paragraph, would you predict Socrates's response to the notion that "The end justifies the means"?

2. Socrates devotes Paragraph 4 to this proposition: death is good. Examine his argument with care, paying particular attention to his logic. You might find it instructive to compare William Cullen Bryant's treatment of the same argument in his famous poem, "Thanatopsis."

3. Socrates asks as a favor from his friends that a certain punishment be inflicted. On whom? Why?

4. In Paragraph 2 what political advice does Socrates offer to those in power, advice frequently ignored by the powerful?

5. We are led to believe that Socrates's remarks are *spoken* language — a speech as opposed to a written essay. What are the characteristics of speech? Do you think of the difference between spoken and written language when you are writing? Does the work of other writers in this collection have the qualities of speech?

Richard Rhodes (b. 1937) grew up in Missouri and Kansas,
where he now lives. He has published fiction, including The
Ungodly *(1973), a novel about the Donner party, and nonfiction,*
including The Inland Ground: An Evocation of the American Middle West *(1970). A first-rate essayist, he has published articles in*
Playboy *and* Esquire, *and is a contributing editor of* Harper's Magazine. *He has taught, edited, and farmed, and has worked in the*
industry he describes in this essay.

57

RICHARD RHODES
Packaged Sentiment

Christmas is come, the holiday season, and with it our annual   1
deluge of cards, whose successful dispersal across the land the Postal
Service heralds to justify failing us for the rest of the year. "By God,
we moved the Christmas cards!" Well, half of all the personal mail
moved annually in the United States is greeting cards. Cards for
Christmas but also cards for New Year's, Valentine's Day, Easter,
Mother's Day, Father's Day, Independence Day and Thanksgiving and
Halloween, the official holidays of the American year. And for the
occasions greeting-card people call "Everyday," though they are not,
births and birthdays, graduations, weddings, anniversaries, showers,
vacations, friendship, promotion, hello, love, thanks, goodbye, illness
and bereavement, and even to have Thought O'You and for a Secret
Pal. We are a nation not of letter writers but of card signers. If the
personal letter is long dead, maimed by the penny post and murdered
by the telephone, the mass-produced card thrives, picturing what we
haven't skill to picture, saying what we haven't words to say. Cards

knot the ties that bind in a land where a fourth of us change residence with every change of calendar and where grown children no longer live at home. They show us at our best, if in borrowed finery. You may buy a card made of pansies and doggerel or you may buy a card made of da Vinci and the Sermon on the Mount. Whoever receives it will understand what you meant, and that you meant well.

2   The Christmas card was an English invention, but the greeting card an American one. One hundred twenty-eight years ago this season, an Englishman distracted by business matters failed to get his Christmas cards written. Boldly he turned an embarrassment into an opportunity, commissioned a paper tableau of Pickwickians, their glasses raised in toast, and inside each engraved and colored folio he printed a verse. His friends' reactions were not recorded. No doubt some found the idea distastefully impersonal and lamented the decline of manners in a declining age. Others, alert for new twists, thought it charming. The sensible saw its efficiency. It met the first requirement of all mechanical inventions: it saved time.

3   We have taken the idea and made it ours. The English send few cards today, and Europeans fewer still. We send cards for everything, mechanizing and standardizing the complex relationships we maintain with one another, to give us time to breathe. We needn't be ashamed of our custom. Elegant mechanizing is what we do best. It is the form our national character has taken. Look at our office buildings raised on narrow pillars ten feet off the ground as if someone had dared us to float a fifty-story building in the air. Compare our white and graceful moon rockets to the Soviet Union's drab boiler plate. Look at our cards, little shuttles of sentiment weaving across the land.

4   Some of the old cards, the nineteenth-century cards that borrowed the Englishman's invention, were masterpieces of reproduction, printed in as many as twelve colors with verses selected in national contests with cash prizes, verses no better than they should be for all the fanfare. The Victorian Age produced German cards that opened up into three-dimensional sleighing scenes of marvelous intricacy, cards with moving parts, cards fringed like a love-seat pillow with gaudy silks, cards as ornate as any gingerbread house. Cards, one presumes, for the wealthy, because the rest of us hadn't begun sending them in today's incredible numbers, today's fifteen or twenty *billion* cards a year. Now that we do, the special effects that delicate handwork once supplied have had to be scaled down, though the cards we send today carry their weight of handwork too, and with it their weight of amusing stories, cautionary tales of American ingenuity gone berserk. I remember a humorous card that required for its gag a small plastic

sack of what it called "belly-button fuzz" stapled below its punch line. No supplier could thumb out enough of the authentic material to meet the demand, so the manufacturer turned to the clothes dryers of a nearby college town, bought up the lint franchise, sterilized the lint to meet health regulations, and bagged it and stapled it on, by hand, and got the effect it was seeking and probably, college towns being college towns, got some belly-button fuzz too. "Attachments," such devices are called — plastic tears, toy scissors, miniature boxes of crayons, feathers, spring-and-paper jumping jacks, pencils, beans, the detritus of industrial civilization shrunk to card size. An attachment will sell a humorous card all by itself if it isn't stolen first, a problem for greeting-card manufacturers as surely as it is a problem for the sellers of screws and beads and hair ribbons in dime stores. Like children we lust to get our hands on little things, finding magic in tiny representations of the lumbering world.

The business of greeting cards began in the ambitions of hungry 5 men, and they improvised as they went. There are schools of nursing and schools of nuclear physics, but there are no schools for the makers of greeting cards, only apprenticeships. When Joyce Hall of country Nebraska began his enterprise in Kansas City, Missouri, more than sixty years ago, there weren't even many kinds of cards. Christmas, Easter, birthdays, and weddings were about the only occasions we announced. Hall, Fred Rust of Rust Craft, and a few people like them had to teach us to send cards by making cards we wanted to send. In that work, Hall's career strikingly parallels the career of another Midwesterner, Walt Disney, for both men learned to parse our emotions and recast them in visual and verbal form. Disney, for example, took some shadowy figures from a fairy tale, clothed them in universals, and gave us the Seven Dwarfs. Hall and his people took our need to signal our degrees of social familiarity and our various notions of good taste and gave us a choice among greeting cards.

For any given social occasion, depending on how well you know 6 someone and what you want him to think of you, you may select a card for him that is Formal, Traditional, Humorous, Floral, Cute, Contemporary, or some other among Hallmark's many categories of mood. Two cards for a friend who is hospitalized give the flavor. One, an embossed vase of flowers, says, "Glad your Operation's Over" on the cover, and inside:

You're thought of so often
As days come and go

That this card comes to tell you,
And then let you know
How much you are wished
A recovery that's quick —
For someone like you
Is too nice to be sick!

The other card, a photograph of a cotton bunny in a flower-bedecked four-poster, opens with, "Hope you'll soon be out of that *blooming bed!*" and carries the flower pun through:

Sure like to see you back in the pink,
So just take it easy, 'cause then
You'll soon be in clover,
Feeling just rosy,
And fresh as a daisy *again!*

Moods and tones and levels, you see. You are not likely to send a Contemporary card to your maiden aunt nor a Formal card to your spouse. The greeting-card people give you a range of choices. It may be a narrower range than you would prefer, but if you are a sender of cards at all, the choices will not be so narrow that you turn away in disgust and write a letter. You may choose frank sentiment; humor ranging from the modestly ethnic (hillbillies, Indians, Dead End Kids — blacks, Italians, and Eastern Europeans are out today, though they used to be a staple) to the heavily punned to the backward compliment to the gentle slap; simple statement, favored for Christmas and sympathy cards, both occasions being to some people matters serious enough for prose; and a number of alternatives between. Visually, you may choose flowers, cartoons, arabesque gilding, photographs, even reproductions of fine art, though few enough of those because few people buy them. Or stylized little children with ink-drop eyes, or encrustations of plastic jewels, or velvet flocking, or metallic glitter. Variations in texture and surface are legion — and the pride of the older generation of greeting-card men, who believed in making a quality product, who learned what would sell by selling, and who relied for their judgment in such matters on what Joyce Hall once called "the vapors of past experience."

7   Even if you have never given thought to such matters as categories of emotion and levels of taste, greeting-card people know you operate by them, and know how many cards to make to meet your needs. Such is the variety, of cards and of needs, that the largest of the manufacturers, Hallmark Cards, would have collapsed a decade ago if the computer hadn't come along to speed their sorting. The company

claims 12,000 products, counting each separate design a product, and the figure is certainly conservative. Twelve thousand different products in quantities of six to perhaps 20,000 different stores: you can do the multiplication yourself, but count in the envelopes; count in as many as ten or twenty different manufacturing operations on every card; count in all the designs being prepared for future publication, designs that pass through hundreds of hands at drawing boards and typewriters and approval committees and lithographic cameras and printing plants; count in all these different bits of information and many more besides, and you arrive at a total that demands the kind of machines that track astronauts to the moon.

And count in one thing more: every display in every store is a modest computer of its own, each of its pockets filled with designs that favor the social and cultural biases of the neighborhood around the store, and among those favored designs the best sellers of the day. "Tailoring," Hallmark calls it — loading the display to favor the preferences of the young or old or black or white or Catholic or Jewish or rich or poor who regularly shop there. The salesman sets up the display with the help of the owner; after that the computer in Kansas City keeps track. The point, of course, is to give you a maximum range of choice among the choices available. Tucked away in the stock drawer below the display, quietly humming, an IBM card meters every design.

Despite appearances, then, greeting-card manufacture is no work of hand coloring performed by elderly ladies in lace. The Hallmark plant in Kansas City occupies two city blocks, and the company doesn't even do its own printing. Times Square would fit nicely inside the new distribution center Hallmark is building on a railroad spur outside of town. More than one printing firm in the United States owes its giant color presses to Hallmark orders, which is why the company gets the kind of quality it is known for — because it has the heft to stop the presses and pull a proof. It claims 400 artists in residence, the largest art department in the world, and if you include the girls who separate out the colors of a design by hand, a procedure that still costs less for certain designs than separating the colors by machine, the claim is fair.

So many different operations go into the production of greeting cards that even a glimpse of them boggles the mind, serene and simple as the cards look when they finally reach the store. Hallmark buys paper by the boxcar, paper of every imaginable texture and weight, parchment, deckle, bond, pebble-grained, leather-grained, cloth-grained, board, brown wrapping, hard-finished, soft-finished, smooth.

Special committees earnestly debate the future popularity of roses or ragamuffins. An artist conceives a group of cards that feature cartoon mice, and the cards sell and the artist is rewarded with a trip to San Francisco. Down in the bowels of the building, behind a secret door, a master photographer labors as he has labored for most of a decade to perfect flat three-dimensional photography using a camera on which Hallmark owns the license, a camera that rolls around in a semicircle on model railroad tracks, its prisms awhirr. In California a contract artist makes dolls of old socks and ships them to Kansas City to be photographed for children's cards. Market-research girls carry cards mounted on black panels to meetings of women's clubs, where the ladies, at a charitable fifty cents a head, choose among different designs with the same verses, or different verses with the same design, helping Hallmark determine the very best that you might care to send. An engineer, a stack of handmade designs before him on his desk, struggles to arrange them on a lithography sheet to get the maximum number of designs per sheet so that they can be printed all at once with minimum waste of paper — "nesting," the process is called. Artists roam the streets of major cities at Christmastime, studying shop windows and the offerings of art galleries to discover new trends in visual design. A deputation of sales managers retreats to an Ozark resort for a multimedia presentation of next year's line. A mechanical genius grown old in the service of the firm remembers the tricks he has taught mere paper cards to do: walking, talking, sticking out their tongues, growling, snoring, squeaking, issuing forth perfume at the scratch of a fingernail across microscopic beads. An engineer sits down at a handwork table and conducts a motion study and designs a system and lines and lines of young girls in gray smocks follow the system to assemble a complicated card by hand, their hands making the memorized motions while they dream of boyfriends or listen to the rhythm of the gluing machines interweaving fugally along the line. A master engraver puts the finishing touches on a die that will punch a dotted line around a paper puppet on a get-well card. A committee of executives meets and decides that the pink of a card isn't cheerful enough and the cartoon figure on another card not sufficiently neuter to appeal both to men and to women. A shipment of paper for a line of children's books is frozen into a harbor in Finland when it should be steaming its way to a printing plant in Singapore. A baby leopard runs loose in the photography department while an editor upstairs sorts through another shipment of amateur verse mailed in by the card lovers of America. He has not found a writer worth encouraging in three years.

Greeting cards aren't simply manufactured, like soap or breakfast cereal. They are rescued from the confusing crosscurrents of American life, every one of them a difficult recovery. John Donne found the King's likeness on a coin: greeting-card manufacturers must discover Everyman's likeness and somehow fix it on paper with all its idiosyncrasies smoothed away.

Hallmark employs far fewer writers than artists, about fifteen or twenty. Unlike designs, verses enjoy a long half-life if they are adjusted for minor changes in the language along the way. These days they are often selected — selected entire, not written — by computer from a stock of the most popular verses of the past. The writers try to think up new words, and from time to time they do. Greeting-card verse has come in for its share of ridicule, which perhaps it deserves, but before it is ridiculed its distinction ought to be explained. Most song lyrics look equally ridiculous when printed bald, because the rhetoric of a song lyric, the source of its emotional impact, is the music that accompanies it. The rhetoric of greeting-card verse is the card, the physical and visual accompaniment to the verse. A few greeting-card makers have caught on to the similarity between song lyrics and greeting-card verse and have begun to borrow effects they can use, as in this verse from one of American Greetings' new "Soft Touch" cards, cards for young people that feature soft-focus photography:

> untold the times i've kissed you
> in the moments i have missed you
> and our love goes on forever . . .
> with you softly on my mind

If that doesn't quite make sense, well, neither do most lyrics away from their music, or greeting-card verses away from their cards. A poem, a real poem, the thing itself, works no better on a greeting card or in a song, because it contains its own orchestration and goes dissonant when larded with the scrapings of Mantovani strings.

Modern young people don't like eight-line rhymed verses, preferring song words or evocative sentences. One card on my desk is captioned merely "Peace," which makes it appropriate to almost every occasion except Halloween. Finding the right words for a card is harder today than it used to be because a generation trained on the film expects the words and images to subtly interlock. Getting new words approved by management is harder still. Like most American corporations of healthy middle age, Hallmark has discovered the benefits of redundant personnel and of a certain resistance to fad. Good ideas don't come along every morning, and they must always be weighed against the success of the old: there are only so many pockets in a greeting-card display. Joyce Hall, a tall, spare man with a W. C. Fields nose and a lifetime of practical experience, used to approve every card Hallmark made, words, music, and all; and his son, Donald Hall, who is now president of the firm, still approves every Contemporary card that gets past his secretary, or did when I worked there. A friend of mine who free-lanced for Hallmark once earned that secretary's enmity with a design she thought in questionable taste. "It's nice, Bill," she told him, "but it's not Hallmark." You cannot be too careful, and who is to say she wasn't right?

13   If the process of selection was once a matter of subjective judgment, it is today at least outwardly scientific. For reasons that only statisticians understand, Kansas City is a superb test market. If products sell in Kansas City, they will sell to the nation, a fact that city sophisticates might soberly consider the next time they buy a card. The formula doesn't always work — the East Coast prefers the word "Pop" to the word "Dad" on its Father cards, for example — but it works often enough to keep Hallmark researchers close to home. Yet market research is often discounted at Hallmark. The vapors of past experience still blow through the halls, and men whose only business experience has been with greeting cards still ignore the information of market tests if it conflicts with the information of the gut.

14   Daring subjectivity was Joyce Hall's genius, and remains a legacy of sorts in the hands of less remarkable men now that he has reluctantly relinquished command. Like every successful self-made man he has found retirement difficult. He is a man of quirks and crotchets and always was, but the enterprise he began out of a suitcase stashed under his bed at the Kansas City YMCA now ranks high on *Fortune* magazine's list of the 500 leading privately owned American corporations. The Hall family still owns the place lock, stock, and barrel. It is one of the few privately owned companies of any size left in Kansas City, where wealthy sons of fathers who sweated their way up from poverty tend to sell out to national conglomerations and pass their time at Martha's Vineyard or Harbor Point or Cannes. "You can teach your children everything but poverty," Hall once said, but he taught his son to care about the family firm; and today Hallmark thrives, branching out into gift books, stationery, party goods, calendars and albums, puzzles, candy, pens, urban redevelopment, retail stores on the Neiman-Marcus model, and whatever other enterprises it can find that fit its

broad conception of its business, which it calls, modestly enough, "social expression."

I could complain against greeting cards. It isn't difficult to do in 15 a world where more people feel pain than feel pleasure. There is even the risk that if I don't complain you will take me for a patsy. The greeting card's contribution to literacy will not be decisive, but I don't believe it does us that much harm. By definition, popular art can only be defended numerically, and to those who equate numbers with mediocrity, to the antipopulists, a numerical defense amounts to a certain conviction. Television is mediocre because it caters to popular taste, and greeting cards too. No. If either of them has a glaring weakness, it is that among their plethora of choices they do not give us all the choices we might want, or need. That is the effect of the marketplace, lopping off the ends of the bell curve, but the marketplace pays our bills. And if you would like to consider an opposing view, consider Joyce Hall's, who remembers this nation when it was largely rural and uneducated, and who believed that one of Hallmark's responsibilities was the elevation of American taste, a view that might seem didactic of him, but I was a country boy too, and the first play I ever saw, chills running down my back, was *Macbeth*, on television's *Hallmark Hall of Fame.*

Hallmark established its considerable reputation with thought 16 and care, spending far less on advertising than most companies that make consumer products do. It sponsors television specials and between the acts simply shows its cards. Can you remember a year when the *Hall of Fame* didn't come in for at least one Emmy? Do you know how many Americans traipsed through art galleries they had never visited before to see the collection of paintings by Winston Churchill that Hallmark shipped around the land? No breath of public scandal has ever blown through the organization. It does not make napalm and until very recently was old-fashioned enough to pay its bills in cash. One of its best men, now retired, a German Jew named Hans Archenhold whose printing plant was seized by the Nazis, came to Kansas City in its gangster years and found the printing industry there a sty of kickbacks and corruption. With the leverage of Hallmark printing orders he helped to clean it up. Hall himself switched his employees from coffee to milk breaks during the Depression, reasoning, in memory of his own hungry years, that they probably ate no breakfast and might not be sure of lunch, and I doubt that many complained of paternalism. By all means rail against the size and impersonality of

American corporations — your arguments will be well taken — but remember also that most are little Swedens now, dispensing profits and medical care and life insurance and retirement funds with a cheerful hand.

17   Today Hallmark's brand identity, an elusive commodity in a competitive society, approaches 100 per cent. Schoolchildren, asked to make cards in class, often draw a crown on the back of their productions or attempt the famous slogan, "When you care enough to send the very best," in sturdy Big Chief print. There are other greeting-card companies, American, Buzza-Cardozo, Rust Craft, and Hallmark's own poor cousin, Ambassador Cards, to name only the biggest, but the one giant has come to stand for them all.

18   Strangely, 80 per cent of the buyers of greeting cards are women. That is why cards are tested at women's clubs. Even cards for men are designed with a woman buyer in mind, featuring scenes so romantically masculine that only the coldest feminine heart would not be touched: pipes and slippers, a red-capped hunter knocking down a brace of ducks, a fleet of galleons in harbor unaccountably full-sailed, knightly shields and lordly crests, racy automobiles, workshop tools, or smiling Dad (Pop) himself. Why do women buy most of the cards? The answer may be simpler than it seems. Men think themselves too busy running the nation to find time for the smaller amenities, but they rationalize. The truth is that they are locked into an office or on a production line all day. Running an office, doing a job, no more takes all day than housework — few of us have brains that run so uniformly by the clock — but when the housework is done the woman who does it is free to go visiting or wander through the shops, while the man must shuffle papers and watch the clock. The woman may feel uncomfortable with her freedom, may feel she buys it at too high a price. It is hers nonetheless, and she uses it, among other good works, to buy cards. The new cards, by the way, the cards for young people, don't draw such sharp distinctions between masculine and feminine roles. They are androgynous. We all are, underneath: the kids have found us out.

19   I suspect we send each other cards partly from guilt, believing we haven't kept our friendships in good repair. If we are gregarious, we are also shy, uneasy as only a people raised in a society straining toward egalitarianism can be. Most of us were never rich and never desperately poor. We never learned our place: we started this country so we wouldn't have to, but our mobility leaves us unsure of where our elbows belong. We are known for our humor, but not for our wit; for

our ability, but not for our style; for our strength, but not for our grace. We find ourselves harried and we fumble, or think we do.

Our guilt is misplaced. Thoreau's three chairs for company and two for friendship nicely defines our human limits. They are no longer limits to which we can comfortably adhere. We would hurt too many feelings if we did, the feelings of the people we work with, of our relatives and our neighbors and the neighbors we left behind. Anyone who has moved recently knows how much sheer matter we accumulate in our houses, but imagine also the long list of acquaintances we have accumulated, back to our earliest years. If we are fond of people at all, we have met thousands in our lives. Perhaps that is why so few of us read. Perhaps our culture is really oral, despite the science fiction of our media, satellites above and wires and presses below and the air itself in fervent vibration. One recalls the theory that ghetto children have difficulty in school not because of deprivation but because of excess, of overstimulation by the teeming world in which they live. It is true to some degree of us all. With China and the Soviet Union, and for much of the same reasons of origin and purpose, we are a national people far more than we are local. Our traditions and our associations extend from ocean to ocean, and our burden of communication too. The Communist nations, not having finished their first industrial revolution, turn to party meetings and rallies to stay in touch; with a more ritualized social structure, we send cards. 20

Making greeting cards to suit us isn't easy. Try to imagine a card that would please both your grandmother and your revolutionary son — and yet your Christmas card probably did. For reasons no one knows, green cards don't sell. Writers of greeting cards must search their verses for unintentional double entendres, and because of that danger, the word "it" used as a direct object is taboo. "Today's your day to get *it!*" It won't do. St. Patrick's Day cards that kid Irish drinking habits elicit indignant letters from Hibernian Societies, a sign that the Irish are ready to melt the rest of the way into the pot. A card is two years in the making: what if hemlines change? Superman cards reached the stores the day the Superman fad collapsed. And what do you say, in a card, in mere words, to a widow whose world has emptied of the life she loved? (You say, in rhymed verse, that words can't express your sympathy.) 21

When I worked at Hallmark I sometimes thought of cards as pretty packages with nothing inside, but I am a year older now and I wonder. Perhaps, ephemeral though they are, they carry a greater weight of emotion to a greater number of people than we can bear to 22 carry ourselves. They are tactful, discreet; they strike the right tone. Their designers sweat blood, believe me, to make them so. Even when they fail we forgive the sender and blame the card, as we forgive a caller a bad connection on the phone. Greeting cards have inertia. Like Santa's bag they hang a little behind. They are innately conservative because the occasions of our lives are too important for fads, of style or of spirit. Hallmark has discovered that the young people who buy its breezily pessimistic Contemporary cards return to more traditional forms when they acquire families and careers. Pessimism becomes a luxury they can no longer afford.

23   We grow older; the cards for our stops along the way await us in the store. They are not dangerous or subversive or mean; they espouse no causes except the old mute causes of life itself, birth and marriage and begetting and death, and these gently. I celebrate them as E. M. Forster celebrated democracy, with a hearty two cheers. Merry Christmas.

___ CONSIDERATIONS _____

1. Study Rhodes's opening paragraph. Show how Rhodes builds that paragraph with the ideas he intends to discuss in the remainder of the essay.

2. What is the difference between sentiment and sentimentality? Find (or make up your own) greeting cards to demonstrate both words.

3. Find passages in which Rhodes is working with material drawn from research. In presenting this material, how does he keep from sounding like a textbook or an encyclopedia?

4. Rhodes compares the leading greeting-card manufacturer with Walt Disney. Do you agree with the parallels he draws? Could you extend them? Is this comparison a commentary or judgment on either Joyce Hall or Walt Disney?

5. Imagine Woody Allen turned loose in the Hallmark greeting-card factory. Dream up a few examples of what Allen's satirical, inventive typewriter might produce.

6. Paragraph 10, beginning "So many different operations . . . ," is the longest in this essay. Why?

Adrienne Rich (b. 1929) was Yale Younger Poet in 1951, publishing her first collection of poetry before she was graduated from college. She married, bore three sons, and wrote more poems. In 1974, she published Poems: Selected and New. *In her forties she became a radical feminist, and in 1976 published her first prose book,* Of Woman Born, *which examines motherhood historically, autobiographically, mythically, and polemically.*

This poem comes from her most recent collection, The Dream of a Common Language *(1978). If poetry exists to allow one spirit access to another, its dream of intimacy allies poetry with love.*

58

ADRIENNE RICH

Origins and History of Consciousness

I

Night-life. Letters, journals, bourbon
sloshed in the glass. Poems crucified on the wall,
dissected, their bird-wings severed
like trophies. No one lives in this room
without living through some kind of crisis.   5

No one lives in this room
without confronting the whiteness of the wall
behind the poems, planks of books,
photographs of dead heroines.

"Origins and History of Consciousness" is reprinted from *The Dream of a Common Language,* Poems 1974–1977, by Adrienne Rich, with the permission of W. W. Norton & Company, Inc. Copyright © 1978 by W. W. Norton & Company, Inc.

Without contemplating last and late
the true nature of poetry. The drive
10   to connect. The dream of a common language.

Thinking of lovers, their blind faith, their
experienced crucifixions,
my envy is not simple. I have dreamed of going to bed
as walking into clear water ringed by a snowy wood
15   white as cold sheets, thinking, *I'll freeze in there.*
My bare feet are numbed already by the snow
but the water
is mild, I sink and float
like a warm amphibious animal
20   that has broken the net, has run
through fields of snow leaving no print;
this water washes off the scent —
You are clear now
of the hunter, the trapper
25   *the wardens of the mind—*

yet the warm animal dreams on
of another animal
swimming under the snow-flecked surface of the pool,
and wakes, and sleeps again.

30   No one sleeps in this room without
the dream of a common language.

II

It was simple to meet you, simple to take your eyes
into mine, saying: these are eyes I have known
from the first. . . . It was simple to touch you
35   against the hacked background, the grain of what we
had been, the choices, years. . . . It was even simple
to take each other's lives in our hands, as bodies.

What is not simple: to wake from drowning
from where the ocean beat inside us like an afterbirth
40   into this common, acute particularity
these two selves who walked half a lifetime untouching —

to wake to something deceptively simple: a glass
sweated with dew, a ring of the telephone, a scream
of someone beaten up far down in the street
causing each of us to listen to her own inward scream   45

knowing the mind of the mugger and the mugged
as any woman must who stands to survive this city,
this century, this life . . .
each of us having loved the flesh in its clenched or loosened beauty
better than trees or music (yet loving those too   50
as if they were flesh — and they are — but the flesh
of beings unfathomed as yet in our roughly literal life).

III

It's simple to wake from sleep with a stranger,
dress, go out, drink coffee,
enter a life again. It isn't simple   55
to wake from sleep into the neighborhood
of one neither strange nor familiar
whom we have chosen to trust. Trusting, untrusting,
we lowered ourselves into this, let ourselves
downward hand over hand as on a rope that quivered   60
over the unsearched. . . . We did this. Conceived
of each other, conceived each other in a darkness
which I remember as drenched in light.
                              I want to call this, life.

But I can't call it life until we start to move   65
beyond this secret circle of fire
where our bodies are giant shadows flung on a wall
where the night becomes our inner darkness, and sleeps
like a dumb beast, head on her paws, in the corner.

Theodore Roethke (1908–1963) grew up in Michigan, and spent the last decades of his life in the Pacific Northwest, where he taught at the University of Washington. Master of many styles, Roethke began by writing tight, short-lined lyrics; eventually he assimilated the long lines and inclusive structures of Walt Whitman, as shown in his posthumous The Far Field *(1963). He was a big, gentle man, funny, and a good mimic. Thousands of former students attest to Roethke's excellence and excitement as a classroom teacher.*

59

THEODORE ROETHKE
Elegy for Jane

MY STUDENT, THROWN BY A HORSE

I remember the neckcurls, limp and damp as tendrils;
And her quick look, a sidelong pickerel smile;
And how, once startled into talk, the light syllables leaped for her,
And she balanced in the delight of her thought,
5   A wren, happy, tail into the wind,
Her song trembling the twigs and small branches.
The shade sang with her;
The leaves, their whispers turned to kissing;
And the mold sang in the bleached valleys under the rose.

10   Oh, when she was sad, she cast herself down into such a pure depth,
Even a father could not find her:
Scraping her cheek against straw;
Stirring the clearest water.

My sparrow, you are not here,
Waiting like a fern, making a spiny shadow.   15
The sides of wet stones cannot console me,
Nor the moss, wound with the last light.

If only I could nudge you from this sleep,
My maimed darling, my skittery pigeon.
Over this damp grave I speak the words of my love: 20
I, with no rights in this matter,
Neither father nor lover.

Lillian Ross (b. 1926) writes for The New Yorker, *where this essay originally appeared. In 1952 she published* Picture, *a documentary account of John Huston filming* The Red Badge of Courage. *The book reads like a novel, and was a precursor of the New Journalism. She has also published* Portrait of Hemingway *(1961),* The Player *(with Helen Ross, 1962), which is about actors, and* Talk Stories *(1966), which collects her contributions to* The New Yorker's *"Talk of the Town." Also in 1966 she published a collection of articles called* Reporting, *from which we take this portion of "The Yellow Bus."*

In the summer of 1960, eighteen members of the senior class of Bean Blossom Township High School, Indiana, drove to New York in their yellow school bus. Mrs. Watts — their English teacher — and Mr. Watts accompanied them, along with their bus driver Ralph Walls and his wife. The senior class, mostly from farms, had saved money for six years in order to take a trip together after graduation. At first, all of them were confused and unhappy in New York, so alien to their background. "No one in the senior class had ever talked to a Jew or to more than one Catholic, or — with the exception of Mary Jane Carter, daughter of the Nazarene minister in Stinesville — had even heard of an Episcopalian." Finally, a few of them weakened and began to like the city. Throughout the article, Lillian Ross never reveals herself. We see and hear only the Bean Blossomers — but we become gradually aware of a gigantic eye and a gigantic ear, observing and recording everything that happens.

60

LILLIAN ROSS
The Yellow Bus

Before dinner that night, Mr. Watts walked through the Times   1
Square area checking prices and menus at likely restaurants. He made
tentative arrangements at The Californian for a five-course steak or
chicken dinner, to cost $1.95 per person, and asked Jay Bowman to go
around taking a vote on the proposition. Half an hour later, Jay
reported to Mr. Watts that some of the boys didn't want to go to The
Californian, because they thought they'd have to do their own ordering. So Mr. Watts talked to the boys in their rooms and explained that
the ordering was taken care of; all they had to say was whether they
wanted steak or chicken. On the next ballot, everybody was in favor of
The Californian. The class walked over. When the fifth course was
finished, it was agreed that the dinner was all right, but several of the
boys said they thought the restaurant was too high-class.

After dinner, it started to rain, and it rained hard. The Wattses   2
and seven of the girls decided that they wanted to see "The Music
Man." The four other girls wanted to see "My Fair Lady." None of the
boys wanted to see a musical show. In the driving rain, the Wattses
and the girls ran to the theatres of their choice, all arriving soaked to
the skin. By good luck, each group was able to buy seats. At "The
Music Man," the Wattses and the seven girls with them sat in the
balcony, in the direct path of an air-conditioning unit that blew icy
blasts on their backs. At "My Fair Lady," the four girls sat in the
balcony, where an air-conditioning unit blew icy blasts at their legs.
The girls liked their shows. The "My Fair Lady" group was transported
by the costumes. Ina Hough, who went to "The Music Man," though
that it was just like a movie, except for the way the scenes changed.

The boys split up, some of them taking the subway down to   3

From *Reporting* (Simon & Schuster). Reprinted by permission; © 1960 by Lillian
Ross. Originally appeared in *The New Yorker*.

Greenwich Village, the others heading for the Empire State Building, where they paid a dollar-thirty for tickets to the observatory and, once up there, found that the fog and rain blotted out the view completely. "We stood there about an hour and a half messin' around, me and my buddies," Jay later told Mrs. Watts. "Wasn't no sense in leavin' at that price." In Greenwich Village, Mike Richardson, Dennis Smith, and Larry Williams walked along the narrow streets in a drizzling rain. All were still wearing their beachcomber outfits. Nobody talked to them. They didn't see anybody they wanted to talk to. They almost went into a small coffeehouse; they changed their minds because the prices looked too high. They went into one shop, a bookstore, and looked at some abstract paintings, which appealed to them. "Sort of interestin', the way they don't look like nothin'," Mike said. Then they took the subway back to Times Square, where they walked around for a while in the rain. Toward midnight, Mike and Dennis told each other they were lonesome for the smell of grass and trees, and, the rain having stopped, they walked up to Central Park, where they stayed for about an hour and got lost.

4   The next morning, a meeting of the class was held in the hotel lobby to take a vote on when to leave New York. Jay Bowman reported that they had enough money to cover an extra day in the city, plus a side trip to Niagara Falls on the way home. Or, he said, they could leave New York when they had originally planned to and go to Washington, D.C., for a day before heading home. The class voted for the extra day in New York and Niagara Falls.

5   "I'm glad," Becky Kiser said, with a large, friendly smile, to Dennis Smith. Several of her classmates overheard her and regarded her with a uniformly deadpan look. "I like it here," she went on. "I'd like to live here. There's so much to see. There's so much to do."

6   Her classmates continued to study here impassively until Dennis took their eyes away from her by saying, "You get a feelin' here of goin' wherever you want to. Seems the city never closes. I'd like to live here, I believe. People from everyplace are here."

7   "Limousines all over the joint," Albert Warthan said.

8   "Seems like you can walk and walk and walk," Dennis went on dreamily. "I like the way the big buildin's crowd you in. You want to walk and walk and never go to sleep."

9   "I hate it," Connie Williams said, with passion.

10   "Oh, man, you're just not lookin' ahead," Mike Richardson said to Dennis. "You got a romantic notion. You're not realistic about it."

11   "This place couldn't hold me," Larry Williams said. "I like the privacy of the farm."

"I want to go to new places," said Becky, who had started it. "I   12
want to go to Europe."

"Only place I want to go is Texas," Larry said. "I got folks in   13
Texas."

"There's no place like home," Mike said. "Home's good enough   14
for me."

"I believe the reason of this is we've lived all of our lives around   15
Stinesville," Dennis said. "If you took Stinesville out of the country,
you wouldn't be hurt. But if you took New York out of the country,
you'd be hurt. The way the guide said, all our clothes and everything
comes from New York."

Becky said, "In Coney Island, I saw the most handsome man I   16
ever saw in my whole life. I think he was a Puerto Rican or something,
too."

Albert said, "When we get back, my pa will say, 'Well, how was   17
it?' I'll say, 'It was fine.' "

"I'd like to come back, maybe stay a month," Jay Bowman said   18
diplomatically. "One thing I'd like to do is come here when I can see a
major-league baseball game."

"I'd like to see a major-league baseball game, but I wouldn't come   19
back just to see *it*," Mike said.

"I hate New York," Connie said.   20

"Back home, everybody says 'Excuse me,' " Nancy Prather said.   21

"I like it here," Dennis said stubbornly.   22

This day was an open one, leaving the boys and girls free to do   23
anything they liked, without prearranged plan or vote. Mike passed
close by the souvenir-and-gift stand on the hotel lobby, and the propri-
etor urged him to take home the Statue of Liberty.

"I'd like to, but it won't fit in my suitcase," Mike said, with a   24
loud laugh.

A group formed to visit the zoo in Central Park, got on the sub-   25
way, had a loud discussion about where to get off, and were taken in
hand by a stranger, who told them the zoo was in the Bronx. Only the
boy named Lynn Dillon listened to the stranger. The others went to
the zoo in Central Park. Lynn stayed on the subway till it reached the
Bronx, and spent the entire day in the Bronx Zoo by himself. The rest
of the zoo visitors, walking north after lunch in the cafeteria, ran into
the Metropolitan Museum of Art and went in. "It was there, and it
was free, so we did it," Nancy Prather said. "There were these suits of
armor and stuff. Nothin' I go for myself."

That morning, the Wattses had tried to get some of the boys and   26
girls to accompany them to the Guggenheim Museum or the Museum

of Modern Art, but nobody had wanted to pay the price of admission. "Why pay fifty cents to see a museum when they got them free?" the class president asked. Mrs. Watts reported afterward that the Guggenheim was the most exciting museum she had ever seen, including all the museums she had seen in Europe on her accredited art tour. "There aren't big crowds in there, for one thing," she said. "And I don't think the building overpowers the paintings at all, as I'd heard." From the Guggenheim, the Wattses went to Georg Jensen's to look at silver, but didn't buy anything. Then they went to the Museum of Modern Art and had lunch in the garden. "Lovely lunch, fabulous garden, fabulous sculpture, but I'm disappointed in the museum itself," Mrs. Watts said. "Everything jammed into that small space! Impossible to get a good view of Picasso's 'Girl Before a Mirror.' "

27   By dinnertime, more than half of the Bean Blossomers had, to their relief, discovered the Automat. Jay Bowman had a dinner consisting of a ham sandwich (forty cents), a glass of milk (ten cents), and a dish of fresh strawberries (twenty cents). Then, with a couple of buddies, he bought some peanuts in their shells and some Cokes, and took them up to his room for the three of them to consume while talking about what to do that night. They decided, because they had not yet had a good view of the city from the Empire State observatory, that they would go back there. They were accompanied by most of the girls and the other boys, and this time the group got a cut rate of sixty-five cents apiece. Dennis went off wandering by himself. He walked up Fifth Avenue to Eighty-fifth Street, over to Park Avenue, down Park to Seventy-second Street, across to the West Side, down Central Park West to Sixty-sixth Street, over behind the Tavern-on-the-Green (where he watched people eating outdoors), and down Seventh Avenue to Times Square, where he stood around on corners looking at the people who bought papers at newsstands.

28   The Wattses had arranged to meet anybody who was interested under the Washington Arch at around nine-thirty for an evening in Greenwich Village. The boys had decided to take a walk up Broadway after leaving the Empire State Building, but the girls all showed up in Washington Square, along with two soldiers and three sailors they had met in the U.S.O. across the street from the Woodstock. The Wattses led the way to a coffeehouse, where everybody had coffee or lemonade. Then the girls and the servicemen left the Wattses, saying they were going to take a ride on the ferry to Staten Island. The Wattses went to the Five Spot, which their jazz friend had told them had good music.

After breakfast the following morning, the bus driver, Ralph 29
Walls, showed up in the hotel lobby for the first time since the group's
arrival in New York and told Jay Bowman to have everyone assembled
at five-forty-five the following morning for departure at six o'clock on
the dot. The driver said that he was spending most of his time sleeping,
and that before they left he was going to do some more sleeping. He
had taken his wife on a boat trip around Manhattan, though, he said,
and he had taken a few walks on the streets. After reminding Jay again
about the exact time planned for the departure, he went back upstairs
to his room.

Mrs. Watts took nine of the girls (two stayed in the hotel to sleep) 30
for a walk through Saks Fifth Avenue, just looking. Mr. Watts took
three of the boys to Abercrombie & Fitch, just looking. Everybody
walked every aisle on every floor in each store, looking at everything
on the counters and in the showcases. Nobody bought anything. The
two groups met at noon under the clock in Grand Central; lunched at
an Automat; walked over to the United Nations Buildings, where they
decided not to take the regular tour; and took a crosstown bus to the
Hudson River and went aboard the liner S.S. Independence, where they
visited every deck and every lounge on the boat, and a good many of
the staterooms. Then they took the bus back to Times Square and
scattered to do some shopping.

Mike Richardson bought all his gifts — eleven dollars' worth — 31
at the hotel stand, taking not only the plaque for his mother but a set
of salt and pepper shakers, with the Statue of Liberty on the salt and
the Empire State Building on the pepper, also for his mother; a Statue
of Liberty ashtray for his father; a George Washington Bridge teapot for
his sister-in-law; a mechanical dog for his niece; a City Hall teapot-
cup-and-saucer set for his grandparents; and a cigarette lighter stamped
with the Great White Way for himself. At Macy's, Becky Kiser bought
a dress, a blouse, and an ankle chain for herself, and a necklace with
matching bracelet and earrings for her mother, a cuff-link-and-tie-clasp
set for her father, and a bracelet for her younger sister. Albert Warthan
bought a miniature camera for himself and a telephone-pad-and-pencil
set stamped with the George Washington Bridge and a Statue of Liberty
thermometer, large-size, as general family gifts, at the hotel stand. Jay
Bowman bought an unset cultured pearl at Macy's for his girl friend in
the junior class, as well as silver-looking earrings for his married sister
and for his mother, and at a store called King of Slims, around the
corner from the hotel, he bought four ties — a red toreador tie (very
narrow) for his older brother, a black toreador tie for his younger

brother, a conservative silk foulard for his father, and a white toreador tie for himself. Dennis Smith bought a Statue of Liberty ashtray for his mother and a Statue of Liberty cigarette lighter for his father. Connie Williams bought two bracelets and a Statue of Liberty pen for herself. The bus driver and his wife spent sixty dollars on clothes for their children, six of whom are girls. Nancy Prather didn't buy anything. The Wattses spent about a hundred dollars in the course of the visit, most of it on meals and entertainment.

32   On their last evening in New York, all the boys and girls, accompanied by the Wattses, went to the Radio City Music Hall, making it in time to see the stage show. Then they packed and went to bed. The bus driver, after an early dinner with his wife at Hector's Cafeteria, brought the yellow school bus over from Tenth Avenue and parked it right in front of the hotel, so that it would be there for the early start.

33   Next morning at five-forty-five, the Bean Blossomers assembled in the lobby; for the first time since the trip had started, nobody was late. The bus pulled out at exactly 6 A.M., and twenty minutes after that, heading west over the George Washington Bridge, it disappeared from the city.

_____ CONSIDERATIONS _____

1. Ross often makes very short statements, as in the opening of Paragraph 2. What effect is produced by such terse sentences? Try combining the first four sentences of that paragraph into one. Read your version and Ross's aloud.

2. In Paragraph 31, Ross has much longer sentences, most of them jammed with facts. She manages these lists of things so that she preserves simple sentence structure. What do you learn of these tourists from the lists of presents?

3. Ross's account of the New York trip is a kind of reportage. Does it remind you of Truman Capote's essay (pages 87–91).

4. How is Ross's use of dialogue like the rest of her essay, particularly in its effect?

Bertrand Russell (1872–1970) was a mathematician, philoso-
pher, and gadfly to generations of English and American readers.
He combined sound scholarship, uncommon intellectual power,
moral zealotry, and the popular touch, espousing such causes as
pacifism, mathematics, and free love. When he was in his nineties
he led the fight in England against nuclear weapons, and cam-
paigned against American involvement in Vietnam.
   In this essay, Russell's intelligence combines with his imagina-
tion to produce clear, handsome prose that explains some
Einsteinian concepts to laymen.

61

BERTRAND RUSSELL
Touch and Sight:
The Earth and the Heavens

Everybody knows that Einstein did something astonishing, but   1
very few people know exactly what it was that he did. It is generally
recognized that he revolutionized our conception of the physical
world, but the new conceptions are wrapped up in mathematical tech-
nicalities. It is true that there are innumerable popular accounts of the
theory of relativity, but they generally cease to be intelligible just at
the point where they begin to say something important. The authors
are hardly to blame for this. Many of the new ideas can be expressed in
non-mathematical language, but they are none the less difficult on
that account. What is demanded is a change in our imaginative picture
of the world — a picture which has been handed down from remote,
perhaps pre-human, ancestors, and has been learned by each one of us

From Bertrand Russell, *ABC of Relativity*, pp. 9–15. Reprinted by permission of
George Allen & Unwin (Publishers) Ltd.

in early childhood. A change in our imagination is always difficult, especially when we are no longer young. The same sort of change was demanded by Copernicus, when he taught that the earth is not stationary and the heavens do not revolve about it once a day. To us now there is no difficulty in this idea, because we learned it before our mental habits had become fixed. Einstein's ideas, similarly, will seem easier to generations which grow up with them; but for us a certain effort of imaginative reconstruction is unavoidable.

2   In exploring the surface of the earth, we make use of all our senses, more particularly of the senses of touch and sight. In measuring lengths, parts of the human body are employed in pre-scientific ages: a "foot," a "cubit," a "span" are defined in this way. For longer distances, we think of the time it takes to walk from one place to another. We gradually learn to judge distance roughly by the eye, but we rely upon touch for accuracy. Moreover it is touch that gives us our sense of "reality." Some things cannot be touched: rainbows, reflections in looking-glasses, and so on. These things puzzle children, whose metaphysical speculations are arrested by the information that what is in the looking-glass is not "real." Macbeth's dagger was unreal because it was not "sensible to feeling as to sight." Not only our geometry and physics, but our whole conception of what exists outside us, is based upon the sense of touch. We carry this even into our metaphors: a good speech is "solid," a bad speech is "gas," because we feel that a gas is not quite "real."

3   In studying the heavens, we are debarred from all senses except sight. We cannot touch the sun, or travel to it; we cannot walk around the moon, or apply a foot-rule to the Pleiades. Nevertheless, astronomers have unhesitatingly applied the geometry and physics which they found serviceable on the surface of the earth, and which they had based upon touch and travel. In doing so, they brought down trouble on their heads, which it was left for Einstein to clear up. It turned out that much of what we learned from the sense of touch was unscientific prejudice, which must be rejected if we are to have a true picture of the world.

4   An illustration may help us to understand how much is impossible to the astronomer as compared with the man who is interested in things on the surface of the earth. Let us suppose that a drug is administered to you which makes you temporarily unconscious, and that when you wake you have lost your memory but not your reasoning powers. Let us suppose further that while you were unconscious you were carried into a balloon, which, when you come to, is sailing with

the wind on a dark night — the night of the fifth of November[1] if you are in England, or of the fourth of July if you are in America. You can see fireworks which are being sent off from the ground, from trains, and from aeroplanes travelling in all directions, but you cannot see the ground or the trains or the aeroplanes because of the darkness. What sort of picture of the world will you form? You will think that nothing is permanent: there are only brief flashes of light, which, during their short existence, travel through the void in the most various and bizarre curves. You cannot touch these flashes of light, you can only see them. Obviously your geometry and your physics and your metaphysics will be quite different from those of ordinary mortals. If an ordinary mortal were with you in the balloon, you would find his speech unintelligible. But if Einstein were with you, you would understand him more easily than the ordinary mortal would, because you would be free from a host of preconceptions which prevent most people from understanding him.

The theory of relativity depends, to a considerable extent, upon 5 getting rid of notions which are useful in ordinary life but not to our drugged balloonist. Circumstances on the surface of the earth, for various more or less accidental reasons, suggest conceptions which turn out to be inaccurate, although they have come to seem like necessities of thought. The most important of these circumstances is that most objects on the earth's surface are fairly persistent and nearly stationary from a terrestrial point of view. If this were not the case, the idea of going on a journey would not seem so definite as it does. If you want to travel from King's Cross to Edinburgh, you know that you will find King's Cross where it has always been, that the railway line will take the course that it did when you last made the journey, and that Waverly Station in Edinburgh will not have walked up to the Castle. You therefore say and think that you have travelled to Edinburgh, not that Edinburgh has travelled to you, though the latter statement would be just as accurate. The success of this common-sense point of view depends upon a number of things which are really of the nature of luck. Suppose all the houses in London were perpetually moving about, like a swarm of bees; suppose railways moved and changed their shapes like avalanches; and finally suppose that material objects were perpetually being formed and dissolved like clouds. There is nothing impossible in these suppositions. But obviously what we call a journey to Edinburgh would have no meaning in such a world. You would begin, no doubt, by asking the taxi-driver: "Where is King's Cross this

---

[1] Guy Fawkes Day, when the English set off fireworks. — ED.

morning?" At the station you would have to ask a similar question about Edinburgh, but the booking-office clerk would reply: "What part of Edinburgh do you mean, sir? Prince's Street has gone to Glasgow, the Castle has moved up into the Highlands, and Waverly Station is under the water in the middle of the Firth of Forth." And, on the journey the stations would not be staying quiet, but some would be travelling north, some south, some east or west, perhaps much faster than the train. Under these conditions you could not say where you were at any moment. Indeed, the whole notion that one is always in some definite "place" is due to the fortunate immobility of most of the large objects on the earth's surface. The idea of "place" is only a rough practical approximation: there is nothing logically necessary about it, and it cannot be made precise.

6   If we were not much larger than an electron, we should not have this impression of stability, which is only due to the grossness of our senses. King's Cross, which to us looks solid, would be too vast to be conceived except by a few eccentric mathematicians. The bits of it that we could see would consist of little tiny points of matter, never coming into contact with each other, but perpetually whizzing around each other in an inconceivably rapid ballet-dance. The world of our experience would be quite as mad as the one in which the different parts of Edinburgh go for walks in different directions. If — to take the opposite extreme — you were as large as the sun and lived as long, with a corresponding slowness of perception, you would again find a higgledy-piggledy universe without permanence — stars and planets would come and go like morning mists, and nothing would remain in a fixed position relatively to anything else. The notion of comparative stability which forms part of our ordinary outlook is thus due to the fact that we are about the size we are, and live on a planet of which the surface is not very hot. If this were not the case, we should not find pre-relativity physics intellectually satisfying. Indeed we should never have invented such theories. We should have had to arrive at relativity physics at one bound, or remain ignorant of scientific laws. It is fortunate for us that we were not faced with this alternative, since it is almost inconceivable that one man could have done the work of Euclid, Galileo, Newton and Einstein. Yet without such an incredible genius physics could hardly have been discovered in a world where the universal flux was obvious to non-scientific observation.

7   In astronomy, although the sun, moon, and stars continue to exist year after year, yet in other respects the world we have to deal

with is very different from that of everyday life. As already observed, we depend exclusively on sight: the heavenly bodies cannot be touched, heard, smelt, or tasted. Everything in the heavens is moving relatively to everything else. The earth is going round the sun, the sun is moving, very much faster than an express train, towards a point in the constellation Hercules, the "fixed" stars are scurrying hither and thither like a lot of frightened hens. There are no well-marked places in the sky, like King's Cross and Edinburgh. When you travel from place to place on the earth, you say the train moves and not the stations, because the stations preserve their topographical relations to each other and the surrounding country. But in astronomy it is arbitrary which you call the train and which the station: the question is to be decided purely by convenience and as a matter of convention.

In this respect, it is interesting to contrast Einstein and Coperni- 8 cus. Before Copernicus, people thought that the earth stood still and the heavens revolved about it once a day. Copernicus taught that "really" the earth rotates once a day, and the daily revolution of sun and stars is only "apparent." Galileo and Newton endorsed this view, and many things were thought to prove it — for example, the flattening of the earth at the poles and the fact that bodies are heavier there than at the equator. But in the modern theory the question between Copernicus and his predecessors is merely one of convenience; all motion is relative, and there is no difference between the two statements: "The earth rotates once a day" and "the heavens revolve about the earth once a day." The two mean exactly the same thing, just as it means the same thing if I say that a certain length is six feet or two yards. Astronomy is easier if we take the sun as fixed than if we take the earth, just as accounts are easier in decimal coinage. But to say more for Copernicus is to assume absolute motion, which is a fiction. All motion is relative, and it is a mere convention to take one body as at rest. All such conventions are equally legitimate, though not all are equally convenient.

There is another matter of great importance, in which astronomy 9 differs from terrestrial physics because of its exclusive dependence upon sight. Both popular thought and old-fashioned physics used the notion of "force," which seemed intelligible because it was associated with familiar sensations. When we are walking, we have sensations connected with our muscles which we do not have when we are sitting still. In the days before mechanical traction, although people could travel by sitting in their carriages, they could see the horses exerting themselves and evidently putting out "force" in the same way as human beings do. Everybody knew from experience what it is to push or pull, or to be pushed or pulled. These very familiar facts made "force" seem a natural basis for dynamics. But Newton's law of gravitation introduced a difficulty. The force between two billiard balls appeared intelligible because we know what it feels like to bump into another person; but the force between the earth and the sun, which are ninety-three million miles apart, was mysterious. Newton himself regarded this "action at a distance" as impossible, and believed that there was some hitherto undiscovered mechanism by which the sun's influence was transmitted to the planets. However, no such mechanism was discovered, and gravitation remained a puzzle. The fact is that the whole conception of "force" is a mistake. The sun does not exert any force on the planets; in Einstein's law of gravitation, the planet only pays attention to what it finds in its own neighborhood. The way in which this works will be explained in a later chapter; for the present we are only concerned with the necessity of abandoning the notion of "force," which was due to misleading conceptions derived from the sense of touch.

10   As physics has advanced, it has appeared more and more that sight is less misleading than touch as a source of fundamental notions about matter. The apparent simplicity in the collision of billiard balls is quite illusory. As a matter of fact the two billiard balls never touch at all; what really happens is inconceivably complicated, but it is more analogous to what happens when a comet penetrates the solar system and goes away again than to what common sense supposes to happen.

11   Most of what we have said hitherto was already recognized by physicists before Einstein invented the theory of relativity. "Force" was known to be merely a mathematical fiction, and it was generally held that motion is a merely relative phenomenon — that is to say, when two bodies are changing their relative position, we cannot say that one is moving while the other is at rest, since the occurrence is merely a change in their relation to each other. But a great labor was required in order to bring the actual procedure of physics into harmony with these new convictions. Newton believed in force and in absolute space and time; he embodied these beliefs in his technical methods, and his methods remained those of later physicists. Einstein invented a new technique, free from Newton's assumptions. But in order to do so he had to change fundamentally the old ideas of space and time, which had been unchallenged from time immemorial. This is what makes both the difficulty and the interest of his theory.

___ CONSIDERATIONS _____

1. Like many other scientists, Russell does not hesitate to use his imagination — and ours — to explain a difficult concept. Find an example of imaginative explanation in this essay, and study it. Does it show us something about our preconceptions of scientists, or does it illustrate a principle of good writing? Or both?

2. "In studying the heavens, we are debarred from all senses except sight," says Russell in Paragraph 3. To increase your awareness of the importance of sight, ask a trustworthy friend to blindfold you and walk you about the campus for a half an hour. Write about the experience in relation to Russell's point.

3. Explain what Russell means when he says that understanding relativity would be easier if it were not for the "grossness of our senses." Has this idea anything to do with what he calls our "common-sense view" of our movements on earth?

4. The Copernican view of the universe was opposed by the established church of the day. Has any opposition risen to meet the Einsteinian view? From whom?

5. Russell's essay popularizes science, a kind of writing which becomes increasingly important as science advances further into territory unexplored by the ordinary citizen. Try your hand at writing a layman's account of a short article in a scientific journal found in your college library.

Richard Selzer (b. 1928) is a general surgeon, a professor of surgery at the Yale Medical School, and a writer. He has published a collection of short stories called Ritual of Surgery *(1974) and a collection of essays called* Mortal Lessons *(1977). His words are clear and serious; he writes with a surgeon's steady hand. In touch with life and death every day, Selzer spares us nothing when he writes. Compassion that does not call attention to itself shines through this work.*

62

RICHARD SELZER

The Discus Thrower

1   I spy on my patients. Ought not a doctor to observe his patients by any means and from any stance, that he might the more fully assemble evidence? So I stand in the doorways of hospital rooms and gaze. Oh, it is not all that furtive an act. Those in bed need only look up to discover me. But they never do.

2   From the doorway of Room 542 the man in the bed seems deeply tanned. Blue eyes and close-cropped white hair give him the appearance of vigor and good health. But I know that his skin is not brown from the sun. It is rusted, rather, in the last stage of containing the vile repose within. And the blue eyes are frosted, looking inward like the windows of a snowbound cottage. This man is blind. This man is also legless — the right leg missing from midthigh down, the left from just below the knee. It gives him the look of a bonsai, roots and branches pruned into the dwarfed facsimile of a great tree.

Propped on pillows, he cups his right thigh in both hands. Now 3
and then he shakes his head as though acknowledging the intensity of
his suffering. In all of this he makes no sound. Is he mute as well as
blind?

The room in which he dwells is empty of all possessions — no 4
get-well cards, small, private caches of food, day-old flowers, slippers,
all the usual kickshaws of the sickroom. There is only the bed, a chair,
a nightstand, and a tray on wheels that can be swung across his lap for
meals.

"What time is it?" he asks. 5

"Three o'clock." 6

"Morning or afternoon?" 7

"Afternoon." 8

He is silent. There is nothing else he wants to know. 9

"How are you?" I say. 10

"Who is it?" he asks. 11

"It's the doctor. How do you feel?" 12

He does not answer right away. 13

"Feel?" he says. 14

"I hope you feel better," I say. 15

I press the button at the side of the bed. 16

"Down you go," I say. 17

"Yes, down," he says. 18

He falls back upon the bed awkwardly. His stumps, unweighted 19
by legs and feet, rise in the air, presenting themselves. I unwrap the
bandages from the stumps, and begin to cut away the black scabs and
the dead, glazed fat with scissors and forceps. A shard of white bone
comes loose. I pick it away. I wash the wounds with disinfectant and
redress the stumps. All this while, he does not speak. What is he
thinking behind those lids that do not blink? Is he remembering a time
when he was whole? Does he dream of feet? Of when his body was not
a rotting log?

He lies solid and inert. In spite of everything, he remains impres- 20
sive, as though he were a sailor standing athwart a slanting deck.

"Anything more I can do for you?" I ask. 21

For a long moment he is silent. 22

"Yes," he says at last and without the least irony. "You can bring 23
me a pair of shoes."

In the corridor, the head nurse is waiting for me. 24

25   "We have to do something about him," she says. "Every morning he orders scrambled eggs for breakfast, and, instead of eating them, he picks up the plate and throws it against the wall."

26   "Throws his plate?"

27   "Nasty. That's what he is. No wonder his family doesn't come to visit. They probably can't stand him any more than we can."

28   She is waiting for me to do something.

29   "Well?"

30   "We'll see," I say.

31   The next morning I am waiting in the corridor when the kitchen delivers his breakfast. I watch the aide place the tray on the stand and swing it across his lap. She presses the button to raise the head of the bed. Then she leaves.

32   In time the man reaches to find the rim of the tray, then on to find the dome of the covered dish. He lifts off the cover and places it on the stand. He fingers across the plate until he probes the eggs. He lifts the plate in both hands, sets it on the palm of his right hand, centers it, balances it. He hefts it up and down slightly, getting the feel of it. Abruptly, he draws back his right arm as far as he can.

33   There is the crack of the plate breaking against the wall at the foot of his bed and the small wet sound of the scrambled eggs dropping to the floor.

34   And then he laughs. It is a sound you have never heard. It is something new under the sun. It could cure cancer.

35   Out in the corridor, the eyes of the head nurse narrow.

36   "Laughed, did he?"

37   She writes something down on her clipboard.

38   A second aide arrives, brings a second breakfast tray, puts it on the nightstand, out of his reach. She looks over at me shaking her head and making her mouth go. I see that we are to be accomplices.

39   "I've got to feed you," she says to the man.

40   "Oh, no you don't," the man says.

41   "Oh, yes I do," the aide says, "after the way you just did. Nurse says so."

42   "Get me my shoes," the man says.

43   "Here's oatmeal," the aide says. "Open." And she touches the spoon to his lower lip.

44   "I ordered scrambled eggs," says the man.

45   "That's right," the aide says.

46   I step forward.

"Is there anything I can do?" I say. 47
"Who are you?" the man asks. 48

In the evening I go once more to that ward to make my rounds. 49
The head nurse reports to me that Room 542 is deceased. She has
discovered this quite by accident, she says. No, there had been no
sound. Nothing. It's a blessing, she says.

I go into his room, a spy looking for secrets. He is still there in 50
his bed. His face is relaxed, grave, dignified. After a while, I turn to
leave. My gaze sweeps the wall at the foot of the bed, and I see the
place where it has been repeatedly washed, where the wall looks very
clean and very white.

____ CONSIDERATIONS ____

1. To appreciate Selzer's feeling for the patient, try rewriting part of the
essay to make it a strictly impersonal record. Probably the first thing you
would change is the first word of Selzer's essay. Why?
2. One brief passage saves "The Discus Thrower" from being an exercise
in despair. Find that passage and discuss.
3. Give some thought to the title of Selzer's essay. What does that tell
you about Selzer's feelings for the man in Room 542?
4. What is the attitude of the nursing staff toward the discus thrower?
How does Selzer show that attitude?
5. If you were visiting Room 542, and the man asked you to bring him a
pair of shoes, what would you say? Why?

William Shakespeare (1564–1616) wrote three long poems and
a sequence of sonnets, as well as the plays for which we know
him best. He was born in Stratford-on-Avon to a middle-class
family, came to London in his twenties, and began his theatrical
career as an actor. His writing for the theater started with plays
based on English history: the three parts of Henry VI *and* Richard
III. The Tempest *was his last play, and by 1611 he had retired to*
Stratford with the money he had made upon the stage.

This sonnet develops a common poetic theme with metaphors
at once profuse and precise.

63

WILLIAM SHAKESPEARE

That time of year thou mayst in me behold

That time of year thou mayst in me behold
When yellow leaves, or none, or few, do hang
Upon those boughs which shake against the cold,
Bare ruined choirs, where late the sweet birds sang.
5 In me thou see'st the twilight of such day
As after sunset fadeth in the west;
Which by and by black night doth take away,
Death's second self, that seals up all in rest.
In me thou see'st the glowing of such fire,
10 That on the ashes of his youth doth lie,
As the deathbed whereon it must expire,
Consumed with that which it was nourished by.
This thou perceiv'st, which makes thy love more strong,
To love that well which thou must leave ere long.

William Stafford (b. 1914) is a poet who grew up in Kansas and teaches now at Lewis and Clark College in Oregon. Traveling through the Dark *won the National Book Award in 1963, and was followed by* The Rescued Year *(1966),* Allegiances *(1970), and* Some Day, Maybe *(1973). In 1977, Stafford collected his poems into one volume called* Stories That Could Be True.

Stafford's poetry and his account of writing his poetry look simple. In a way, they are *simple, but their simplicity deepens as long as you look at it. His poetry is simple and deep, rather than complex and superficial. Reading about his way of writing, you feel the style of the man as intensely in his prose as in his poems.*

64

WILLIAM STAFFORD
A Way of Writing

A writer is not so much someone who has something to say as he 1
is someone who has found a process that will bring about new things
he would not have thought of if he had not started to say them. That
is, he does not draw on a reservoir; instead, he engages in an activity
that brings to him a whole succession of unforeseen stories, poems,
essays, plays, laws, philosophies, religions, or — but wait!

Back in school, from the first when I began to try to write things, 2
I felt this richness. One thing would lead to another; the world would
give and give. Now, after twenty years or so of trying, I live by that
certain richness, an idea hard to pin, difficult to say, and perhaps offensive to some. For there are strange implications in it.

One implication is the importance of just plain receptivity. When 3
I write, I like to have an interval before me when I am not likely to be

"A Way of Writing" by William Stafford from *Field*, Spring 1970. Reprinted by permission of *Field*, Oberlin College, Oberlin, Ohio.

interrupted. For me, this means usually the early morning, before others are awake. I get pen and paper, take a glance out the window (often it is dark out there), and wait. It is like fishing. But I do not wait very long, for there is always a nibble — and this is where receptivity comes in. To get started I will accept anything that occurs to me. Something always occurs, of course, to any of us. We can't keep from thinking. Maybe I have to settle for an immediate impression: it's cold, or hot, or dark, or bright, or in between! Or — well, the possibilities are endless. If I put down something, that thing will help the next thing come, and I'm off. If I let the process go on, things will occur to me that were not at all in my mind when I started. These things, odd or trivial as they- may be, are somehow connected. And if I let them string out, surprising things will happen.

4   If I let them string out. . . . Along with initial receptivity, then, there is another readiness: I must be willing to fail. If I am to keep on writing, I cannot bother to insist on high standards. I must get into action and not let anything stop me, or even slow me much. By "standards" I do not mean "correctness" — spelling, punctuation, and so on. These details become mechanical for anyone who writes for a while. I am thinking about what many people would consider "important" standards, such matters as social significance, positive values, consistency, etc. I resolutely disregard these. Something better, greater, is happening! I am following a process that leads so wildly and originally into new territory that no judgment can at the moment be made about values, significance, and so on. I am making something new, something that has not been judged before. Later others — and maybe I myself — will make judgments. Now, I am headlong to discover. Any distraction may harm the creating.

5   So, receptive, careless of failure, I spin out things on the page. And a wonderful freedom comes. If something occurs to me, it is all right to accept it. It has one justification: it occurs to me. No one else can guide me. I must follow my own weak, wandering, diffident impulses.

6   A strange bonus happens. At times, without my insisting on it, my writings become coherent; the successive elements that occur to me are clearly related. They lead by themselves to new connections. Sometimes the language, even the syllables that happen along, may start a trend. Sometimes the materials alert me to something waiting in my mind, ready for sustained attention. At such times, I allow myself to be eloquent, or intentional, or for great swoops (treacherous! not to be trusted!) reasonable. But I do not insist on any of that; for I

know that back of my activity there will be the coherence of my self, and that indulgence of my impulses will bring recurrent patterns and meanings again.

This attitude toward the process of writing creatively suggests a 7 problem for me, in terms of what others say. They talk about "skills" in writing. Without denying that I do have experience, wide reading, automatic orthodoxies and maneuvers of various kinds, I still must insist that I am often baffled about what "skill" has to do with the precious little area of confusion when I do not know what I am going to say and then I find out what I am going to say. That precious interval I am unable to bridge by skill. What can I witness about it? It remains mysterious, just as all of us must feel puzzled about how we are so inventive as to be able to talk along through complexities with our friends, not needing to plan what we are going to say, but never stalled for long in our confident forward progress. Skill? If so, it is the skill we all have, something we must have learned before the age of three or four.

A writer is one who has become accustomed to trusting that 8 grace, or luck, or — skill.

Yet another attitude I find necessary: most of what I write, like 9 most of what I say in casual conversation, will not amount to much. Even I will realize, and even at the time, that it is not negotiable. It will be like practice. In conversation I allow myself random remarks — in fact, as I recall, that is the way I learned to talk — , so in writing I launch many expendable efforts. A result of this free way of writing is that I am not writing for others, mostly; they will not see the product at all unless the activity eventuates in something that later appears to be worthy. My guide is the self, and its adventuring in the language brings about communication.

This process-rather-than-substance view of writing invites a 10 final, dual reflection:

1) Writers may not be special — sensitive or talented in any usual sense. They are simply engaged in sustained use of a language skill we all have. Their "creations" come about through confident reliance on stray impulses that will, with trust, find occasional patterns that are satisfying.

2) But writing itself is one of the great, free human activities. There is scope for individuality, and elation, and discovery, in writing. For the person who follows with trust and forgiveness what occurs to him, the world remains always ready and deep, an inexhaustible environment, with the combined vividness of an actuality and flexibility

of a dream. Working back and forth between experience and thought, writers have more than space and time can offer. They have the whole unexplored realm of human vision.

A sample daily-writing sheet and the poem as revised.

15 December 1969

at the fountain on Main Street I saw
our shadows. It did not drink, but
waited on cement and pretty while I drank.
They were two people and but one shadow.
Two people in love there but one shadow.
I looked at ferns out where a bird
flying past made a shadow on the day.
There is a place in the air where too much
used to fly. Once I crawled through
grassblades to hear the sound of their shadows.
One of the shadows moved, and it was
the earth where a mole was passing.
I could hear little paws in the dirt,
and fur brush along the tunnel, a few,
somehow, the mole shadow.
Out in places like Wyoming some of the shadows
are cut out and pasted on fossils.
There are mountains that erode when
clouds drag across them. You can hear
the tick of the light breaking edges off white stones.
In my prayers I let yesterday begin
and then go behind this time now. Every heart
pumps from a well full of shadows.
In churches their hearts pump from wells
full of shadows.
In churches they pump sermons from
wells full of shadows.

Shadows

I

Out in places like Wyoming some of the shadows

are cut out and pasted on fossils.

There are mountains that erode when
clouds drag across them. You can hear ~~the tick~~ the tick

~~the tick~~ of the light breaking edges off white stones.

At ~~the~~ a fountain on Main Street I saw

our shadow. It did not drink but

waited on cement and water while I drank.

There were two people and but one shadow.

I looked up so hard outward that a bird

flying past made a shadow on the sky.X,

There is a place in the air where our house

~~used to be.~~

Once I crawled through grassblades to hear

the sounds of their shadows. One of the shadows

moved, and it was the earth where a mole

was passing. I could hear little

paws in the dirt, and fur brush along

the tunnel, and even, somehow, the mole shadow.

In churches ~~their~~ when hearts pump sermons

from wells full of shadows.

In my prayers I let yesterday begin

and then go behind this hour now,

SHADOWS

Out in places like Wyoming some of the shadows
are cut out and pasted on fossils.
There are mountains that erode when
clouds drag across them. You hear the tick
of sunlight breaking edges off white stones.

At a fountain on Main Street I saw
our shadow. It did not drink but
waited on cement and water while I drank.
There were two people and but one shadow.
I looked up so hard outward that a bird
flying past made a shadow on the sky.
There is a place in the air where
our old house used to be.

Once I crawled through grassblades to hear
the sounds of their shadows. One shadow
moved, and it was the earth where a mole
was passing. I could hear little
paws in the dirt, and fur brush along
the tunnel, and even, somehow, the mole shadow.

In my prayers I let yesterday begin
and then go behind this hour now,
in churches where hearts pump sermons
from wells full of shadows.

___ CONSIDERATIONS _____

1. Stafford is clearly and openly talking about himself — how *he* writes,
what writing means to *him* — and yet most readers agree that he successfully
avoids the egotism or self-consciousness that sours many first-person essays.
Compare his style with three or four other first-person pieces in this book to
see how he does it.

2. In his first paragraph, Stafford tells of an idea that might be called
writing as discovery. Thinking back through your own writing, can you recall
this experience — when, after struggling to write an essay or letter that you
had to write, you discovered something you *wanted* to write? What did you
do about it? More important, what might you do next time it happens?

3. What, according to Stafford, is more important to a writer than "social significance, or positive values, or consistency"?

4. Stafford is talking about writing a poem. How do his discoveries and conclusions bear on *your* problems in writing an essay? Be specific.

5. Do the opening and closing paragraphs differ in style? If so, what is the difference, and why does Stafford allow it?

6. Study the three versions of Stafford's poem "Shadows." Do you find anything that belies the easygoing impression his essay gives of Stafford at work? Explain.

Jonathan Swift (1667–1745) was a priest, a poet, and a master of English prose, who wrote Gulliver's Travels. *Some of his strongest satire took the form of reasonable defense of the unthinkable, like his argument in favor of abolishing Christianity in the British Isles. Born in Dublin, he was angry all his life at England's misuse and mistreatment of the subject Irish people. In 1729, he made this modest proposal for solving the Irish problem.*

65

JONATHAN SWIFT
A Modest Proposal

For Preventing the Children of Poor People in Ireland
from Being a Burden to Their Parents or Country,
and for Making Them Beneficial to the Public

1   It is a melancholy object to those who walk through this great town or travel in the country, when they see the streets, the roads, and cabin doors, crowded with beggars of the female sex, followed by three, four, or six children, all in rags and importuning every passenger for an alms. These mothers, instead of being able to work for their honest livelihood, are forced to employ all their time in strolling to beg sustenance for their helpless infants, who, as they grow up, either turn thieves for want of work, or leave their dear native country to fight for the Pretender in Spain, or sell themselves to the Barbadoes.

2   I think it is agreed by all parties that this prodigious number of children in the arms, or on the backs, or at the heels of their mothers, and frequently of their fathers, is in the present deplorable state of the kingdom a very great additional grievance; and therefore whoever could find out a fair, cheap, and easy method of making these children sound, useful members of the commonwealth would deserve so well of the public as to have his statue set up for a preserver of the nation.

But my intention is very far from being confined to provide only   3
for the children of professed beggars; it is of a much greater extent, and
shall take in the whole number of infants at a certain age who are born
of parents in effect as little able to support them as those who demand
our charity in the streets.

As to my own part, having turned my thoughts for many years   4
upon this important subject, and maturely weighed the several
schemes of other projectors, I have always found them grossly mistaken in their computation. It is true, a child just dropped from its dam
may be supported by her milk for a solar year, with little other nourishment; at most not above the value of two shillings, which the
mother may certainly get, or the value in scraps, by her lawful occupation of begging; and it is exactly at one year old that I propose to
provide for them in such a manner as instead of being a charge upon
their parents or the parish, or wanting food and raiment for the rest of
their lives, they shall on the contrary contribute to the feeding, and
partly to the clothing, of many thousands.

There is likewise another great advantage in my scheme, that it   5
will prevent those voluntary abortions, and that horrid practice of
women murdering their bastard children, alas, too frequent among us,
sacrificing the poor innocent babes, I doubt, more to avoid the expense
than the shame, which would move tears and pity in the most savage
and inhuman breast.

The number of souls in this kingdom being usually reckoned one   6
million and a half, of these I calculate there may be about two hundred
thousand couples whose wives are breeders; from which number I
subtract thirty thousand couples who are able to maintain their own
children, although I apprehend there cannot be so many under the
present distress of the kingdom; but this being granted, there will
remain an hundred and seventy thousand breeders. I again subtract
fifty thousand for those women who miscarry, or whose children die
by accident or disease within the year. There only remain an hundred
and twenty thousand children of poor parents annually born. The question therefore is, how this number shall be reared and provided for,
which, as I have already said, under the present situation of affairs, is
utterly impossible by all the methods hitherto proposed. For we can
neither employ them in handicraft or agriculture; we neither build
houses (I mean in the country) nor cultivate land. They can very seldom pick up a livelihood by stealing till they arrive at six years old,
except where they are of towardly parts; although I confess they learn
the rudiments much earlier, during which time they can however be

looked upon only as probationers, as I have been informed by a principal gentleman in the country of Cavan, who protested to me that he never knew above one or two instances under the age of six, even in a part of the kingdom so renowned for the quickest proficiency in that art.

7   I am assured by our merchants that a boy or a girl before twelve years old is no salable commodity; and even when they come to this age they will not yield above three pounds, or three pounds and half a crown at most on the Exchange; which cannot turn to account either to the parents or the kingdom, the charge of nutriment and rags having been at least four times that value.

8   I shall now therefore humbly propose my own thoughts, which I hope will not be liable to the least objection.

9   I have been assured by a very knowing American of my acquaintance in London, that a young healthy child well nursed is at a year old a most delicious, nourishing, and wholesome food, whether stewed, roasted, baked, or boiled; and I make no doubt that it will equally serve in a fricassee or a ragout.

10   I do therefore humbly offer it to public consideration that of the hundred and twenty thousand children, already computed, twenty thousand may be reserved for breed, whereof only one fourth part to be males, which is more than we allow to sheep, black cattle, or swine; and my reason is that these children are seldom the fruits of marriage, a circumstance not much regarded by our savages, therefore one male will be sufficient to serve four females. That the remaining hundred thousand may at a year old be offered in sale to the persons of quality and fortune through the kingdom, always advising the mother to let them suck plentifully in the last month, so as to render them plump and fat for a good table. A child will make two dishes at an entertainment for friends; and when the family dines alone, the fore or hind quarter will make a reasonable dish, and seasoned with a little pepper or salt will be very good boiled on the fourth day, especially in winter.

11   I have reckoned upon a medium that a child just born will weigh twelve pounds, and in a solar year if tolerably nursed increaseth to twenty-eight pounds.

12   I grant this food will be somewhat dear, and therefore very proper for landlords, who, as they have already devoured most of the parents, seem to have the best title to the children.

13   Infant's flesh will be in season throughout the year, but more plentiful in March, and a little before and after. For we are told by a grave author, an eminent French physician, that fish being a prolific

diet, there are more children born in Roman Catholic countries about nine months after Lent than at any other season; therefore, reckoning a year after Lent, the markets will be more glutted than usual, because the number of popish infants is at least three to one in this kingdom; and therefore it will have one other collateral advantage, by lessening the number of Papists among us.

I have already computed the charge of nursing a beggar's child (in 14 which list I reckon all cottagers, laborers, and four fifths of the farmers) to be about two shillings per annum, rags included; and I believe no gentleman would repine to give ten shillings for the carcass of a good fat child, which, as I have said, will make four dishes of excellent nutritive meat, when he hath only some particular friend or his own family to dine with him. Thus the squire will learn to be a good landlord, and grow popular among the tenants; the mother will have eight shillings net profit, and be fit for work till she produces another child.

Those who are more thrifty (as I must confess the times require) 15 may flay the carcass; the skin of which artificially dressed will make admirable gloves for ladies, and summer boots for fine gentlemen.

As to our city of Dublin, shambles may be appointed for this 16 purpose in the most convenient parts of it, and butchers we may be assured will not be wanting; although I rather recommend buying the children alive, and dressing them hot from the knife as we do roasting pigs.

A very worthy person, a true lover of his country, and whose 17 virtues I highly esteem, was lately pleased in discoursing on this matter to offer a refinement upon my scheme. He said that many gentlemen of his kingdom, having of late destroyed their deer, he conceived that the want of venison might be well supplied by the bodies of young lads and maidens, not exceeding fourteen years of age nor under twelve, so great a number of both sexes in every county being now ready to starve for want of work and service; and these to be disposed of by their parents, if alive, or otherwise by their nearest relations. But with due deference to so excellent a friend and so deserving a patriot, I cannot be altogether in his sentiments; for as to the males, my American acquaintance assured me from frequent experience that their flesh was generally tough and lean, like that of our schoolboys, by continual exercise, and their taste disagreeable; and to fatten them would not answer the charge. Then as to the females, it would, I think with humble submission, be a loss to the public, because they soon would become breeders themselves: and besides, it is not improbable that some scrupulous people might be apt to censure such a practice (although indeed very unjustly) as a little bordering upon cruelty; which, I confess, hath always been with me the strongest objection against any project, how well soever intended.

18   But in order to justify my friend, he confessed that this expedient was put into his head by the famous Psalmanazar, a native of the island Formosa, who came from thence to London above twenty years ago, and in conversation told my friend that in his country when any young person happened to be put to death, the executioner sold the carcass to persons of quality as a prime dainty; and that in his time the body of a plump girl of fifteen, who was crucified for an attempt to poison the emperor, was sold to his Imperial Majesty's prime minister of state, and other great mandarins of the court, in joints from the gibbet, at four hundred crowns. Neither indeed can I deny that if the same use were made of several plump young girls in this town, who without one single groat to their fortunes cannot stir abroad without a chair, and appear at the playhouse and assemblies in foreign fineries which they never will pay for, the kingdom would not be the worse.

19   Some persons of a desponding spirit are in great concern about that vast number of poor people who are aged, diseased, or maimed, and I have been desired to employ my thoughts what course may be taken to ease the nation of so grievous an encumbrance. But I am not in the least pain upon that matter, because it is very well known that they are every day dying and rotting by cold and famine, and filth and vermin, as fast as can be reasonably expected. And as to the younger laborers, they are now in almost as hopeful a condition. They cannot get work, and consequently pine away for want of nourishment to a degree that if at any time they are accidentally hired to common labor, they have not strength to perform it; and thus the country and themselves are happily delivered from the evils to come.

20   I have too long digressed, and therefore shall return to my subject. I think the advantages by the proposal which I have made are obvious and many, as well as of the highest importance.

21   For first, as I have already observed, it would greatly lessen the number of Papists, with whom we are yearly overrun, being the principal breeders of the nation as well as our most dangerous enemies; and who stay at home on purpose to deliver the kingdom to the Pretender, hoping to take their advantage by the absence of so many good Protestants, who have chosen rather to leave their country than to stay at home and pay tithes against their conscience to an Episcopal curate.

22   Secondly, the poorer tenants will have something valuable of their own, which by law may be made liable to distress, and help to

pay their landlord's rent, their corn and cattle being already seized and money a thing unknown.

Thirdly, whereas the maintenance of an hundred thousand chil- 23 dren, from two years old and upwards, cannot be computed at less than ten shillings a piece per annum, the nation's stock will be thereby increased fifty thousand pounds per annum, besides the profit of a new dish introduced to the tables of all gentlemen of fortune in the kingdom who have any refinement in taste. And the money will circulate among ourselves, the goods being entirely of our own growth and manufacture.

Fourthly, the constant breeders, besides the gain of eight shillings 24 sterling per annum by the sale of their children, will be rid of the charge of maintaining them after the first year.

Fifthly, this food would likewise bring great custom to taverns, 25 where the vintners will certainly be so prudent as to procure the best receipts for dressing it to perfection, and consequently have their houses frequented by all the fine gentlemen, who justly value themselves upon their knowledge in good eating; and a skillful cook, who understands how to oblige his guests, will contrive to make it as expensive as they please.

Sixthly, this would be a great inducement to marriage, which all 26 wise nations have either encouraged by rewards or enforced by laws and penalties. It would increase the care and tenderness of mothers toward their children, when they were sure of a settlement for life to the poor babes, provided in some sort by the public, to their annual profit instead of expense. We should see an honest emulation among the married women, which of them could bring the fattest child to the market. Men would become as fond of their wives during the time of their pregnancy as they are now of their mares in foal, their cows in calf, or sows when they are ready to farrow; nor offer to beat or kick them (as is too frequent a practice) for fear of a miscarriage.

Many other advantages might be enumerated. For instance, the 27 addition of some thousand carcasses in our exportation of barreled beef, the propagation of swine's flesh, and improvements in the art of making good bacon, so much wanted among us by the great destruction of pigs, too frequent at our tables, which are no way comparable in taste or magnificence to a well-grown, fat, yearling child, which roasted whole will make a considerable figure at a lord mayor's feast or any other public entertainment. But this and many others I omit, being studious of brevity.

Supposing that one thousand families in this city would be con- 28 stant customers for infants' flesh, besides others who might have it at merry meetings, particularly weddings and christenings, I compute that Dublin would take off annually about twenty thousand carcasses, and the rest of the kingdom (where probably they will be sold somewhat cheaper) the remaining eighty thousand.

29   I can think of no one objection that will possibly be raised against this proposal, unless it should be urged that the number of people will be thereby much lessened in the kingdom. This I freely own, and it was indeed one principal design in offering it to the world. I desire the reader will observe, that I calculate my remedy for this one individual kingdom of Ireland and for no other that ever was, is, or I think ever can be upon earth. Therefore let no man talk to me of other expedients: of taxing our absentees at five shillings a pound: of using neither clothes nor household furniture except what is of our own growth and manufacture: of utterly rejecting the materials and instruments that promote foreign luxury: of curing the expensiveness of pride, vanity, idleness, and gaming in our women: of introducing a vein of parsimony, prudence, and temperance: of learning to love our country, in the want of which we differ even from Laplanders and the inhabitants of Topinamboo: of quitting our animosities and factions, nor acting any longer like the Jews, who were murdering one another at the very moment their city was taken: of being a little cautious not to sell our country and conscience for nothing: of teaching landlords to have at least one degree of mercy toward their tenants: lastly, of putting a spirit of honesty, industry, and skill into our shopkeepers; who, if a resolution could now be taken to buy only our native goods, would immediately unite to cheat and exact upon us in the price, the measure, and the goodness, nor could ever yet be brought to make one fair proposal of just dealing, though often and earnestly invited to it.

30   Therefore I repeat, let no man talk to me of these and the like expedients, till he hath at least some glimpse of hope that there will ever be some hearty and sincere attempt to put them in practice.

31   But as to myself, having been wearied out for many years with offering vain, idle, visionary thoughts, and at length utterly despairing of success, I fortunately fell upon this proposal, which, as it is wholly new, so it hath something solid and real, of no expense and little trouble, full in our own power, and whereby we can incur no danger in disobliging England. For this kind of commodity will not bear exportation, the flesh being of too tender a consistence to admit a long continuance in salt, although perhaps I could name a country which would be glad to eat up our whole nation without it.

After all, I am not so violently bent upon my own opinion as to   32
reject any offer proposed by wise men, which shall be found equally
innocent, cheap, easy, and effectual. But before something of that kind
shall be advanced in contradiction to my scheme, and offering a better,
I desire the author or authors will be pleased maturely to consider two
points. First, as things now stand, how they will be able to find food
and raiment for an hundred thousand useless mouths and backs. And
secondly, there being a round million of creatures in human figure
throughout this kingdom, whose sole subsistence put into a common
stock would leave them in debt two millions of pounds sterling, adding
those who are beggars by profession to the bulk of farmers, cottagers,
and laborers, with their wives and children who are beggars in effect;
I desire those politicians who dislike my overture, and may perhaps be
so bold to attempt an answer, that they will first ask the parents of
these mortals whether they would not at this day think it a great
happiness to have been sold for food at a year old in this manner I
prescribe, and thereby have avoided such a perpetual scene of misfor-
tunes as they have since gone through by the oppression of landlords,
the impossibility of paying rent without money or trade, the want of
common sustenance, with neither house nor clothes to cover them
from the inclemencies of the weather, and the most inevitable pros-
pect of entailing the like or greater miseries upon their breed forever.

I profess, in the sincerity of my heart, that I have not the least   33
personal interest in endeavoring to promote this necessary work, having no other motive than the public good of my country, by advancing
our trade, providing for infants, relieving the poor, and giving some
pleasure to the rich. I have no children by which I can propose to get a
single penny; the youngest being nine years old, and my wife past
childbearing.

_____ CONSIDERATIONS _____

   1. The biggest risk a satirist runs is that his reader will not understand
that he is reading satire; that he will be too literal-minded. Can you imagine a
reader missing the satiric nature of Swift's "A Modest Proposal"? It has happened many times. What might such a reader think of the author? Consider
the same problem with regard to Ambrose Bierce (pages 60–63) or Mark Twain
(pages 413–417).
   2. One clue to the satire is Swift's choice of diction in certain passages.
In Paragraph 4, for example, note the phrase, "just dropped from its dam," in

reference to a newborn child. How do these words make a sign to the reader? Look for other such words.

3. How soon after Paragraph 9, in which he makes explicit his modest proposal, does Swift tip his hand and make it impossible for a careful reader to take him literally?

4. What words and phrases does Swift use to give the impression of straightforward seriousness?

5. How does Swift turn his satirical talent against religious intolerance?

6. What is the chief target of his satire toward the end of the essay?

Thomas Szasz (b. 1920) came to the United States in 1938 from his native Hungary. (His last name is pronounced Soz.) He is a medical doctor, psychiatrist, and psychoanalyst with ideas that pass as heresies among many of his colleagues. Szasz apparently enjoys this position: one of his many books is Heresies *(1976), from which this selection is taken. Szasz has written much.* Heresies *was one of three books he published in 1976; in 1977 he published two,* The Theology of Medicine *and* Psychiatric Slavery; *in 1978 he issued* The Myth of Psychotherapy. *He delights in the role of devil's advocate, ridiculing conventional wisdom with consistent acerbity.*

66

THOMAS SZASZ
Laws Make Crimes

The free exit of people from the Soviet Union is prohibited. The Soviet Union has a problem with people leaving the country, which it calls "defection." 1

The free entry of opiates into the United States is prohibited. The United States has a problem with opiates coming into the country, which it calls "trafficking in dope." 2

The United States recognizes that its citizens have an inalienable right to leave their country. The United States therefore has no such problem as "defection." 3

Similarly, if the United States recognized that its citizens also have an inalienable right to self-medication (a right of which they were deprived in 1914), there would be no illegal inflow of heroin into the 4 country. The United States would therefore have no such problem as "trafficking in dope."

5   Of course, some people would still take drugs some other people did not want them to take. But this would no more constitute "drug abuse" than leaving the country constitutes "border abuse."

6   In short, if a government believes that its citizens have no right to leave their country, it will generate policies which, in turn, will create the "problem of defection." Similarly, if a government believes that its citizens have no right to use "dangerous drugs," it will generate policies which, in turn, will create the "problem of drug abuse." Many national and social "problems" are thus created not by what people do, but by the way governments *define* what they do and by the policies which such definitions impose on rulers and ruled alike.

7   Confronted with such totalitarian laws, most people in the "free" world assert that the prohibitions are criminal and that the victims are the citizens whose freedom they curtail. Yet, confronted with similar therapeutic laws — which prohibit certain movements in the chemical and sexual, rather than in the geographical, sphere — most people in the "free" world assert that the prohibitions are merely unfortunate or unwise because they create "crimes without victims." This is self-deception of the worst sort: it is the unwillingness to see and acknowledge the malevolent tyranny of one's own rulers, and, where it applies, of one's own conscience, on whose behest a "free" people deprive themselves of a liberty whose burden they are too weak to bear.

___ CONSIDERATIONS _____

1. Szasz draws a strict parallel between policies in the Soviet Union and the United States as a basis for his argument. Read what Robert Gorham Davis has to say about false analogy (pages 119–120) and decide whether Szasz's parallel is valid.

2. In effect, Szasz argues that creating laws creates crime. If students decided to require everyone who attends class to wear pink pajamas, would that cause a problem? How far do you think Szasz would go with his argument? For instance, what about the law making it a crime to kill another person? Would you make a modest proposal that murder be decriminalized?

3. If Szasz would not extend his argument to all laws, how would he determine which laws are vulnerable?

4. What does this author describe as "self-deception of the worst sort"? Do you agree?

5. Does Szasz's position resemble Walter Lippmann's, who criticizes the power of the majority (pages 233–241)?

Studs Terkel (b. 1912) has been an actor on stage and television, and has conducted a successful radio interview show in Chicago. His best known books, collections of interviews, are Division Street America *(1966),* Hard Times *(1970), and* Working *(1974) — from which we take this example of American speech. In 1977, he published* Talking to Myself, *his autobiography.*

67

STUDS TERKEL

Phil Stallings, Spot Welder

He is a spot-welder at the Ford assembly plant on the far South 1
Side of Chicago. He is twenty-seven years old; recently married. He
works the third shift: 3:30 P.M. *to midnight.*

"I start the automobile, the first welds. From there it goes to 2
another line, where the floor's put on, the roof, the trunk hood, the
doors. Then it's put on a frame. There is hundreds of lines.

"The welding gun's got a square handle, with a button on the 3
top for high voltage and a button on the bottom for low. The first is to
clamp the metal together. The second is to fuse it.

"The gun hangs from a ceiling, over tables that ride on a track. 4
It travels in a circle, oblong, like an egg. You stand on a cement
platform, maybe six inches from the ground."

I stand in one spot, about two- or three-feet area, all night. The 5
only time a person stops is when the line stops. We do about thirty-
two jobs per car, per unit. Forty-eight units an hour, eight hours a day.

Thirty-two times forty-eight times eight. Figure it out. That's how many times I push that button.

6   The noise, oh it's tremendous. You open your mouth and you're liable to get a mouthful of sparks. (Shows his arms) That's a burn, these are burns. You don't compete against the noise. You go to yell and at the same time you're straining to maneuver the gun to where you have to weld.

7   You got some guys that are uptight, and they're not sociable. It's too rough. You pretty much stay to yourself. You get involved with yourself. You dream, you think of things you've done. I drift back continuously to when I was a kid and what me and my brothers did. The things you love most are the things you drift back into.

8   Lots of times I worked from the time I started to the time of the break and I never realized I had even worked. When you dream, you reduce the chances of friction with the foreman or with the next guy.

9   It don't stop. It just goes and goes and goes. I bet there's men who have lived and died out there, never seen the end of that line. And they never will — because it's endless. It's like a serpent. It's just all body, no tail. It can do things to you . . . (Laughs.)

10   Repetition is such that if you were to think about the job itself, you'd slowly go out of your mind. You'd let your problems build up, you'd get to a point where you'd be at the fellow next to you — his throat. Every time the foreman came by and looked at you, you'd have something to say. You just strike out at anything you can. So if you involve yourself by yourself, you overcome this.

11   I don't like the pressure, the intimidation. How would you like to go up to someone and say, "I would like to go to the bathroom?" If the foreman doesn't like you, he'll make you hold it, just ignore you. Should I leave this job to go to the bathroom I risk being fired. The line moves all the time.

12   I work next to Jim Grayson and he's preoccupied. The guy on my left, he's a Mexican, speaking Spanish, so it's pretty hard to understand him. You just avoid him. Brophy, he's a young fella, he's going to college. He works catty-corner from me. Him and I talk from time to time. If he ain't in the mood, I don't talk. If I ain't in the mood, he knows it.

13   Oh sure, there's tension here. It's not always obvious, but the whites stay with the whites and the coloreds stay with the coloreds. When you go into Ford, Ford says, "Can you work with other men?" This stops a lot of trouble, 'cause when you're working side by side with a guy, they can't afford to have guys fighting. When two men

don't socialize, that means two guys are gonna do more work, know what I mean?

I don't understand how come more guys don't flip. Because you're 14 nothing more than a machine when you hit this type of thing. They give better care to that machine than they will to you. They'll have more respect, give more attention to that machine. And you *know* this. Somehow you get the feeling that the machine is better than you are. (Laughs.)

You really begin to wonder. What price do they put on me? Look 15 at the price they put on the machine. If that machine breaks down, there's somebody out there to fix it right away. If I break down, I'm just pushed over to the other side till another man takes my place. The only thing they have on their mind is to keep that line running.

I'll do the best I can. I believe in an eight-hour pay for an eight- 16 hour day. But I will not try to outreach my limits. If I can't cut it, I just don't do it. I've been there three years and I keep my nose pretty clean. I never cussed anybody or anything like that. But I've had some real brushes with foremen.

What happened was my job was overloaded. I got cut and it got 17 infected. I got blood poisoning. The drill broke. I took it to the fore-man's desk. I says, "Change this as soon as you can." We were running specials for XL hoods. I told him I wasn't a repair man. That's how the conflict began. I says, "If you want, take me to the Green House." Which is a superintendent's office — disciplinary station. This is when he says, "Guys like you I'd like to see in the parking lot."

One foreman I know, he's about the youngest out here, he has 18 this idea: I'm it and if you don't like it, you know what you can do. Anything this other foreman says, he usually overrides. Even in some cases, the foremen don't get along. They're pretty hard to live with, even with each other.

Oh yeah, the foreman's got somebody knuckling down on him, 19 putting the screws to him. But a foreman is still free to go to the bathroom, go get a cup of coffee. He doesn't face the penalties. When I first went in there, I kind of envied foremen. Now, I wouldn't have a foreman's job. I wouldn't give 'em the time of the day.

When a man becomes a foreman, he has to forget about even 20 being human, as far as feelings are concerned. You see a guy there bleeding to death. So what, buddy? That line's gotta keep goin'. I can't live like that. To me, if a man gets hurt, first thing you do is get him some attention.

About the blood poisoning. It came from the inside of a hood 21 rubbin' against me. It caused quite a bit of pain. I went down to the medics. They said it was a boil. Got to my doctor that night. He said blood poisoning. Running fever and all this. Now I've smartened up.

22   They have a department of medics. It's basically first aid. There's no doctor on our shift, just two or three nurses, that's it. They've got a door with a sign on it that says Lab. Another door with a sign on it: Major Surgery. But my own personal opinion, I'm afraid of 'em. I'm afraid if I were to get hurt, I'd get nothin' but back talk. I got hit square in the chest one day with a bar from a rack and it cut me down this side. They didn't take x-rays or nothing. Sent me back on the job. I missed three and a half days two weeks ago. I had bronchitis. They told me I was all right. I didn't have a fever. I went home and my doctor told me I couldn't go back to work for two weeks. I really needed the money, so I had to go back the next day. I woke up still sick, so I took off the rest of the week.

23   I pulled a muscle on my neck, straining. This gun, when you grab this thing from the ceiling, cable, weight, I mean you're pulling everything. Your neck, your shoulders, and your back. I'm very surprised more accidents don't happen. You have to lean over, at the same time holding down the gun. This whole edge here is sharp. I go through a shirt every two weeks, it just goes right through. My coveralls catch on fire. I've had gloves catch on fire. (Indicates arms) See them little holes? That's what sparks do. I've got burns across here from last night.

24   I know I could find better places to work. But where could I get the money I'm making? Let's face it, $4.32 an hour. That's real good money now. Funny thing is, I don't mind working at body construction. To a great degree, I enjoy it. I love using my hands — more than I do my mind. I love to be able to put things together and see something in the long run. I'll be the first to admit I've got the easiest job on the line. But I'm against this thing where I'm being held back. I'll work like a dog until I get what I want. The job I really want is utility.

25   It's where I can stand and say I can do any job in this department, and nobody has to worry about me. As it is now, out of say, sixty jobs, I can do almost half of 'em. I want to get away from standing in one spot. Utility can do a different job every day. Instead of working right there for eight hours I could work over there for eight, I could work the other place for eight. Every day it would change. I would be around more people. I go out on my lunch break and work on the fork truck for a half-hour — to get the experience. As soon as I got it down pretty good, the foreman in charge says he'll take me. I don't want the other guys to see me. When I hit that fork lift, you just stop your thinking

and you concentrate. Something right there in front of you, not in the past, not in the future. This is real healthy.

I don't eat lunch at work. I may grab a candy bar, that's enough. 26 I wouldn't be able to hold it down. The tension your body is put under by the speed of the line . . . When you hit them brakes, you just can't stop. There's a certain momentum that carries you forward. I could hold the food, but it wouldn't set right.

Proud of my work? How can I feel pride in a job where I call a 27 foreman's attention to a mistake, a bad piece of equipment, and he'll ignore it. Pretty soon you get the idea they don't care. You keep doing this and finally you're titled a troublemaker. So you just go about your work. You *have* to have pride. So you throw it off to something else. And that's my stamp collection.

I'd break both my legs to get into social work. I see all over so 28 many kids really gettin' a raw deal. I think I'd go into juvenile. I tell kids on the line, "Man, go out there and get that college." Because it's too late for me now.

When you go into Ford, first thing they try to do is break your 29 spirit. I seen them bring a tall guy where they needed a short guy. I seen them bring a short guy where you have to stand on two guys' backs to do something. Last night, they brought a fifty-eight-year-old man to do the job I was on. That man's my father's age. I know damn well my father couldn't do it. To me, this is humanely wrong. A job should be a job, not a death sentence.

The younger worker, when he gets uptight, he talks back. But 30 you take an old fellow, he's got a year, two years, maybe three years to go. If it was me, I wouldn't say a word, I wouldn't care what they did. 'Cause, baby, for another two years I can stick it out. I can't blame this man. I respect him because he had enough will power to stick it out for thirty years.

It's gonna change. There's a trend. We're getting younger and 31 younger men. We got this new Thirty and Out. Thirty years seniority and out. The whole idea is to give a man more time, more time to slow down and live. While he's still in his fifties, he can settle down in a camper and go out and fish. I've sat down and thought about it. I've got twenty-seven years to go. (Laughs.) That's why I don't go around causin' trouble or lookin' for a cause.

The only time I get involved is when it affects me or it affects a 32 man on the line in a condition that could be me. I don't believe in lost causes, but when it all happened . . . (He pauses, appears bewildered.)

The foreman was riding the guy. The guy either told him to go 33 away or pushed him, grabbed him . . . You can't blame the guy — Jim Grayson. I don't want nobody stickin' their finger in my face. I'd've probably hit him beside the head. The whole thing was: Damn it, it's about time we took a stand. Let's stick up for the guy. We stopped the line. (He pauses, grins.) Ford lost about twenty units. I'd figure about five grand a unit — whattaya got? (Laughs.)

34   I said, "Let's all go home." When the line's down like that, you can go up to one man and say, "You gonna work?" If he says no, they can fire him. See what I mean? But if nobody was there, who the hell were they gonna walk up to and say, "Are you gonna work?" Man, there woulda been nobody there! If it were up to me, we'd gone home.

35   Jim Grayson, the guy I work next to, he's colored. Absolutely. That's the first time I've seen unity on that line. Now it's happened once, it'll happen again. Because everybody just sat down. Believe you me. (Laughs.) It stopped at eight and it didn't start till twenty after eight. Everybody and his brother were down there. It was really nice to see, it really was.

____ CONSIDERATIONS _____

1. Terkel is famous for his ability to catch the voice of the poeple he interviews. Study the language of Phil Stallings and list some of the features of his voice.

2. In addition to diction, what about this selection takes it out of the category of "essay"?

3. How does Stallings show that the company puts a higher value on its machines than on its men?

4. Does Stallings agree with what Caroline Bird says in her essay on the value of college (pages 64–73)?

5. What occurrence on the line, described toward the end of the interview, reveals Stallings' social consciousness?

6. Interview someone you find interesting, or, if you're too shy, some imaginary character.

Lewis Thomas (b. 1913) is a medical doctor, teacher, and writer, who lives in New York, where he was born, and where he is now president of the Memorial Sloan-Kettering Cancer Center. Earlier, he taught medicine at the University of Minnesota, was department chairman and dean at New York University-Bellevue, and was a dean at Yale Medical School. We take this essay from Lives of a Cell, *which won a National Book Award in 1975.* The New England Journal of Medicine *originally printed the articles collected in that volume, articles that at the same time make contributions to medicine and to literature. His scientific mind, like the best minds in whatever field, extends itself by language to investigate everything human, and to speculate beyond the human.*

68

LEWIS THOMAS
Ceti

Tau Ceti is a relatively nearby star that sufficiently resembles our sun to make its solar system a plausible candidate for the existence of life. We are, it appears, ready to begin getting in touch with Ceti, and with any other interested celestial body in more remote places, out to the edge. CETI is also, by intention, the acronym of the First International Conference on Communication with Extraterrestrial Intelligence, held in 1972 in Soviet Armenia under the joint sponsorship of the National Academy of Sciences of the United States and the Soviet Academy, which involved eminent physicists and astronomers from various countries, most of whom are convinced that the odds for the existence of life elsewhere are very high, with a reasonable probability that there are civilizations, one place or another, with technologic mastery matching or exceeding ours.

2   On this assumption, the conferees thought it likely that radio-astronomy would be the generally accepted mode of interstellar communication, on grounds of speed and economy. They made a formal recommendation that we organize an international cooperative program, with new and immense radio telescopes, to probe the reaches of deep space for electromagnetic signals making sense. Eventually, we would plan to send out messages on our own and receive answers, but at the outset it seems more practical to begin by catching snatches of conversation between others.

3   So, the highest of all our complex technologies in the hardest of our sciences will soon be engaged, full scale, in what is essentially biologic research — and with some aspects of social science, at that.

4   The earth has become, just in the last decade, too small a place. We have the feeling of being confined — shut in; it is something like outgrowing a small town in a small county. The views of the dark, pocked surface of Mars, still lifeless to judge from the latest photographs, do not seem to have extended our reach; instead, they bring closer, too close, another unsatisfactory feature of our local environment. The blue noonday sky, cloudless, has lost its old look of immensity. The word is out that the sky is not limitless; it is finite. It is, in truth, only a kind of local roof, a membrane under which we live, luminous but confusingly refractile when suffused with sunlight; we can sense its concave surface a few miles over our heads. We know that it is tough and thick enough so that when hard objects strike it from the outside they burst into flames. The color photographs of the earth are more amazing than anything outside: we live inside a blue chamber, a bubble of air blown by ourselves. The other sky beyond, absolutely black and appalling, is wide-open country, irresistible for exploration.

5   Here we go, then. An extraterrestrial embryologist, having a close look at us from time to time, would probably conclude that the morphogenesis of the earth is coming along well, with the beginnings of a nervous system and fair-sized ganglions in the form of cities, and now with specialized, dish-shaped sensory organs, miles across, ready to receive stimuli. He may well wonder, however, how we will go about responding. We are evolving into the situation of a Skinner pigeon in a Skinner box, peering about in all directions, trying to make connections, probing.

6   When the first word comes in from outer space, finally, we will probably be used to the idea. We can already provide a quite good explanation for the origin of life, here or elsewhere. Given a moist planet with methane, formaldehyde, ammonia, and some usable min-

erals, all of which abound, exposed to lightning or ultraviolet irradiation at the right temperature, life might start off almost anywhere. The tricky, unsolved thing is how to get the polymers to arrange in membranes and invent replication. The rest is clear going. If they follow our protocol, it will be anaerobic life at first, then photosynthesis and the first exhalation of oxygen, then respiring life and the great burst of variation, then speciation, and, finally, some kind of consciousness. It is easy, in the telling.

I suspect that when we have recovered from the first easy acceptance of signs of life from elsewhere, and finished nodding at each other, and finished smiling, we will be in shock. We have had it our way, relatively speaking, being unique all these years, and it will be hard to deal with the thought that the whole, infinitely huge, spinning, clocklike apparatus around us is itself animate, and can sprout life whenever the conditions are right. We will respond, beyond doubt, by making connections after the fashion of established life, floating out our filaments, extending pili, but we will end up feeling smaller than ever, as small as a single cell, with a quite new sense of continuity. It will take some getting used to. 7

The immediate problem, however, is a much more practical, down-to-earth matter, and must be giving insomnia to the CETI participants. Let us assume that there is, indeed, sentient life in one or another part of remote space, and that we will be successful in getting in touch with it. What on earth are we going to talk about? If, as seems likely, it is a hundred or more light years away, there are going to be some very long pauses. The barest amenities, on which we rely for opening conversations — Hello, are you there?, from us, followed by Yes, hello, from them — will take two hundred years at least. By the time we have our party we may have forgotten what we had in mind. 8

We could begin by gambling on the rightness of our technology and just send out news of ourselves, like a mimeographed Christmas letter, but we would have to choose our items carefully, with durability of meaning in mind. Whatever information we provide must still make sense to us two centuries later, and must still seem important, or the conversation will be an embarrassment to all concerned. In two hundred years it is, as we have found, easy to lose the thread. 9

Perhaps the safest thing to do at the outset, if technology permits, is to send music. This language may be the best we have for explaining what we are like to others in space, with least ambiguity. I would vote for Bach, all of Bach, streamed out into space, over and over again. We would be bragging, of course, but it is surely excusable for us to put the best possible face on at the beginning of such an acquaintance. We 10 can tell the harder truths later. And, to do ourselves justice, music would give a fairer picture of what we are really like than some of the other things we might be sending, like *Time,* say, or a history of the U.N. or Presidential speeches. We could send out our science, of course, but just think of the wincing at this end when the polite comments arrive two hundred years from now. Whatever we offer as today's items of liveliest interest are bound to be out of date and irrelevant, maybe even ridiculous. I think we should stick to music.

11   Perhaps, if the technology can be adapted to it, we should send some paintings. Nothing would better describe what this place is like, to an outsider, than the Cézanne demonstrations that an apple is really part fruit, part earth.

12   What kinds of questions should we ask? The choices will be hard, and everyone will want his special question first. What are your smallest particles? Did you think yourselves unique? Do you have colds? Have you anything quicker than light? Do you always tell the truth? Do you cry? There is no end to the list.

13   Perhaps we should wait a while, until we are sure we know what we want to know, before we get down to detailed questions. After all, the main question will be the opener: Hello, are you there? If the reply should turn out to be Yes, hello, we might want to stop there and think about that, for quite a long time. .

_____ CONSIDERATIONS _____

1. If you were to decide on our first communication with life in outer space, what message would you send? Why?

2. Why must people working on interplanetary communication keep time in mind?

3. Like Loren Eiseley (see pages 140–146), Thomas skillfully uses figurative language to help us see what he is talking about. Consider, for example, his description of our sky in Paragraph 4.

4. Point out some stylistic features in Thomas's essay that account for the highly informal, even jaunty tone.

5. Thomas touches on the shock we will feel when we have proof that mankind is not, after all, unique. What does he mean by saying "we will end up feeling smaller than ever, as small as a single cell, with quite a new sense of continuity"?

6. Why Bach rather than The Beatles or Bob Dylan?

7. How seriously do science fiction stories like *Star Wars* confront the questions raised by Thomas?

Henry David Thoreau (1817–1862) is one of the greatest American writers, and Walden *one of the great American books. Thoreau attended Concord Academy, in the Massachusetts town where he was born and lived. Then he went to Harvard and completed his formal education, which was extensive in mathematics, literature, Greek, Latin, and French — and included smatterings of Spanish and Italian and some of the literature of India and China. He and his brother founded a school that lasted four years, and then he was a private tutor to a family. He also worked for his father, manufacturing pencils. But mostly Thoreau walked, meditated, observed nature, and wrote.*

A friend of Ralph Waldo Emerson's, Thoreau was influenced by the older man, and by Transcendentalism — a doctrine that recognized the unity of man and nature. For Thoreau, an idea required testing by life itself; it never remained merely mental. In his daily work on his journals, and in the books he carved from them — A Week on the Concord and Merrimack Rivers *(1849) as well as* Walden *(1854) — he observed the detail of daily life, human and natural, and he speculated on the universal laws he could derive from this observation.*

The paragraphs below come from Walden, *the book Thoreau wrote about his experience of living by himself, alone in the natural world, on the shores of Walden Pond in Concord. He had resolved — this civilized man of the nineteenth century, learned and cultured and educated — "to drive life into a corner, and reduce it to its lowest terms, and, if it be proven to be mean, why then to get the whole and genuine meanness of it, and publish its meanness to the world; and if it were sublime, to know it by experience, and be able to give a true account of it."*

"To know it by experience, and be able to give a true account of it" *— these words could be carved on Thoreau's gravestone. "To give a true account" he became a great writer, a master in particular of the long, inclusive sentence, which, built of many descriptive phrases and subordinate clauses, controls the position of observed detail, and sets the parts of a world in clear relation to each other.*

69

HENRY DAVID THOREAU
To Build My House

1   Near the end of March, 1845, I borrowed an axe and went down to the woods by Walden Pond, nearest to where I intended to build my house, and began to cut down some tall arrowy white pines, still in their youth, for timber. It is difficult to begin without borrowing, but perhaps it is the most generous course thus to permit your fellow-men to have an interest in your enterprise. The owner of the axe, as he released his hold on it, said that it was the apple of his eye; but I returned it sharper than I received it. It was a pleasant hillside where I worked, covered with pine woods, through which I looked out on the pond, and a small open field in the woods where pines and hickories were springing up. The ice in the pond was all dark colored and saturated with water. There were some slight flurries of snow during the days that I worked there; but for the most part when I came out on to the railroad, on my way home, its yellow sand heap stretched away gleaming in the hazy atmosphere, and the rails shone in the spring sun, and I heard the lark and pewee and other birds already come to commence another year with us. They were pleasant spring days, in which the winter of man's discontent was thawing as well as the earth, and the life that had lain torpid began to stretch itself. One day, when my axe had come off and I had cut a green hickory for a wedge, driving it with a stone, and had placed the whole to soak in a pond hole in order to swell the wood, I saw a striped snake run into the water, and he lay on the bottom, apparently without inconvenience, as long as I staid there, or more than a quarter of an hour; perhaps because he had not yet fairly come out of the torpid state. It appeared to me that for a like reason men remain in their present low and primitive condition;

but if they should feel the influence of the spring of springs arousing them, they would of necessity rise to a higher and more ethereal life. I had previously seen the snakes in frosty mornings in my path with portions of their bodies still numb and inflexible, waiting for the sun to thaw them. On the 1st of April it rained and melted the ice, and in the early part of the day, which was very foggy, I heard a stray goose groping about over the pond and cackling as if lost, or like the spirit of the fog.

So I went on for some days cutting and hewing timber, and also studs and rafters, all with my narrow axe, not having many communicable or scholar-like thoughts, singing to myself — 2

> Men say they know many things;
> But lo! they have taken wings, —
> The arts and sciences,
> And a thousand appliances;
> The wind that blows
> Is all that any body knows.

I hewed the main timbers six inches square, most of the studs on two sides only, and the rafters and floor timbers on one side, leaving the rest of the bark on, so that they were just as straight and much stronger than sawed ones. Each stick was carefully mortised or tenoned by its stump, for I had borrowed other tools by this time. My days in the woods were not very long ones; yet I usually carried my dinner of bread and butter, and read the newspaper in which it was wrapped, at noon, sitting amid the green pine boughs which I had cut off, and to my bread was imparted some of their fragrance, for my hands were covered with a thick coat of pitch. Before I had done I was more the friend than the foe of the pine tree, though I had cut down some of them, having become better acquainted with it. Sometimes a rambler in the wood was attracted by the sound of my axe, and we chatted pleasantly over the chips which I had made.

By the middle of April, for I made no haste in my work, but rather made the most of it, my house was framed and ready for the raising. I had already bought the shanty of James Collins, an Irishman who worked on the Fitchburg Railroad, for boards. James Collins' shanty was considered an uncommonly fine one. When I called to see it he was not at home. I walked about the outside, at first unobserved from within, the window was so deep and high. It was of small dimensions, 3 with a peaked cottage roof, and not much else to be seen, the dirt being raised five feet all around as if it were a compost heap. The roof was the soundest part, though a good deal warped and made brittle by the sun. Doorsill there was none, but a perennial passage for the hens under the door board. Mrs. C. came to the door and asked me to view it from the inside. The hens were driven in by my approach. It was dark, and had a dirt floor for the most part, dank, clammy, and aguish, only here a board and there a board which would not bear removal. She lighted a lamp to show me the inside of the roof and the walls, and also that the board floor extended under the bed, warning me not to step into the cellar, a sort of dust hole two feet deep. In her own words, they were "good boards overhead, good boards all around and a good window," — of two whole squares originally, only the cat had passed out that way lately. There was a stove, a bed, and a place to sit, an infant in the house where it was born, a silk parasol, gilt-framed looking-glass, and a patent new coffee mill nailed to an oak sapling, all told. The bargain was soon concluded, for James had in the meanwhile returned. I to pay four dollars and twenty-five cents tonight, he to vacate at five tomorrow morning, selling to nobody else meanwhile: I to take possession at six. It were well, he said, to be there early, and anticipate certain indistinct but wholly unjust claims on the score of ground rent and fuel. This he assured me was the only encumbrance. At six I passed him and his family on the road. One large bundle held their all, — bed, coffee-mill, looking glass, hens, — all but the cat, she took to the woods and became a wild cat, and, as I learned afterward, trod in a trap set for woodchucks, and so became a dead cat at last.

4   I took down this dwelling the same morning, drawing the nails, and removed it to the pond side by small cart-loads, spreading the boards on the grass there to bleach and warp back again in the sun. One early thrush gave me a note or two as I drove along the woodland path. I was informed treacherously by a young Patrick that neighbor Seeley, an Irishman, in the intervals of the carting, transferred the still tolerable, straight, and drivable nails, staples, and spikes to his pocket, and then stood when I came back to pass the time of day, and look freshly up, unconcerned, with spring thoughts, at the devastation; there being a dearth of work, as he said. He was there to represent spectatordom, and help make this seemingly insignificant event one with the removal of the gods of Troy.

5   I dug my cellar in the side of a hill sloping to the south, where a woodchuck had formerly dug his burrow, down through sumach and

blackberry roots, and the lowest stain of vegetation, six feet square by seven deep, to a fine sand where potatoes would not freeze in any winter. The sides were left shelving, and not stoned; but the sun having never shone on them, the sand still keeps its place. It was but two hours' work. I took particular pleasure in this breaking of ground, for in almost all latitudes men dig into the earth for an equable temperature. Under the most splendid house in the city is still to be found the cellar where they store their roots as of old, and long after the superstructure has disappeared posterity remark its dent in the earth. The house is still but a sort of porch at the entrance of a burrow.

At length, in the beginning of May, with the help of some of my acquaintances, rather to improve so good an occasion for neighborliness than from any necessity, I set up the frame of my house. No man was ever more honored in the character of his raisers than I. They are destined, I trust, to assist at the raising of loftier structures one day. I began to occupy my house on the 4th of July, as soon as it was boarded and roofed, for the boards were carefully feather-edged and lapped, so that it was perfectly impervious to rain; but before boarding I laid the foundation of a chimney at one end, bringing two cartloads of stones up the hill from the pond in my arms. I built the chimney after my hoeing in the fall, before a fire became necessary for warmth, doing my cooking in the mean while out of doors on the ground, early in the morning: which mode I still think is in some respects more convenient and agreeable than the usual one. When it stormed before my bread was baked, I fixed a few boards over the fire, and sat under them to watch my loaf, and passed some pleasant hours in that way. In those days, when my hands were much employed, I read but little, but the least scraps of paper which lay on the ground, my holder, or tablecloth, afforded me as much entertainment, in fact answered the same purpose as the Iliad.

It would be worth the while to build still more deliberately than I did, considering, for instance, what foundation a door, a window, a cellar, a garret, have in the nature of man, and perchance never raising any superstructure until we found a better reason for it than our temporal necessities even. There is some of the same fitness in a man's building his own house that there is in a bird's building its own nest. Who knows but if men constructed their dwellings with their own hands, and provided food for themselves and families simply and honestly enough, the poetic faculty would be universally developed, as

birds universally sing when they are so engaged? But alas! we do like
cowbirds and cuckoos, which lay their eggs in nests which other birds
have built, and cheer no traveller with their chattering and unmusical
notes. Shall we forever resign the pleasure of construction to the carpenter? What does architecture amount to in the experience of the
mass of men? I never in all my walks came across a man engaged in so
simple and natural an occupation as building his house. We belong to
the community. It is not the tailor alone who is the ninth part of a
man, it is as much the preacher, and the merchant, and the farmer.
Where is this division of labor to end? and what object does it finally
serve? No doubt another *may* also think for me; but it is not therefore
desirable that he should do so to the exclusion of my thinking for
myself.

8   True, there are architects so called in this country, and I have
heard of one at least possessed with the idea of making architectural
ornaments have a core of truth, a necessity, and hence a beauty, as if it
were a revelation to him. All very well perhaps from his point of view,
but only a little better than the common dilettantism. A sentimental
reformer in architecture, he began at the cornice, not at the foundation.
It was only how to put a core of truth within the ornaments, that every
sugar plum in fact might have an almond or caraway seed in it, —
though I hold that almonds are most wholesome without the sugar —
and not how the inhabitant, the indweller, might build truly within
and without, and let the ornaments take care of themselves. What
reasonable man ever supposed that ornaments were something outward and in the skin merely, — that the tortoise got his spotted shell,
or the shellfish its mother-o'-pearl tints by such a contract as the
inhabitants of Broadway their Trinity Church? But a man has no more
to do with the style of architecture of his house than a tortoise with
that of its shell: nor need the soldier be so idle as to try to paint the
precise *color* of his virtue on his standard. The enemy will find it out.
He may turn pale when the trial comes. This man seemed to me to
lean over the cornice, and timidly whisper his half truth to the rude
occupants who really knew it better than he. What of architectural
beauty I now see, I know has gradually grown from within outward,
out of the necessities and character of the indweller, who is the only
builder — out of some unconscious truthfulness, and nobleness, without ever a thought for the appearance; and whatever additional beauty
of this kind is destined to be produced will be preceded by a like
unconscious beauty of life. The most interesting dwellings in this

country, as the painter knows, are the most unpretending, humble log huts and cottages of the poor commonly; it is the life of the inhabitants whose shells they are, and not any peculiarity in their surfaces merely, which makes them *picturesque;* and equally interesting will be the citizen's suburban box, when his life shall be as simple and as agreeable to the imagination, and there is as little straining after effect in the style of his dwelling. A great proportion of architectural ornaments are literally hollow, and a September gale would strip them off, like borrowed plumes, without inquiry to the substantials. They can do without *architecture* who have no olives nor wines in the cellar. What if an equal ado were made about the ornaments of style in literature, and the architects of our bibles spent as much time about their cornices as the architects of our churches do? So are made the *belles-lettres* and the *beaux-arts* and their professors. Much it concerns a man, forsooth, how a few sticks are slanted over him or under him and what colors are daubed upon his box. It would signify somewhat, if, in any earnest sense, *he* slanted them and daubed it; but the spirit having departed out of the tenant, it is of a piece with constructing his own coffin, — the architecture of the grave, and "carpenter," is but another name for "coffin-maker." One man says, in his despair or indifference to life, take up handful of the earth at your feet, and paint your house that color. Is he thinking of his last and narrow house? Toss up a copper for it as well. What an abundance of leisure he must have! Why do you take up a handful of dirt? Better paint your house your own complexion; let it turn pale or blush for you. An enterprise to improve the style of cottage architecture! When you have got my ornaments ready I will wear them.

Before winter I built a chimney, and shingled the sides of my 9 house, which were already impervious to rain, with imperfect and sappy shingles made of the first slice of the log, whose edges I was obliged to straighten with a plane.

I have thus a tight shingled and plastered house, ten feet wide by 10 fifteen long, and eight-feet posts, with a garret and a closet, a large window on each side, two trap doors, one door at the end, and a brick fireplace opposite. The exact cost of my house, paying the usual price for such materials as I used, but not counting the work, all of which was done by myself, was as follows; and I give the details because very few are able to tell exactly what their houses cost, and fewer still, if any, the separate cost of the various materials which compose them: —

Boards	$8 03½,	mostly shanty boards.
Refuse shingles for roof		
and sides,	4 00	
Laths,	1 25	
Two second-hand		
windows with glass,	2 43	
One thousand old brick,	4 00	
Two casks of lime,	2 40	That was high.
Hair,	0 31	More than I needed.
Mantle-tree iron,	0 15	
Nails,	3 90	
Hinges and screws,	0 14	
Latch,	0 10	
Chalk,	0 01	
Transportation,	1 40	I carried a good part on my back.
In all,	$28 12½	

11   These are all the materials excepting the timber, stones and sand, which I claimed by squatter's right. I have also a small wood-shed adjoining, made chiefly of the stuff which was left after building the house.

12   I intend to build me a house which will surpass any on the main street in Concord in grandeur and luxury, as soon as it pleases me as much and will cost me no more than my present one.

13   I thus found that the student who wishes for a shelter can obtain one for a lifetime at an expense not greater than the rent which he now pays annually. If I seem to boast more than is becoming, my excuse is that I brag for humanity rather than for myself; and my shortcomings and inconsistencies do not affect the truth of my statement. Notwithstanding much cant and hypocrisy, — chaff which I find it difficult to separate from my wheat, but for which I am as sorry as any man, — I will breathe freely and stretch myself in this respect, it is such a relief to both the moral and physical system; and I am resolved that I will not through humility become the devil's attorney. I will endeavor to speak a good word for the truth. At Cambridge College the mere rent of a student's room, which is only a little larger than my own, is thirty dollars each year, though the corporation had the advantage of building thirty-two side by side and under one roof, and the occupant suffers

the inconvenience of many and noisy neighbors, and perhaps a residence in the fourth story. I cannot but think that if we had more true wisdom in these respects, not only less education would be needed, because, forsooth, more would already have been acquired, but the pecuniary expense of getting an education would in a great measure vanish. Those conveniences which the student requires at Cambridge or elsewhere cost him or somebody else ten times as great a sacrifice of life as they would with proper management on both sides. Those things for which the most money is demanded are never the things which the student most wants. Tuition, for instance, is an important item in the term bill, while for the far more valuable education which he gets by associating with the most cultivated of his contemporaries no charge is made. The mode of founding a college is, commonly, to get up a subscription of dollars, and cents, and then following blindly the principles of a division of labor to its extreme, a principle which should never be followed but with circumspection, — to call in a contractor who makes this a subject of speculation, and he employs Irishmen or other operatives actually to lay the foundation, while the students that are to be are said to be fitting themselves for it; and for these oversights successive generations have to pay. I think that it would be *better than this,* for the students, or those who desire to be benefited by it, even to lay the foundation themselves. The student who secures his coveted leisure and retirement by systemically shirking any labor necessary to man obtains but an ignoble and unprofitable leisure, defrauding himself of the experience which alone can make leisure fruitful. "But," says one, "you do not mean that the students should go to work with their hands instead of their heads?" I do not mean that exactly, but I mean something which he might think a good deal like that; I mean that they should not *play* life, or *study* it merely, while the community supports them at this expensive game, but earnestly *live* it from beginning to end. How could youths better learn to live than by at once trying the experiment of living? Methinks this would exercise their minds as much as mathematics. If I wished a boy to know something about the arts and sciences, for instance, I would not pursue the common course, which is merely to send him into the neighborhood of some professor, where any thing is professed and practised but the art of life; — to survey the world through a telescope or a microscope, and never with his natural eye; to study chemistry, and not learn how his bread is made, or mechanics, and not learn how it is earned; to discover new satellites to Neptune, and not detect the motes in his eyes, or to what vagabond he is a satellite himself; or to be devoured by the monsters that swarm all around him, while contemplating the monsters in a drop of vinegar. Which would have advanced the most at the end of a month, — the boy who had made his own jackknife from the ore which he had dug and smelted, reading as much as would be necessary for this, — or the boy who had attended the lectures on metallurgy at the Institute in the mean while, and had received a Rogers' penknife from his father? Which would be most likely to cut his fingers? . . . To my astonishment I was informed on leaving college that I had studied navigation! — why, if I had taken one turn down the harbor I should have known more about it. Even the *poor* student studies and is taught only *political* economy, while that economy of living which is synonymous with philosophy is not even sincerely professed in our colleges. The consequence is, that while he is reading Adam Smith, Ricardo, and Say, he runs his father in debt irretrievably.

14   As with our colleges, so with a hundred "modern improvements;" there is an illusion about them; there is not always a positive advance. The devil goes on exacting compound interest to the last for his early share and numerous succeeding investments in them. Our inventions are wont to be pretty toys, which distract our attention from serious things. They are but too improved means to an improved end, an end which was already but too easy to arrive at; as railroads lead to Boston or New York. We are in great haste to construct a magnetic telegraph from Maine to Texas; but Maine and Texas, it may be, have nothing important to communicate. Either is in such a predicament as the man who was earnest to be introduced to a distinguished deaf woman, but when he was presented, and one end of her ear trumpet was put into his hand, had nothing to say. As if the main object were to talk fast and not to talk sensibly. We are eager to tunnel under the Atlantic and bring the old world some weeks nearer to the new; but perchance the first news that will leak through into the broad flapping American ear will be that the Princess Adelaide has the whooping cough. After all, the man whose horse trots a mile in a minute does not carry the most important messages; he is not an evangelist, nor does he come round eating locusts and wild honey. I doubt if Flying Childers[1] ever carried a peck of corn to mill.

---

[1] According to Walter Harding, Secretary of the Thoreau Society, Flying Childers was a famous race horse in 18th century England, owned by a Mr. Childers of Carr House, and reputed to have been able to run a mile in one minute. — ED.

——— CONSIDERATIONS ————————————————————————

1. Like many of his contemporaries, Thoreau kept extensive journals and from these culled prized sentences upon which he built many paragraphs, essays, and portions of books, including *Walden*. In this selection from *Walden*, pick three of four sentences you think especially memorable. Explain why they seem exceptional.

2. Thoreau's sentences are rarely short and simple, and yet they are renowned for clarity. Study an especially complex sentence and observe how he manages its several parts. Rewrite it by breaking it down into three or four short sentences. Compare and contrast the two versions.

3. Thoreau is describing a specific project — how he built his house — yet he does not hesitate to include reflections on such large subjects as human nature. Finding an example, comment on his success in combining the particular and the general.

4. When did Thoreau move into his house? Is anything symbolic about that date and that circumstance? What do you understand by "symbolic"?

5. What did Thoreau read during the early days of his occupancy? What is his curious remark about that reading material (remember that Thoreau was a student of classical literature)?

6. Why does Thoreau give us the cost of the materials for his house? In what way does that list expose an important thematic thread that is woven through the selection?

James Thurber (1894–1961) was born in Columbus, Ohio, the scene of many of his funniest stories. He graduated from Ohio State University, and after a period as a newspaper man in Paris, began to work for The New Yorker. *For years his comic writing and his cartoons — drawings of sausage-shaped dogs and of men and women forever at battle — were fixtures of that magazine. His collections of essays, short stories, and cartoons include* The Owl in the Attic and Other Perplexities *(1931),* The Seal in the Bedroom and Other Predicaments *(1932),* My Life and Hard Times *(1933),* Men, Women, and Dogs *(1943), and* Alarms and Diversions *(1957). He also wrote an account of life on* The New Yorker *staff,* The Years with Ross *(1959).*

An elegant stylist, Thurber was always fussy about language. "Which" is an example not only of his fascination with language — which became obsessive at times — but also of his humor.

70

JAMES THURBER
Which

1   The relative pronoun "which" can cause more trouble than any other word, if recklessly used. Foolhardy persons sometimes get lost in which-clauses and are never heard of again. My distinguished contemporary, Fowler, cites several tragic cases, of which the following is one: "It was rumoured that Beaconsfield intended opening the Conference with a speech in French, his pronunciation of which language leaving everything to be desired . . ." That's as much as Mr. Fowler quotes because, at his age, he was afraid to go any farther. The young man who originally got into that sentence was never found. His fate, how-

ever, was not as terrible as that of another adventurer who became involved in a remarkable which-mire. Fowler has followed his devious course as far as he safely could on foot: "Surely what applies to games should also apply to racing, the leaders of which being the very people from whom an example might well be looked for . . ." Not even Henry James could have successfully emerged from a sentence with "which," "whom," and "being" in it. The safest way to avoid such things is to follow in the path of the American author, Ernest Hemingway. In his youth he was trapped in a which-clause one time and barely escaped with his mind. He was going along on solid ground until he got into this: "It was the one thing of which, being very much afraid — for whom has not been warned to fear such things — he . . ." Being a young and powerfully built man, Hemingway was able to fight his way back to where he had started, and begin again. This time he skirted the treacherous morass in this way: "He was afraid of one thing. This was the one thing. He had been warned to fear such things. Everybody has been warned to fear such things." Today Hemingway is alive and well, and many happy writers are following along the trail he blazed.

What most people don't realize is that one "which" leads to 2 another. Trying to cross a paragraph by leaping from "which" to "which" is like Eliza crossing the ice. The danger is in missing a "which" and falling in. A case in point is this: "He went up to a pew which was in the gallery, which brought him under a colored window which he loved and always quieted his spirit." The writer, worn out, missed the last "which" — the one that should come just before "always" in that sentence. But supposing he had got it in! We would have: "He went up to a pew which was in the gallery, which brought him under a colored window which he loved and which always quieted his spirit." Your inveterate whicher in this way gives the effect of tweeting like a bird or walking with a crutch, and is not welcome in the best company.

It is well to remember that one "which" leads to two and that 3 two "whiches" multiply like rabbits. You should never start out with the idea that you can get by with one "which." Suddenly they are all around you. Take a sentence like this: "It imposes a problem which we either solve, or perish." On a hot night, or after a hard day's work, a man often lets himself get by with a monstrosity like that, but suppose he dictates that sentence bright and early in the morning. It comes to him typed out by his stenographer and he instantly senses that something is the matter with it. He tries to reconstruct the sentence, still clinging to the "which," and gets something like this: "It imposes a problem which we either solve, or which, failing to solve, we must perish on account of." He goes to the water-cooler, gets a drink, sharpens his pencil, and grimly tries again. "It imposes a problem which we either solve or which we don't solve and . . ." He begins once more: "It imposes a problem which we either solve, or which we do not solve, and from which . . ." The more times he does it the more "whiches" he gets. The way out is simple: "We must either solve this problem, or perish." Never monkey with "which." Nothing except getting tangled up in a typewriter ribbon is worse.

—— CONSIDERATIONS ————————————————————

1. James Thurber concentrates on one word from an important class of function words. These relative pronouns often complicate life for the writer wishing to write clear sentences more complex than "I see Spot. Spot is a dog. Spot sees me." What other words belong to this class? Do you find any of them tripping you up in your sentences?

2. A grammar lesson may seem a peculiar place to find humor, but humor is Thurber's habit, whatever his subject. How does he make his treatment of the relative pronoun "which" entertaining?

3. The "Fowler" Thurber mentions is H. W. Fowler, author of *A Dictionary of Modern English Usage,* a trusted standby for writers through its many editions. It is also opinionated, sophisticated, and tartly amusing. Discover its worth for yourself by consulting a copy in your college library.

4. "One 'which' leads to another" is a play on the old saying, "One drink leads to another." Consider how changing one word can revive a thought that George Orwell would call a hackneyed phrase. See how it is done by substituting a key word in several familiar sayings.

5. The two writers Thurber mentions, Henry James and Ernest Hemingway, are not idly chosen. Why not?

Mark Twain is the pseudonym of Samuel Clemens (1835–1910) who wrote Tom Sawyer *(1876),* Huckleberry Finn *(1884), and other novels, as well as short stories, essays, and an autobiography. Born in Missouri, he settled with his wife in Hartford, Connecticut; at his best he wrote out of his midwestern past. Twain's humor disguised his gloom, and the misanthrophy that grew in his later years. The lightness of this essay's tone thinly covers Twain's rage and contempt. His sense of man's littleness makes his vision modern.*

71

MARK TWAIN
Was the World Made for Man?

Alfred Russell Wallace's revival of the theory that this earth is at the centre of the stellar universe, and is the only habitable globe, has aroused great interest in the world / LITERARY DIGEST

For ourselves we do thoroughly believe that man, as he lives just here on this tiny earth, is in essence and possibilities the most sublime existence in all the range of non-divine being — the chief love and delight of God. / Chicago "INTERIOR" *(Presb.)*

I seem to be the only scientist and theologian still remaining to   1
be heard from on this important matter of whether the world was made for man or not. I feel that it is time for me to speak.

I stand almost with the others. They believe the world was made   2
for man, I believe it likely that it was made for man; they think there

is proof, astronomical mainly, that it was made for man, I think there is evidence only, not proof, that it was made for him. It is too early, yet, to arrange the verdict, the returns are not all in. When they are all in, I think they will show that the world was made for man; but we must not hurry, we must patiently wait till they are all in.

3   Now as far as we have got, astronomy is on our side. Mr. Wallace has clearly shown this. He has clearly shown two things: that the world was made for man, and that the universe was made for the world — to stiddy it, you know. The astronomy part is settled, and cannot be challenged.

4   We come now to the geological part. This is the one where the evidence is not all in, yet. It is coming in, hourly, daily, coming in all the time, but naturally it comes with geological carefulness and deliberation, and we must not be impatient, we must not get excited, we must be calm, and wait. To lose our tranquillity will not hurry geology; nothing hurries geology.

5   It takes a long time to prepare a world for man, such a thing is not done in a day. Some of the great scientists, carefully ciphering the evidences furnished by geology, have arrived at the conviction that our world is prodigiously old, and they may be right, but Lord Kelvin is not of their opinion. He takes a cautious, conservative view, in order to be on the safe side, and feels sure it is not so old as they think. As Lord Kelvin is the highest authority in science now living, I think we must yield to him and accept his view. He does not concede that the world is more than a hundred million years old. He believes it is that old, but not older. Lyell believed that our race was introduced into the world 31,000 years ago, Herbert Spencer makes it 32,000. Lord Kelvin agrees with Spencer.

6   Very well. According to these figures it took 99,968,000 years to prepare the world for man, impatient as the Creator doubtless was to see him and admire him. But a large enterprise like this has to be conducted warily, painstakingly, logically. It was foreseen that man would have to have the oyster. Therefore the first preparation was made for the oyster. Very well, you cannot make an oyster out of whole cloth, you must make the oyster's ancestor first. This is not done in a day. You must make a vast variety of invertebrates, to start with — belemnites, trilobites, Jebusites, Amalekites, and that sort of fry; and put them to soak in a primary sea, and wait and see what will happen. Some will be a disappointment — the belemnites, the Ammonites and such; they will be failures, they will die out and become extinct, in the course of the nineteen million years covered by

the experiment, but all is not lost, for the Amalekites will fetch the homestake; they will develop gradually into encrinites, and stalacites, and blatherskites, and one thing and another as the mighty ages creep on and the Archaean and the Cambrian Periods pile their lofty crags in the primordial seas, and at last the first grand stage in the preparation of the world for man stands completed, the oyster is done. An oyster has hardly any more reasoning power than a scientist has; and so it is reasonably certain that this one jumped to the conclusion that the nineteen million years was a preparation for *him*; but that would be just like an oyster, which is the most conceited animal there is, except man. And anyway, this one could not know, at that early date, that he was only an incident in a scheme, and that there was some more to the scheme, yet.

The oyster being achieved, the next thing to be arranged for in 7 the preparation of the world for man was fish. Fish and coal — to fry it with. So the Old Silurian seas were opened up to breed the fish in, and at the same time the great work of building Old Red Sandstone mountains eighty thousand feet high to cold-storage their fossils in was begun. This latter was quite indispensable, for there would be no end of failures again, no end of extinctions — millions of them — and it would be cheaper and less trouble to can them in the rocks than keep tally of them in a book. One does not build the coal beds and eighty thousand feet of perpendicular Old Red Sandstone in a brief time — no, it took twenty million years. In the first place, a coal bed is a slow and troublesome and tiresome thing to construct. You have to grow prodigious forests of tree-ferns and reeds and calamites and such things in a marshy region; then you have to sink them under out of sight and let them rot; then you have to turn the streams on them, so as to bury them under several feet of sediment, and the sediment must have time to harden and turn to rock; next you must grow another forest on top, then sink it and put on another layer of sediment and harden it; then more forest and more rock, layer upon layer, three miles deep — ah, indeed it is a sickening slow job to build a coal-measure and do it right!

So the millions of years drag on; and meantime the fish culture is 8 lazying along and frazzling out in a way to make a person tired. You have developed ten thousand kinds of fishes from the oyster; and come to look, you have raised nothing but fossils, nothing but extinctions. There is nothing left alive and progressive but a ganoid or two and perhaps half a dozen asteroids. Even the cat wouldn't eat such.

Still, it is no great matter; there is plenty of time, yet, and they 9 will develop into something tasty before man is ready for them. Even a ganoid can be depended on for that, when he is not going to be called on for sixty million years.

10   The Paleozoic time limit having now been reached, it was necessary to begin the next stage in the preparation of the world for man, by opening up the Mesozoic Age and instituting some reptiles. For man would need reptiles. Not to eat, but to develop himself from. This being the most important detail of the scheme, a spacious liberality of time was set apart for it — thirty million years. What wonders followed! From the remaining ganoids and asteroids and alkaloids were developed by slow and steady and painstaking culture those stupendous saurians that used to prowl about the steamy world in those remote ages, with their snaky heads reared forty feet in the air and sixty feet of body and tail racing and thrashing after. All gone, now, alas — all extinct, except the little handful of Arkansawrians left stranded and lonely with us here upon this far-flung verge and fringe of time.

11   Yes, it took thirty million years and twenty million reptiles to get one that would stick long enough to develop into something else and let the scheme proceed to the next step.

12   Then the pterodactyl burst upon the world in all his impressive solemnity and grandeur, and all Nature recognized that the Cenozoic threshold was crossed and a new Period open for business, a new stage begun in the preparation of the globe for man. It may be that the pterodactyl thought the thirty million years had been intended as a preparation for himself, for there was nothing too foolish for a pterodactyl to imagine, but he was in error, the preparation was for man. Without doubt the pterodactyl attracted great attention, for even the least observant could see that there was the making of a bird in him. And so it turned out. Also the makings of a mammal, in time. One thing we have to say to his credit, that in the matter of picturesqueness he was the triumph of his Period; he wore wings and had teeth, and was a starchy and wonderful mixture altogether, a kind of long-distance premonitory symptom of Kipling's marine:

> 'E isn't one o' the reg'lar Line, nor 'e isn't one of the crew,
> 'E's a kind of a giddy harumfrodite — soldier an' sailor too!

13   From this time onward for nearly another thirty million years the preparation moved briskly. From the pterodactyl was developed the bird; from the bird the kangaroo, from the kangaroo the other marsupials; from these the mastodon, the megatherium, the giant sloth, the Irish elk, and all that crowd that you make useful and instructive

fossils out of — then came the first great Ice Sheet, and they all retreated before it and crossed over the bridge at Bering Strait and wandered around over Europe and Asia and died. All except a few, to carry on the preparation with. Six Glacial Periods with two million years between Periods chased these poor orphans up and down and about the earth, from weather to weather — from tropic swelter at the poles to Arctic frost at the equator and back again and to and fro, they never knowing what kind of weather was going to turn up next; and if ever they settled down anywhere the whole continent suddenly sank under them without the least notice and they had to trade places with the fishes and scramble off to where the seas had been, and scarcely a dry rag on them; and when there was nothing else doing a volcano would let go and fire them out from wherever they had located. They led this unsettled and irritating life for twenty-five million years, half the time afloat, half the time aground, and always wondering what it was all for, they never suspecting, of course, that it was a preparation for man and had to be done just so or it wouldn't be any proper and harmonious place for him when he arrived.

And at last came the monkey, and anybody could see that man   14
wasn't far off, now. And in truth that was so. The monkey went on developing for close upon five million years, and then turned into a man — to all appearances.

Such is the history of it. Man has been here 32,000 years. That it   15
took a hundred million years to prepare the world for him is proof that that is what it was done for. I suppose it is. I dunno. If the Eiffel Tower were now representing the world's age, the skin of paint on the pinnacle-knob at its summit would represent man's share of that age; and anybody would perceive that that skin was what the tower was built for. I reckon they would, I dunno.

_____ CONSIDERATIONS _____

1. How and when does Twain let us know what he is up to in this essay?

2. Twain urges us, as we study the history of man and the world, to be patient, to be calm, to jump to no conclusions. Note how he uses the oyster (Paragraph 6) and the pterodactyl (Paragraph 12) to strengthen his point.

3. Among Twain's characteristics as a humorist was his fondness for inventing words. Make a list of half a dozen invented words and consider how they are funny and what part they play in his satire.

4. "Was the World Made for Man?" begins with two epigraphs: quotations selected by the author and used to state or hint at the central theme or

image of the piece. What other authors in this book use epigraphs? To learn the uses and limitations of this literary device, select epigraphs for one or two essays in this book. Consult Barlett's *Quotations* for a little assistance.

5. One characteristic of satire is the use of gross exaggeration (see Jonathan Swift's "A Modest Proposal," pages 378–385). Is exaggeration a feature of Twain's essay?

6. Twain uses the Eiffel Tower to help us get some idea of the length of time and the complexity of man's history. Setting aside his satirical motives for a moment, observe that Twain is doing what every good writer tries to do: he presents abstractions in concrete terms. Try the technique yourself by inventing a concrete way of giving a child some notion of infinity, or eternity, or the distance from here to the sun.

7. Read Lewis Thomas's essay, "Ceti" (pages 395–398), and then decide whether that scientist would agree or disagree with Twain's "scientific" account of the evolution of man. Don't lose sight of the fact that Thomas, too, has a sense of humor.

*John Updike (b. 1932) grew up in Pennsylvania and went to
Harvard, where he edited the humor magazine, the* Lampoon. *On
a fellowship year at Oxford, Updike sold a poem to* The New
Yorker *and began his long relationship with that magazine. First
he worked on the staff of* The New Yorker, *contributing to the
"Talk of the Town." When he quit to free-lance, he continued to
write stories, poems, reviews, and articles for the magazine.* The
Poorhouse Fair *(1959), his first novel, appeared in the same year as
his first collection of stories,* The Same Door, *from which we take
"Ace in the Hole." This story appears to be the seed of his second
novel,* Rabbit, Run *(1960) — also about an ex–basketball star with
a deteriorating marriage.*

*Updike has published stories, novels, poems, and two miscel-
laneous collections,* Assorted Prose *(1965) and* Picked-up Pieces
(1975). Among his best-known novels are The Centaur *(1963) and*
Couples *(1968). In "Ace in the Hole," Updike writes with his
usual precision and finish, and with a final image that illuminates
everything that has gone before it, gilding the dross of the present
with a recollected gold.*

72

JOHN UPDIKE
Ace in the Hole

No sooner did his car touch the boulevard heading home than
Ace flicked on the radio. He needed the radio, especially today. In the
seconds before the tubes warmed up, he said aloud, doing it just to hear
a human voice, "Jesus. She'll pop her lid." His voice, though familiar,
irked him; it sounded thin and scratchy, as if the bones in his head
were picking up static. In a deeper register Ace added, "She'll murder

me." Then the radio came on, warm and strong, so he stopped worrying. The Five Kings were doing "Blueberry Hill"; to hear them made Ace feel so sure inside that from the pack pinched between the car roof and the sun shield he plucked a cigarette, hung it on his lower lip, snapped a match across the rusty place on the dash, held the flame in the instinctive spot near the tip of his nose, dragged, and blew out the match, all in time to the music. He rolled down the window and snapped the match so it spun end-over-end into the gutter. "Two points," he said, and cocked the cigarette toward the roof of the car, sucked powerfully, and exhaled two plumes through his nostrils. He was beginning to feel like himself, Ace Anderson, for the first time that whole day, a bad day. He beat time on the accelerator. The car jerked crazily. "On Blueberry Hill," he sang, "my heart stood still. The wind in the wil-low tree" — he braked for a red light — "played love's suh-*weet* melodee — "

"Go, Dad, bust your lungs!" a kid's voice blared. The kid was riding in a '52 Pontiac that had pulled up beside Ace at the light. The profile of the driver, another kid, was dark over his shoulder.

Ace looked over at him and smiled slowly, just letting one side of his mouth lift a little. "Shove it," he said, good-naturedly, across the little gap of years that separated them. He knew how they felt, young and mean and shy.

But the kid, who looked Greek, lifted his thick upper lip and spat out the window. The spit gleamed on the asphalt like a half-dollar.

"Now isn't that pretty?" Ace said, keeping one eye on the light. "You miserable wop. You are *mis*erable." While the kid was trying to think of some smart comeback, the light changed. Ace dug out so hard he smelled burned rubber. In his rear-view mirror he saw the Pontiac lurch forward a few yards, then stop dead, right in the middle of the intersection.

The idea of them stalling their fat tin Pontiac kept him in a good humor all the way home. He decided to stop at his mother's place and pick up the baby, instead of waiting for Evey to do it. His mother must have seen him drive up. She came out on the porch holding a plastic spoon and smelling of cake.

"You're out early," she told him.

"Friedman fired me," Ace told her.

"Good for you," his mother said. "I always said he never treated you right." She brought a cigarette out of her apron pocket and tucked it deep into one corner of her mouth, the way she did when something pleased her.

Ace lighted it for her. "Friedman was O.K. personally," he said. "He just wanted too much for his money. I didn't mind working Saturdays, but until eleven, twelve Friday nights was too much. Everybody has a right to some leisure."

"Well, I don't dare think what Evey will say, but I, for one, thank dear God you had the brains to get out of it. I always said that job had no future to it — no future of any kind, Freddy."

"I guess," Ace admitted. "But I wanted to keep at it, for the family's sake."

"Now, I know I shouldn't be saying this, but any time Evey — this is just between us — any time Evey thinks she can do better, there's room for you *and* Bonnie right in your father's house." She pinched her lips together. He could almost hear the old lady think, *There, I've said it.*

"Look, Mom, Evey tries awfully hard, and anyway you know she can't work that way. Not that *that* — I mean, she's a realist, too . . ." He let the rest of the thought fade as he watched a kid across the street dribbling a basketball around a telephone pole that had a backboard and net nailed on it.

"Evey's a wonderful girl of her own kind. But I've always said, and your father agrees, Roman Catholics ought to marry among themselves. Now I know I've said it before, but when they get out in the greater world — "

"*No*, Mom."

She frowned, smoothed herself, and said, "Your name was in the paper today."

Ace chose to let that go by. He kept watching the kid with the basketball. It was funny how, though the whole point was to get the ball up into the air, kids grabbed it by the sides and squeezed. Kids just didn't think.

"Did you hear?" his mother asked.

"Sure, but so what?" Ace said. His mother's lower lip was coming at him, so he changed the subject. "I guess I'll take Bonnie."

His mother went into the house and brought back his daughter, wrapped in a blue blanket. The baby looked dopey. "She fussed all day," his mother complained. "I said to your father, 'Bonnie is a dear little girl, but without a doubt she's her mother's daughter.' You were the best-natured boy."

"Well I *had* everything," Ace said with an impatience that made his mother blink. He nicely dropped his cigarette into a brown flowerpot on the edge of the porch and took his daughter into his arms. She was getting heavier, solid. When he reached the end of the cement walk, his mother was still on the porch, waving to him. He was so close he could see the fat around her elbow jiggle, and he only lived a half block up the street, yet here she was, waving to him as if he was going to Japan.

At the door of his car, it seemed stupid to him to drive the measly half block home. His old coach, Bob Behn, used to say never to ride where you could walk. Cars were the death of legs. Ace left the ignition keys in his pocket and ran along the pavement with Bonnie laughing and bouncing at his chest. He slammed the door of his landlady's house open and shut, pounded up the two flights of stairs, and was panting so hard when he reached the door of his apartment that it took him a couple of seconds to fit the key into the lock.

The run must have tuned Bonnie up. As soon as he lowered her into the crib, she began to shout and wave her arms. He didn't want to play with her. He tossed some blocks and a rattle into the crib and walked into the bathroom, where he turned on the hot water and began to comb his hair. Holding the comb under the faucet before every stroke, he combed his hair forward. It was so long, one strand curled under his nose and touched his lips. He whipped the whole mass back with a single pull. He tucked in the tufts around his ears, and ran the comb straight back on both sides of his head. With his fingers he felt for the little ridge at the back where the two sides met. It was there, as it should have been. Finally, he mussed the hair in front enough for one little lock to droop over his forehead, like Alan Ladd. It made the temple seem lower than it was. Every day, his hair-line looked higher. He had observed all around him how blond men went bald first. He remembered reading somewhere, though, that baldness shows virility.

On his way to the kitchen he flipped the left-hand knob of the television. Bonnie was always quieter with the set on. Ace didn't see how she could understand much of it, but it seemed to mean something to her. He found a can of beer in the refrigerator behind some brownish lettuce and those hot dogs Evey never got around to cooking. She'd be home any time. The clock said 5:12. She'd pop her lid.

Ace didn't see what he could do but try and reason with her. "Evey," he'd say, "you ought to thank God I got out of it. It had no future to it at all." He hoped she wouldn't get too mad, because when she was mad he wondered if he should have married her, and doubting that made him feel crowded. It was bad enough, his mother always crowding him. He punched the two triangles in the top of the beer can, the little triangle first, and then the big one, the one he drank from. He hoped Evey wouldn't say anything that couldn't be forgotten. What women didn't seem to realize was that there were things you knew but shouldn't say.

He felt sorry he had called the kid in the car a wop.

Ace balanced the beer on a corner where two rails of the crib met and looked under the chairs for the morning paper. He had trouble finding his name, because it was at the bottom of a column on an inside sports page, in a small article about the county basketball statistics:

> "Dusty" Tremwick, Grosvenor Park's sure-fingered center, copped the individual scoring honors with a season's grand (and we do mean grand) total of 376 points. This is within eighteen points of the all-time record of 394 racked up in the 1949–1950 season by Olinger High's Fred Anderson.

Ace angrily sailed the paper into an armchair. Now it was Fred Anderson; it used to be Ace. He hated being called Fred, especially in print, but then the sportswriters were all office boys anyway, Behn used to say.

"Do not just ask for shoe polish," a man on television said, "but ask for *Emu Shoe Gloss,* the *only* polish that absolutely *guarantees* to make your shoes look shinier than new." Ace turned the sound off, so that the man moved his mouth like a fish blowing bubbles. Right away, Bonnie howled, so Ace turned it up loud enough to drown her out and went into the kitchen, without knowing what he wanted there. He wasn't hungry; his stomach was tight. It used to be like that when he walked to the gymnasium alone in the dark before a game and could see the people from town, kids and parents, crowding in at the lighted doors. But once he was inside, the locker room would be bright and hot, and the other guys would be there, laughing it up and towel-slapping, and the tight feeling would leave. Now there were whole days when it didn't leave.

A key scratched at the door lock. Ace decided to stay in the kitchen. Let *her* find *him.* Her heels clicked on the floor for a step or two; then the television set went off. Bonnie began to cry. "Shut up, honey," Evey said. There was a silence.

"I'm home," Ace called.

"No kidding. I thought Bonnie got the beer by herself."

Ace laughed. She was in a sarcastic mood, thinking she was Lauren Bacall. That was all right, just so she kept funny. Still smiling, Ace eased into the living room and got hit with, "What are *you* smirking about? Another question: What's the idea running up the street with Bonnie like she was a football?"

"You saw that?"

"Your mother told me."

"You saw her?"

"Of course I saw her. I dropped by to pick up Bonnie. What the hell do you think? — I read her tiny mind?"

"Take it easy," Ace said, wondering if Mom had told her about Friedman.

"Take it easy? Don't coach *me.* Another question: Why's the car out in front of her place? You give the car to her?"

"Look, I parked it there to pick up Bonnie, and I thought I'd leave it there."

"Why?"

"Whaddeya mean, why? I just did. I just thought I'd walk. It's not that far, you know."

"No, I don't know. If you'd been on your feet all day a block would look like one hell of a long way."

"Okay. I'm sorry."

She hung up her coat and stepped out of her shoes and walked around the room picking up things. She stuck the newspaper in the wastebasket.

Ace said, "My name was in the paper today."

"They spell it right?" She shoved the paper deep into the basket with her foot. There was no doubt; she knew about Friedman.

"They called me Fred."

"Isn't that your name? What *is* your name anyway? Hero J. Great?"

There wasn't any answer, so Ace didn't try any. He sat down on the sofa, lighted a cigarette, and waited.

Evey picked up Bonnie. "Poor thing stinks. What does your mother do, scrub out the toilet with her?"

"Can't you take it easy? I know you're tired."

"You should. I'm always tired."

Evey and Bonnie went into the bathroom; when they came out, Bonnie was clean and Evey was calm. Evey sat down in an easy chair beside Ace and rested her stocking feet on his knees. "Hit me," she said, twiddling her fingers for the cigarette.

The baby crawled up to her chair and tried to stand, to see what he gave her. Leaning over close to Bonnie's nose, Evey grinned, smoke leaking through her teeth, and said, "Only for grownups, honey."

"Eve," Ace began, "there was no future in that job. Working all Saturday, and then Friday nights on top of it."

"I know. Your mother told *me* all that, too. All I want from you is what happened."

She was going to take it like a sport, then. He tried to remember how it *did* happen. "It wasn't my fault," he said. "Friedman told me to back this '51 Chevvy into the line that faces Church Street. He just bought it from an old guy this morning who said it only had thirteen thousand on it. So in I jump and start her up. There was a knock in the engine like a machine gun. I almost told Friedman he'd bought a squirrel, but you know I cut that smart stuff out ever since Palotta laid me off."

"You told me that story. What happens in this one?"

"Look, Eve. I *am* telling ya. Do you want me to go out to a movie or something?"

"Suit yourself."

"So I jump in the Chevvy and snap it back in line, and there was a kind of scrape and thump. I get out and look and Friedman's running over, his arms going like *this*" — Ace whirled his own arms and laughed — "and here was the whole back fender of a '49 Merc mashed in. Just looked like somebody took a planer and shaved off the bulge, you know, there at the back." He tried to show her with his hands. "The Chevvy, though, didn't have a dent. It even gained some paint. But *Friedman,* to *hear* him — Boy, they can rave when their pocketbook's hit. He said" — Ace laughed again — "never mind."

Evey said, "You're proud of yourself."

"No, listen. I'm not happy about it. But there wasn't a thing I could *do.* It wasn't my driving at all. I looked over on the other side, and there was just two or three inches between the Chevvy and a Buick. *Nobody* could have gotten into that hole. Even if it had hair on it." He thought this was pretty good.

She didn't. "You could have looked."

"There just wasn't the *space.* Friedman said stick it in; I stuck it in."

"But you could have looked and moved the other cars to make more room."

"I guess that would have been the smart thing."

"I guess, too. Now what?"

"What do you mean?"

"I mean now what? Are you going to give up? Go back to the Army? Your mother? Be a basketball pro? What?"

"You know I'm not tall enough. Anybody under six-six they don't want."

"Is that so? Six-six? Well, please listen to this, Mr. Six-Foot-Five-and-a-Half: I'm fed up. I'm ready as Christ to let you run." She stabbed her cigarette into an ashtray on the arm of the chair so hard the ashtray jumped to the floor. Evey flushed and shut up.

What Ace hated most in their arguments was these silences after Evey had said something so ugly she wanted to take it back. "Better ask the priest first," he murmured.

She sat right up. "If there's one thing I don't want to hear about from you it's priests. You let the priests to me. You don't know a damn thing about it. Not a damn thing."

"Hey, look at Bonnie," he said, trying to make a fresh start with his tone.

Evey didn't hear him. "If you think," she went on, "if for one rotten moment you think, Mr. Fred, that the be-all and end-all of my life is you and your hot-shot stunts — "

"Look, Mother," Ace pleaded, pointing at Bonnie. The baby had picked up the ashtray and put it on her head for a hat and was waiting for praise.

Evey glanced down sharply at the child. "Cute," she said. "Cute as her daddy."

The ashtray slid from Bonnie's head and she patted where it had been and looked around puzzled.

"Yeah, but watch," Ace said. "Watch her hands. They're really terrific hands."

"You're nuts," Evey said.

"No, honest. Bonnie's great. She's a natural. Get the rattle for her. Never mind, I'll get it." In two steps, Ace was at Bonnie's crib, picking the rattle out of the mess of blocks and plastic rings and bean-bags. He extended the rattle toward his daughter, shaking it delicately. Made wary by this burst of attention, Bonnie reached with both hands; like two separate animals they approached from opposite sides and touched the smooth rattle simultaneously. A smile bubbled up on her face. Ace tugged weakly. She held on, and then tugged back. "She's a natural," Ace said, "and it won't do her any good because she's a girl. Baby, we got to have a boy."

"I'm not your baby," Evey said, closing her eyes.

Saying "Baby" over and over again, Ace backed up to the radio and, without turning around, switched on the volume knob. In the moment before the tubes warmed up, Evey had time to say, "Wise up, Freddy. What shall we do?"

The radio came in on something slow: dinner music. Ace picked Bonnie up and set her in the crib. "Shall we dance?" he asked his wife, bowing.

"I want to talk."

"Baby. It's the cocktail hour."

"This is getting us no place," she said, rising from her chair, though.

"Fred Junior. I can see him now," he said, seeing nothing.

"We will have no Juniors."

In her crib, Bonnie whimpered at the sight of her mother being seized. Ace fitted his hand into the natural place on Evey's back and she shuffled stiffly into his lead. When, with a sudden injection of saxophones, the tempo quickened, he spun her out carefully, keeping the beat with his shoulders. Her hair brushed his lips as she minced in, then swung away, to the end of his arm; he could feel her toes dig into the carpet. He flipped his own hair back from his eyes. The music ate through his skin and mixed with the nerves and small veins; he seemed to be great again, and all the other kids were around them, in a ring, clapping time.

———— CONSIDERATIONS ————————————

1. Updike often uses minute physical observations. Do you find any of these in "Ace in the Hole"? How do they contribute to the story's effect?

2. How old is Ace? What information in the story prompts you to make a guess? What kind of age do you mean — chronological, mental, emotional? How important is his age to the story?

3. What are Ace's *real* interests? Wife? Child? Job? Future career? How does Updike help you discriminate between Ace's casual and lasting interests?

4. Which is most important to Ace — the past, the present, or the future? Cite evidence. Of what thematic significance is this question?

5. If you were a marriage counselor, would you have any advice for this young couple? Would you say that their marriage is in trouble? What are the chances that they would even consider consulting a marriage counselor? For your answers use the story itself.

6. What importance has play had in Ace's life? What particulars in the story reveal his attitude toward play, sport, games, fun, diversions, recreation?

7. Compare the reactions of Ace's mother and his wife to his losing the job. How do their different attitudes toward this event reveal important things about Ace's life at this time?

Eudora Welty (b. 1909) lives in her native Jackson, Mississippi, where she continues to write, deliberately and slowly, her perfect stories and novels. A Curtain of Green *(1941) collected stories to make her first volume; now there is a* Selected Stories *available from the Modern Library. Her novels include* Losing Battles *(1970) and* The Optimist's Daughter *(1972), which won her a Pulitzer Prize.*

Here is one of her stories, and a useful essay she wrote about it years later, recently collected in her newest book, The Eye of the Story *(1978).*

_73_

EUDORA WELTY
A Worn Path

It was December — a bright frozen day in the early morning. Far out in the country there was an old Negro woman with her head tied in a red rag, coming along a path through the pinewoods. Her name was Phoenix Jackson. She was very old and small and she walked slowly in the dark pine shadows, moving a little from side to side in her steps, with the balanced heaviness and lightness of a pendulum in a grandfather clock. She carried a thin, small cane made from an umbrella, and with this she kept tapping the frozen earth in front of her. This made a grave and persistent noise in the still air, that seemed meditative, like the chirping of a solitary little bird.

She wore a dark striped dress reaching down to her shoetops, and an equally long apron of bleached sugar sacks, with a full pocket; all neat and tidy, but every time she took a step she might have fallen over her shoelaces, which dragged from her unlaced shoes. She looked straight ahead. Her eyes were blue with age. Her skin had a pattern all its own of numberless branching wrinkles and as though a whole little tree stood in the middle of her forehead, but a golden color ran underneath, and the two knobs of her cheeks were illuminated by a yellow burning under the dark. Under the red rag her hair came down on her neck in the frailest of ringlets, still black, and with an odor like copper.

Now and then there was a quivering in the thicket. Old Phoenix said, "Out of my way, all you foxes, owls, beetles, jack rabbits, coons, and wild animals! . . . Keep out from under these feet, little bobwhites. . . . Keep the big wild hogs out of my path. Don't let none of those come running my direction. I got a long way." Under her small black-freckled hand her cane, limber as a buggy whip, would switch at the brush as if to rouse up any hiding things.

On she went. The woods were deep and still. The sun made the pine needles almost too bright to look at, up where the wind rocked. The cones dropped as light as feathers. Down in the hollow was the mourning dove — it was not too late for him.

The path ran up a hill. "Seem like there is chains about my feet, time I get this far," she said, in the voice of argument old people keep to use with themselves. "Something always take a hold on this hill — pleads I should stay."

After she got to the top she turned and gave a full, severe look behind her where she had come. "Up through pines," she said at length. "Now down through oaks."

Her eyes opened their widest and she started down gently. But before she got to the bottom of the hill a bush caught her dress.

Her fingers were busy and intent, but her skirts were full and long, so that before she could pull them free in one place they were caught in another. It was not possible to allow the dress to tear. "I in the thorny bush," she said. "Thorns, you doing your appointed work. Never want to let folks past — no sir. Old eyes thought you was a pretty little *green* bush."

Finally, trembling all over, she stood free, and after a moment dared to stoop for her cane.

"Sun so high!" she cried, leaning back and looking, while the thick tears went over her eyes. "The time getting all gone here."

At the foot of this hill was a place where a log was laid across the creek.

"Now comes the trial," said Phoenix.

Putting her right foot out, she mounted the log and shut her eyes.

Lifting her skirt, leveling her cane fiercely before her, like a festival figure in some parade, she began to march across. Then she opened her eyes and she was safe on the other side.

"I wasn't as old as I thought," she said.

But she sat down to rest. She spread her skirts on the bank around her and folded her hands over her knees. Up above her was a tree in a pearly cloud of mistletoe. She did not dare to close her eyes, and when a little boy brought her a little plate with a slice of marble-cake on it she spoke to him. "That would be acceptable," she said. But when she went to take it there was just her own hand in the air.

So she left that tree, and had to go through a barbed-wire fence. There she had to creep and crawl, spreading her knees and stretching her fingers like a baby trying to climb the steps. But she talked loudly to herself: she could not let her dress be torn now, so late in the day, and she could not pay for having her arm or her leg sawed off if she got caught fast where she was.

At last she was safe through the fence and risen up out in the clearing. Big dead trees, like black men with one arm, were standing in the purple stalks of the withered cotton field. There sat a buzzard.

"Who you watching?"

In the furrow she made her way along.

"Glad this not the season for bulls," she said, looking sideways, "and the good Lord made his snakes to curl up and sleep in the winter. A pleasure I don't see no two-headed snake coming around that tree, where it come once. It took a while to get by him, back in the summer."

She passed through the old cotton and went into a field of dead corn. It whispered and shook, and was taller than her head. "Through the maze now," she said, for there was no path.

Then there was something tall, black, and skinny there, moving before her.

At first she took it for a man. It could have been a man dancing in the field. But she stood still and listened, and it did not make a sound. It was as silent as a ghost.

"Ghost," she said sharply, "who be you the ghost of? For I have heard of nary death close by."

But there was no answer, only the ragged dancing in the wind.

She shut her eyes, reached out her hand, and touched a sleeve. She found a coat and inside that an emptiness, cold as ice.

"You scarecrow," she said. Her face lighted. "I ought to be shut up for good," she said with laughter. "My senses is gone. I too old. I the oldest people I ever know. Dance, old scarecrow," she said, "while I dancing with you."

She kicked her foot over the furrow, and with mouth drawn down shook her head once or twice in a little strutting way. Some husks blew down and whirled in streamers about her skirts.

Then she went on, parting her way from side to side with the cane, through the whispering field. At last she came to the end, to a wagon track, where the silver grass blew between the red ruts. The quail were walking around like pullets, seeming all dainty and unseen.

"Walk pretty," she said. "This the easy place. This the easy going."

She followed the track, swaying through the quiet bare fields, through the little strings of trees silver in their dead leaves, past cabins silver from weather, with the doors and windows boarded shut, all like old women under a spell sitting there. "I walking in their sleep," she said, nodding her head vigorously.

In a ravine she went where a spring was silently flowing through a hollow log. Old Phoenix bent and drank. "Sweetgum makes the water sweet," she said, and drank more. "Nobody knows who made this well, for it was here when I was born."

The track crossed a swampy part where the moss hung as white as lace from every limb. "Sleep on, alligators, and blow your bubbles." Then the track went into the road.

Deep, deep the road went down between the high green-colored banks. Overhead the live-oaks met, and it was as dark as a cave.

A black dog with a lolling tongue came up out of the weeds by the ditch. She was meditating, and not ready, and when he came at her she only hit him a little with her cane. Over she went in the ditch, like a little puff of milk-weed.

Down there, her senses drifted away. A dream visited her, and she reached her hand up, but nothing reached down and gave her a pull. So she lay there and presently went to talking. "Old woman," she said to herself, "that black dog come up out of the weeds to stall you off, and now there he sitting on his fine tail, smiling at you."

A white man finally came along and found her — a hunter, a young man, with his dog on a chain.

"Well, Granny!" he laughed. "What are you doing there?"

"Lying on my back like a June-bug waiting to be turned over, mister," she said, reaching up her hand.

He lifted her up, gave her a swing in the air, and set her down, "Anything broken, Granny?"

"No sir, them old dead weeds is springy enough," said Phoenix, when she had got her breath. "I thank you for your trouble."

"Where do you live, Granny?" he asked, while the two dogs were growling at each other.

"Away back yonder, sir, behind the ridge. You can't even see it from here."

"On your way home?"

"No, sir, I going to town."

"Why that's too far! That's as far as I walk when I come out myself, and I get something for my trouble." He patted the stuffed bag he carried, and there hung down a little closed claw. It was one of the bobwhites, with its beak hooked bitterly to show it was dead. "Now you go on home, Granny!"

"I bound to go to town, mister," said Phoenix. "The time come around."

He gave another laugh, filling the whole landscape. "I know you colored people! Wouldn't miss going to town to see Santa Claus!"

But something held Old Phoenix very still. The deep lines in her face went into a fierce and different radiation. Without warning she had seen with her own eyes a flashing nickel fall out of the man's pocket on to the ground.

"How old are you, Granny?" he was saying.

"There is no telling, mister," she said, "no telling."

Then she gave a little cry and clapped her hands, and said, "Git on away from here, dog! Look! Look at that dog!" She laughed as if in admiration. "He ain't scared of nobody. He a big black dog." She whispered, "Sick him!"

"Watch me get rid of that cur," said the man. "Sick him, Pete! Sick him!"

Phoenix heard the dogs fighting and heard the man running and throwing sticks. She even heard a gunshot. But she was slowly bending forward by that time, further and further forward, the lids stretched down over her eyes, as if she were doing this in her sleep. Her chin was lowered almost to her knees. The yellow palm of her hand came out from the fold of her apron. Her fingers slid down and along the ground under the piece of money with the grace and care they would have in lifting an egg from under a sitting hen. Then she slowly straightened up, she stood erect, and the nickel was in her apron pocket. A bird flew by. Her lips moved. "God watching me the whole time. I come to stealing."

The man came back, and his own dog panted about them. "Well,

I scared him off that time," he said, and then he laughed and lifted his gun and pointed it at Phoenix.

She stood straight and faced him.

"Doesn't the gun scare you?" he said, still pointing it.

"No, sir, I seen plenty go off closer by, in my day, and for less what I done," she said, holding utterly still.

He smiled, and shouldered the gun. "Well, Granny," he said, "you must be a hundred years old, and scared of nothing. I'd give you a dime if I had any money with me. But you take my advice and stay home, and nothing will happen to you."

"I bound to go on my way, mister," said Phoenix. She inclined her head in the red rag. Then they went in different directions, but she could hear the gun shooting again and again over the hill.

She walked on. The shadows hung from the oak trees to the road like curtains. Then she smelled wood-smoke, and smelled the river, and she saw a steeple and the cabins on their steep steps. Dozens of little black children whirled around her. There ahead was Natchez shining. Bells were ringing. She walked on.

In the paved city it was Christmas time. There were red and green electric lights strung and crisscrossed everywhere, and all turned on in the daytime. Old Phoenix would have been lost if she had not distrusted her eyesight and depended on her feet to know where to take her.

She paused quietly on the sidewalk, where people were passing by. A lady came along in the crowd, carrying an armful of red-, green-, and silver-wrapped presents; she gave off perfume like the red roses in hot summer, and Phoenix stopped her.

"Please, missy, will you lace up my shoe?" She held up her foot.

"What do you want, Grandma?"

"See my shoe," said Phoenix. "Do all right for out in the country, but wouldn't look right to go in a big building."

"Stand still then, Grandma," said the lady. She put her packages down carefully on the sidewalk beside her and laced and tied both shoes tightly.

"Can't lace 'em with a cane," said Phoenix. "Thank you, missy. I doesn't mind asking a nice lady to tie up my shoe when I gets out on the street."

Moving slowly and from side to side, she went into the stone building and into a tower of steps, where she walked up and around and around until her feet knew to stop.

She entered a door, and there she saw nailed up on the wall the document that had been stamped with the gold seal and framed in the gold frame which matched the dream that was hung up in her head.

"Here I be," she said. There was a fixed and ceremonial stiffness over her body.

"A charity case, I suppose," said an attendant who sat at the desk before her.

But Phoenix only looked above her head. There was sweat on her face; the wrinkles shone like a bright net.

"Speak up, Grandma," the woman said. "What's your name? We must have your history, you know. Have you been here before? What seems to be the trouble with you?"

Old Phoenix only gave a twitch to her face as if a fly were bothering her.

"Are you deaf?" cried the attendant.

But then the nurse came in.

"Oh, that's just old Aunt Phoenix," she said. "She doesn't come for herself — she has a little grandson. She makes these trips just as regular as clockwork. She lives away back off the Old Natchez Trace." She bent down. "Well, Aunt Phoenix, why don't you just take a seat? We won't keep you standing after your long trip." She pointed.

The old woman sat down, bolt upright in the chair.

"Now, how is the boy?" asked the nurse.

Old Phoenix did not speak.

"I said, how is the boy?"

But Phoenix only waited and stared straight ahead, her face very solemn and withdrawn into rigidity.

"Is his throat any better?" asked the nurse. "Aunt Phoenix, don't you hear me? Is your grandson's throat any better since the last time you came for the medicine?"

With her hand on her knees, the old woman waited, silent, erect and motionless, just as if she were in armor.

"You mustn't take up our time this way, Aunt Phoenix," the nurse said. "Tell us quickly about your grandson, and get it over. He isn't dead, is he?"

At last there came a flicker and then a flame of comprehension across her face, and she spoke.

"My grandson. It was my memory had left me. There I sat and forgot why I made my long trip."

"Forgot?" The nurse frowned. "After you came so far?"

Then Phoenix was like an old woman begging a dignified forgiveness for waking up frightened in the night. "I never did go to school

— I was too old at the Surrender," she said in a soft voice. "I'm an old woman without an education. It was my memory fail me. My little grandson, he is just the same, and I forgot it in the coming."

"Throat never heals, does it?" said the nurse, speaking in a loud, sure voice to Old Phoenix. By now she had a card with something written on it, a little list. "Yes. Swallowed lye. When was it — January — two — three years ago —"

Phoenix spoke unasked now. "No, missy, he not dead, he just the same. Every little while his throat begin to close up again, and he not able to swallow. He not get his breath. He not able to help himself. So the time come around, and I go on another trip for soothing medicine."

"All right. The doctor said as long as you came to get it you could have it," said the nurse. "But it's an obstinate case."

"My little grandson, he sit up there in the house all wrapped up, waiting by himself," Phoenix went on. "We is the only two left in the world. He suffer and it don't seem to put him back at all. He got a sweet look. He going to last. He wear a little patch quilt and peep out, holding his mouth open like a little bird. I remembers so plain now. I not going to forget him again, no, the whole enduring time. I could tell him from all the others in creation."

"All right." The nurse was trying to hush her now. She brought her a bottle of medicine. "Charity," she said, making a check mark in a book.

Old Phoenix held the bottle close to her eyes and then carefully put it into her pocket.

"I thank you," she said.

"It's Christmas time, Grandma," said the attendant. "Could I give you a few pennies out of my purse?"

"Five pennies is a nickel," said Phoenix stiffly.

"Here's a nickel," said the attendant.

Phoenix rose carefully and held out her hand. She received the nickel and then fished the other nickel out of her pocket and laid it beside the new one. She stared at her palm closely, with her head on one side.

Then she gave a tap with her cane on the floor.

"This is what come to me to do," she said. "I going to the store and buy my child a little windmill they sells, made out of paper. He going to find it hard to believe there such a thing in the world. I'll march myself back where he waiting, holding it straight up in this hand."

She lifted her free hand, gave a little nod, turned round, and walked out of the doctor's office. Then her slow step began on the stairs, going down.

_____ CONSIDERATIONS _____

1. " 'Up through pines. . . . Now down through oaks.' " Old Phoenix talked continually to herself on her long worn path to town. Her running comments make us a party to her consciousness of the land as she moves through it. Read Wendell Berry's "A Native Hill" (pages 41–51), and speculate on what he would say about Old Phoenix's sense of place.

2. Some features of Old Phoenix's long journey might bring to mind Everyman's difficult travel through life. Do specific passages suggest that Old Phoenix's journey is symbolic or archetypal?

3. Would you say that Old Phoenix is senile? Is she in excellent control of her thoughts? What evidence can you find for your answer?

4. Is the grandson alive or dead? After you answer this question, read Welty's own comments on the story in the next selection.

5. Who was the little boy with the slice of marble-cake? Why does he appear and disappear so abruptly?

6. Eudora Welty makes no comment in the story on Old Phoenix's encounter with the white man. Do the details of that encounter reveal anything about relations between whites and blacks?

7. What do you learn of Old Phoenix's sense of morality, and sense of humor, and feeling of personal worth?

74

EUDORA WELTY
The Point of the Story

A story writer is more than happy to be read by students; the fact 1
that these serious readers think and feel something in response to his
work he finds life-giving. At the same time he may not always be able
to reply to their specific questions in kind. I wondered if it might
clarify something, for both the questioners and myself, if I set down a
general reply to the question that comes to me most often in the mail,
from both students and their teachers, after some classroom discussion. The unrivaled favorite is this: "Is Phoenix Jackson's grandson
really *dead?*" It refers to a short story I wrote years ago called "A Worn
Path," which tells of a day's journey an old woman makes on foot from
deep in the country into town and into a doctor's office on behalf of
her little grandson; he is at home, periodically ill, and periodically she
comes for his medicine; they give it to her as usual, she receives it and
starts the journey back.

I had not meant to mystify readers by withholding any fact; it is 2
not a writer's business to tease. The story is told through Phoenix's
mind as she undertakes her errand. As the author at one with the
character as I tell it, I must assume that the boy is alive. As the reader,
you are free to think as you like, of course: the story invites you to
believe that no matter what happens, Phoenix for as long as she is able
to walk and can hold to her purpose will make her journey. The *possibility* that she would keep on even if he were dead is there in her
devotion and its single-minded, single-track errand. Certainly the *artistic* truth, which should be good enough for the fact, lies in Phoenix's
own answer to that question. When the nurse asks, "He isn't dead, is
he?" she speaks for herself: "He still the same. He going to last."

3   The grandchild is the incentive. But it is the journey, the going of the errand, that is the story, and the question is not whether the grandchild is in reality alive or dead. It doesn't affect the outcome of the story or its meaning from start to finish. But it is not the question itself that has struck me as much as the idea, almost without exception implied in the asking, that for Phoenix's grandson to be dead would somehow make the story "better."

4   It's *all right,* I want to say to the students who write to me, for things to be what they appear to be, and for words to mean what they say. It's all right, too, for words and appearances to mean more than one thing — ambiguity is a fact of life. A fiction writer's responsibility covers not only what he presents as the facts of a given story but what he chooses to stir up as their implications; in the end, these implications, too, become facts, in the larger, fictional sense. But it is not all right, not in good faith, for things not to mean what they say.

5   The grandson's plight was real and it made the truth of the story, which is the story of an errand of love carried out. If the child no longer lived, the truth would persist in the "wornness" of the path. But his being dead can't increase the truth of the story, can't affect it one way or the other. I think I signal this, because the end of the story has been reached before old Phoenix gets home again: she simply starts back. To the question "Is the grandson really dead?" I could reply that it doesn't make any difference. I could also say that I did not make him up in order to let him play a trick on Phoenix. But my best answer would be: "Phoenix is alive."

6   The origin of a story is sometimes a trustworthy clue to the author — or can provide him with the clue — to its key image; maybe in this case it will do the same for the reader. One day I saw a solitary old woman like Phoenix. She was walking; I saw her, at middle distance, in a winter country landscape, and watched her slowly make her way across my line of vision. That sight of her made me write the story. I invented an errand for her, but that only seemed a living part of the figure she was herself: what errand other than for someone else could be making her go? And her going was the first thing, her persisting in her landscape was the real thing, and the first and the real were what I wanted and worked to keep. I brought her up close enough, by imagination, to describe her face, make her present to the eyes, but the full-length figure moving across the winter fields was the indelible one and the image to keep, and the perspective extending into the vanishing distance the true one to hold in mind.

7   I invented for my character as I wrote, some passing adventures — some dreams and harassments and a small triumph or two, some

jolts to her pride, some flights of fancy to console her, one or two
encounters to scare her, a moment that gave her cause to feel ashamed,
a moment to dance and preen — for it had to be a journey, and all these
things belonged to that, parts of life's uncertainty.

A narrative line is in its deeper sense, of course, the tracing out of   8
a meaning, and the real continuity of a story lies in this probing forward. The real dramatic force of a story depends on the strength of the
emotion that has set it going. The emotional value is the measure of
the reach of the story. What gives any such content to "A Worn Path"
is not its circumstances but its subject: the deep-grained habit of love.

What I hoped would come clear was that in the whole surround   9
of this story, the world it threads through, the only certain thing at all
is the worn path. The habit of love cuts through confusion and stum-
bles or contrives its way out of difficulty, it remembers the way even
when it forgets, for a dumbfounded moment, its reason for being. The
path is the thing that matters.

Her victory — old Phoenix's — is when she sees the diploma in   10
the doctor's office, when she finds "nailed up on the wall the document that had been stamped with the gold seal and framed in the gold
frame, which matched the dream that was hung up in her head." The
return with the medicine is just a matter of retracing her own footsteps. It is the part of the journey, and of the story, that can now go
without saying.

In the matter of function, old Phoenix's way might even do as a   11
sort of parallel to your way of work if you are a writer of stories. The
way to get there is the all-important, all-absorbing problem, and this
problem is your reason for undertaking the story. Your only guide, too,
is your sureness about your subject, about what this subject is. Like
Phoenix, you work all your life to find your way, through all the obstructions and the false appearances and the upsets you may have
brought on yourself, to reach a meaning — using inventions of your
imagination, perhaps helped out by your dreams and bits of good luck.
And finally too, like Phoenix, you have to assume that what you are
working in aid of is life, not death.

But you would make the trip anyway — wouldn't you? — just on   12
hope.

___ CONSIDERATIONS _____

1. Welty says that Old Phoenix's return trip is "the part of the journey,
and of the story, that can now go without saying." If you were writing this

story would you choose a different place to end it? Would you follow Old Phoenix all the way back into the hills? Would you show us the grandson? Why?

2. How does Welty feel about writers who intentionally mystify their readers?

3. Does "A Worn Path" illustrate what Welty means when she says, "A narrative line is in its deeper sense . . . the tracing out of a meaning"?

4. In Paragraph 4, Welty touches on the "factuality" of a work of fiction. This introduces a fascinating (if maddening) question: what is the difference between fiction and nonfiction?

5. Another Southern writer, William Faulkner, wrote a short novel, *As I Lay Dying*, that can be read as a fuller version of "A Worn Path." It too is based on "an errand of love," as Welty puts it. Read the novel and discuss its parallels with Welty's story.

6. What do you think of Welty's response to the question about her story? Do her comments constitute the kind of critical analysis that Robert Gorham Davis mentions in Paragraph 8, page 118?

E. B. White (b. 1899) was born in Mount Vernon, New York, graduated from Cornell in 1921, and joined the staff of The New Yorker *in 1926. For many years, he wrote the brief essay which led off that magazine's "Talk of the Town" and edited other "Talk" segments. In 1929, White collaborated with James Thurber on a book called* Is Sex Necessary? *and from time to time he has published collections of essays and poems, most of them taken from* The New Yorker *and* Harper's. *Some of his best-known collections are* One Man's Meat *(1942),* The Second Tree from the Corner *(1953), and* The Points of My Compass *(1962). He is also the author of children's books, most notably* Stuart Little *(1945) and* Charlotte's Web *(1952), and the celebrated book on prose,* The Elements of Style *(with William Strunk, Jr., 1959). In 1937, he retired from* The New Yorker *and moved to a farm in Maine, where he continues to edit* The New Yorker's *"newsbreaks" — those minimal, devastating comments attached to the proofhacks and other errors printed at the bottom of* The New Yorker's *columns. And he continues his slow, consistent writing of superb prose. In recent years, the collected* Letters of E. B. White *(1976) and* Essays of E. B. White *(1977) have reconfirmed this country's infatuation with this versatile author. A special citation from the Pulitzer Prize Committee in 1978 celebrated the publication of White's letters.*

75

E. B. WHITE
Once More to the Lake

1   One summer, along about 1904, my father rented a camp on a lake in Maine and took us all there for the month of August. We all got ringworm from some kittens and had to rub Pond's Extract on our arms and legs night and morning, and my father rolled over in a canoe with all his clothes on; but outside of that the vacation was a success and from then on none of us ever thought there was any place in the world like that lake in Maine. We returned summer after summer — always on August 1st for one month. I have since become a salt-water man, but sometimes in summer there are days when the restlessness of the tides and the fearful cold of the sea water and the incessant wind that blows across the afternoon and into the evening make me wish for the placidity of a lake in the woods. A few weeks ago this feeling got so strong I bought myself a couple of bass hooks and a spinner and returned to the lake where we used to go, for a week's fishing and to revisit old haunts.

2   I took along my son, who had never had any fresh water up his nose and who had seen lily pads only from train windows. On the journey over to the lake I began to wonder what it would be like. I wondered how time would have marred this unique, this holy spot — the coves and streams, the hills that the sun set behind, the camps and the paths behind the camps. I was sure that the tarred road would have found it out and I wondered in what other ways it would be desolated. It is strange how much you can remember about places like that once you allow your mind to return into the grooves that lead back. You remember one thing, and that suddenly reminds you of another thing.

I guess I remembered clearest of all the early mornings, when the lake was cool and motionless, remembered how the bedroom smelled of the lumber it was made of and of the wet woods whose scent entered through the screen. The partitions in the camp were thin and did not extend clear to the top of the rooms, and as I was always the first up I would dress softly so as not to wake the others, and sneak out into the sweet outdoors and start out in the canoe, keeping close along the shore in the long shadows of the pines. I remembered being very careful never to rub my paddle against the gunwale for fear of disturbing the stillness of the cathedral.

The lake had never been what you would call a wild lake. There were cottages sprinkled around the shores, and it was in farming country although the shores of the lake were quite heavily wooded. Some of the cottages were owned by nearby farmers, and you would live at the shore and eat your meals at the farmhouse. That's what our family did. But although it wasn't wild, it was a fairly large and undisturbed lake and there were places in it which, to a child at least, seemed infinitely remote and primeval.

I was right about the tar: it led to within half a mile of the shore. But when I got back there, with my boy, and we settled into a camp near a farmhouse and into the kind of summertime I had known, I could tell that it was going to be pretty much the same as it had been before — I knew it, lying in bed the first morning, smelling the bedroom, and hearing the boy sneak quietly out and go off along the shore in a boat. I began to sustain the illusion that he was I, and therefore, by simple transposition, that I was my father. This sensation persisted, kept cropping up all the time we were there. It was not an entirely new feeling, but in this setting it grew much stronger. I seemed to be living a dual existence. I would be in the middle of some simple act, I would be picking up a bait box or laying down a table fork, or I would be saying something, and suddenly it would be not I but my father who was saying the words or making the gesture. It gave me a creepy sensation.

We went fishing the first morning. I felt the same damp moss covering the worms in the bait can, and saw the dragonfly alight on the tip of my rod as it hovered a few inches from the surface of the water. It was the arrival of this fly that convinced me beyond any doubt that everything was as it always had been, that the years were a mirage and there had been no years. The small waves were the same, chucking the rowboat under the chin as we fished at anchor, and the boat was the same boat, the same color green and the ribs broken in

3

4

5

the same places, and under the floor-boards the same fresh-water leavings and débris — the dead helgramite, the wisps of moss, the rusty discarded fishhook, the dried blood from yesterday's catch. We stared silently at the tips of our rods, at the dragonflies that came and went. I lowered the tip of mine into the water, tentatively, pensively dislodging the fly, which darted two feet away, poised, darted two feet back, and came to rest again a little farther up the rod. There had been no years between the ducking of this dragonfly and the other one — the one that was part of memory. I looked at the boy, who was silently watching his fly, and it was my hands that held his rod, my eyes watching. I felt dizzy and didn't know which rod I was at the end of.

6   We caught two bass, hauling them in briskly as though they were mackerel, pulling them over the side of the boat in a businesslike manner without any landing net, and stunning them with a blow on the back of the head. When we got back for a swim before lunch, the lake was exactly where we had left it, the same number of inches from the dock, and there was only the merest suggestion of a breeze. This seemed an utterly enchanted sea, this lake you could leave to its own devices for a few hours and come back to, and find that it had not stirred, this constant and trustworthy body of water. In the shallows, the dark, water-soaked sticks and twigs, smooth and old, were undulating in clusters on the bottom against the clean ribbed sand, and the track of the mussel was plain. A school of minnows swam by, each minnow with its small individual shadow, doubling the attendance, so clear and sharp in the sunlight. Some of the other campers were in swimming, along the shore, one of them with a cake of soap, and the water felt thin and clear and unsubstantial. Over the years there had been this person with the cake of soap, this cultist, and here he was. There had been no years.

7   Up to the farmhouse to dinner through the teeming, dusty field, the road under our sneakers was only a two-track road. The middle track was missing, the one with the marks of the hooves and splotches of dried, flaky manure. There had always been three tracks to choose from in choosing which track to walk in; now the choice was narrowed down to two. For a moment I missed terribly the middle alternative. But the way led past the tennis court, and something about the way it lay there in the sun reassured me; the tape had loosened along the backline, the alleys were green with plantains and other weeds, and the net (installed in June and removed in September) sagged in the dry noon, and the whole place steamed with midday heat and hunger and emptiness. There was a choice of pie for dessert, and one was blueberry

and one was apple, and the waitresses were the same country girls, there having been no passage of time, only the illusion of it as in a dropped curtain — the waitresses were still fifteen; their hair had been washed, that was the only difference — they had been to the movies and seen the pretty girls with the clean hair.

Summertime, oh summertime, pattern of life indelible, the fade-proof lake, the woods unshatterable, the pasture with the sweetfern and the juniper forever and ever, summer without end; this was the background, and the life along the shore was the design, the cottagers with their innocent and tranquil design, their tiny docks with the flagpole and the American flag floating against the white clouds in the blue sky, the little paths over the roots of the trees leading from camp to camp and the paths leading back to the outhouses and the can of lime for sprinkling, and at the souvenir counters at the store the miniature birch-bark canoes and the post cards that showed things looking a little better than they looked. This was the American family at play, escaping the city heat, wondering whether the newcomers in the camp at the head of the cove were "common" or "nice," wondering whether it was true that the people who drove up for Sunday dinner at the farmhouse were turned away because there wasn't enough chicken. 8

It seemed to me, as I kept remembering all this, that those times and those summers had been infinitely precious and worth saving. There had been jollity and peace and goodness. The arriving (at the beginning of August) had been so big a business in itself, at the railway station the farm wagon drawn up, the first smell of the pine-laden air, the first glimpse of the smiling farmer, and the great importance of the trunks and your father's enormous authority in such matters, and the feel of the wagon under you for the long ten-mile haul, and at the top of the last long hill catching the first view of the lake after eleven months of not seeing this cherished body of water. The shouts and cries of the other campers when they saw you, and the trunks to be unpacked, to give up their rich burden. (Arriving was less exciting nowadays, when you sneaked up in your car and parked it under a tree near the camp and took out the bags and in five minutes it was all over, no fuss, no loud wonderful fuss about trunks.) 9

Peace and goodness and jollity. The only thing that was wrong now, really, was the sound of the place, an unfamiliar nervous sound of the outboard motors. This was the note that jarred, the one thing that would sometimes break the illusion and set the years moving. In those other summertimes all motors were inboard; and when they were at a little distance, the noise they made was a sedative, an ingre- 10 dient of summer sleep. They were one-cylinder and two-cylinder engines, and some were make-and-break and some were jump-spark, but they all made a sleepy sound across the lake. The one-lungers throbbed and fluttered, and the twin-cylinder ones purred and purred, and that was a quiet sound too. But now the campers all had outboards. In the daytime, in the hot mornings, these motors made a petulant, irritable sound; at night, in the still evening when the afterglow lit the water, they whined about one's ears like mosquitoes. My boy loved our rented outboard, and his great desire was to achieve singlehanded mastery over it, and authority, and he soon learned the trick of choking it a little (but not too much), and the adjustment of the needle valve. Watching him I would remember the things you could do with the old one-cylinder engine with the heavy flywheel, how you could have it eating out of your hand if you got really close to it spiritually. Motor boats in those days didn't have clutches, and you would make a landing by shutting off the motor at the proper time and coasting in with a dead rudder. But there was a way of reversing them, if you learned the trick, by cutting the switch and putting it on again exactly on the final dying revolution of the flywheel, so that it would kick back against compression and begin reversing. Approaching a dock in a strong following breeze, it was difficult to slow up sufficiently by the ordinary coasting method, and if a boy felt he had complete mastery over his motor, he was tempted to keep it running beyond its time and then reverse it a few feet from the dock. It took a cool nerve, because if you threw the switch a twentieth of a second too soon you would catch the flywheel when it still had speed enough to go up past center, and the boat would leap ahead, charging bull-fashion at the dock.

11   We had a good week at the camp. The bass were biting well and the sun shone endlessly, day after day. We would be tired at night and lie down in the accumulated heat of the little bedrooms after the long hot day and the breeze would stir almost imperceptibly outside and the smell of the swamp drift in through the rusty screens. Sleep would come easily and in the morning the red squirrel would be on the roof, tapping out his gay routine. I kept remembering everything, lying in bed in the mornings — the small steamboat that had a long rounded stern like the lip of a Ubangi, and how quietly she ran on the moonlight sails, when the older boys played their mandolins and the girls sang and we ate doughnuts dipped in sugar, and how sweet the music was on the water in the shining night, and what it had felt like to think about girls then. After breakfast we would go up to the store and

the things were in the same place — the minnows in a bottle, the plugs and spinners disarranged and pawed over by the youngsters from the boys' camp, the fig newtons and the Beeman's gum. Outside, the road was tarred and cars stood in front of the store. Inside, all was just as it had always been, except there was more Coca Cola and not so much Moxie and root beer and birch beer and sarsaparilla. We would walk out with a bottle of pop apiece and sometimes the pop would backfire up our noses and hurt. We explored the streams, quietly, where the turtles slid off the sunny logs and dug their way into the soft bottom; and we lay on the town wharf and fed worms to the tame bass. Everywhere we went I had trouble making out which was I, the one walking at my side, the one walking in my pants.

One afternoon while we were there at that lake a thunderstorm 12 came up. It was like the revival of an old melodrama that I had seen long ago with childish awe. The second-act climax of the drama of the electrical disturbance over a lake in America had not changed in any important respect. This was the big scene, still the big scene. The whole thing was so familiar, the first feeling of oppression and heat and a general air around camp of not wanting to go very far away. In midafternoon (it was all the same) a curious darkening of the sky, and a lull in everything that had made life tick; and then the way the boats suddenly swung the other way at their moorings with the coming of a breeze out of the new quarter, and the premonitory rumble. Then the kettle drum, then the snare, then the bass drum and cymbals, then crackling light against the dark, and the gods grinning and licking their chops in the hills. Afterward the calm, the rain steadily rustling in the calm lake, the return of light and hope and spirits, and the campers running out in joy and relief to go swimming in the rain, their bright cries perpetuating the deathless joke about how they were getting simply drenched, and the children screaming with delight at the new sensation of bathing in the rain, and the joke about getting drenched linking the generations in a strong indestructible chain. And the comedian who waded in carrying an umbrella.

When the others went swimming my son said he was going in 13 too. He pulled his dripping trunks from the line where they had hung all through the shower, and wrung them out. Languidly, and with no thought of going in, I watched him, his hard little body, skinny and bare, saw him wince slightly as he pulled up around his vitals the small, soggy, icy garment. As he buckled the swollen belt suddenly my groin felt the chill of death.

_____ CONSIDERATIONS _____

1. A master of the personal essay, E. B. White transforms an exercise in memory into something universal, timeless, and profound. Study Paragraph 4 to see how.

2. White rejuvenates bits and pieces of language that have become worn and lackluster through repetition. Can you find an example of this technique in Paragraph 2?

3. White notes many changes at the old summer place, but he is more moved by the sameness. Locate examples of his feeling of sameness and consider how these examples contribute to his themes.

4. The author expresses a predictable dislike of outboard motors on the otherwise quiet lake. Does he avoid stereotype when he writes about motors elsewhere in this essay?

5. What is the chief device White uses in his description of the thunderstorm in Paragraph 12?

6. How is the last sentence of the essay a surprise? How has White prepared us for it?

Walter White (1893–1955) was born in Atlanta, Georgia, where he observed the race riot he describes in this essay taken from his autobiography. He was fair in complexion, and could have chosen to deny his African ancestors. Instead, disgusted by the bigotry he encountered in his early years, he devoted his life to the struggle for civil rights. An early official of the NAACP, he was its chief officer from 1931 until his death. As one of his duties with the NAACP, he investigated lynchings and race riots. During his investigations, he sometimes chose to pass as white, in order to ask questions. A dangerous strategy. In 1929 he published Rope and Faggot — A Biography of Judge Lynch. *But his best writing is his autobiography,* A Man Called White *(1948), where the restraint and delicacy of his style contrast with the violence of his story to make a prose that accumulates eloquence and dignity.*

76

WALTER WHITE
The Atlanta Riot

There were nine light-skinned Negroes in my family: mother, father, five sisters, an older brother, George, and myself. The house in which I discovered what it meant to be a Negro was located on Houston Street, three blocks from the Candler Building, Atlanta's first skyscraper, which bore the name of the ex-drug clerk who had become a millionaire from the sale of Coca-Cola. Below us lived none but Negroes; toward town all but a very few were white. Ours was an eight-room, two-story frame house which stood out in its surroundings not because of its opulence but by contrast with the drabness and unpaintedness of the other dwellings in a deteriorating neighborhood.

1

2   Only Father kept his house painted, the picket fence repaired, tne board fence separating our place from those on either side white-washed, the grass neatly trimmed, and flower beds abloom. Mother's passion for neatness was even more pronounced and it seemed to me that I was always the victim of her determination to see no single blade of grass longer than the others or any one of the pickets in the front fence less shiny with paint than its mates. This spic-and-span-ness became increasingly apparent as the rest of the neighborhood became more down-at-heel, and resulted, as we were to learn, in sullen envy among some of our white neighbors. It was the violent expression of that resentment against a Negro family neater than themselves which set the pattern of our lives.

3   On a day in September 1906, when I was thirteen, we were taught that there is no isolation from life. The unseasonably oppressive heat of an Indian summer day hung like a steaming blanket over Atlanta. My sisters and I had casually commented upon the unusual quietness. It seemed to stay Mother's volubility and reduced Father, who was more taciturn, to monosyllables. But, as I remember it, no other sense of impending trouble impinged upon our consciousness.

4   I had read the inflammatory headlines in the *Atlanta News* and the more restrained ones in the *Atlanta Constitution* which reported alleged rapes and other crimes committed by Negroes. But these were so standard and familiar that they made — as I look back on it now — little impression. The stories were more frequent, however, and con-sisted of eight-column streamers instead of the usual two- or four-column ones.

5   Father was a mail collector. His tour of duty was from three to eleven P.M. He made his rounds in a little cart into which one climbed from a step in the rear. I used to drive the cart for him from two until seven, leaving him at the point nearest our home on Houston street, to return home either for study or sleep. That day Father decided that I should not go with him. I appealed to Mother, who thought it might be all right, provided Father sent me home before dark because, she said, "I don't think they would dare start anything before nightfall." Father told me as we made the rounds that ominous rumors of a race riot that night were sweeping the town. . . .

6   During the afternoon preceding the riot little bands of sullen evil-looking men talked excitedly on street corners all over downtown Atlanta. Around seven o'clock my father and I were driving toward a mail box at the corner of Peachtree and Houston Streets when there came from near-by Pryor Street a roar the like of which I had never

heard before, but which sent a sensation of mingled fear and excitement coursing through my body. I asked permission of Father to go and see what the trouble was. He bluntly ordered me to stay in the cart. A little later we drove down Atlanta's main business thoroughfare, Peachtree Street. Again we heard the terrifying cries, this time near at hand and coming toward us. We saw a lame Negro bootblack from Herndon's barber shop pathetically trying to outrun a mob of whites. Less than a hundred yards from us the chase ended. We saw clubs and fists descending to the accompaniment of savage shouting and cursing. Suddenly a voice cried, "There goes another nigger!" Its work done, the mob went after new prey. The body with the withered foot lay dead in a pool of blood on the street.

Father's apprehension and mine steadily increased during the 7 evening, although the fact that our skins were white kept us from attack. Another circumstance favored us — the mob had not yet grown violent enough to attack United States government property. But I could see Father's relief when he punched the time clock at eleven P.M. and got into the cart to home. He wanted to go the back way down Forsyth Street, but I begged him, in my childish excitement and ignorance, to drive down Marietta to Five Points, the heart of Atlanta's business district, where the crowds were densest and the yells loudest. No sooner had we turned into Marietta Street, however, than we saw careening toward us an undertaker's barouche. Crouched in the rear of the vehicle were three Negroes clinging to the sides of the carriage as it lunged and swerved. On the driver's seat crouched a white man, the reins held taut in his left hand. A huge whip was gripped in his right. Alternately he lashed the horses and, without looking backward, swung the whip in savage swoops in the faces of members of the mob as they lunged at the carriage determined to seize the three Negroes.

There was no time for us to get of its path, so sudden and swift 8 was the appearance of the vehicle. The hub cap of the right rear wheel of the barouche hit the right side of our much lighter wagon. Father and I instinctively threw our weight and kept the cart from turning completely over. Our mare was a Texas mustang which, frightened by the sudden blow, lunged in the air as Father clung to the reins. Good fortune was with us. The cart settled back on its four wheels as Father said in a voice which brooked no dissent, "We are going home the back way and not down Marietta."

But again on Pryor Street we heard the cry of the mob. Close to 9 us and in our direction ran a stout and elderly woman who cooked at a downtown white hotel. Fifty yards behind, a mob which filled the street from curb to curb was closing in. Father handed the reins to me and, though he was of slight stature, reached down and lifted the woman into the cart. I did not need to be told to lash the mare to the fastest speed she could muster.

10   The church bells tolled the next morning for Sunday service. But no one in Atlanta believed for a moment that the hatred and lust for blood had been appeased. Like skulls on a cannibal's hut the hats and caps of victims of the mob the night before had been hung on the iron hooks of telegraph poles. None could tell whether each hat represented a dead Negro. But we knew that some of those who had worn hats would never again wear any.

11   Later in the afternoon friends of my father's came to warn of more trouble that night. They told us that plans had been perfected for a mob to form on Peachtree Street just after nightfall to march down Houston Street to what the white people called "Darktown," three blocks or so below our house, to "clean out the niggers." There had never been a firearm in our house before that day. Father was reluctant even in those circumstances to violate the law, but he at last gave in at Mother's insistence.

12   We turned out the lights, as did all our neighbors. No one removed his clothes or thought of sleep. Apprehension was tangible. We could almost touch its cold and clammy surface. Toward midnight the unnatural quiet was broken by a roar that grew steadily in volume. Even today I grow tense in remembering it.

13   Father told Mother to take my sisters, the youngest of them only six, to the rear of the house, which offered more protection from stones and bullets. My brother George was away, so Father and I, the only males in house, took our places at the front windows. The windows opened on a porch along the front side of the house, which in turn gave onto a narrow lawn that sloped down to the street and a picket fence. There was a crash as Negroes smashed the street lamp at the corner of Houston and Piedmont Avenue down the street. In a very few minutes the vanguard of the mob, some of them bearing torches, appeared. A voice which we recognized as that of the son of the grocer with whom we had traded for many years yelled, "That's where the nigger mail carrier lives! Let's burn it down! It's too nice for a nigger to live in!" In the eerie light Father turned his drawn face toward me. In a voice as quiet as though he were asking me to pass him the sugar at the breakfast table, he said, "Son, don't shoot until the first man puts his foot on the lawn and then — don't you miss!"

14   In the flickering light the mob swayed, paused, and began to flow

toward us. In that instant there opened within me a great awareness; I knew then who I was. I was a Negro, a human being with an invisible pigmentation which marked me a person to be hunted, hanged, abused, discriminated againt, kept in poverty and ignorance, in order that those whose skin was white would have readily at hand a proof of their superiority, a proof patent and inclusive, accessible to the moron and the idiot as well as to the wise man and the genius. No matter how low a white man fell, he could always hold fast to the smug conviction that he was superior to two-thirds of the world's population, for those two-thirds were not white.

It made no difference how intelligent or talented my millions of   15 brothers and I were, or how virtuously we lived. A curse like that of Judas was upon us, a mark of degradation fashioned with heavenly authority. There were white men who said Negroes had no souls, and who proved it by the Bible. Some of these now were approaching us, intent upon burning our house.

Theirs was a world of contrasts in values: superior and inferior,   16 profit and loss, cooperative and noncooperative, civilized and aboriginal, white and black. If you were on the wrong end of the comparison, if you were inferior, if you were noncooperative, if you were aboriginal, if you were black, then you were marked for excision, expulsion, or extinction. I was a Negro; I was therefore that part of history which opposed the good, the just, and the enlightened. I was a Persian, falling before the hordes of Alexander, I was a Carthaginian, extinguished by the Legions of Rome. I was a Frenchman at Waterloo, an Anglo-Saxon at Hastings, a Confederate at Vicksburg. I was defeated, wherever and whenever there was a defeat.

Yet as a boy there in the darkness amid the tightening fright, I   17 knew the inexplicable thing — that my skin was as white as the skin of those who were coming at me.

The mob moved toward the lawn. I tried to aim my gun, wonder-   18 ing what it would feel like to kill a man. Suddenly there was a volley of shots. The mob hesitated, stopped. Some friends of my father's had barricaded themselves in a two-story brick building just below our house. It was they who had fired. Some of the mobsmen, still blood-thirsty, shouted, "Let's go get the nigger." Others, afraid now for their safety, held back. Our friends, noting the hesitation, fired another volley. The mob broke and retreated up Houston Street.

In the quiet that followed I put my gun aside and tried to relax.   19 But a tension different from anything I had ever known possessed me. I was gripped by the knowledge of my identity, and in the depths of my soul I was vaguely aware that I was glad of it. I was sick with loathing for the hatred which had flared before me that night and come so close to making me a killer; but I was glad I was not one of those who hated; I was glad I was not one of those made sick and murderous by pride. I was glad I was not one of those whose story is in the history of the world, a record of bloodshed, rapine, and pillage. I was glad my mind and spirit were part of the races that had not fully awakened, and who therefore still had before them the opportunity to write a record of virtue as a memorandum to Armageddon.

20 It was all just a feeling then, inarticulate and melancholy, yet reassuring in the way that death and sleep are reassuring, and I have clung to it now for nearly half a century.

___ **CONSIDERATIONS** ___

1. The color of a man's skin, the cut of a family's front-yard lawn, the paint on a picket fence — all this is appearance. How does Walter White use appearances to give his narrative essay drama?

2. The first sentence in Paragraph 3 might well be called the thesis of White's essay. What advantage does he gain by placing it there instead of beginning with it?

3. What was the most important thing White learned from that race riot in Atlanta in 1906?

4. If you notice yourself tensing as you read White's account, study what he does to build suspense.

5. Compare and contrast White's account with an equally dramatic event in the childhood of Langston Hughes (pages 198–200). Are the two writers more different than alike in their style and tone? Explain.

6. How and where in his essay does White try to express consciousness of his place in humanity's long history?

Walt Whitman (1819–1892) is often called the greatest poet of America. We represent him here by a casual note in prose, for when the writer is Whitman, even a casual note may display the fresh observation of great writing. His view of Abraham Lincoln, so unlike the contemporary view of him as a second-rate bumbler, foreshadows the vision of subsequent generations.

77

WALT WHITMAN
On Abraham Lincoln

August 12th. — I see the President almost every day, as I happen to live where he passes to or from his lodgings out of town. He never sleeps at the White House during the hot season, but has quarters at a healthy location some three miles north of the city, the Soldiers' home, a United States military establishment. I saw him this morning about 8½ coming in to business, riding on Vermont avenue, near L street. He always has a company of twenty-five or thirty cavalry, with sabres drawn and held upright over their shoulders. They say this guard was against his personal wish, but he let his counselors have their way. The party makes no great show in uniform or horses. Mr. Lincoln on the saddle generally rides a good-sized, easy-going gray horse, is dress'd in plain black, somewhat rusty and dusty, wears a black stiff hat, and looks about as ordinary in attire, &c., as the commonest man. A lieutenant, with yellow straps, rides at his left, and following behind, two by two, come the cavalry men, in their yellow-striped jackets. They are generally going at a slow trot, as that is the pace set them by the one they wait upon. The sabres and accoutrements clank, and the entirely unornamental *cortège* as it trots towards Lafayette square arouses no sensation, only some curious stranger stops and gazes. I see very plainly Abraham Lincoln's dark brown face, with the deep-cut lines, the eyes, always to me with a deep latent sadness in the expression. We have got so that we exchange bows, and very cordial ones. Sometimes the President goes and comes in an open barouche. The cavalry always accompany him, with drawn sabres. Often I notice as he goes out evenings — and sometimes in the morning, when he returns early — he turns off and halts at the large and handsome residence of the Secretary of War, on K street, and holds conference there. If in his barouche, I can see from my window he does not alight, but sits in his vehicle, and Mr. Stanton comes out to attend him. Sometimes one of his sons, a boy of ten or twelve, accompanies him, riding at his right on a pony. Earlier in the summer I occasionally saw the President and his wife, toward the latter part of the afternoon, out in a barouche, on a pleasure ride through the city. Mrs. Lincoln was dress'd in complete black, with a long crape veil. The equipage is of the plainest kind, only two horses, and they nothing extra. They pass'd me once very close, and I saw the President in the face fully, as they were moving slowly, and his look, though abstracted, happen'd to be directed steadily in my eye. He bow'd and smiled, but far beneath his smile I noticed well the expression I have alluded to. None of the artists or pictures has caught the deep, though subtle and indirect expression of this man's face. There is something else there. One of the great portrait painters of two or three centuries ago is needed.

_____ CONSIDERATIONS _____

1. Reading Whitman's poem, "When Lilacs Last in the Dooryard Bloom'd," will reveal the poet's profound feeling for Lincoln, a feeling only suggested in this brief account.

2. Whitman's notes illustrate the selection of detail that every writer makes. Note the details that Whitman records, then make a list of details that he may have seen in Lincoln's cortège but did not write down. How conscious are you of what you select to include in your writing?

3. Is Whitman's an "objective" description of Lincoln? Is any description 100 percent objective? Why? Why not?

William Carlos Williams (1883–1963) lived all his life in Rutherford, New Jersey, where he was a pediatrician, and where he wrote his poems. He used American speech for his poems, plain talk in spoken rhythms, and he believed strongly in the accurate poetic rendition of people and things around us. People who love his poems quarrel over which of William Carlos Williams's sense organs work best in his poems: the eyes or the ears.

78

WILLIAM CARLOS WILLIAMS
To Waken an Old Lady

Old age is
a flight of small
cheeping birds
skimming
bare trees   5
above a snow glaze.
Gaining and failing
they are buffeted
by a dark wind —
But what?   10
On harsh weedstalks
the flock has rested,
the snow
is covered with broken
seedhusks   15
and the wind tempered
by a shrill
piping of plenty.

*Garry Wills (b. 1934) was educated as a classicist and writes
mostly about politics. He teaches at John Hopkins, writes for
newspapers and magazines, and publishes many books, including*
Nixon Agonistes *(1970) and* Bare Ruined Choirs *(1972). Here we
reprint a portion of his prologue to* Inventing America *(1978), in
which Wills studies the intellectual influences on Thomas Jefferson in writing the Declaration of Independence. Consult the texts
of Jefferson (pages 211–216) and Lincoln (pages 231–232) as you
consider Wills's remarks, which as always compel the reader into
freshness — as if we read familiar words for the first time, without
their cloaks of history.*

79

GARRY WILLS
The Myth of the Declaration

1   Americans like, at intervals, to play this dirty trick upon themselves: Pollsters are sent out to canvass men and women on certain
doctrines and to shame them when these doctrines are declared — as
usually happens — unacceptable. Shortly after, the results are published: Americans have, once again, failed to subscribe to some phrase
or other from the Declaration of Independence. The late political scientist Willmoore Kendall called this game "discovering America." He
meant to remind us that running men out of town on a rail is at least
as much an American tradition as declaring unalienable rights. A good
point; but *should* that be our heritage? Shouldn't we, as Americans,
subscribe to the creed that (we are told) *made* us Americans?

2   Maybe. Still, do we really think we can find people, running
around alive in the street, who believe in the psychology of Louis de

Jaucourt, the contract theory of David Hume, the mechanics of benevolence as elaborated by Francis Hutcheson? And, if not, how can we ask people in good conscience to endorse a document of eighteenth-century science based on such beliefs? What are we asserting if we agree to the document? That it is eloquent, or part of our heritage, or noble in its aspiration? Or that it is *right?*

Obviously, to judge from the use made of the responses, good   3
Americans are supposed to take the latter view. When many, or even most, refuse to agree with the Declaration's teaching, we are urged to fear that something has gone wrong with America; that it has ceased in part to be itself — i.e., to think as it ought. In 1975, the lieutenant governor of Pennsylvania wrote around to scholars for a list of appropriate modern leaders who might re-enact the signing of the Declaration on July 4, 1976. If he meant to re-enact what actually happened, he should have begun the signings on August 2 and continued them into November. But, even apart from that, the man was asking for the impossible, for a resurrection of the dead. Most of those brought in for such a ceremony would not know what on earth they were admitting to. And those who might know, and still wanted to sign, would have to justify their act in ways so devious as to defeat speculation on their motives.

It is not surprising that we should misunderstand the Declara-   4
tion. It is written in the lost language of the Enlightenment. It is dark with unexamined lights. Besides, we have a very powerful document from the nineteenth century to help us along in our error. What the State of Pennsylvania was contemplating in 1975, the President of the United States had already accomplished in 1863 — the recontracting of our society on the basis of the Declaration as our fundamental charter. This was accomplished by the principal political stylist of his day — indeed, of our entire history. Abraham Lincoln was a great and conscious verbal craftsman. The man who writes, "The world will little note, nor long remember, what we do here," has done his best — by mere ripple and interplay of liquids — to make sure the world will remember; as it has.[1]

Lincoln was a great artist of America's romantic period. The pop-   5
ular image of the man — pacing long corridors at night, moody, fearing madness — is Byronic in all but its American setting. And his literary

---

[1] The phrase quoted has a musical pattern dear to Lincoln — preliminary eddyings that yield to lapidary monosyllables: "We shall nobly save, or meanly lose, the last best hope of earth."

kinship in America is established by the style itself: "The mystic cords of memory, stretching from every battlefield and patriot grave to every living heart and hearthstone, all over this broad land, will yet swell the chorus of the Union, when again touched, as surely they will be, by the better angels of our nature." That is purest Israfel; Lincoln's is the style of a soberer Edgar Poe, with touches of Emerson. It achieves a democratic-oracular tone.

6   He obviously gave some thought to the first six words of his most famous exordium: "Four score and seven years ago . . ." In the 1950s, a satirist rewrote the Gettysburg Address in Eisenhowerese: "About eighty-some years ago, I think — I'll have Sherm look that up for you if you need it. . . ." That was funny in its way. But so, in its way, is Lincoln's own exordium. "Four score and seven" is a very stilted way of saying eighty-seven. Lincoln himself, speaking at Springfield in 1857, talked of the Declaration's passage "some eighty years ago" (which eerily anticipates the Eisenhower version). And later in the speech Lincoln cited the exact figure: "eighty-one years ago." That is the plain blunt way of counting back — and it is said (by those who have not given the matter much attention) that Lincoln's style charmed by its plainness.

7   Admittedly, "Four score and seven" rolls — it has less the accountant's style than the prophet's. You hear it and don't immediately start subtracting eighty-seven from 1863. ("Let's see, that gives us 1776.") And Lincoln had good reason to prefer that you hold off, for a while, on the computation till he made his case for it. It was not a necessary, or even obvious, number to choose for our date of national origin.

8   It is customary to settle for a vague justification of Lincoln's language as achieving dignity by periphrasis. But what, precisely, makes "four score" so dignified? One thing. The English Bible. That does the trick. Only in "three-score and ten" for the allotted life of man was "score" commonly used for twice-ten in the Victorian era. Lincoln is stirring biblical echoes in his opening phrase, and he keeps on stirring as he goes.

9   "Four score and seven years ago our fathers brought forth . . ." Fathers is another religious term. Faith of our Fathers. The language of the hymnal. Pilgrim Fathers. Washington as Father of his Country. "Fathers" of the Constitution. But Lincoln is not talking about the founders, in the sense of the framers, the men of 1787; if he were, he would have been forced to say "Three score and sixteen years ago" or "Four score minus four years ago," which is better history but inferior music.

"Our fathers *brought forth* . . ." Just what does that mean? Not   10
simply that they introduced something onto this continent. If so,
where was it before they brought it in? And how could it be called a
new nation if merely transferred? No, "bring forth" cannot mean anything like "introduce from abroad." Lincoln is talking about generation on the spot. The nation is rightly called new because it is brought
forth maieutically, by midwifery; it is not only new, but newborn. The
suggested image is, throughout, of a *hieros gamos,* a marriage of male
heaven ("our fathers") and female earth ("this continent"). And it is a
miraculous conception, a virgin birth. The nation is conceived by a
mental act, in the spirit of liberty, and *dedicated* (as Jesus was in the
temple) to a proposition. The proposition to which it is dedicated
forms the bridge back from Lincoln to Jefferson, from the Address to
the Declaration — "the proposition that all men are created equal."

Lincoln was a master of the Bible's extraordinary hold on the   11
Protestant imagination of nineteenth-century America. Edmund Wilson says that its patterns, already deep in his literary imagination,
printed themselves ever more insistently on his mind as he grew into
a Christic vision of his own office and the nation's ordeal. But earlier
texts show how easily he thought of America as having been virgin-
born. In his 1854 Peoria address, he had already used the Magnificat[2]
to describe America's special status among nations:

> Let us re-adopt the Declaration of Independence, and — with it
> — the practises and policy which harmonize with it. Let North and
> South, let all America, let all lovers of liberty everywhere, join in
> the great and good work. If we do this, we shall not only have saved
> the Union, but shall have so saved it, as to make and to keep it
> forever worthy of the saving. We shall have so saved it, that the
> succeeding millions of free happy people, the world over, shall rise
> up and call us blessed to the latest generation.

We shall, that is, be Mary of the Magnificat, guarding the thing born to
us by a miracle. He picked up this theme again during the war, in his
December 1, 1862, address to Congress: "The fiery trial through which
we pass will light us down, in honor or dishonor, to the latest generation." The opening of St. Luke's Gospel is to the Gettysburg Address
what the Book of Isaiah is to "The Battle Hymn of the Republic."

That is why Lincoln chose his peculiar, his biblically shrouded,   12
figure "four score and seven." The figure takes us back to 1776, the
year of the Declaration, of the self-evident truth that all men are created equal. But there are some fairly self-evident objections to that

---

[2] See Luke 1:48. — Ed.

mode of calculating. All thirteen original colonies subscribed to the Declaration with instructions to their delegates that this was *not* to imply formation of a single nation. If anything, July 4, 1776, produced twelve new nations (with a thirteenth coming in on July 15) — conceived in liberty perhaps, but more dedicated to the proposition that the colonies they severed from the mother country were equal to each other than that their *inhabitants* were equal.

13   So resistant to union were these colonies that their first experiment at it — the (articled) Confederation — failed. Still, that *was* an attempt upon single nationhood; so 1777, the date of the Articles, has a better claim to be the moment when a new nation was brought forth than does 1776. In that case, Lincoln would have to say, "Four score and six years ago . . ." But the Articles did not become a universally accepted instrument of government until 1781. So a better historian would amend to "Four score and two years ago . . ." And even then, as I say, the Confederation failed. It was more in the nature of a league between sovereignties than the creation of a new state. For that we have to wait not only six more years, to the drafting of the Constitution, a date that gives us "Four score minus four years ago . . ."; but, more properly, eight years — to the Constitution's final ratification, the seating of a Congress, and inauguration of a President. So Lincoln's best date would have been 1789 — "Four score minus six years ago . . ." Those dissatisfied with the bicentennial celebrations of 1776 had only to wait thirteen years for a more appropriate date to be honored.

14   The mere idea of a sudden "birth" for America is very misleading. In the first place, the continent was not all that "virgin." It had not only Indians to be pitchforked toward the interior, but long-standing colonial governments which had reached a high degree of self-rule. Benjamin Harrison V arrived at the Continental Congress of 1774 as a member of the Virginia Assembly, in which Benjamin Harrison I had sat — and Benjamin Harrison II, *and* Benjamin Harrison III, *and* Benjamin Harrison IV. These were men with a century of governing behind them. America was already old before she got a chance to be "born" from an idea, as the myth of virgin birth demands.

15   The Declaration lends itself to that myth in ways the Articles or the Constitution could never do. They are messier enterprises, with the stamp of compromise upon them. To this the Articles add a note of failure and the Constitution adds a note of illegality. The convention that drew up our Constitution went far beyond its mandate; in effect, smuggled a new nation in upon the continent rather than bringing it forth by intellectual impregnation. The founding legend begins to look more like a case of Sabine rape than virginal conception.

Of course, to Lincoln — and to those progressive historians who   16
fleshed out his insight — the compromises of the Constitution were a
natural struggling of the flesh, unable to live up to the pure spirit of
the nation's Idea. The Church may at times not live up to the demands
of Faith, but Faith was given us entire at the outset. We move, here,
from nineteenth-century Fundamentalism to liberal Protestantism, to
the idea of a development in the Church's living of doctrinal truth. At
Springfield, Lincoln put it this way:

> They [the Declaration's signers] meant simply to declare the
> right, so that enforcement of it might follow as fast as circum-
> stances should permit. They meant to set up a standard maxim for
> free society, which would be familiar to all, and revered by all;
> constantly looked to, constantly labored for, and even though
> never perfectly attained, constantly approximated, and thereby
> constantly spreading and deepening its influence and augmenting
> the happiness and value of life to all people of all colors every-
> where. The assertion that "all men are created equal" was of no
> practical use in effecting our separation from Great Britain; and it
> was placed in the Declaration not for that, but for future use. Its
> authors meant it to be — as, thank God, it is now proving itself —
> a stumbling block [like St. Paul's preaching at Galatians 5:11] to
> all those who in after times might seek to turn a free people back
> into the hateful paths of despotism.

The *new* nation was not conceived in blood and conquest, like   17
other nations, nor by mere accident or legal convenience. There was a
necessity in its conception. But does this extraordinary birth of itself
make the nation too etherial to survive in our real world? "Now we
are engaged in a great civil war testing whether that nation, or any
nation so conceived and so dedicated, can long endure." We move from
St. Luke to St. John, to the hour and the power of darkness. Lincoln
hints here, as he did elsewhere, at the Civil War as the nation's cruci-
fixion. The country set apart by miraculous birth undergoes its supreme test and achieves — resurrection: "that this nation under God
shall have a *new birth* of freedom." The nation must be twice-born,
according to the gospel pattern, to become a sign for the nations, a
pledge that "government of the people, by the people, and for the
people shall not perish from the earth."

Well, now, that is a very nice myth. It flatters us with our special   18
status, our central importance to all men's aspirations. If we tried to
live up to its implications, we might all be better human beings. So
what's the matter with keeping the myth?

19   Useful falsehoods are dangerous things, often costing something down the road. We can already tot up some of the things this myth has cost us. To begin with, the cult of the Declaration as our mystical founding document led to a downgrading of the actual charter that gives us our law. The Constitution has often been treated as a falling off from the original vision of 1776, a betrayal of the Revolution — a compromising of the *proposition* to which (after being conceived in liberty) we were dedicated. That view of things was bad history and has been revealed as such. . . . But the surprising thing is that even scholars held and taught that view for so long — long enough for it to persist in the popular mind. That shows the power of our favored myth to distort facts.

20   There are subtler and more important results of the myth. A belief in our extraordinary birth, outside the processes of time, has led us to think or ourselves as a nation apart, with a special destiny, the hope of all those outside America's shores. This feeling, of course, antedated Lincoln. It was part of the Puritan ideal, of the city set on a hilltop. It turned George Washington into a Moses during the revolutionary period. It arose from Protestant America's strong feeling of kinship with the chosen people of its Old Testament. It returned in visions of manifest destiny at the beginning of this century. But Lincoln's was the most profound statement of this belief in a special American fate. His version of it was not pinned to a narrow Puritanism or imperialism, but simply to the Declaration itself. Its power is mythic, not sectarian. Lincoln did not join a separate religion to politics; he made his politics religious. And that is why his politics has survived the attack on less totally fused forms of "civil religion."

21   After his election in 1860, Lincoln said on his way to Washington: "It [the Revolution] was not the mere matter of separation of the colonies from the motherland, but [of] that sentiment in the Declaration of Independence, which gave liberty not alone to the people of this country, but hope to all the world, for all future time. It was that which gave promise that in due time the weights would be lifted from the shoulders of all men, and that all should have an equal chance. This is the sentiment embodied in the Declaration of Independence."

22   One way we felt we should save the world was to stay pure of it. If we were set apart, we should stay apart, to influence others precisely because we would not join them in the ruck of things. On the other hand, *when* we intervened in the affairs of the world, it would have to be for the highest and most total reasons — to save and transform the world, to give it a new life patterned after ours; to make the world safe

for democracy, to free the captives, to bring self-determination to others. In 1960, John F. Kennedy adapted a phrase from Lincoln — who was, in turn, adapting the Bible — to say that the world cannot exist half-slave and half-free. The possession parable of the house divided against itself was used by Lincoln to show that the North must prevail over the South's demoniac "possession" by slavery. Kennedy expanded that to make us willing to throw Communist devils out of Russia, China, Cuba, or Vietnam.

Since we had a special mission, we could assume special powers. President Woodrow Wilson, invading Mexico because its electoral arrangements displeased him, said that our bayonets would teach the country to elect good men, say, like Woodrow Wilson. The virtue of our aims sanctified the means — so we could indulge in a righteous Hiroshima or two, in napalm and saturation bombing, in a Diem coup, or a Chile *putsch*. Lincoln spoke of shed American blood as expiatory and cleansing, as a washing in the blood of the Lamb; and if we shed even our own blood, might we not shed that of others for their salvation? 23

This touches only one manifestation of our messianic sense, our willingness to redeem men in blood. The heart of that urge comes from our dedication to a *proposition*. In 1921, when Gilbert Chesterton applied for entry to America as a visiting lecturer, he was amused by the questions he had to answer. Was he an anarchist? A polygamist? Did he advocate the overthrow of America by force? "I have stood on the other side of Jordan, in the land ruled by a rude Arab chief, where the police looked so like brigands that one wondered what the brigands looked like. But they did not ask me whether I had come to subvert the power of the Shereef; and they did not exhibit the faintest curiosity about my personal views on the ethical basis of civil authority." Only America, the land of the free, asked him what he thought about the kind of freedom it was peddling — and asked him not as a settler or possible immigrant, but merely as a visitor. He especially loved the idea that subverters of the nation would serenely declare, on a question form, their intention to subvert. 24

Chesterton, being as generous as he could to this odd inquisition, granted that America, with its ambition of combining the most disparate ingredients in one republic, had to have a mold of some kind: "The experiment of a democracy of diverse races has been compared to a melting pot. But even that metaphor implies that the pot itself is of a certain shape and a certain substance; a pretty solid substance. The melting pot must not melt." Chesterton rightly called the mold reli- 25 gious, and looked for the source of our religion in the Declaration of Independence (as that was understood by Lincoln): "America is the only nation in the world that is founded on a creed. That creed is set forth with dogmatic and even theological lucidity in the Declaration of Independence, perhaps the only piece of practical politics that is also theoretical politics and also great literature."

26   Certainly Lincoln felt that the Declaration's importance was doctrinal, a test of virtue and citizenship: "All honor to Jefferson — to the man who, in the concrete pressure of a struggle for national independence by a single people, had the coolness, forecast, and capacity to introduce into a merely revolutionary document, an abstract truth, and so to embalm it there, that today and in all coming days, it shall be a rebuke and a stumbling block to the very harbingers of reappearing tyranny and oppression" (Letter to H. L. Pierce, 1859). America is the American *idea* for Lincoln, and that idea is contained in the Declaration: "I have insisted that, in legislating for new countries where it [slavery] does not exist, there is no just rule other than of moral and abstract right. With reference to those new countries, those maxims as to the right of people to 'life, liberty, and the pursuit of happiness' were the just rules to be constantly referred to" (1858). Again, after being elected President, he said in Philadelphia: "I have never had a feeling politically that did not spring from the sentiments embodied in the Declaration of Independence. I have often pondered over the toils that were endured by the officers and soldiers of the army, who achieved that Independence. I have often inquired of myself what great principle or idea it was that kept this Confederacy so long together." Speaking to the New Jersey Senate at the same period, he said: "I am exceedingly anxious that this Union, the Constitution, and the liberties of the people shall be perpetuated in accordance with the original idea for which the struggle was made." These assertions are inoffensive to most Americans — which explains why things like the House Un-American Activities Committee were inoffensive for so long.

27   If there is an American *idea*, then one must subscribe to it in order to be an American. One must sort out one's *mental* baggage to "declare" it on entry to the country. To be fully American, one must adopt this idea wholeheartedly, proclaim it, prove one's devotion to it. Unless we know what our fellows *think*, we do not know whether they are American at all, much less whether they are *truly* American. Indeed, since the idea is so pure and abstract, we must all be constantly striving toward it, trying to become *more* American. A Chesterton might well be shocked to find himself put under inquest before touch-

ing these religious shores; he had never been accused, at home, of "un-English activities." But here, to tell someone "That is not the American way" is to say, in effect, that the person addressed is not entirely American — not worthy of citizenship; a kind of second-class American or disguised interloper. Uncovering heresy under such disguises was the aim of America's loyalty oaths, security tests, black lists. Even the questions asked by pollsters who quiz Americans on their dedication to the Declaration are a politer kind of loyalty oath. The implication is that those who answer "wrong" prove that we are not inculcating our creed well enough. This very activity leans back toward the tradition Willmoore Kendall described. It rides the unorthodox out on a rail, of ridicule at least, if not of actual violence.

This whole way of thinking would, on many grounds, have been 28 alien to Thomas Jefferson. He was not, like Lincoln, a nineteenth-century romantic living in the full glow of transcendentalism (that school of faintly necrophiliac spirituality). He was an eighteenth-century empiricist, opposed to generalizations and concentrating on particular realities. With Locke, he had rejected innate ideas. He considered Plato's self-existent Ideas the great delusion of Western history. He did not believe one could "embalm" an idea in a text, lay it away in some heaven of the mind, for later generations to be constantly aspiring after. He denied that a spiritual ideal could be posed over-against some fleshly struggle toward it. He did not think material circumstances an obstacle to Reality. They, and they alone, *were* reality for him. He would not have accepted Lincoln's mystique of national union as a transcendentally "given" imperative.

He would never encourage people to yearn back toward some 29 ideal of perfection delivered to their forbears. He opposed "entailing" opinions on a later generation; he wanted constitutions revised often, since accumulated knowledge must make later generations wiser than that which drew up *any* old document. Even when trying to placate John Adams, he would not yield on this vital point:

> One of the questions you know on which our parties took different sides, was on the improvability of the human mind, in science, in ethics, in government, etc. Those who advocated reformation of institutions, *pari passu*,[3] with the progress of science, maintained that no definite limits could be assigned to that progress. The enemies of reform, on the other hand, denied improvement, and advocated steady adherence to the principles, practices and institu-

---

[3] Equally and simultaneously. — ED.

tions of our fathers, which they represented as the consummation of wisdom, and *akmé*[4] of excellence, beyond which the human mind could never advance. Altho' in the passage of your answer alluded to, you expressly disclaim the wish to influence the freedom of enquiry, you predict that that will produce nothing more worthy of transmission to posterity, than the principles, institutions, and systems of education received from their ancestors. I do not consider this as your deliberate opinion. You possess, yourself, too much science, not to see how much is still ahead of you, unexplained and unexplored. Your own consciousness must place you as far before our ancestors, as in the rear of our posterity (Cappon, 332).

30   To the extent that Chesterton read the Declaration as "dogmatic and even theological," he was misreading it. Jefferson would take such terms as an insult if applied to his draft. He thought most theology an enemy to man's freedom, and he opposed any religious tests for holding office or citizenship.

31   The dry intellectual formulae of the eighteenth century were traced in fine acids of doubt, leaving them difficult to decipher across the intervals of time and fashion. When the Declaration is read in Lincoln's romantic glass, darkly, its content becomes entirely a victim of guess and bias. Proof of this is easily obtained: Lincoln congratulates Jefferson for not being "merely" practical, for laying up a timeless truth, usable in future ages, though his own contemporaries could not recognize it. That praise includes almost everything Jefferson opposed. For him, the highest test of a thing was its immediate practicality to the living generation.

32   I have concentrated, here, on misreadings that derive from Lincoln, or are strengthened by his views, not because I think all our errors traceable to Gettysburg. Far from it. My point is that this is only one of *many* intervening filters that distort the text. The Declaration is not only part of our history; we are part of its history. We have cited it, over the years, for many purposes, including the purpose of deceiving ourselves; and it has become a misshapen thing in our minds. Jefferson never intended it for a spiritual Covenant; but it has traveled in an Ark that got itself more revered the more it was battered.

33   The best way to honor the spirit of Jefferson is to use his doubting intelligence again on his own text. Only skepticism can save him from his devotees, return us to the drier air of his scientific maxims, all

---

[4] Acme. — ED.

drawn with the same precision that went into his architectural sketches. The pollster on the street wants us to "endorse" Jefferson's Declaration. But Jefferson would be the first to ask what such an exercise could mean. Despite his hostility to Plato, he liked Socrates and thought the unexamined life not worth living. Even more, the unexamined document is not worth signing. The Declaration has been turned into something of a blank check for idealists of all sorts to fill in as they like. We had better stop signing it (over and over) and begin reading it. I do not mean seeing it. I mean reading it.

──── CONSIDERATIONS ────────────────────────────

1. Wills describes Lincoln as "a great artist," and says that "those who have not given the matter much attention" claim that Lincoln's style "charmed by its plainness." Select one example used by Wills to support his opinion that Lincoln was a great stylist, reread the Gettysburg Address, and evaluate his assertion.

2. What does Wills think gives the phrase "four score" its dignity? Take the opportunity offered by this question to compare the two versions of Ecclesiastes (pages 53–59).

3. "Some of us," wrote George Orwell in his satire, *Animal Farm*, "are more equal than others." What kind of equality was intended by the Declaration of Independence, according to Wills? See Paragraph 12.

4. In Paragraph 18 the author describes Lincoln's idealistic view of the founding of America as a myth and asks "So what's the matter with keeping the myth?" Can you think of any myths that are part of your heritage as a twentieth-century American? What are your views on the preservation or the destruction of these myths?

5. How does Wills argue that Lincoln completely misunderstood the Declaration of Independence? Does your reading of the declaration and the Gettysburg Address make you agree with Wills?

6. Throughout his essay, Wills uses the terms "Enlightenment" and "Romantic," counting on those terms to help his readers understand the difference he is drawing between Jefferson and Lincoln. Look up these words in a literary dictionary — Benet's *Reader's Encyclopedia*, for example — and discuss how Wills uses them.

Thomas Wolfe (1900–1938) wrote enormous autobiographical novels, most notably Look Homeward, Angel *(1929) and* Of Time and the River *(1935), and two published posthumously,* The Web and the Rock *(1939) and* You Can't Go Home Again *(1940). He was born and grew up in Asheville, North Carolina, entered the University of North Carolina at fifteen, attended Harvard, and taught at New York University. Wolfe was a huge man, and he wrote hugely. His novels were unending journals of total recall. He sometimes wrote twenty thousand words — about sixty pages in* A Writer's Reader — *at one sitting. Patient editors, especially Maxwell Perkins at Scribners, spent months carving each of his novels from packing cases full of disorganized manuscript. The finished novels were highly emotional, lyrical accounts of childhood, youth, and early manhood. Wolfe wrote one book about his unique method of writing,* The Story of a Novel *(1936). He died of complications following an attack of pneumonia, two weeks before he would have turned thirty-eight.*

The journal from which these selections come was written shortly before his final illness and death. He had given a talk at Purdue University in Indiana, and then had traveled to the Pacific Northwest looking for some relatives on his mother's side. He took a notebook with him, thinking that later he might work his notes up into a book. Only these notes survive, presented here line by line, transcribed from the novelist's nearly illegible handwriting.

Brilliant descriptions, intense evocation — and no discipline or structure. Of course one would not expect discipline or structure from any *writer in an unedited, posthumously published journal. This journal may serve as a model for students who wish to learn to write rapidly — in order to loosen up, and to accumulate detail and color, idea and recollection — before applying to their writing the formal disciplines of sentence, paragraph, and essay.*

80

THOMAS WOLFE
Journal Entries

MONDAY JUNE 20 (CRATER LAKE)

Left Portland, University Club, 8:15 sharp —   1
Fair day, bright sunlight, no cloud in sky —
Went South by East through farmlands of upper
Willamette and around base of Mount Hood
which was glowing in brilliant sun — Then
climbed and crossed Cascades, and came down
with suddenness of knife into the dry lands of the
Eastern slope — Then over high plateau and
through bare hills and canyons and irrigated
farmlands here and there, low valley, etc., and
into Bent at 12:45 — 200 miles in 4½
hours —

Then lunch at hotel and view of the 3 Sisters and   2
the Cascade range — then up to the Pilot Butte
above the town — the great plain stretching
infinite away — and unapproachable the great line
of the Cascades with their snowspired sentinels
Hood, Adams, Jefferson, 3 sisters, etc, and out of
Bend at 3 and then through the vast and level
pinelands — somewhat reminiscent of the South
for 100 miles then down through the noble pines
to the vast plainlike valley of the Klamath? — the

virgin land of Canaan all again — the far-off
ranges — infinite — Oregon and the Promised
Land — then through the valley floor — past Indian
reservation — Capt Jack — the Modocs — the great
trees open approaching vicinity of the Park —
the entrance and the reservation — the forester —
the houses — the great snow patches underneath
the trees — then the great climb upwards — the
foresting, administration — up and up again —
through the passes the great plain behind and at
length the incredible crater of the lake — the hotel
and a certain cheerlessness in spite of cordialness
— dry tongues vain-licking for a feast — the return,
the cottages, the college boys and girls who serve
and wait — the cafeteria and the souvenirs —
the great crater fading coldly in incredible
cold light — at

3   length departure — and the forest rangers down
below — long, long talks — too long with them
about "our wonders", etc — then by darkness the
sixty or seventy miles down the great dim
expanse of Klamath Lake, the decision to stay
here for the night — 3 beers, a shower, and this,
reveille at 5:30 in the morning — and so to bed!
       First day: 404 miles

4   The gigantic unconscious humor of the situation
— C "making every national park" without
seeing any of them — the main thing is to "make
them" — and so on and on tomorrow

TUESDAY JUNE 21, 1938 (YOSEMITE)

5   Dies Irae: Wakened at 5:30 — dragged weary
bones erect, dressed, closed baggage, was ready
shortly before six, and we were off again "on
the dot" — at six oclock. So out of Klamath,
the lakes red, and a thread of silver river in
the desert, and immediately

the desert, sage brush, and bare, naked, hills,   6
giant-molded, craterous, cupreous, glaciated
blasted — a demonic heath with reaches of great
pine, and volcanic glaciation, cupreous, fiendish,
desert, blasted — the ruins of old settlers home-
steads, ghost towns and the bleak little facades
of long forgotten postoffices lit bawdily by blazing
rising sun and the winding mainstreet, the
deserted station of the incessant railway — all
dominated now by the glittering snow — pale
masses of

Mount Shasta — pine lands, canyons, sweeps and   7
rises, the naked crateric hills and the volcanic
lava masses and then Mount Shasta omnipresent
— Mount Shasta all the time — always Mt. Shasta
— and at last the town named Weed (with a
divine felicity) — and breakfast at Weed at 7:45 —
and the morning bus from Portland and the
tired people tumbling out and *in* for breakfast

and away from Weed and towering Shasta at   8
8:15 — and up and climbing and at length into
the passes of the lovely timbered Siskiyous
and now down into canyon of the Sacramento
in among the lovely timbered Siskiyous and all
through the morning down and down and down
the canyon, and the road snaking, snaking
always with a thousand little punctual gashes,
and the freight trains and the engines turned
backward with the cabs in *front*

down below along the lovely Sacramento snaking   9
snaking snaking — and at last into the town of
Redding and the timber fading, hills fading,
cupreous lavic masses fading — and almost at
once the mighty valley of the Sacramento — as
broad as a continent — and all through the morning through the great floor of that great plain
like valley — the vast fields thick with straw
grass lighter

10   than Swedes hair — and infinitely far and
unapproachable the towns down the mountain
on both sides — and great herds of fat brown
steers in straw light fields — a dry land, with
a strange hot heady fragrance and fertility —
and at last no mountains at all but the great
sun-bright, heat-hazed, straw-light plain and
the straight marvel of the road on which the
car rushes

11   on like magic and no sense of speed at 60 miles
an hour — At 11:30 a brief halt at ——— to look at
the hotel — and great palms now, and spanish
tiles and arches and pilasters and a patio in
the hotel and swimming pool — and on again and
on again across the great, hot, straw light plain,
and great fields mown new and scattered with
infinite bundles of baled hay and

12   occasional clumps of greenery and pastures and
house and barns where water is and as Sacramento
nears a somewhat greener land, more unguent,
and better houses now, and great fat herds of
steers innumerable and lighter and more sun —
ovenhot towns and at length through the heat-
haze the slopes of Sacramento and over an
enormous viaduct across a flat

13   and marshy land and planes flying, and then
the far flung filling stations, hot dog stores,
3 Little Pigs, and Bar B-Q's of a California
town and then across the Sacramento into town —
the turn immediate and houses new and mighty
palms and trees and people walking. and the
State house with its gold leaf dome
and spaghetti at the first Greeks that we find,
and on out again immediate —

14   pressing on — past state house — and past street
by street of leafy trees and palms and pleasant
houses and out from town now — but traffic
flashing past now — and loaded trucks and

whizzing cars — no more the lovely 50 mile
stretches and 60 miles an hour — but down across
the backbone of the state — and the whole backbone
of the state — cars and towns and farms
and people
flashing by — and still that same vast
billowy plain — no light *brown* now — the
San Joaquin Valley now — and bursting with
Gods plenty — orchards — peaches — apricots —
and vineyards — orange groves — Gods plenty of
the best — and glaring litle towns sown thick
with fruit packing houses — ovenhot, glittering
in the hot and shining air — town

      after town — each in the middle of Gods plenty —   15
and at length the turn at ——— toward Yosemite —
90 miles away — the barren, crateric, lavic, volcanic
blasted hills — but signs now telling us we can't
get in now across the washed out road save
behind the conductor — and now too late — already
5 of six and the last conductor leaves

      at six and we still 50 miles away — and telephone   16
calls now to rangers, superintendents and so
forth, a filling station and hot cabins, and the
end of a day of blazing heat and the wind
stirring in the sycamores about the cabins, and
on again now, and almost immediately the broken
ground, the straw light mouldings, the rises to
the crater hills and soon

      among them — climbing, climbing into timber —   17
and down down down into pleasant timbered
mountain folds — get no sensation yet and winding
in and out — and little hill towns here and there
and climbing, climbing, climbing, mountain
lodges, cabins, houses, and so on, and now in
terrific mountain folds, close packed, precipitous,
lapped together and down and over, down again

      along breath taking curves and steepnesses and   18
sheer drops down below into a canyon cut a

mile below by great knifes blade — and at the
bottom the closed gate — the little store — calls upon
the phone again, and darkness and the sending
notes, and at last success — upon our own heads
be the risk but we may enter — and we do —
and so slowly up

19   we go along the washed out road — finding it
not near so dangerous as we feared — and at
length past the bad end and the closed gate and
release — and up now climbing and the sound of
mighty waters in the gorge and the sheer black-
nesses of beetling masses and the stars — and
presently the entrance and the rangers house —
a free pass now — and up and up — and boles of
trees terrific, cloven rock above the road

20   and over us and dizzy masses night black as a
cloud, a sense of the imminent terrific and at
length the valley of the Yosemite; roads forking
darkly, but the perfect sign — and now a smell
of smokes and of gigantic tentings and enormous
trees and gigantic cliff walls night black all
around and above the sky-bowl of starred night —
and Currys Lodge and

21   smoky gaiety and wonder — hundreds of young
faces and voices — the offices, buildings stores,
the dance floor crowded with its weary hundreds
and the hundreds of tents and cabins and the
absurdity of the life and the immensity of all —
and 1200 little shop girls and stenogs and new-
weds and schoolteachers and boys — all, God
bless their

22   little lives, necking, dancing, kissing, feeling,
and embracing in the great darkness of the giant
redwood trees — and the sound of the dark gigantic fall
of water — and so to bed!
        And 535 miles today!

_____ **CONSIDERATIONS** _____

1. Judging from the kinds of things he recorded in his journal, what were Wolfe's chief interests during the journey? What was he searching for? Why did he bother to keep a journal?

2. How many periods can you find in this selection? How does that number help account for the sense of speed and constant motion we get from the journal? What other characteristics of Wolfe's prose here contribute to that sense?

3. Does Wolfe depend much in his journal on figurative language, or is this selection chiefly literal and matter-of-fact?

4. How much of a typical American tourist was Wolfe? How often does he break out of such a stereotype? As you consider these questions, think of the phrases "see America first," "the American dream," and "middle-class values."

5. Write journal entries of your own about a trip you've made, imitating Wolfe's style. How do an imitation and a parody differ?

Virginia Woolf (1882–1941) is best known as a novelist. The
Voyage Out *appeared in 1915, followed by* Night and Day *(1919),*
Jacob's Room *(1922),* Mrs. Dalloway *(1925),* To The Lighthouse
(1927), Orlando *(1928),* The Waves *(1931),* The Years *(1937), and*
Between the Acts, *published shortly before her death. Daughter of
Sir Leslie Stephen, Victorian critic and essayist who edited the*
Dictionary of National Biography, *she was educated at home, and
began her literary career as a critic for the* Times Literary Supple-
ment. *She wrote essays regularly until her death; four volumes of
her* Collected Essays *appeared in the United States in 1967. More
recently, her publishers have issued three volumes of her collected
letters.*

*With her sister Vanessa, a painter, her husband Leonard Woolf,
an editor and writer, and Vanessa's husband Clive Bell, an art
critic, Virginia lived at the center of the Bloomsbury group—artists and intellectuals who gathered informally to talk and to
amuse each other, and whose unconventional ideas and habits,
when they were known, shocked the stolid British public. John
Maynard Keynes, the economist, was a member of the varied
group, which also included the biographer Lytton Strachey, the
novelist E. M. Forster, and eventually the American poet living in
England, T. S. Eliot. With her husband, Virginia Woolf founded*
The Hogarth Press, *a small firm dedicated to publishing superior
work. Among its authors were T. S. Eliot and Virginia herself.*

A recent biography — Virginia Woolf *— by her nephew Quentin
Bell gives an intimate picture of the whole group. Of all the
Bloomsbury people, Virginia was perhaps the most talented.
Throughout most of her life, she struggled against recurring mental illness, which brought with it intense depression and suicidal
impulses. When she was fifty-nine, the desire to die overcame the
desire to live.*

*This essay illustrates her preoccupation with describing the
essence of events, rather than their outward appearance.*

81

VIRGINIA WOOLF

The Death of the Moth

Moths that fly by day are not properly to be called moths; they do not excite that pleasant sense of dark autumn nights and ivy-blossom which the commonest yellow underwing asleep in the shadow of the curtain never fails to rouse in us. They are hybrid creatures, neither gay like butterflies nor sombre like their own species. Nevertheless the present specimen, with his narrow hay-coloured wings, fringed with a tassel of the same colour, seemed to be content with life. It was a pleasant morning, mid-September, mild, benignant, yet with a keener breath than of the summer months. The plough was already scoring the field opposite the window, and where the share had been, the earth was pressed flat and gleamed with moisture. Such vigour came rolling in from the fields and the down beyond that it was difficult to keep the eyes strictly turned upon the book. The rooks too were keeping one of their annual festivities; soaring round the tree-tops until it looked as if a vast net with thousands of black knots in it has been cast up into the air; which, after a few moments sank slowly down upon the trees until every twig seemed to have a knot at the end of it. Then, suddenly, the net would be thrown into the air again in a wider circle this time, with the utmost clamour and vociferation, as though to be thrown into the air and settle slowly down upon the tree-tops were a tremendously exciting experience.

The same energy which inspired the rooks, the ploughmen, the horses, and even, it seemed, the lean bare-backed downs, sent the moth fluttering from side to side of his square of the window-pane. One

479

could not help watching him. One was, indeed, conscious of a queer feeling of pity for him. The possibilities of pleasure seemed that morning so enormous and so various that to have only a moth's part in life, and a day moth's at that, appeared a hard fate, and his zest in enjoying his meagre opportunities to the full, pathetic. He flew vigorously to one corner of his compartment, and, after waiting there a second, flew across to the other. What remained for him but to fly to a third corner and then to a fourth? That was all he could do, in spite of the size of the downs, the width of the sky, the far-off smoke of houses, and the romantic voice, now and then, of a steamer out at sea. What he could do he did. Watching him, it seemed as if a fibre, very thin but pure, of the enormous energy of the world had been thrust into his frail and diminutive body. As often as he crossed the pane, I could fancy that a thread of vital light became visible. He was little or nothing but life.

3   Yet, because he was so small, and so simple a form of the energy that was rolling in at the open window and driving its way through so many narrow and intricate corridors in my own brain and in those of other human beings, there was something marvellous as well as pathetic about him. It was as if someone had taken a tiny bead of pure life and decking it as lightly as possible with down and feathers, had set it dancing and zigzagging to show us the true nature of life. Thus displayed one could not get over the strangeness of it. One is apt to forget all about life, seeing it humped and bossed and garnished and cumbered so that it has to move with the greatest circumspection and dignity. Again, the thought of all that life might have been had he been born in any other shape caused one to view his simple activities with a kind of pity.

4   After a time, tired by his dancing apparently, he settled on the window ledge in the sun, and the queer spectacle being at an end, I forgot about him. Then, looking up, my eye was caught by him. He was trying to resume his dancing, but seemed either so stiff or so awkward that he could only flutter to the bottom of the window-pane; and when he tried to fly across it he failed. Being intent on other matters I watched these futile attempts for a time without thinking, unconsciously waiting for him to resume his flight, as one waits for a machine, that has stopped momentarily, to start again without considering the reason for its failure. After perhaps a seventh attempt he slipped from the wooden ledge and fell, fluttering his wings, on to his back on the window-sill. The helplessness of his attitude roused me. It flashed upon me that he was in difficulties; he could no longer raise himself; his legs struggled vainly. But, as I stretched out a pencil,

meaning to help him to right himself, it came over me that the failure and awkwardness were the approach of death. I laid the pencil down again.

The legs agitated themselves once more. I looked as if for the enemy against which he struggled. I looked out of doors. What had happened there? Presumably it was midday, and work in the fields had stopped. Stillness and quiet had replaced the previous animation. The birds had taken themselves off to feed in the brooks. The horses stood still. Yet the power was there all the same, massed outside indifferent, impersonal, not attending to anything in particular. Somehow it was opposed to the little hay-coloured moth. It was useless to try to do anything. One could only watch the extraordinary efforts made by those tiny legs against an oncoming doom which could, had it chosen, have submerged an entire city, not merely a city, but masses of human beings; nothing, I knew, had any chance against death. Nevertheless after a pause of exhaustion the legs fluttered again. It was superb this last protest, and so frantic that he succeeded at last in righting himself. One's sympathies, of course, were all on the side of life. Also, when there was nobody to care or to know, this gigantic effort on the part of an insignificant little moth, against a power of such magnitude, to retain what no one else valued or desired to keep, moved one strangely. Again, somehow, one saw life, a pure bead. I lifted the pencil again, useless though I knew it to be. But even as I did so, the unmistakable tokens of death showed themselves. The body relaxed, and instantly grew stiff. The struggle was over. The insignificant little creature now knew death. As I looked at the dead moth, this minute wayside triumph of so great a force over so mean an antagonist filled me with wonder. Just as life had been strange a few minutes before, so death was now as strange. The moth having righted himself now lay most decently and uncomplaining composed. O yes, he seemed to say, death is stronger than I am.

_____ **CONSIDERATIONS** _____

1. Writers are often concerned about the *point of view* they use in their work. By that they mean, not their own attitude toward their characters or situations, but the authority through whom the reader gets information. John McPhee's account of a tennis game, for example, changes its point of view from player to player (pages 243–247). Do you find any shifting or mixing of point of view in "The Death of the Moth"?

2. Study the extended image of the rooks (British word for crow) at the end of Woolf's first paragraph. Is it literal or figurative? Does it help you *see?* How does it contribute to a larger idea in this essay?

3. As Woolf watched the moth's last moments, her feelings about it grew. Is her essay sentimental? Consult a literary dictionary or handbook to clarify "sentimentality," and to understand why that trait is so widely considered a fault. Compare Richard Rhodes's essay on greeting cards (pages 335–346) with the Woolf essay.

4. An important part of Woolf's essay is her treatment of the sequence of events. Is the essay then narrative instead of descriptive? How practical or useful is it to hold rigidly to such categories?

5. As she demonstrates her descriptive and narrative skills, Woolf does something that lifts the essay above mere reporting. How does she do it?

Richard Wright (1908–1960) was born on a plantation in Natchez, Mississippi. A restless and unruly child, at fifteen he left home and supported himself doing unskilled work, gradually improving his employment until he became a clerk in a post office. In this essay from his autobiography Black Boy *(1944) he writes about an occasion that transformed his life. By chance he became obsessed with the notion of reading H. L. Mencken, the iconoclastic editor and essayist. (See Mencken's "Gamalielese" on pages 274–277.) He schemed and plotted to borrow Mencken's books from the library, and when he succeeded his career as a writer began.*

Determined to be a writer, Richard Wright worked on the Federal Writer's Project, wrote for the New Masses, *and finally won a prize from* Story *magazine for a short novel called* Uncle Tom's Children. *The following year, he was awarded a Guggenheim Fellowship, and in 1940 he published his novel* Native Son, *which has become an American classic. In 1946 he emigrated to Paris, where he lived until his death. His later novels included* The Outsider *(1953) and* The Long Dream *(1958). In 1977, his publisher issued the second half of* Black Boy, *entitled* American Hunger.

82

RICHARD WRIGHT
The Library Card

One morning I arrived early at work and went into the bank lobby where the Negro porter was mopping. I stood at a counter and picked up the Memphis *Commercial Appeal* and began my free reading of the press. I came finally to the editorial page and saw an article dealing with one H. L. Mencken. I knew by hearsay that he was the editor of 1 the *American Mercury,* but aside from that I knew nothing about him. The article was a furious denunciation of Mencken, concluding with one, hot, short sentence: Mencken is a fool.

2   I wondered what on earth this Mencken had done to call down upon him the scorn of the South. The only people I had ever heard denounced in the South were Negroes, and this man was not a Negro. Then what ideas did Mencken hold that made a newspaper like the *Commercial Appeal* castigate him publicly? Undoubtedly he must be advocating ideas that the South did not like. Were there, then, people other than Negroes who criticized the South? I knew that during the Civil War the South had hated northern whites, but I had not encountered such hate during my life. Knowing no more of Mencken than I did at that moment, I felt a vague sympathy for him. Had not the South, which had assigned me the role of a non-man, cast at him its hardest words?

3   Now, how could I find out about this Mencken? There was a huge library near the riverfront, but I knew that Negroes were not allowed to patronize its shelves any more than they were the parks and playgrounds of the city. I had gone into the library several times to get books for the white men on the job. Which of them would now help me to get books? And how could I read them without causing concern to the white men with whom I worked? I had so far been successful in hiding my thoughts and feelings from them, but I knew that I would create hostility if I went about this business of reading in a clumsy way.

4   I weighed the personalities of the men on the job. There was Don, a Jew; but I distrusted him. His position was not much better than mine and I knew that he was uneasy and insecure; he had always treated me in an offhand, bantering way that barely concealed his contempt. I was afraid to ask him to help me to get books; his frantic desire to demonstrate a racial solidarity with the whites against Negroes might make him betray me.

5   Then how about the boss? No, he was a Baptist and I had the suspicion that he would not be quite able to comprehend why a black boy would want to read Mencken. There were other white men on the job whose attitudes showed clearly that they were Kluxers or sympathizers, and they were out of the question.

6   There remained only one man whose attitude did not fit into an anti-Negro category, for I had heard the white men refer to him as a "Pope lover." He was an Irish Catholic and was hated by the white Southerners. I knew that he read books, because I had got him volumes

from the library several times. Since he, too, was an object of hatred, I
felt that he might refuse me but would hardly betray me. I hesitated,
weighing and balancing the imponderable realities.

One morning I paused before the Catholic fellow's desk.   7

"I want to ask you a favor," I whispered to him.   8

"What is it?"   9

"I want to read. I can't get books from the library. I wonder if   10
you'd let me use your card?"

He looked at me suspiciously.   11

"My card is full most of the time," he said.   12

"I see," I said and waited, posing my question silently.   13

"You're not trying to get me into trouble, are you, boy?" he asked,   14
staring at me.

"Oh, no, sir."   15

"What book do you want?"   16

"A book by H. L. Mencken."   17

"Which one?"   18

"I don't know. Has he written more than one?"   19

"He has written several."   20

"I didn't know that."   21

"What makes you want to read Mencken?"   22

"Oh, I just saw his name in the newspaper," I said.   23

"It's good of you to want to read," he said. "But you ought to read   24
the right things."

I said nothing. Would he want to supervise my reading?   25

"Let me think," he said. "I'll figure out something."   26

I turned from him and he called me back. He stared at me quiz-   27
zically.

"Richard, don't mention this to the other white men," he said.   28

"I understand," I said. "I won't say a word."   29

A few days later he called me to him.   30

"I've got a card in my wife's name," he said. "Here's mine."   31

"Thank you, sir."   32

"Do you think you can manage it?"   33

"I'll manage fine," I said.   34

"If they suspect you, you'll get in trouble," he said.   35

"I'll write the same kind of notes to the library that you wrote   36
when you sent me for books," I told him. "I'll sign your name."

He laughed.   37

"Go ahead. Let me see what you get," he said.   38

That afternoon I addressed myself to forging a note. Now, what   39 were the names of books written by H. L. Mencken? I did not know any of them. I finally wrote what I thought would be a foolproof note: *Dear Madam: Will you please let this nigger boy* — I used the word "nigger" to make the librarian feel that I could not possibly be the author of the note — *have some books by H. L. Mencken?* I forged the white man's name.

40   I entered the library as I had always done when on errands for whites, but I felt that I would somehow slip up and betray myself. I doffed my hat, stood a respectful distance from the desk, looked as unbookish as possible, and waited for the white patrons to be taken care of. When the desk was clear of people, I still waited. The white librarian looked at me.

41   "What do you want, boy?"

42   As though I did not possess the power of speech, I stepped forward and simply handed her the forged note, not parting my lips.

43   "What books by Mencken does he want?" she asked.

44   "I don't know, ma'am," I said, avoiding her eyes.

45   "Who gave you this card?"

46   "Mr. Falk," I said.

47   "Where is he?"

48   "He's at work, at the M ——— Optical Company," I said. "I've been in here for him before."

49   "I remember," the woman said. "But he never wrote notes like this."

50   Oh, God, she's suspicious. Perhaps she would not let me have the books? If she had turned her back at that moment, I would have ducked out the door and never gone back. Then I thought of a bold idea.

51   "You can call him up, ma'am," I said, my heart pounding.

52   "You're not using these books, are you?" she asked pointedly.

53   "Oh, no, ma'am. I can't read."

54   "I don't know what he wants by Mencken," she said under her breath.

55   I knew now that I had won; she was thinking of other things and the race question had gone out of her mind. She went to the shelves. Once or twice she looked over her shoulder at me, as though she was still doubtful. Finally she came forward with two books in her hand.

56   "I'm sending him two books," she said. "But tell Mr. Falk to come in next time, or send me the names of the books he wants. I don't know what he wants to read."

57   I said nothing. She stamped the card and handed me the books. Not daring to glance at them, I went out of the library, fearing that the

woman would call me back for further questioning. A block away from the library I opened one of the books and read a title: *A Book of Prefaces.* I was nearing my nineteenth birthday and I did not know how to pronounce the word "preface." I thumbed the pages and saw strange words and strange names. I shook my head, disappointed. I looked at the other book; it was called *Prejudices.* I knew what that word meant; I had heard it all my life. And right off I was on guard against Mencken's books. Why would a man want to call a book *Prejudices?* The word was so stained with all my memories of racial hate that I could not conceive of anybody using it for a title. Perhaps I had made a mistake about Mencken? A man who had prejudices must be wrong.

When I showed the books to Mr. Falk, he looked at me and frowned. 58

"That librarian might telephone you," I warned him. 59

"That's all right," he said. "But when you're through reading those books, I want you to tell me what you get out of them." 60

That night in my rented room, while letting the hot water run over my can of pork and beans in the sink, I opened *A Book of Prefaces* and began to read. I was jarred and shocked by the style, the clear, clean, sweeping sentences. Why did he write like that? And how did one write like that? I pictured the man as a raging demon, slashing with his pen, consumed with hate, denouncing everything American, extolling everything European or German, laughing at the weaknesses of people, mocking God, authority. What was this? I stood up, trying to realize what reality lay behind the meaning of the words . . . Yes, this man was fighting, fighting with words. He was using words as a weapon, using them as one would use a club. Could words be weapons? Well, yes, for here they were. Then, maybe, perhaps, I could use them as a weapon? No. It frightened me. I read on and what amazed me was not what he said, but how on earth anybody had the courage to say it. 61

Occasionally I glanced up to reassure myself that I was alone in the room. Who were these men about whom Mencken was talking so passionately? Who was Anatole France? Joseph Conrad? Sinclair Lewis, Sherwood Anderson, Dostoevski, George Moore, Gustave Flaubert, Maupassant, Tolstoy, Frank Harris, Mark Twain, Thomas Hardy, Arnold Bennett, Stephen Crane, Zola, Norris, Gorky, Bergson, Ibsen, Balzac, Bernard Shaw, Dumas, Poe, Thomas Mann, O. Henry, Dreiser, H. G. Wells, Gogol, T. S. Eliot, Gide, Baudelaire, Edgar Lee Masters, Stendhal, Turgenev, Huneker, Nietzsche, and scores of others? Were these men real? Did they exist or had they existed? And how did one pronounce their names? 62

63   I ran across many words whose meanings I did not know, and I either looked them up in a dictionary or, before I had a chance to do that, encountered the word in a context that made its meaning clear. But what strange world was this? I concluded the book with the conviction that I had somehow overlooked something terribly important in life. I had once tried to write, had once reveled in feeling, had let my crude imagination roam, but the impulse to dream had been slowly beaten out of me by experience. Now it surged up again and I hungered for books, new ways of looking and seeing. It was not a matter of believing or disbelieving what I read, but of feeling something new, of being affected by something that made the look of the world different.

64   As dawn broke I ate my pork and beans, feeling dopey, sleepy. I went to work, but the mood of the book would not die; it lingered, coloring everything I saw, heard, did. I now felt that I knew what the white men were feeling. Merely because I had read a book that had spoken of how they lived and thought, I identified myself with that book. I felt vaguely guilty. Would I, filled with bookish notions, act in a manner that would make the whites dislike me?

65   I forged more notes and my trips to the library became frequent. Reading grew into a passion. My first serious novel was Sinclair Lewis's *Main Street.* It made me see my boss, Mr. Gerald, and identify him as an American type. I would smile when I saw him lugging his golf bags into the office. I had always felt a vast distance separating me from the boss, and now I felt closer to him, though still distant. I felt now that I knew him, that I could feel the very limits of his narrow life. And this had happened because I had read a novel about a mythical man called George F. Babbitt.

66   The plots and stories in the novels did not interest me so much as the point of view revealed. I gave myself over to each novel without reserve, without trying to criticize it; it was enough for me to see and feel something different. And for me, everything was something different. Reading was like a drug, a dope. The novels created moods in which I lived for days. But I could not conquer my sense of guilt, my feeling that the white men around me knew that I was changing, that I had begun to regard them differently.

67   Whenever I brought a book to the job, I wrapped it in newspaper — a habit that was to persist for years in other cities and under other circumstances. But some of the white men pried into my packages when I was absent and they questioned me.

68   "Boy, what are you reading those books for?"

69   "Oh, I don't know, sir."

"That's deep stuff you're reading, boy."   70
"I'm just killing time, sir."   71
"You'll addle your brains if you don't watch out."   72
I read Dreiser's *Jennie Gerhardt* and *Sister Carrie* and they re-   73
vived in me a vivid sense of my mother's suffering; I was overwhelmed. I grew silent, wondering about the life around me. It would
have been impossible for me to have told anyone what I derived from
these novels, for it was nothing less than a sense of life itself. All my
life had shaped me for the realism, the naturalism of the modern novel,
and I could not read enough of them.

Steeped in new moods and ideas, I bought a ream of paper and   74
tried to write; but nothing would come, or what did come was flat
beyond telling. I discovered that more than desire and feeling were
necessary to write and I dropped the idea. Yet I still wondered how it
was possible to know people sufficiently to write about them? Could
I ever learn about life and people? To me, with my vast ignorance, my
Jim Crow station in life, it seemed a task impossible of achievement.
I now knew what being a Negro meant. I could endure the hunger. I
had learned to live with hate. But to feel that there were feelings denied
me, that the very breath of life itself was beyond my reach, that more
than anything else hurt, wounded me. I had a new hunger.

In buoying me up, reading also cast me down, made me see what   75
was possible, what I had missed. My tension returned, new, terrible,
bitter, surging, almost too great to be contained. I no longer *felt* that
the world about me was hostile, killing; I *knew* it. A million times I
asked myself what I could do to save myself, and there were no answers. I seemed forever condemned, ringed by walls.

I did not discuss my reading with Mr. Falk, who had lent me his   76
library card; it would have meant talking about myself and that would
have been too painful. I smiled each day, fighting desperately to maintain my old behavior, to keep my disposition seemingly sunny. But
some of the white men discerned that I had begun to brood.

"Wake up there, boy!" Mr. Olin said one day.   77
"Sir!" I answered for the lack of a better word.   78
"You act like you've stolen something," he said.   79
I laughed in the way I knew he expected me to laugh, but I re-   80
solved to be more conscious of myself, to watch my every act, to guard
and hide the new knowledge that was dawning within me.

If I went north, would it be possible for me to build a new life   81
then? But how could a man build a life upon vague, unformed yearn-
ings? I wanted to write and I did not even know the English language.

I bought English grammars and found them dull. I felt that I was getting a better sense of the language from novels than from grammars. I read hard, discarding a writer as soon as I felt that I had grasped his point of view. At night the printed page stood before my eyes in sleep.

82   Mrs. Moss, my landlady, asked me one Sunday morning:

83   "Son, what is this you keep on reading?"

84   "Oh, nothing. Just novels."

85   "What you get out of 'em?"

86   "I'm just killing time," I said.

87   "I hope you know your own mind," she said in a tone which implied that she doubted if I had a mind.

88   I knew of no Negroes who read the books I liked and I wondered if any Negroes ever thought of them. I knew that there were Negro doctors, lawyers, newspapermen, but I never saw any of them. When I read a Negro newspaper I never caught the faintest echo of my preoccupation in its pages. I felt trapped and occasionally, for a few days, I would stop reading. But a vague hunger would come over me for books, books that opened up new avenues of feeling and seeing, and again I would forge another note to the white librarian. Again I would read and wonder as only the naïve and unlettered can read and wonder, feeling that I carried a secret, criminal burden about with me each day.

89   That winter my mother and brother came and we set up housekeeping, buying furniture on the installment plan, being cheated and yet knowing no way to avoid it. I began to eat warm food and to my surprise found that regular meals enabled me to read faster. I may have lived through many illnesses and survived them, never suspecting that I was ill. My brother obtained a job and we began to save toward the trip north, plotting our time, setting tentative dates for departure. I told none of the white men on the job that I was planning to go north; I knew that the moment they felt I was thinking of the North they would change toward me. It would have made them feel that I did not like the life I was living, and because my life was completely conditioned by what they said or did, it would have been tantamount to challenging them.

90   I could calculate my chances for life in the South as a Negro fairly clearly now.

91   I could fight the southern whites by organizing with other Negroes, as my grandfather had done. But I knew that I could never win that way; there were many whites and there were but few blacks. They were strong and we were weak. Outright black rebellion could never win. If I fought openly I would die and I did not want to die. News of lynchings were frequent.

I could submit and live the life of a genial slave, but that was   92
impossible. All of my life had shaped me to live by my own feelings,
and thoughts. I could make up to Bess and marry her and inherit the
house. But that, too, would be the life of a slave; if I did that, I would
crush to death something within me, and I would hate myself as much
as I knew the whites already hated those who had submitted. Neither
could I ever willingly present myself to be kicked, as Shorty had done.
I would rather have died than do that.

I could drain off my restlessness by fighting with Shorty and   93
Harrison. I had seen many Negroes solve the problem of being black
by transferring their hatred of themselves to others with a black skin
and fighting them. I would have to be cold to do that, and I was not
cold and I could never be.

I could, of course, forget what I had read, thrust the whites out of   94
my mind, forget them; and find release from anxiety and longing in
sex and alcohol. But the memory of how my father had conducted
himself made that course repugnant. If I did not want others to violate
my life, how could I voluntarily violate it myself?

I had no hope whatever of being a professional man. Not only had   95
I been so conditioned that I did not desire it, but the fulfillment of
such an ambition was beyond my capabilities. Well-to-do Negroes
lived in a world that was almost as alien to me as the world inhabited
by whites.

What, then, was there? I held my life in my mind, in my con-   96
sciousness each day, feeling at times that I would stumble and drop it,
spill it forever. My reading had created a vast sense of distance between
me and the world in which I lived and tried to make a living, and that
sense of distance was increasing each day. My days and nights were
one long, quiet, continuously contained dream of terror, tension, and
anxiety. I wondered how long I could bear it.

—— CONSIDERATIONS ————————————————————

1. How do you heat a can of beans if you don't have a hot plate in your
room? How is Wright's answer to this question an autobiographical fact that
might affect your appreciation of his essay?

2. Compare Walter White's account of physical persecution of blacks in
Atlanta (pages 449–454) with this record of cultural discrimination in Memphis. Consider what the two men learned from their rather different experiences.

3. Compare what Wright had to endure to use the public library with
your own introduction to the same institution. How do you account for the

motivation Wright needed to break the barriers between him and freedom to read?

4. The word Wright uses throughout to refer to his own race is no longer widely accepted. Why? What other words have been used at other times in American history? What difference does a name make?

5. Notice how Wright uses dialogue in this essay. How do you decide when to use dialogue? What are its purposes?

6. The authors mentioned by Wright in his essay would make a formidable reading program for anyone. If you were to lay out such a program for yourself, what titles would you include? Why?

A Rhetorical Index

The various writing patterns — argument and persuasion, description, exposition, and narration — are well illustrated by the many essays, stories, journal entries, and poems in *A Writer's Reader*. Of course any classification of good writing according to type is suspect because good writers inevitably merge the types, and good writing will not submit to pigeonholing. This index, then, is only one arrangement. Yet anyone looking for models or examples for study and imitation may well begin here.

A word about the subcategories. We index two sorts of argument — formal and implicit — because some selections represent obvious attempts to present a strong case, often in high style, whereas other arguments are indirect, below the surface, perhaps never said outright. Under "Description" we index not only whole selections but also sections within selections that primarily describe places, persons, or miscellaneous phenomena. Expository selections include pieces illustrating the various rhetorical patterns, example, classification and division, cause and effect, comparison and contrast, process analysis, and definition. Here, too, both whole selections and individual paragraphs are listed. Narration includes autobiographical narrative essays, stories, nonfiction nonautobiographical narratives, and narrative poems.

Throughout the index we have starred short selections (under 1200 words). Numbers in parentheses refer to the paragraph numbers within selections, when parts of whole essays are indexed. Finally, there are listings of all the nonessay materials in the reader — short stories, journal entries, and poems.

ARGUMENT AND PERSUASION

Formal, Overt
  *BACON, *Of Marriage and Single Life*, 24–25
  *BAXTER, *Why Shouldn't We Change Sex?*, 37–39

EXPOSITION

Analogy (see Comparison, Contrast, Analogy)

Cause and Effect

JOURNALS, DIARIES, NOTEBOOKS, SHORT TAKES

SHORT STORIES

POEMS

To the Student

Part of our job as educational publishers is to try to improve the textbooks we publish. Thus, when revising we take into account the experience of both instructors and students with the previous edition. At some time in the future your instructor will be asked to comment extensively on *A Writer's Reader*, Second Edition, but right now we want to hear from you. After all, though your instructor assigned this book, you are the one for whom it is intended (and the one who paid for it).

Please help us by completing this questionnaire and returning it to College English Developmental Group, Little, Brown and Company, 34 Beacon Street, Boston, Mass. 02106.

School _____Course Title _____

Instructor's Name_____

Other Books Assigned _____

Tell us about the readings.

	KEEP	DROP	DID NOT READ
ADAMS, *Winter and Summer*	____	____	____
AGEE, *Knoxville, Summer 1915*	____	____	____
ALLEN, *Selections from the Allen Notebooks*	____	____	____
ANGELOU, *Mr. Red Leg*	____	____	____
ARNOLD, *Dover Beach*	____	____	____
BACON, *On Marriage and Single Life*	____	____	____

	KEEP	DROP	DID NOT READ
LIPPMANN, *Why Should the Majority Rule?*	___	___	___
McPHEE, *Ashe and Graebner*	___	___	___
MAILER, *A Walk on the Moon*	___	___	___
MARVELL, *To His Coy Mistress*	___	___	___
MEAD, *On Ruth Benedict*	___	___	___
MENCKEN, *Gamalielese*	___	___	___
MOMADAY, *The Way to Rainy Mountain*	___	___	___
MORRIS, *Odd Balls*	___	___	___
NIN, *Journal Entry*	___	___	___
OLSEN, *I Stand Here Ironing*	___	___	___
ORR, *Washing My Face*	___	___	___
ORWELL, *Politics and the English Language*	___	___	___
PARRISH, *Welcome to Vietnam*	___	___	___
PESEROFF, *The Hardness Scale*	___	___	___
PIRSIG, *The Church of Reason*	___	___	___
PLATO, *Socrates to His Accusers*	___	___	___
RHODES, *Packaged Sentiment*	___	___	___
RICH, *Origins and History of Consciousness*	___	___	___
ROETHKE, *Elegy for Jane*	___	___	___
ROSS, *The Yellow Bus*	___	___	___
RUSSELL, *Touch and Sight*	___	___	___
SELZER, *The Discus Thrower*	___	___	___
SHAKESPEARE, *That time of year . . .*	___	___	___
STAFFORD, *A Way of Writing*	___	___	___
SWIFT, *A Modest Proposal*	___	___	___
SZASZ, *Laws Make Crimes*	___	___	___
TERKEL, *Phil Stallings, Spot Welder*	___	___	___
THOMAS, *Ceti*	___	___	___
THOREAU, *To Build My House*	___	___	___
THURBER, *Which*	___	___	___
TWAIN, *Was the World Made for Man?*	___	___	___
UPDIKE, *Ace in the Hole*	___	___	___
WELTY, *A Worn Path*	___	___	___
WELTY, *The Point of the Story*	___	___	___

	KEEP	DROP	DID NOT READ
WHITE, E. B., *Once More to the Lake*	——	——	——
WHITE, W., *The Atlanta Riot*	——	——	——
WHITMAN, *On Abraham Lincoln*	——	——	——
WILLIAMS, *To Waken an Old Lady*	——	——	——
WILLS, *The Myth of the Declaration*	——	——	——
WOLFE, *Journal Entries*	——	——	——
WOOLF, *The Death of the Moth*	——	——	——
WRIGHT, *The Library Card*	——	——	——

Did you use the Rhetorical Index? _____

How might it be improved? _____

_____

_____

Were the Introductions and Considerations that accompany each selection helpful? _____ How might they be improved? _____

_____

_____

Should we add more stories and poems? _____

Please add any further comments or suggestions. _____

_____

_____

_____

Date _____ Your Name _____

_____

Mailing Address